OUR LADY OF
CLASS STRUGGLE

OUR LADY OF CLASS STRUGGLE

THE CULT OF THE VIRGIN MARY IN HAITI

Terry Rey

Africa World Press, Inc.

P.O. Box 1892
Trenton, NJ 08607

P.O. Box 48
Asmarà, ERITREA

Africa World Press, Inc.

P.O. Box 1892
Trenton, NJ 08607

P.O. Box 48
Asmara, ERITREA

Cover design: Jonathan Gullery
Book design: Wanjiku Ngugi

Library of Congress Cataloging-in-Publication Data

Rey, Terry
   Our lady of class struggle : the cult of the Virgin Mary in Haiti
/ by Terry Rey.
     p.   cm.
   Includes bibliographical references and index.
  ISBN 0-86543-694-0. – ISBN 0-86543-695-9 (pbk.)
   1. Mary, Blessed Virgin, Saint--Cult--Haiti. 2. Religion and
sociology--Haiti.   I. Title.
BT652.H2R48 1998
306.6'3291'097294--dc21   98-31306
                                    CIP

Pour Connie Francès, les enfants, et les bankoko…

CONTENTS

ACKNOWLEDGMENTS

Support for the research and writing of this book came in many forms from many people, and much more thanksgiving is in order than I can possibly express here. To begin, nonetheless, no one has taught me more about Haitian culture than my wife, Connie Francès, herself a Haitian, and she rightly heads the list of my supporters. It is to her, our children, Nathaniel Joseph and Thoraya Marie (who were both born in Haiti during my research), and to our parents, Victor Joseph, Marie-France Jean-Felix, Sergio Rey, and Linda Rey, that this book is dedicated in gratitude.

As this project originally was developed as a doctoral dissertation for the Department of Religion at Temple University, much gratitude is directed toward North Philadelphia, where I received consistent and generous financial support during my years as a doctoral student. For this immeasurable fortune I owe more than a word of special thanks to Barbara Campbell, Karen Addison-Williams, and Jack Nelson. The guidance I received from my dissertation committee is inestimable, and is a root of whatever scholarly merits that this book has; many thanks, thus, to Katie Cannon, John Raines, and Leonard Swidler of Temple University, and François Hoffmann of Princeton University.

In Haiti, I enjoyed the friendship of Ira Lowenthal and Drexel Woodson, who greatly enriched both my understanding of "the magic island" and this project considerably. I am also intellectually indebted to a number of Catholic clergy in Port-au-Prince who graciously shared their thoughts with me about the place of the Virgin in the lives of the Haitian people. In particular, I would like to thank Soeur Marie-Paul Salgado of *Les Filles de Marie*, Père Roger Hallee of *Les Oblats de Marie Imaculée*, and Père René Soler of *Le Petit Séminaire Collège St. Martial*. Two other Catholic priests shared ideas and a number of key contacts in the *Tilegliz* community, but asked that their names not appear in the book; respecting their wishes, I thank them nonetheless. Thanks also to Elie Destiné and Joel Jean-Baptiste for their assistance with my research on the island of La Gonâve and in the Jacmel area respectively. Several students in my *Sociologie des religions* class in *La Faculté d'Ethnologie* at the State University in Port-au-Prince also conducted interviews on my behalf and taught me an important thing or two about a topic on which I sometimes consider myself an expert; my appreciation is theirs. Also, I was privileged to count Rachel Beauvoir-Dominique among my colleagues at *La Fac*, and I have profited from her understanding of both Vodou and the cult of the Virgin in Haiti. Special thanks as well to Janice Hall for kindly granting me access to the Gregory Bogat Collection at Union School in Port-au-Prince, to Peter Frisch for opening to me the archives at *La Maison Deschamps*, and to Frère Ernest Even for his kind and knowledgeable help with sources at the *Bibliotèque de Saint Louis de Gonzague.*

And those to whom I am most indebted—those who taught me the most—I am deeply grateful: Marie-Carmel, Guertha, and to all of the Haitian people who openly shared with me their profound beliefs about the Mother of God— *ak tout ke'm, mèsi.* To those whom I have neglected to mention here, please accept my apology, for I am thankful nonetheless. Neither you nor anyone acknowledged here are responsible for the errors and inaccuracies contained in this text, which are the only things for which I take full and sole credit, and for which I can proclaim with confidence, *se fòt mwen!*

CHAPTER ONE

INTRODUCTION

Das ewig weibliche zieht uns heran.
The eternal feminine draws us on.
—Goethe

Roch nan dlo pa kon doulè roch nan soley.
The stone in the water knows not the pain of the stone in the sun.
—Haitian proverb

Jipon lavyej plen koukouy.
The Virgin's slip is full of fireflies.
—Haitian proverb

This book is an ethnological study of the cult of the Virgin Mary in Haiti. It is by definition sociomariological[1] for its attempt to understand sociologically the meaning of one of the most important forms of religious devotion in the world, discussed here in its Haitian manifestation. In particular, it is also a contribution to the study of Haitian religion because of its extensive historical, empirical, and theoretical analyses of the Virgin's place in the lives of the Haitian people—rich and poor alike. In the Haitian religious field, Mary holds an elevated place that few other spiritual beings or symbols have attained. Could one go so far as to say that devotion to the Virgin Mary is a central aspect of Haitian culture? Insofar as Catholicism—however blended with Vodou that it may in this case be—is a leading characteristic of "Haitian-ness," then, yes, for Haitian Catholicism consists largely, as we shall demonstrate in the pages that follow, in Marian devotion.

Religious images abound in Haiti. Whether in the bustling streets of the capital or in some remote mountain village, one religious symbol or another is rarely far from view. Arguably the names and images of the Virgin Mary are the most common of these diffuse spiritual representations that color the Haitian world. A tour of Port-au-Prince, for example, carries the sojourner by pharmacies, gas stations, schools, restaurants, beauty salons, gambling booths, grocery stores, and of course churches named after or portraying some Marian manifestation. En route, one crosses paths with countless buses, taxis, trucks, and private cars adorned with either the miraculous Marian decal or paintings of Madonnas or their titles. Indeed, perhaps in no other country are representations of the Virgin Mary more pervasive.

As several writers have remarked, it is especially in poor "Catholic countries" that the cult of the Virgin Mary is the most prominent form of religious devotion. Deservedly, there has been a great deal of scholarly attention paid in particular to the devotion of Mexicans and Mexican-Americans to *Nuestra Señora de Guadalupe*, the Marian icon that has received papal sanction as patroness of Latin America. Through my own experience and research in Haiti, I am convinced that for Haitians and Haitian-Americans, *Notre Dame du Perpétuel Secours* is as central and vital a spiritual force as Guadalupe is for Mexican and Mexican-American Catholics; both icons serve the needs of a people who are, in the main, oppressed, and both are assimilated in popular religious consciousness with "pagan" goddess figures. Unfortunately, however, there has thus far been no extensive scholarly effort to understand Haitian—or even Caribbean—Marianism, thus leaving us to take our cue from leading studies of continental Latin American Marianism.

Scholarly texts treating Marian devotion in South and Central America, Mexico, and Hispanic communities in the United States are heavily influenced by liberation theology and—rightly, in my judgment—thus emphasize the history of oppression to which poor Latin American Catholics have been subjected. Such emphasis guides inquiry to a consideration of how the poor's Marian devotion takes the form of both an endeavor (through syncretism and symbolic appropriation) in indigenous cultural maintenance and a representation of "the flag of all the great movements of independence, betterment and liberty."[2] Scholars like Leonardo Boff, Virgil Elizondo, and Ivone Gebara and Maria Clara Bingemer have shown that popular Marian devotion in Latin America can and—depending upon the historical moment and a variety of circumstances— sometimes does emerge as a potent ideologicoreligious critique of, and an effective challenge to, social, economic, political, cultural, and/or sexual oppression.

As each of these writers points out, the discussion of any facet of popular Catholicism in Latin America demands reference to the phenomenon of base communities (CEB: *comunidades de base*). Although it is true, as Daniel Levine[3] notes, that CEB's are anything but uniform across Latin America's national borders, by accounts from several nations, Marian devotion appears to be a significant component to the political force of the CEB movement at large. According to Boff, "In the *comunidades de base*, whenever the political dimension of faith is discussed, special appreciation of Mary's role of denunciation and proclamation (*denúncia y anúncia*) stands out as a key aspect of the people's devotion to her."[4] The Haitian case, as we shall discuss particularly in chapters four and five, is consistent with Boff's description, as among Haiti's popular masses over the last fifteen years, CEB's have especially flourished, similarly professing Mary to be on their side in their struggle against domination and oppression.

Sociohistorical discussions of Latin American Marianism also reveal the tendency of society's dominant—be they politically, culturally, economically, sexually, religiously, or militarily dominant— to manipulate the symbol of the Virgin and Marian devotion to legitimize the status quo and thereby perpetuate their positions of privilege and power. Latin American elites, as has been the case since the Spanish conquistadors and missionaries first arrived in the New World, "institutionalize Christianity itself, with all its symbols and concepts, and reduce it to the service of their selfish cause."[5] Toward this cause, the symbol of Mary, along with the concepts (virtues?) which orthodoxy has promoted through her (submission, obedience, female subordination, etc.), has been a weapon of choice. As the next chapter will demonstrate, Haitian history offers some of the most illustrious examples imaginable of this phenomenon.

Hence, guided by the insights of Boff and other liberation theologians into this legitimization/liberation duality of Latin American Marianism, this study undertakes the disclosure of similar features in the Haitian case. It, thus, emphasizes with these writers the striking "coincidence of mariocentricism with national economic weakness."[6] What is rarely addressed in this context, however, is the equally striking fact that in impoverished nations such as Haiti and Mexico, it is not only the economically weak who demonstrate a pronounced devotion to the Virgin Mary. Indeed, the economic elite in Haiti are possessed of a Marian piety that is as appreciable as that of the under-class, and wealthy Haitians worship among the poor at every major Marian feast celebration and pilgrimage throughout the country. At first glance, Marianism would seem one of the few cultural elements that traverse Haiti's infamous and stark class division. However, as our fieldwork reveals, the Virgin of the poor, who orchestrated the return from exile of President Jean-Bertrand Aristide[7] and wills a revolutionary wealth redistribution for Haitian society, is hardly the same as the Virgin of the elite, who would rather console the under-classes into resignation to their worldly lot, while providing the elite with "the psychological reassurance of legitimacy,"[8] to adopt a term from Max Weber to which we shall return in earnest below.

This divergence between popular and elite perceptions of Mary represents but one level on which is played out the struggle that has characterized the development and structure of Marianism in all ages in many cultures. Besides taking the form of a class-based contest over the meaning and representation of the Virgin, the struggle over Catholicism's most important feminine symbol has also been a gendered struggle, an ecclesial struggle, and a political struggle. In the gendered struggle, the Church hierarchy has employed the Mary symbol and myth to reinforce Catholicism's epic misogynist portrayal of human society and the subjugation of women. This is a central theme of Marina Warner's essential study of the history of the Marian cult, *Alone of All Her Sex*:

> The Virgin Mary is not the innate archetype of female nature, the dream incarnate; she is the instrument of a dynamic argument from the Catholic Church about the structure of society, presented in a God-given code . . . an

undiminished certainty that women are subordinate to men....[9]

On the theological front of the gendered struggle, feminist theologians like Rosemary Radford Ruether, Mary Daly, and Catharina Halkes have clearly exposed the sexism inherent to orthodox Catholic Mariology. While this has led "many feminist theologians [to argue] that Mary is not salvageable,"[10] others, meanwhile, keep the faith in the possibility of recasting Mary as a symbol propitious to the liberation of women. Halkes, to this end, links the political potency of Mary's Magnificat—which has been reclaimed by liberation theology for political and ecclesiological argument—to prospects for a feminist Mariology. "Consequently, [socio-political] liberation by a female symbol can have a positive influence on the conscientization of women and the struggle against machismo, the dominant male vanity, which is still so present."[11] The political dimension of the struggle over the Virgin is anything but irrelevant to the ecclesial dimension. Both are, in fact, significant facets of the culture of domination and subjugation that has characterized Latin American history. Orthodoxy's interests in maintaining doctrinal unity in the name of ecclesial supremacy and the domination of the laity have usually been pursued in the form of an alliance with the politically and economically dominant, who have at least as much interest in promoting obedient resignation in the masses. This pursuit often involves an assault against sometimes politically subversive indigenous or syncretic popular forms of religious expression. The present study endeavors to disclose especially this form of struggle over the symbol of Mary and Marian devotion in the Haitian religious field.

The overarch of this multiform struggle over Mary is the quest for power and domination: of men over women, of the rich over the poor, of whites (or mulattoes) over blacks and native Americans, and of the Catholic hierarchy over the laity and indigenous religions or heresy. Sociomariology must, therefore, focus careful attention on the relationship between power and the uses of the symbol of the Virgin Mary and Marian devotion. Furthermore, it must keep sight of the fact that struggle implies, of course, the presence of two or more conflicting forces. In the sociomariological context, this means that those who are to be subjugated through the elite's manipulation of Mary themselves can respond with their own forms of Mariology that sometimes emerge as politically subversive.

Therefore, given this study's principal concern with the conflicting forces and ideological functions of Marianism in Haiti's past and present, theoretical guidance from those thinkers who are concerned with the relationships between religion, class, and oppression is prerequisite. For this reason, since "nowhere does Durkheim confront the possibility that religious beliefs may have an ideological function legitimizing the domination of one group or class over another,"[12] Emile Durkheim and most of his followers are irrelevant to the present concerns. Instead, this study is oriented theoretically through a careful consideration of the writings on religion of Antonio Gramsci, Max Weber, and Pierre Bourdieu, who each lay "stress on the variations of religious expression among social groups"[13] and on religion's ideological contribution to the legitimation and perpetuation of social inequalities and structures of domination.

Thus oriented by the theoretical insights of these and other thinkers, the present study proposes to explain the meaning of Haitian Marianism, particularly focusing on the different ways poor and rich Haitians perceive and employ the symbol of the Virgin Mary. As such, social theory serves this study as a paradigm through which to consider these and other relevant issues, and then test them against the data produced through extensive fieldwork among agents from virtually every walk of life in Haiti. Such is the *raison d'être* of sociological theory: the theoretical engagement of the socially empirical. "Theoretical discussion and debate alone and without reference to substantive issues are, of course, sterile," writes Malcolm Hamilton. "The purpose of theory is to promote understanding of the substantive."[14]

The substantive in the present case is the Marian devotion of the Haitian people, which is a particular manifestation of Catholicism's cult of Mary. This cult, as already noted, ranks among the most prominent forms of religious expression in the world. It is thus no surprise that "whole libraries have been written about Mary down the centuries in the form of sermons, theological writings, devotional literature, historical or literary works."[15] Given the diffusion of texts about Mary, it is "surprising, then," notes Michael Carroll, "that scholarly studies of the Mary cult are so few. The general neglect of the Mary cult by sociologists of religion seems especially surprising, given their great concern over the past fifteen years with the study of other religious cults."[16] This book is intended as a single contribution toward filling this considerable gap in the sociology of religion. While, obviously, this contribution's main component is its explanation of the various forms of the Haitian incarnation of the Mary cult, our study's findings will expand our broader understanding of the place of the Mother of God in the religious lives of Catholics the world over.

Why a Class-based Analysis?

In his classic 1941 study *The Haitian People*, James Leyburn remarks that "probably the most striking phenomenon in the country is its division into two social groups. So rigidly are the class lines set that caste is the only word to describe the effective separation of aristocrats from the masses."[17] While Leyburn's option for the word "caste" is tenuous, few would argue that class division is not at least one of the "most striking" aspects of Haitian society, or that the separation between the elite and the masses is not "effective." As Michel-Rolph Trouillot affirms, "Haiti is undeniably a society split into two."[18] Lyonel Paquin agrees that "[t]he population of Haiti is divided into two distinct categories: the ruling class—and the "asservis," the oppressed or the masses."[19] And while this division is not so insurmountable as to rank as a division between castes, it is formidable enough to reasonably assert that the masses and the elite live in two different worlds. In effect, each practices religion differently, perceiving of the same symbols differently and using these symbols toward divergent and sometimes overtly adversarial ends. This study focuses on the Virgin Mary's journey across Haiti's often turbulent social history—a history that is strongly marked by class struggle. At least as much as anything else, class struggle, as it turns out, has dictated the forms that Haitian Marianism has taken over the years, much as it has virtually every feature of Haitian cultural expression.

The haves/have-nots dichotomy, while oversimplifying what is in reality a complex matter, accurately reflects what has been since the slave era the dominant characteristic of Haitian society and the primary source of the nation's many and great difficulties. Eminent anthropologist of Caribbean cultures Sidney Mintz makes this point clear:

> The origins of these difficulties lie in the past.... Haiti's rulers have siphoned off surpluses for two centuries without contributing even nominally to the education of the people or the growth of new sources of income. Rulers who profit from stasis are disinclined to risk change.[20]

Agreeing that Haiti's class struggle has its roots deeply entrenched in the slave era, Trouillot writes that "if history reveals anything it is the very extent to which the stakes have long been different for various groups in Haiti: the history of Haiti is one of sharply opposed interests." He elaborates that this centuries-old conflict of interests is manifest as the "two structural features" of Haitian society:

> the total rejection of the majority by the very groups that exert political and economic control, and the role of the state as the key mechanism of both rejection and control. Simply put, the Haitian elites made a choice early on that the maintenance of their lifestyle was more important than the survival of the majority. That choice, in turn, meant using the state both to suck up the economic output of the majority and to stop the majority from crying out too loudly.[21]

As will be demonstrated in the next chapter, it is not only the state, but also the Catholic Church that the Haitian elite have effectively employed toward these very same ends.

Ira Lowenthal, a student of Mintz and an anthropologist whose own experience in Haiti spans three decades, lucidly illustrates the constancy of Haiti's class strife across a quarter millennia:

> The Haitian Revolution...was actually fought in the name of two quite different kinds of "freedom," by two equally distinct but by no means equal groups. Almost one-half million slaves—fully half of whom had themselves been born in Africa, enslaved and transported—fought for personal liberation, to free themselves from the oppression of

plantation servitude and all that it represented. Some 30,000 *affranchis*, or free men and women of color—whose aggregate holdings at the time included 1/3 of the colony's land and more than 1/4 of its slaves—fought, on the other hand, for political and economic freedom from French colonialism, in order to extend and consolidate their own control over the country's vast wealth and productivity. In the final analysis, the slaves victory was to prove illusory, while the *affranchis* and their descendants have prevailed for almost two centuries. Today, the heirs of these groups still live side by side in a country that they have never truly shared, cohabitants, but not yet truly fellow citizens, facing the millennium in a nation riven by strife that has its still-living roots in the brutal realities of 18th century slavery and colonization.[22]

In light of the centuries-deep roots of this formidable rift in Haitian society, it is clear that studies of any aspect of Haitian culture that ignore the question of class risk serious distortion. While in Haiti rich and poor alike *do* share certain cultural features that make them each Haitian, they nevertheless stand in perpetual conflict in this explosive nation, often being Haitian in quite different ways. This conflictual divergence has indelibly marked virtually every aspect of Haitian culture. "Thus while it would be wrong to suggest that elites and masses fully share the same culture," comments Trouillot, "it is equally misleading to divide Haiti into two cultural spheres. The fundamental cultural divide is not based on huge differences in cultural repertoire but on the uses of those differences that exist to create a social wall that few can cross."[23] In the pages that follow, especially in chapters four, five, and six, we shall examine in particular both the Virgin Mary's foundational place in this social wall, as well as her subversive value to those who would like to break it down.

A class-based analysis allows for just such a disclosure of the distinctive ideological functions of Marianism for each the elite and the masses. To speak of such an analysis, of course, invokes the name of Karl Marx and presupposes reference to his enormous influence on the social sciences. In effect, class, according to many social theorists, is one of the most important structural determinants of human society. While other tenets of Marxism have been superseded or discarded, the notion that class matters, and that it matters a great deal, is irrefutable. In the religious field, the operative effects of class division reveal themselves in the forms of what are in reality different religions among members of the same church or movement.

Scholarly notice of differences between popular and official religion dates back at least as early as the eighteenth century in David Hume's contrast of "the monotheism of the enlightened few with the implicitly polytheistic tendencies of the uninstructed "vulgar" masses."[24] Building on such insight, Marx and Engels, a century later, developed the forceful argument that "religion had a double function of compensating the suffering of the poor with promises of spiritual wealth, while simultaneously legitimating the wealth of the dominant class."[25] This "double function" of religion has been very pronounced in Haitian history, with the Virgin Mary operating most efficiently as a key symbol for each function. This fact alone justifies the employment of a class-based paradigm toward the understanding of Haitian Marianism.

Preferencing a neo-Marxist paradigm over other forms of analysis (feminist, Afrocentric, etc.) by no means belittles the insights that other perspectives might offer into the meaning of Haitian Marianism. To be sure, when Gramsci argues that Catholicism "is in reality a multiplicity of distinct and often contradictory religions,"[26] he not only illustrates his point with reference to "bourgeois Catholicism" and "workers' Catholicism," but to "women's Catholicism" as well, suggesting that a gender-based paradigm could be fruitfully employed for the sociological study of any Catholic devotion. While a comparison of gender differences in Haitian Marian devotion would have uncovered important anomalies that my own analysis misses, the comparison of class differences is more compelling if for no other reason than that poor Haitian women share more in common with poor Haitian men than they do with affluent Haitian women. This is not to suggest that the present study ignores gender considerations. On the contrary, the two case studies presented in this book are of Haitian women, whose needs, concerns, and inspiration for Marian devotion are sometimes clearly gender-specific. While acknowledging this in places, this study does not explore its implications to any great length, centering attention instead on Haitians' class-specific needs, concerns, and impetuses for Marian devotion.

Terminology

There are a number of terms throughout this book that are potentially weighted with misleading connotations. It is, therefore, important that they be clarified at the outset of this study, which is the purpose of the following list of definitions:

Marianism–In certain conservative Protestant circles "Marianism" is a pejorative term that connotes devotion that heretically elevates the Virgin Mary to goddess status. In the context of this study, however, Marianism refers to any form of religious devotion centered upon or guided by beliefs about the Virgin Mary—however orthodox or heretical. More generally, Marianism is to Mary as Buddhism is to Buddha. Just as there are popular forms of Buddhism that transform the Buddha into the supreme intercessory deity, there are popular forms of Marianism that supremely objectify the Virgin. That such forms of belief may be heretical is beside the point. This term's adjectival rendition, "Marian," modifies a noun as being "of the Virgin Mary;" e.g., Marian devotion, Marian icons, etc. Any mariocentric or mariologically maximalist connotations of these terms should be repudiated in the reading of the present text, unless otherwise indicated.

Often I employ the terms "popular Marianism" and "elite Marianism." Being that one of the central aims of this project is to disclose the differences between the Marian devotion of wealthy Haitians and poor Haitians, definitive referential designations for each are indispensable. It is therefore requisite to specify that by elite Marianism I mean the usually relatively orthodox Mariology of the dominant sectors of Haitian society. Contrariwise, by popular Marianism or popular Mariology I mean respectively the Marian devotion of the Haitian under-class and their understanding of the Virgin Mary or their conception of traditional Marian concepts and symbols.

Mariology–Theology means literally "talk about God" (*theo-logos*). Yet not just any talk about God constitutes theology. Used commonly and correctly, theology refers to the systematic study of those things that pertain to God. Similarly, Mariology, which literally refers to talk about Mary (*mario-logos*), refers to the study of that which pertains to the Virgin Mary. Furthermore, a theologian is to theology what a mariologian (or mariologist) is to Mariology. Although Mariology is thus a formal subdivision of theology, it is plausible to speak of the Mariology of individual believers or the laity, as I often do in the second part of the book. In this sense, Mariology refers to the belief content of adherents' Marianism.

Vodou–Vodou is the religion of the majority of the Haitian people. Beside the roughly seven million Haitians in Haiti, here are over one million Haitians living in diasporic communities in places like New York, Montreal, and Miami, where one finds Vodou temples and services similar to those in Haiti. As a religion, Vodou satisfies the religious needs of its adherents just as Lutheranism does for Lutherans, Islam for Muslims, and so on. As such, Vodou deserves as much respect as any other religion. So much should go without saying, but in the case of Vodou, which is one of the most maligned and misunderstood religions in the world, such an explanation is unfortunately necessary. For the ignorant, the term popularly conjures up images of diabolical superstition and nefarious black magic. For those who practice or open-mindedly study Vodou, however, it is in reality a dignified spiritual path, "a religion of major stature, rare poetic vision and artistic expression,"[27] which has been shaped by the Haitian experience of reality in all of its sacredness and profanity.

Etymologically, the word Vodou derives from the Fon word "*vodu*," meaning "sacred being," "sacred thing," or "spirit." From the litany of variations of the term, with Leslie Desmangles and others I choose "Vodou" "because it is phonetically more correct, and because it corresponds to the nomenclature used by the Haitians themselves for their own religion."[28] Also following Desmangles, I have opted to employ the French word *Vodouisant* to refer to a Vodou practitioner instead of the English term "Voodooist," out of both concern for eloquence and discomfort with the English term. Furthermore, just as the word "Christian" serves either to designate a follower of Jesus or as an adjective modifier, the word Vodouisant can also be used as an adjective (e.g., Vodouisant belief).

Elite–The terms "elite," "upper-class," "bourgeois," "wealthy," and "affluent" are used interchangeably in this book to refer to those in Haiti who are, in a word, rich. Among upper-class informants, I encountered considerable disdain for the designation "bourgeois" (or its Creole variant *boujwa*,) which in Haiti—especially since Jean-Bertrand Aristide's rise to popularity and his fiery rhetoric promotive of class struggle—carries negative connotations. Several insisted on being referred to as members of *la classe favorisée* (the favored class). There are also a number of complications with the term "elite." On one survey questionnaire a woman circled both "elite" and "middle class," explaining that there are actually members of the elite who are poor: "Being elite means being a member of an elite family and has nothing really to do with money." It would seem that in this sense elite refers to a caste. I do not use the term in her sense; in this book the term should be taken to mean, quite simply, wealthy.

Poor–In reference to the poor, the terms "lower-class," "under-class," "popular masses," and, rarely, "proletariat" are used interchangeably. The term of choice for the Haitian poor in Creole is *pèp* (the people). Regarding "class," throughout the text I often preface the term with the adjective "socioeconomic," recognizing with Nicos Poulantzas that "purely economic criteria are not sufficient to determine and locate social classes:"[29]

> The economic place of the social agent has a *principal* role in determining social classes. But from that we cannot conclude that this economic sphere is sufficient to determine social classes. Marxism states that the economic does indeed have the determinant role in a mode of production or a social formation; but the political and the ideological (the superstructure) also have an important role .... We can thus say that a social class is defined by its *place* in the ensemble of social practices, i.e., by its place in the ensemble of the division of labour which includes political and ideological relations. This place corresponds to *the structural determination of classes*, i.e., the manner in which determination by the structure...operates on class practices—for classes have existence only in the class struggle.[30]

Poulantzas' specification that social class and class practice are in part structurally determined by "relations of production, politico-ideological domination/subordination" relativizes the neo-Marxist understanding of class to the Haitian case, where a peasantry and a mostly unemployed poor urban mass, as opposed to a true proletariat, comprises the bulk of the under-class that stands in opposition to the dominant, the bourgeoisie. This opposition is indeed structured along the lines of political and ideological domination/subordination and it conditions class practice and determination. Moreover, implicit in the term class as I use it here is Poulantzas' assertion that "classes have existence only in the class struggle," a reality that is increasingly evident in Haiti.

Popular religion–Spanish theologian Luis Maldonado is correct in stating that "popular religion is an *extremely complex reality*, comprising a multiplicity of elements."[31] As such, no single angle of approach or theoretical paradigm is in itself entirely effective for the analysis of popular religion. In an oft-cited article, Natalie Zemon Davis notes that a variety of methodological or theoretical perspectives may be soundly employed together to understand religion in its popular manifestations. "Some may look for historical circumstances which inspire new fear and trembling; some, following Durkheim, will look for features of social organization or disorganization which call forth new gods, demons or witches; some, with Marx and Engels, will turn to class attitudes and aspirations; and some, with Freud and Erik Erikson, will turn to relations within the family."[32] Obviously, the preference in the present study is a Marxist-based theoretical approach,[33] one seeking to identify those class-distinct and/or class-determined religious needs and interests that inform and shape each poor and wealthy Haitians' perception and uses of the symbol of the Virgin Mary.

Vittorio Lanternari cautions against a too facile, overly class-reductionist use of the term "popular religion:"

> Popular religion in all its manifestations cannot be adequately understood in terms of class [alone]. The demarcation line between popular and official religion passes through factors of ethnic and cultural identity, as well as

through factors of class. There is no such thing as a single, unchanging popular religion.[34]

Given such "an extremely complex reality," it might be advisable to discard the term "popular religion" altogether, replacing it perhaps with Antonio Gramsci's less misused "religion of the people," though probably little would be gained by doing so. In any case, while acknowledging that in Haiti, as elsewhere, wealthy individuals participate in popular religious celebrations among the poor, it does not follow that they are actually doing the same thing as the poor; i.e., that their beliefs, their motivations, and their perceptions of the celebration's rites and symbols are comparable to those of the poor. Moreover, popular religious expression is, it may be convincingly argued, mainly the creation of the poor and oppressed masses, whose religious needs and political interests are quite different from, and are sometimes overtly opposed to, those of the wealthy. In this study, then, when discussing popular religion, with Maldonado and others, I take the term "popular" refers to "that part of the population which considers itself to be in opposition to the classes which are better off, have more education and power."[35] Like liberation theologian Paulo Suess, then, I understand popular religion to be "the religious expression of the poor, lay people who live in the margins of the dominant."[36]

How This Book Is Organized

This book is divided into eight chapters. Chapter one employs Pierre Bourdieu's sociological theory of religion to trace the history of religion in Haiti. Bourdieu's work is particularly apposite to the concerns of this project since it emphasizes struggle as a structural determinate of the religious field, and since it endeavors to uncover the means by which religion aids the perpetuation of social structures of domination and subordination. A central aim of this chapter is to illustrate how the Haitian religious field has been extensively conditioned by the epic struggle between the Catholic Church hierarchy and Vodou, which in a broader context are generally allied politically and ideologically with the dominant sectors of Haitian society and the under-class respectively. In effect, religion's role in Haitian history—in both the legitimation of the status quo and the resistance to domination and oppression—is the central theme in chapter two.

Chapter three discusses generally the historical development of Marian dogma and devotion in Catholicism. This discussion is followed by a survey of some of the leading thought on Mary as found in the writings of several contemporary theologians and sociologists of religion, namely Leonardo Boff, Edward Schillibeekcx, Hans Kung, Rosemary Radford Ruether, Mary Daly, and Andrew Greeley.

Chapter four traces the history of Marianism in Haiti, highlighting cases where the symbol of the Virgin Mary and Marian devotion have been either manipulated by the dominant toward the legitimization and perpetuation of their power and privilege, or appropriated and/or syncretized with Vodouisant elements to promote resistance among the subjugated.

Chapter Five addresses the question of Mary's syncretism with Ezili, the Vodou spirit of love and sensuality. While some writers are of the opinion that popularly Haitians so thoroughly conflate Catholic saints with Vodou's *lwas* (spirits) that there is no true distinction between them, this chapter argues that the identification of Ezili with the Virgin Mary is highly superficial, and that the two spiritual beings remain, in the final analysis, for most Haitians *essentially* distinct.

Chapters six and seven—each presenting a case study and a class-distinct analysis of the forms of Marian devotion and the ideological substructures of the Mariology of the Haitian under-class and the elite respectively—employ leading theories on the relationship between religion and class, especially those of Gramsci and Weber, testing them against both the data generated through over 400 interviews and remarks made during participant/observation at Marian feasts and pilgrimages throughout Haiti. These two chapters also note differences between the Marianism of the Haitian poor and that of the rich, emphasizing the divergent ideological functions that Marianism performs for each class.

A brief conclusion, chapter eight, summarily reiterates some of the key elements discussed throughout the book, providing reflection and some closing thoughts on the meaning of Haitian Marianism.

NOTES

1. The term "socio-Mariology" was coined by Scandinavian Catholic theologian Kari Borresen: "Mary in Catholic Theology," in Hans Küng, and Jürgen Moltmann, (eds.), *Mary in the Churches, Concilium*, 168, 1983 (New York: Seabury), pp. 48-55. The term is useful insofar as it serves to replace the more cumbersome "sociological study of Marianism," which convey more or less the same meaning.

2. Virgil Elizondo, "Popular Religion as Support of Identity; a Pastoral-Psychological Case-Study Based on the Mexican American Experience in the United States," in Norbert Greinacher, and Norbert Metz, (eds.), *Popular Religion, Concilium*, 186, 1986 (Edinburgh: T. & T. Clark), pp. 36-43, p. 39.

3. See Daniel H. Levine, *Popular Voices in Latin American Catholicism* (Princeton University Press, 1992), p. 45. "Widely varying kinds of organizations are often lumped together and presented under this heading. What passes for a base community in El Salvador or Brazil often bears little resemblance to groups of the same name encountered in Colombia or Argentina. Conversely, a group that meets all of the normal definitions may not call itself a base community."

4. Leonardo Boff, *The Maternal Face of God: The Feminine and Its Religious Expressions* (New York: Harper and Row, 1987), p. 188

5. Ibid., p. 191.

6. Boressen, "Mary in Catholic Theology," p. 54

7. President Aristide was overthrown in a September 1991 military coup d'état. He return to Haiti in October 1994 in the context of a UN military occupation of Haiti.

8. Max Weber, *The Sociology of Religion* (Boston: Beacon, 1964), p. 107.

9. Marina Warner, *Alone of All Her Sex: The Myth and Cult of the Virgin Mary* (New York: Vintage, 1983), p. 10.

10. Maruice Hammington, *Hail Mary? The Struggle for Ultimate Womanhood in Catholicism* (London & New York: Routledge, 1995), p. 162. "Many feminists want to forget Mary and concentrate on other issues, such as revisiting the language used for divinity or recovering women's spirituality. One could argue that this entire investigation has been a rationale for moving beyond Mary. However, deconstruction must occur before a reconstruction is possible. Mary is such a complex religious figure that to attempt any reworking of

her image without fully addressing her history is to fail to appreci-
ate her religious potency." With this point in mind, chapter two of
the present study provides a survey of the history and development
of Marian doctrine and devotion.

11. Catharina Halkes, "Mary in My Life," in Catharina Halkes and Edward Schillibeeckx, *Mary: Yesterday, Today, Tomorrow*, pp. 47-82,
p. 66.

12. Bryan Morris, *Anthropological Studies of Religion: An Introductory Text* (Cambridge: Cambridge University Press, 1987), p. 122

13. Ibid.

14. Malcolm B. Hamilton, *The Sociology of Religion: Theoretical and
Comparative Perspectives* (London & New York: Routledge, 1995),
p. vii.

15. Marianne Merkx, "Introduction," in Schillibeeckx, and Halkes,
(eds.), *Mary*, pp. 1-11, p. 1.

16. Michael P. Carroll, *The Cult of the Virgin Mary: Psychological Origins* (Princeton: Princeton University Press, 1986) p. ix.

17. James Leyburn, *The Haitian People* (New Haven: Yale University
Press, 1941), p. 3.

18. Michel-Rolph Trouillot, *Haiti, State Against Nation: The Origins
and Legacy of Duvalierism* (New York: Monthly Review Press,
1986), p. 19.

19. Lyonel Paquin, *The Haitians: Class and Color Politics* (Brooklyn:
Multi-Type, 1983), p. 213.

20. Sidney W. Mintz, "Can Haiti Change?" *Foreign Affairs*, v. 74, n. 1,
1995, pp. 73-86, p. 86.

21. Michel-Rolph Trouillot, "Haiti's Nightmare and the Lessons of History," *NACLA Report on the Americas*, v. XXVII, n. 4, 1994, pp.
46-52, p. 48.

22. Ira P. Lowenthal, "Haiti, A House Divided," unpublished manuscript, 1996, p. 1. Cited with author's permission.

23. Trouillot, "Haiti's Nightmare and the Lessons of History," p. 48.

24. Ellen Badone, "Introduction," in Ellen Badone (ed.), *Religious Orthodoxy and Popular Faith in European Society* (Princeton:
Princeton University Press, 1990), p. 3-22, p. 4.

25. Bryan S. Turner, *Religion and Social Theory: Materialist Perspectives* (London: Heinemann, 1983), p. 80.

26. Antonio Gramsci, *Selections from the Prison Notebooks* (New York:
International Publishers, 1971), p. 420.

27. Maya Deren, *The Divine Horsemen: The Living Gods of Haiti* (New
York: Dell, 1970), p. 15.

28. Leslie G. Desmangles, *The Faces of the Gods: Vodou and Roman*

Catholicism in Haiti (Chapel Hill, NC & London: The University of North Carolina Press, 1992), pp. xi-xii.

29. Nicos Poulantzas, "On Social Classes," in Anthony Giddens, and David Held, (eds.), *Classes, Power, and Conflict* (Berekey, Ca: University of California Press, 1982), pp. 101-111, 107.

30. Ibid., p. 101.

31. Luis Maldonado, "Popular Religion: Its Dimensions, Levels and Types," in Greinacher and Mette, (eds.), *Popular Religion*, 1986, pp. 3-11, p. 4.

32. Natalie Zemon Davis, "Some Tasks and Themes in the Study of Popular Religion,' in Charles Trinkhaus and H.A. Oberman, eds., *The Pursuit of Holiness in late Medieval and Renaissance Religion* (Leiden: E. J. Brill, 1974), pp. 307-36, p. 314.

33. By "Marxist-based," I mean a syncretic paradigm molding key theories on popular religion from Gramsci, Weber, Bourdieu, and James Scott. Each of these thinkers is clearly and indelibly influenced by Marx. Despite Weber's vendetta against Marxist theory, in the end his sociology of religion turns is nearly as materialist as that of Marx, and clearly places class at the center of its concerns.

34. Vittorio Lanternari, "La religion populaire: perspective historique et anthropopogiqe." *Archives des science sociales de la religion*, 27, 1982, pp. 121-143, p. 133. This and all translations mine.

35. Maldonado, "Popular Religion," p. 5.

36. Paulo Suess, "The Creative and Normative Role of Popular Religion in the Church," in Greinacher and Mette, (eds.), *Popular Religion*, pp. 122-31, p. 124.

CHAPTER TWO

RATTLES AND CROSSES, SUGAR AND PAIN:
HISTORY AND STRUCTURE OF THE HAITIAN RELIGIOUS FIELD

Pierre Bourdieu's Social Theory of Religion

This chapter employs the social theory of Pierre Bourdieu to trace the history and illustrate the structure of the Haitian religious field. The history of religion in Haiti, while relatively complex, may be centrally reconstructed around its principal structural determinant, which is a singular conflict pitting orthodox Catholicism against Vodou. Until very recently, the Catholic Church hierarchy has been almost exclusively allied economically and politically with the elite sectors of Haitian society, while Vodou, Haiti's popular religion, has been socially marginalized and assailed by the Church/elite alliance as an ensemble of archaic superstitions that precludes the nation's progress and acceptance by the "civilized" world. The recent proliferation of Protestant sects and a long history of spiritualist movements notwithstanding, the religious field in Haiti has been dominated by Catholicism and Vodou, themselves neither mutually distinct nor clearly divisible in Haitian religious life. Yet despite the popular conflation of Catholic and Vodou symbols—the Virgin Mary/Ezili being among the most important—and despite the fact that Vodou itself consists in part of certain Catholic liturgical, theological, and ritualistic elements, there has long been waged a sometimes violent struggle in Haiti between orthodoxy and heresiarchy over the production and administration of religious capital, such as sacraments, community membership, and the assurance of salvation, enlightenment, or holiness; i.e., of "the goods of salvation."[1]

French sociologist Pierre Bourdieu offers the social scientist a number of tremendously helpful "thinking tools" that facilitate the investigation of human practice. Several of his central concepts—in particular, habitus, capital, field, and symbolic violence—are fruitfully applicable to the study of any realm of human social activity, the religious included. Most relevant to understanding Haitian religious history, for example, is Bourdieu's assertion that the religious field, like any other, is an arena of competition (*concurrence*), wherein agents and institutions struggle for the production, accumulation, and control of legitimate forms of capital particular to the religious field (i.e., for forms of religious capital), and struggle to engender in the laity the perception of certain forms of religious capital as legitimate. In the religious field, competition squares itself mainly between the orthodox hierarchy on the one hand and the heresiarch and his/her following (heresiarchy) on the other. This conflict is translatable in the Haitian context as the Catholic Church versus the Vodou priest (*oungan*/masculine or *mambo*/feminine) and his/her followers, who are locked in a struggle over the legitimate production and administration of religious capital and the lay audience (consumers) to whom it is marketed. Religious symbols and the salvational and ideological forces invested therein represent key forms of religious capital, and in the Haitian religious field the symbols of the Virgin Mary and Ezili are unsurpassed in importance and, thus, are highly contested in the struggle.

This book's concern with class renders Bourdieu's theory of practice all the more relevant since "the whole of Bourdieu's work may be interpreted as a materialist anthropology of the specific contribution that various forms of symbolic violence make to the reproduction and transformation of structures of domination."[2] By symbolic violence is meant "the imposition of systems of symbols and meaning (i.e., culture) upon groups or classes in such a way that they are experienced as legitimate."[3] Moreover, Bourdieu's theory of practice encourages using class as a primary category of analysis "since the history of the individual is never anything other than a specification of the collective history of his group or class, each individual system of dispositions may be seen as a structural variant of all other group or class habitus."[4]

I by no means am asserting in this book that class theories, once applied, offer the final or ultimate explanation of either Haitian religious history or of Haitian Marianism. As stated in the introductory chapter, these theories are deemed useful for the careful attention that they pay to the relationship between socioeconomics, politics, and religious belief and practice, and their for their disclosure of religion's role as a weapon of symbolic violence. These theories are enumerated in places throughout the text for the purpose of testing their validity and soundness against the findings of my own fieldwork in order to produce arguments (but not final explanations) as to how we may better understand religion in Haiti. In speaking, for instance, of forms of *legitimierende Macht* (legitimizing power) that the Catholic hierarchy provided colonial domination, I am of course generalizing and I do not mean to deny that some individual Catholic missionaries made sincere, well-intentioned efforts to cater to the spiritual or intellectual advancement of the colonized. I would argue, however, that they were the exceptions, and their efforts, however noble, were overshadowed by the Church/crown alliance that buttressed European imperialism.

In the colonial era, one of the most striking components of this alliance and of the Church's campaign to monopolize the production and administration of religious capital was its age old declaration *"extra ecclesiam nulla salus"* ("outside the Church none are saved"). This infamous dictum, for over 1500 years considered dogmatic truth by Catholic orthodoxy, was the most effective sharpening stone for some of the Church's most destructive weapons of symbolic violence, like ex communication and anathema, as well as the tragic exclusivism and paternalism that has forever characterized Christian missions. This doctrine also rendered the entire transatlantic slave trade palatable to the European conscience, as, after all, an enslaved Christian in New Spain was considered incomparably better off soteriologically speaking than a free "pagan" in Africa.[5] Bourdieu's sociology of religion allows us to disclose these and less obvious ways in which religion has been used in Haitian history to perpetrate symbolic violence.

While acknowledging the great sophistication of Bourdieu's theory of practice that effectively stymies any effort to summarize compactly or categorize his thought, it is hoped that this survey of his most important concepts (habitus, field, capital, symbolic violence, etc.) and their operative functions in the religious domain is at least adequate to permit our present attempt to use Bourdieu to orient our history and sociology of religion in Haiti. Thus, to summarize, the religious field is one of many distinct, yet interrelative fields that together constitute human society. Fields are characterized and structured principally by the struggle or competition that takes place within them. A dominant religious orthodoxy, one in a position of reciprocal support with the power brokers in the economic and political fields, then, is in a clearly advantageous position to promote the misrecognition of inordinate holdings of capital as legitimate. As will be shown later in this chapter, this has especially been the case in the history of the Haitian religious field, which could almost be the subject of the following commentary from Bourdieu:

> In a society divided into classes, the structure of the systems of representation and the religious practices particular to different groups or classes contribute to the perpetuation and the reproduction of the social order...through promoting its sanction, because, even though presenting itself as officially one and indivisible [institutional orthodoxy] is actually organized in relation to two polar positions; 1) the systems of practices and of representations (*religiosité dominante*) that tend *to justify the existence of the dominant classes as dominant*; and 2) the system of practices and representations (*religiosité dominée*) that tend *to impose upon the subjugated the recognition of the legitimacy of the domination founded upon the misrecognition of the arbitrariness of domination and its modes of symbolic expression (e.g., the lifestyle and religiosity of the dominant)....*[6]

Bourdieu highlights what is ultimately at stake for orthodoxy and its religious specialists or clergy, which constitutes their primary interest: "the monopoly over the legitimate production of religious capital," and the "institutionalization of their dominance in the religious field."[7] Most crucial in this regard is orthodoxy's capacity to dupe the masses into accepting structures of domination as legitimate: "Competition for religious power owes its specificity...to the fact that what is at stake is the monopoly of the legitimate exercise of the power to modify, in a deep and lasting fashion, the practice and worldview of lay people, by imposing on and inculcating in them a particular religious habitus."[8] The extent to which orthodoxy succeeds in inculcating a pliant religious habitus in the laity determines both the measure of control and domination of them by elites in all fields, and the margin of victory gained in its struggle against the heresiarch. In consequence, if the laity's religious habitus disposes them to recognize as legitimate and effective the unique sacramental powers of orthodoxy's religious specialists, they remain consumers of orthodox forms of religious capital and submit to domination by the Church and its economic and political co-elites. The heresiarch's appeal to agents in the religious field will rise in proportion to the degree of failure in orthodoxy's attempt to inculcate in the laity a religious habitus in accord with the dominant world view, for renegade religious interests, those uncontrolled by orthodoxy, develop in the laity and lead them to "take their business elsewhere." I intend no pun whatsoever in here using this colloquial expression, for it very well reflects the economic logic at the structural heart of the religious field.

Of course, all is not lost if the religious specialists are not entirely successful in their efforts of religious habitus-inculcation in the laity, for they almost never are fully successful. In reality, provided the margin of failure remains unyielding of religious (or—consequently or concomitantly—sociopolitical) revolution, orthodoxy still maintains a "de facto monopoly" over legitimate religious capital administration. The diffuse variety of habiti among religious consumers which the Church's catholic expansion entails only demands, according to the economic logic that structures the field, coloring the product anew (a la Vatican II) to keep consumers interested, while not sacrificing ultimate hegemonic dominance:

> The nearer the body of religious priests is to holding de facto monopoly of the administration of the goods of sal-

vation in a class divided society, the more divergent, indeed contradictory, are the religious interests to which its preaching and pastoral activities must respond and the more these activities and the agents carrying them out tend to become diversified....[9]

The Haitian Religious Field at the Dawn of Colonialism

Caribbean history does not begin in 1492; neither does the history of the Haitian religious field. A rich religious culture flourished in Hispaniola prior to the arrival of the island's most famous visitor in 1492, yet the Spanish found no value in the traditions of the Tainos and Caribs. Worse yet, once convinced of the futility of effectively enslaving them to maximize the profitability of their capitalistic planting and mining endeavors, they found no value in the Amerindians themselves:

> The "lovable, tractable, peaceable, gentle, decorous Indians," as Columbus had described them in letters home, sickened and died at a rate that even appalled the Europeans. Estimates of their numbers reach as high as eight million. But by 1510, only 50,000 remained on the island. Less than thirty years later the native population could be counted in the hundreds, and the French chronicler Moreau-de Saint-Mery would later note that, late in the seventeenth century, "there remained not a single Indian when the French came to wrest the island from the Spanish."[10]

While the virtual extermination of an entire people might seem the most effective means of eliminating potentially formidable adversaries from the religious field, indigenously produced religious capital has ever-remained operative in the Haitian Vodou, albeit in an indirect, transmuted way. Religious beliefs and practices often do, as it were, outlive the people who produce them. Regarding this phenomenon in Haiti, Maya Deren argues that "parallels enough exist, even on first viewing, to support the hypothesis of a powerful Indian strain in the Petro side of Vaudoun, and many of the traits of Vaudoun are more readily explained in these terms than by reference to Africa."[11] As examples of Amerindian religious survivals,

Deren refers to the *asson* (rattle) of the Vodou priest, certain ceremonial dances, elements of Vodou's vocabulary, and the traits and
functions of particular Vodou spirits (*lwas*) who are not convincingly traceable to Africa. The salient point here is that escaped African and Creole slaves developed relations with Amerindians who
were also fleeing the same unspeakable brutality at the hands of the
colonizers. Together they established maroon settlements in the
mountains.[12] It is likely that among and between the substantial
variety of African ethnic groups and the native Hispaniolans in the
maroon communities a significant transference and adjustment of
religious capital took place. The fact that Amerindian religious
elements have survived in Haitian Vodou while their original producers have not is clear testimony to the considerable credence given
by African and Creole maroons to Amerindian forms of religious
capital.

When Columbus drove a cross into the sands of the island's
northwest coast, he in effect initiated Catholic orthodoxy's entry
into the Hispaniola, a symbolic gesture that pried open the door for
European religious imperialism in the Americas. Catholicism's quest
to monopolize the newfound religious marketplace was inaugurated
when the Genoan explorer saw fit to return to Spain with seven
Amerindians to be baptized. Rome wasted no time in institutional-
izing the religious plunder, for just months after Columbus' return
"in 1493, Pope Alexander VI accorded to Spain the rights to all
lands it discovered west of a line of demarcation between the Azores
and Cape Verde, on condition that the inhabitants found there would
be instructed in the principles of Catholicism."[13] Thus armed with a
form of religious capital of no lesser import than the papal sanction
of their mercantilist undertakings, the Spanish proceeded to seize
control of the island, and orthodoxy embarked on its campaign to
achieve "the complete monopolization of religious production"[14] in
Hispaniola.

The Church's chief adversary in the Haitian religious field was
yet to emerge on the scene. In effect, the nascence of Vodou awaited
the arrival of hundreds of thousands of enslaved Africans and its
crystallization in the resistance to enslavement that would forge it
into Haiti's popular religion. Métraux, whose *Voodoo in Haiti* remains among the strongest studies of Haitian Vodou, reminds us
that Vodou, like any religion, was shaped in part by its environ-

ment, which in the Haitian case was dominated by the slave regime and the plantation economy of the colonial exploitation that has marked modern Western civilization: "It is too often forgotten that Voodoo, for all its African heritage, belongs to the modern world and is part of our civilization."[15] Ironically, for all the Church's efforts to monopolize production of capital in the Haitian religious field, it would in reality unknowingly make an indispensable contribution to the development of Vodou. It is in this light that we should understand Métraux's assertion.

Spanish Missions

From the time of the initial arrival of the Spanish until the Treaty of Ryswick in 1697, the Spanish controlled the entire island of Hispaniola, then ceded its western third, what is today Haiti, to the French. From 1697 until Haiti's independence from France in 1804, the French colony in Hispaniola was called Saint-Domingue. The Spanish colony first requested priests in 1498, and seven years later the Order of St. Francis arrived, followed by the Dominicans, who, in 1512, founded the Convent of St. Croix.[16] The rapid growth of Catholic missions in Hispaniola led Pope Julian II to divide the island into three bishoprics in 1511. "In 1547 Clement VII added to the dignity of the Santo Domingo mission by declaring it the seat of ecclesial power for the area of the West Indies, extending its jurisdiction eastward to Trinidad and westward to the isthmus of Panama, including the southern tip of Florida."[17]

Christian missionary endeavors in colonial contexts are perhaps the clearest example in history of a religious institution's efforts to gain "the monopoly of the control of the legitimate exercise of the power to modify, in a deep and lasting fashion, the practice and world-view of lay people, by imposing on and inculcating in them a particular religious habitus."[18] For Bourdieu, the dogmatic proclamation "*extra ecclesiam nulla salus*"—the leading motivation for Christian missions—epitomized this agenda and, as noted above, served as the Church's most effective weapon of symbolic violence. If "those who fail to join the Catholic Church before death" would ineluctably "perish in eternal fire," as the Council of Florence put it some fifty years prior to Columbus' stumbling upon Hispaniola, then the New World with its unbaptized multitudes represented an extraordinary challenge to the Counter Reformation's missionary spirit.

The transatlantic slave trade—the very crime out of which Haiti was born—was possible only because of this papally-sanctioned religious imperialism. The use of the proclamation "*extra ecclesiam nulla salus*" to justify the theft, exportation, and exploitation of African human beings is shocking evidence of how religious capital transforms itself into political and economic capital, as Hurbon illustrates:

> In the name of the necessity of everywhere implanting the Church, the unique source of salvation virtual crusades were effected. On the one hand, colonization found its *raison d'être* in the superiority of Western civilization, while on the other, the missionary enterprise was explained in terms of the superiority of the Christian religion over pagan religions.[19]

Further illustrating the Church's outright promotion of slavery, in colonial Hispaniola many priests actually owned slaves. By no means the exception, for example, "the Dominican fathers of Petite Rivière de Leogane owned a sugar refinery and maintained over 200 slaves. Thus they openly participated in the slave regime."[20] By some estimates, the Church actually owned three-fourths of all slaves in the colonial French Antilles, which is hardly astonishing in light of the fact that one of the first colonial agents to suggest importing enslaved Africans to replace the rapidly depleting Amerindian labor force was Father Bartolemé de las Casas.[21]

Central to the debate over the enslavement of Native Americans and Africans was the question of whether these people were as human as Europeans and privy to the same lofty moral considerations, a question obviously rooted in the prevalent racist assumptions of the colonizers. The question spilled over into a theological debate among missionaries in Hispaniola and elsewhere, particularly regarding whether Amerindians and Africans were human enough to partake of the Church's teachings and sacraments, or of the key forms of religious capital it produced, i.e., "the goods of salvation." Underlying the arguments against accepting them at "the Lord's table" was an attempt to use the sacraments and official acceptance into the ecclesiological community as "weapons of symbolic violence," so as to concretize and justify the exceedingly rigid social divisions at the base of Hispaniola's economic order. As part of the "strategy of slavocracy [*sic*]," according to Vincent Bakpetu Thompson, "[b]oth religious and educational barriers were used by some slave owners to keep slaves in their assigned place in the social hierarchy."[22] The Church's legitimization of this order was in part effected by the distinction won by those who were accepted into its fold, and by seating the dominant in the pews closest to the altar.

The "structural divisiveness" of Hispaniola's plantation society was entrenched in proportion to the rapid growth in profits that the colony yielded for Church and crown. As Bourdieu explains, orthodoxy plays a critical role in the fragmentation of society and the legitimation and anchoring of what are in fact arbitrary social:

> Due to the fact that symbolic systems retain their structure, as is seen in the case of religion, through the systematic application of a singular principle of division and can only organize the natural and social worlds through cutting them up into antagonistic classes...through a logic of inclusion and exclusion, they are predisposed by their very structure to serve simultaneously the functions of inclusion and exclusion, of association and dissociation, of integration and disintegration: these social functions... always tend to transform themselves into political functions.[23]

With such a divisive structural function inherent to religion's "symbolic systems," it is clear how well the Catholic Church could serve the establishment and maintenance of the radical social divisions upon which colonial exploitation and plantation economics depended. The exclusion of the subjugated from full participation in the ecclesial community was an effective means of symbolically legitimizing and reinforcing these divisions.

The inescapable moral dilemma that slavery presented orthodoxy's religious specialists and their allied economic elite in the New World endured throughout the history of plantation slavery in the Americas. The same dilemma, in fact, also perplexed Christian apologists for slavery in the southern United States. As christianization was a condition of enslavement, the question arose as to how much religious capital the enslaved should be allowed to access. Especially confounding matters were the liberative themes inherent to Christianity. "Discussion on this point became so bitter that in 1537 Pope Paul III issued a special bull stating that native Americans were henceforth to be considered by all as rational human beings capable of receiving the holy sacraments the same as any white man."[24] As was the case with the reforms inspired by Las Casas, this result also came too late for the indigenous peoples of Hispaniola. The question as to what degree of religious capital to offer enslaved Africans and Creoles, however, would continue to plague the ruling classes for the duration of the colonial era.

For the balance of the period of Spanish rule over the western third of the island, the Catholic clergy would remain an important element of colonial society, serving a range of important roles, such as teachers, scientists, engineers, builders, historians and, most important, guardians of morality. During this period, "[t]he enthusiasm for missionary activity did not fluctuate from 1510 to 1685. Numerous congregations were invited to send missionaries to the island, and no doubt the clergy worked tenaciously in the performance of their often unrewarding tasks."[25] Yet the harsh and dangerous conditions that the missionaries faced,[26] coupled with a growing population of antagonistic French settlers, led to a sharp decline in missionary activity by the end of the seventeenth century.

African Influx — Vodou Genesis

Clearly, Haitian culture's strongest roots are African, and Catholic orthodoxy's greatest adversary in the competition for the control of religious capital, Vodou, would emerge out of the enslaved Africans' experience of, and religious response to, their situation. As alluded to above, the decimation of Hispaniola's indigenous population left the Spanish colonists and their regal and papal supporters back in Europe to look to Africa as a boundless source of replacement labor. As early as 1502 Africans were shipped to Hispaniola.[27] The first enslaved Africans in the Caribbean were imported from Latin Europe's slave market, which was already over half a century old in Portugal. "Not until pleas from the Indies by religious prelates were they imported directly from Africa."[28] This direct importation of enslaved Africans to the Caribbean was underway by 1518. It was the Portuguese who furnished most of Hispaniola's African slaves throughout the sixteenth century, for they fully dominated the Guinea, Kongo, and Angola slave markets, thanks in no small part to the papal sanction granted them in 1454.

While the transatlantic slave trade to Hispaniola was inaugurated by the Spanish, the amount of slaves they actually imported would amount to what seemed few in comparison to the numbers the French would have forcefully brought to Saint-Domingue, once having gained control of the colony and establishing a plantation economy. By 1680, on the eve of the Treaty of Ryswick and the transfer of Saint-Domingue to the French, there were 2,000 enslaved Africans and Creoles in Saint-Domingue, a figure that would increase ten fold by the end of the century. To further trace the unfolding of these staggering demographics through the course of the eighteenth century is telling: "In 1779 the figure exceeded 100,000; in 1789, 600,000 slaves toiled for Saint-Domingue's prosperity."[29]

To understand the genesis of Haitian Vodou, it is important to consider the ethnic backgrounds of the enslaved Africans brought to Saint-Domingue, most of whom "came from the region of the Gulf of Benin, known till quite recently as the 'slave Coast.'" An important number, especially during the last thirty years of imports, also came from the war-torn Kongo kingdom. "But [excepting these thirty years] the annual intake from the African coast consisted mainly of Blacks from Dahomey and Nigeria."[30] The religious traditions of these ethnic groups (chiefly Fon, Yoruba and Kongo, among many others) are what nurtured the new religion, which was destined to become Catholicism's chief competitor in the Haitian religious field. The intercourse of the various African (and certain native American, Creole, and Catholic) religious cultures that collided in Saint-Domingue would eventually become Haitian Vodou, which is, thus, not an African religion, but an African-derived religion. We may turn to a lengthy passage from Deren for insight into this phenomenon:

Inevitably, and even deliberately (for the colonists were concerned to minimize the strength of a people who outnumbered them), the tribes were broken up and scattered through the island of Haiti. Yet all these West Africans had certain basic beliefs in common: ancestor worship, the use of song, drums and dancing in the religious rituals, the possession of the worshipper by the god.... They integrated, around this core of what they had in common, the great diversity of their tribal systems. Obviously, since each people had a complete religious system with its own set of major deities, there was much overlapping to be resolved.... And yet, because Vaudoun was a collective creation, it did not exact the abandonment of one tribal deity in favor of another. On the contrary, it seemed rather to delight in as generous an inclusion as possible.[31]

How should we understand this generosity of inclusion, so pivotal to the genesis of Haitian Vodou? One possible approach to this question, and, for that matter, to the broader question of the nature of the universal phenomenon of religious inculturation, lies in Bourdieu's theory of practice, particularly in his notion of the religious habitus and the particular religious interests and values it embodies. The enslaved Africans came to Hispaniola, obviously, with a decidedly African religious habitus, one tolerant of religious diversity and change to a degree largely unrealized among Semitic religions, with their traditions of exclusivism and absolutist truth claims. Only such an expansive religious tolerance—and the almost alacritous adaptability characteristic of traditional African religions—could explain the remarkable fact that, despite the great array of colors in the African cultural spectrum, "there is much more kinship between the various peoples of Africa than might appear at first," and especially "in religious belief there is great similarity."[32] South African theologian Gabriel Setiloane sees such similarity as the result of "much traffic and interchange between the groups...and, in any case, Africans themselves recognize that they are bana ba thari e ntsho: 'Children of one mother.'"[33]

John Mbiti, a leading expert on African traditional religions and philosophies, agrees that there is great similarity among different African belief systems, and he suggests that this is explicable in terms of a practical exchange of religious ideas and practices. "This exchange of ideas is spontaneous, and is probably more noticeable in practical matters like rainmaking and witchcraft and dealing with misfortunes. In such cases, expert knowledge may be borrowed and later assimilated from neighboring peoples."[34] The salient point is that the African religious habitus is characterized by a high level of tolerance of other religions and the credence it gives to alien forms of religious capital. The enslaved African, therefore, arrived in Hispaniola possessed of a religious habitus already accustomed to adapting new forms of religious capital as deemed fit and practical.

This African tradition of borrowing and adopting useful forms of alien religious capital is evident in the genesis of Vodou as a religion during the colonial and revolutionary periods in Haiti. Laguerre's discussion of "the evolution of colonial Voodoo" supports this argument: "Catholicism was perceived by some as the 'magic of the white'.... Some slaves adopted Catholicism only as a magical ritual, auxiliary to their ancestors, cults." He refers to this process as "eco-socialization"—"a continual adaptation to a milieu in continual process of Creolisation"—concluding that:

> Colonial Voodoo syncretism was more a magical than a profoundly religious one. By this I mean that more than anything else, there was a simple accumulation of gestures (the sign of the cross), formulae (psalms, Catholic prayers), images of saints and other cultic objects. The magical syncretism was a kind of precaution: it was thought to be better to rely upon two magics instead of one.[35]

Religion and Slavery in Saint-Domingue

The French first began to arrive in Hispaniola around 1625 and immediately represented something of a dilemma for the Spanish clergy because of their "execrable morality," which consisted in widespread concubinage and other licentious practices, along with the mistreatment of slaves. French Protestants posed an additional challenge to the colony's waxing Catholic hegemony. The Huguenots, as they were called, had fled persecution in Europe and settled on the island of La Tortue off Hispaniola's northwest coast, where they remained for a decade, introducing a third substantial competitor into the religious field. They even managed to install a Protestant governor, Le Vasseur, whose governorship came to an abrupt halt with his assassination. "Afterward the governorship was restored to a Catholic, Monsieur de Fontenay. Hispaniola became a less congenial place for Protestants to live, let alone to govern, beginning in 1685 with the promulgation of the *Code Noir*, or Black Code, which outlawed the exercise of any other religion other than Catholicism and forbade the employment of Protestants in any colony."[36] While Catholicism already enjoyed extensive power in the colony, as evidenced by the numerous decrees passed outlawing the practice of Vodou and by the expulsion of Jews from French colonies in 1683, the *Code Noir* served as a sort of formalized license for orthodoxy's ventures in the religious and economic fields.

Illustrative of the deep historical roots of the steadfast alliance between the Catholic Church and the economic elite in Haiti, the first eight of the Code's sixty articles concern the reinforcement of orthodoxy's effort to dominate the religious field; the remaining articles concerned measures for treating and confining slaves (slave meetings, for instance, were outlawed) in order to maintain the exploitation of the slaves upon which the plantation system and the elite's position of domination so obviously depended. "One can say that the *Code Noir* gave a juridical foundation for colonial exploitation and constituted an essential factor in the 'Cane Revolution,' for thereafter the prosperity of Saint-Domingue become increasingly tied to sugar production totally dependent upon slave labor."[37]

Anne Greene correctly remarks that the enormous advantage over other religions that the *Code Noir* granted to Catholicism represents one of the chief structural determinants in the Haitian religious field to this day:

> The initial official establishment of the Catholic Church in Hispaniola as instituted by the *Code Noir* has had historical repercussions. As the authorized religion throughout the French colonial period, it has continued to enjoy a preeminent position much of the time since independence. When its hegemony has been threatened the Church has referred to its original mandate and objected strenuously. Consequently, adherents of Voodoo, Freemasons, and Protestants have been regarded as interlopers and obstacles

for the Church in the accomplishment of its designated mission.[38]

That mission was, in Bourdieu's terms, "the monopoly over the administration of the goods of salvation and the legitimate exercise of religious power,"[39] or total domination of the religious field as well as the providence of the ecclesial legitimation of the radical social inequalities of the slave regime.

As already noted above, Bourdieu sees religion as characterized in part by a "structural divisiveness," which fragments the social world into "antagonistic classes." It is precisely this end that Articles 3 through 11 of the *Code Noir* served. These articles, as Hurbon remarks, "aimed at maintaining a complete distinction between slaves and the king's subjects even on the level of religious practices such as marriages and funerals; for the slaves, it was the slave master...who must scrupulously tend to their spiritual edification."[40] Moreover, the colonial hegemonic alliance of administration and Church managed to inculcate in the habitus of the slave population the perception of Christian baptism as a form of religious capital that rendered one superior to the unbaptized. Among the enslaved Creoles and Bosals (African-born) of Haiti:

> [r]eligion also became a divisive factor. For instance, a French missionary in the Antilles in the seventeenth century, Jean Baptiste Labat, recorded that African slaves who had already been christianized refused to eat with new arrivals from Africa on the basis that the latter were non-Christians.[41]

The Church thus effectively served to secure the misrecognition, and hence the recognition, of these social inequalities, "[b]ecause it was in the very heart of the Church that masters and slaves learned to recognize their respective social positions."[42]

The terrible injustice of slavery, however, was simply beyond what any degree of misrecognition could conceal. While the Church's sanction of the trade led to a recognition of slavery as "normal" among those whom it benefited, the oppressed victims of this horrid crime would offer resistance at every stage, from their abduction from the mother continent to its culmination in the Haitian Revolution.[43]

Under French colonial rule the plantation system in Saint-Domingue became one of the most profitable business ventures that the world had ever witnessed. At its height the colony was producing three-fourths of the world's sugar supply and generating more revenue than all of England's thirteen continental North American colonies combined:

> As the plantation economy reached staggering proportions, so too did the demand for chattel labor; Saint-Domingue became the chief port-of-call for the slave trade.... The small territory was home to almost half of all slaves held in the Caribbean.[44]

Thus, eighteenth century Haitian history saw the enormous growth of both the population of enslaved Africans and Creoles and the plantation economy, along with the entrenchment of the slave regime instituted to sustain them. The Church, ever dedicated to its alliance with the throne and the colony's economic elite, continued to provide two indispensable forms of religious capital throughout this period: (1) the ecclesial legitimization of the slave trade, and (2) the moral sanction of colonial Saint-Domingue's radical social divisions. The internal stability of the entire plantation economy depended to no small degree on these forms of religious capital.

Religion and Revolution in Saint-Domingue

Of increasing concern to the colonial regime was the fact that the more disproportionate the ratio of slaves to whites became, the greater the likelihood of insurgence. Whereas only twenty years earlier "just" 100,000 slaves toiled on Saint-Domingue's plantations, by the end of the seventeenth century there were well over half-a-million slaves in the colony, while whites numbered a mere 30,000. From the earliest days of the enslavement of African peoples in Hispaniola, the dominant sector recognized in the traditional religions of the subjugated a capacity for rebellious inspiration, and therefore took great pains to cripple any efforts among the Africans and Creoles to practice their traditional religions. "Simply stated, it was hardly for apostolic zeal that the whites of Saint-Domingue outlawed Vodou, but for reasons of security. As Joinville-Gauban explained: 'The masters imperatively oppose the exercise of this pagan African worship which renders the subject insubordinate, because he believes himself protected by some hidden spirit, and thus is capable of the most reprehensible actions.'"[45]

It is quite evident that the planters of Saint-Domingue lived in almost constant fear of retribution at the hands of those they had so brutally exploited. Resistance, usually orchestrated by maroons, began taking on more violent forms with greater frequency: the burning of plantations, poisoning of livestock, assaults on whites and their tractable slaves. Vodou played an inspirational role in such acts of insurgence, as *oungans* were often the leaders of rebellious activity, none more celebrated than Makandal and Boukman. According to Métraux, Makandal was an African who, having been maimed on a slave plantation, fled to the mountains to become a maroon leader. There he "took command of a band of fugitive slaves whom he soon turned into fanatics, persuading them 'that he was immortal and inspiring them with such fear and respect that they thought it an honor to serve him on bended knee and to worship him as they normally worshipped the god of whom he professed to be the mouthpiece.'"[46] Eventually, Makandal was captured at a Vodou ceremony and condemned to burning at the stake. His execution was an event accompanied by great religious enthusiasm among his supporters, many of them believing that he escaped his execution by transforming himself into a fly. Whatever his worldly fate, Makandal has been immortalized as a *lwa* in the Vodou pantheon.[47]

Perhaps nothing better illustrates Vodou's capacity for political empowerment, liberative inspiration, and unification than the celebrated Vodou ceremony at Bois Caïman of August 14, 1791. Accounts of Boukman's inspirational sermon and the various rites performed on the occasion are repeated in numerous texts and articles on Haitian history, culture, and religion. Inclusion here of yet another is, nonetheless, necessitated by Bois Caïman's paramount importance in Haitian religious history, and useful for our purposes since an analysis of his sermon demonstrates effectively Vodou's capacity to engender resistance.

While probably much exaggeration and mythic legend considerably distorts our view of what occurred on that August evening, it does seem that "Boukman, inspirer of the revolt which provided the initial spark for the independence struggle in 1791, was also an *oungan* and served the Petro lwas."[48] It is believed that Boukman, while a slave, had worked as a carriage driver and something of a foreman, positions that brought him into unusually frequent contact with many other slaves, hence giving him a unique opportunity for political consciousness raising. Having escaped, Boukman organized the impressive, well-attended ceremony that would forever change Haitian history. Culling some of the common elements from a number of accounts, the following is a rough sketch of the event:

> It was a stormy evening on August 14, 1791, when hundreds, perhaps thousands, of slaves and maroons gathered at Bois Caiman at Boukman's behest. With lightning, thunder, pouring rain, torches, and darkness serving as a dramatic backdrop, and to the hypnotic, driving rhythms of drums summoning the spirits, an elderly dark woman drew all attention. A respectful fascination swept the congregation as she plunged a cutlass into the throat of a black pig. The sacrifice complete, the participants partook of the pig's blood, swore allegiance to Boukman, and eagerly listened to his sermon:

> "The God who created the sun which gives us light,
> Who rouses the waves and rules the storm,
> Though hidden in the clouds, he watches us.
> He sees all that the white man does.
> The God of the white man inspires him with crime,
> But our God calls upon us to do good works.
> Our God who is good to us orders us to revenge our wrongs.
> He will direct our arms and aid us.
> Throw away the symbol of the God of the whites
> Who has so often caused us to weep,
> And listen to the voice of liberty, which speaks in the hearts
> of us all."[49]

Judging from the text of Boukman's sermon, it becomes clear how Eugene Genovese could refer to the Haitian Revolution as a "holy war." While there is some reason to question the exactitude, if not the authenticity, of this passage, it is likely that Boukman's and his followers' interpretation of the struggle consisted, at least in part, of a belief that Catholic hegemony threatened the ancestral spirits of Africa, and that, therefore, liberation from the chains of enslavement was not all that was at stake. In *Religions of the Oppressed*, Vittorio Lanternari outlines a number of principal characteristics of religious movements that both crystallize in response to oppression and domination, and, concurrently or subsequently, offer a springboard for resistance or insurgence. Vodou—or at least colonial Vodou—is among the "religions of the oppressed" that Lanternari analyzes, and it, as much as any of the others subjects of his studies, exhibits the central traits of all such movements: (1) the rise of prophets who may also serve a role of insurgent leadership; (2) the resistance to the destruction of traditional forms of religious expression; (3) the effort to fully distinguish itself from the religion of the oppressor; and 4) a "theodicy of compensation" (to use Weber's term) which envisions the meek as being on the brink of inheriting, if not the earth, something altogether desirable, like freedom, while the dominant are believed to be doomed to some hellish fate.

Colonial Vodou neatly fits Lanternari's schema, which is more evident in light of his claim that "if the indigenous way of life has been subjugated to misery, persecution, and other adversities, the people seek relief from their frustrations and sufferings in religious ways—in many cases even before attempting to do so by political means." In such cases, the "political means" then "become permeated by a deeply religious spirit."[50] Lanternari's study, thus, suggests that Vodou and the Haitian Revolution are only exceptional by virtue of their singular success. The fact that Vodou was the inspirational force for liberative struggle among an oppressed people, however, is quite consistent with other cases of such cross-cultural domination. For Lanternari, "premonitory religious movements are at the root of almost all cases of political or social uprisings of third world peoples."[51] The revolutionary capacity of popular religion—as also suggested by Antonio Gramsci—is a theme that will be treated again below. For now, it is noteworthy that the Haitian Revolution represents one of the greatest examples in human history of this capacity actualized.

Religiously inspired liberation movements, as Lanternari illustrates, are set into motion by the "creative influence" of the prophet. In the Haitian case, that prophet was Boukman. Within weeks of his

legendary Bois Caïman ceremony, his followers slaughtered scores
of whites and destroyed numerous plantations and sugar refineries.
The Haitian Revolution had officially begun. Consequently, the
shape of the Haitian religious field underwent enormous change in
revolutionary era (1791-1804)—that much is an understatement.

The Church did, of course, strike back against slave resistance.
In 1777, for instance, Father Charles-François de Constance, head
of Capuchin missions in the Caribbean, produced a document entitled *Reglement de discipline pour les negres adressé aux cures
des iles françaises de l'Amérique* (Rule of Discipline for Blacks
Addressed to the Curates of the French Isles of America) in the
name of "the public interest, the interest of slave owners, and of the
salvation of souls," all of which could be facilitated through the
development of a catechism for the enslaved population. The document also suggests using the Church itself "as a place of penitential
discipline for maroon slaves." Two examples of such penitential
discipline will suffice: (1) Each Sunday (the slaves' only day off),
for a period of between three and six months, a slave accused by
his/her master of intransigence would be forced to pass the day
kneeling at the Church gate. (2) On Easter Sunday, a special address was to be made to slaves considered recalcitrant: "Unfaithful
and evil servant, you have slackened in your service to your master.... In order to expose you to the peril of the loss of salvation and
life, we condemn you by the authority of our minister to make pen-
ance." Still more terrible vitriol was reserved for those suspected of
poisonings: "Sordid malefactor, odious to God, unworthy to be
counted among men, crueler that the ferocious beast...the atrocity
of your crime merits for you death and all torments."[52]

In spite of the wealth of measures at the Church's and the planters' disposal to control the colony's enslaved population, rebellious
activity was on a steady rise, most of it the work of maroon raiders.
Makandal was but a precursor of the remarkable historical events
that would occur between 1791 and 1804, over which Vodou would
exert "a preponderant influence."[53] As Harold Courlander puts it,
"the fact cannot be denied that Vodoun was the cement which bound
together the members of the conspiracy and that it served as a catalyst when the time for action came."[54] Most historians are in accord
on this point, which they have already well and clearly demonstrated.
Thus, we will forego a detailed analysis of the irreplaceable unify-

ing and inspirational role Vodou played in history's only successful slave revolt. Rather, one long and informative passage from Laguerre will serve to succinctly sum up how, to cite Jean Price-Mars's famous pronouncement, "1804 est issu du Vodoun":

> In their settlements, maroons openly and freely practiced Voodoo. Voodoo allowed them to be aware of their enslaved condition. The political and messianic significance of Voodoo was a unifying factor in the struggle for liberation. Strengthened by Voodoo spirits and conscious of their power, the maroons destroyed plantations in Cul de Sac in 1691 and in the north in 1696. Until the emancipation these maroons remained the political consciousness of the slaves. Prophets arose who presented themselves as messengers of Voodoo spirits.... It was Voodoo indeed that allowed the slaves to unify and motivate their activities against the colonists.[55]

The need for a unifying political force around which to structure the fight for freedom served to crystallize Vodou as a religion. Laguerre suggests that it was on the eve of the revolution, in response to this need, that "Voodoo abandoned its secrecy and appeared openly as an arm for the revolutionary ideology...and now appeared as an organized religion." Consequently, "the Catholic Church lost ground."[56] Thus the Haitian religious field took on a significantly different complexion at this most critical juncture. Catholicism's position of dominance, for a variety of reasons, was greatly weakened, and Vodou emerged as a more organized, and hence formidable, adversary in the competition in the religious field.

What were the main factors in the Church's radical decline preceding the revolution? A lack of organization was certainly one factor, as different orders employed different policies in the absence of an effective bishopric. The infamous immorality of their priests, moreover, must have undercut the credence of their religious message. Also, their demands on the slaves' time for religious instruction caused strain on the clergy's relationship with the planters, who began to regard Catholicism as "a needless nuisance and expense."[57] Yet the main reason for the decline of orthodoxy's dominance was the rise in subversive violence against the colonizer, with whom, for obvious reasons, Catholic priests were identified, they themselves, thus, increasingly becoming targets of violent attacks. Simply put, by the late-eighteenth century the Church was recognized as a culprit in the barbarous crimes of oppression committed against the enslaved masses. One former slave, Pompée Valentin, who would become a state minister under King Henry Christophe, offers a first-hand account:

> the priests were so much the paid instruments employed by the colonists to hold us in a state of abjection, to disallow us from shaking the bonds of slavery; these priests incessantly recounted to us in the sermons that the whites were of a superior nature than we; they preached to us of respect, submission...they thus molded us into slaves and inured us to support these very bonds.[58]

It was only a matter of time before the growing realization of slaves like Valentin engendered an aggressive liberation struggle, which would understandably involve an offensive against the Church.

The earliest rumblings of rebellion also caused further rift among the rank of orthodoxy's religious specialists, as, according to Laguerre, "[a]fter the first revolts of the slaves, priests of the Catholic Church were divided. Some followed gangs of revolting slaves."[59] Perhaps nothing is more exemplary of the Church's prerevolutionary fall than the cases of priests abandoning their parishes to support the very people whom for years had been subjugated thanks in part to the Church's legitimization of the slave regime. After listing several such renegade priests, Hurbon adds that a group of nuns from *Notre Dame du Cap* also joined a group of rebel slaves, and continues:

> Even sometimes certain priests (*curés*) participated in negotiations between slaves and masters. It can only thus be asserted that the clergy was divided into two camps at the time of the insurrection. In the particular context of the slaves' approach to liberty by their own means, the Church could only but literally disappear as the united ally of the white colonists.[60]

In the face of growing danger, priests began to flee the colony in droves, particularly following the insurrection of November 1791, where slaves and maroons burned a number of churches throughout the country were burned. Patently demonstrative of the insurgents' association of the Church with their bondage and oppression, "[w]hen slaves revolted, Churches and Church possessions were often targeted."[61] Orthodoxy had ultimately failed in its attempt to secure the misrecognition of the legitimacy of its and the slave regime's position of dominance. Defeated, almost all of its religious specialist abandoned the field, left the island, and returned to France. Violent slaughter and, one supposes, some sort of martyrdom awaited most of those who remained. By 1797, there were a mere dozen priests remaining in Saint-Domingue.

As the revolution unfolded, *oungans* continued to play an important leadership role. Some argue that Toussaint L'Ouverture was himself a servant of Ogun Feraille, the Vodou spirit of iron and warfare; others insist that he was an orthodox Catholic. Whatever the case may be, it is certain that the great revolutionary hero recognized the potency of Vodou's political dimension, which he probably exploited in the name of victory. Recognition of the very wellspring of inspiration for insurgence that Vodou offered the struggle for liberty led Toussaint and his two immediate successors, Jean-Jacques Dessalines and Henry Christophe, to institute legislation aimed at keeping its political strength in check. Some Vodouisants who broke these laws were actually shot. As Jean Price-Mars comments, "with what jealous care the leaders, at the dawn of victory, declared war on the ancestral beliefs."[62] Hoffmann proposes two reasons for the Haitian founding fathers' ostensible apostasy: First, they deemed it important, in the name of international acceptance, to appear Catholic and hence "civilized." Second, they feared "that Vodou might inspire new popular revolts against their tyrannical power."[63] Rémy Bastien adds a third: "Catholicism was seen as a necessary instrument of evolution since its clergy could be persuaded to operate along the lines of national policy."[64] In any case, so impressive was Vodou's inspirational and revolutionary capacity during the freedom struggle that once Haitian independence was won, the nation's first leaders saw it as a threat to the state's stability and took measures to subdue it.

In summary, the emergence of inspirational maroon leaders, the crystallization of Vodou as a potent political force, and the exposure of the Church's complicity in the brutal oppression that raged in colonial Saint-Domingue were all important forces, borne of the religious field, in the events leading up to the Haitian Revolution. A radically altered religious field would now take shape in the young Haitian nation in the absence of any adequate orthodox Catholic presence from 1804 to 1860.

The Haitian Religious Field during the "Great Schism": 1804 – 1860

In the history of the Haitian religious field, the period dating from 1804 to 1860 was marked by the absence of any substantial orthodox Catholic presence in the country. Three appreciable ramifications of this would forever influence the nature of Haitian religious life: (1) Vodou was free to become Haiti's popular religion, clearly the religion of choice for the masses, who were able to practice it openly as never before, in spite of early state efforts to discourage them; (2) roughly two generations of Haitians were raised without any formal Catholic instruction, hence their religious *habiti* developed relatively devoid of any significant orthodox Catholic dispositions; and (3) Haitians were left to freely adapt Catholic forms of religious capital, allowing for the "veritable seizure of Catholicism by Vodou"[65] and forever entrenching Catholic elements in Vodou's own system of symbols, beliefs, and rituals; in other words, the popular conception of Catholic symbols, theology, and rituals would be irreversibly filtered through, and conflated with, their correspondents in Vodou.   As Desmangles puts it, "the longer this schism lasted, the further Haitians parted from the teachings of the church. By the time the break was healed in 1860, it was too late: Haitian religion had become a strange assortment of Vodou and Catholic beliefs."[66]

As noted above, the tumultuous upheaval of the revolution, along with the widespread attacks on anything or anyone associated with the Church hierarchy, left Haiti with no more than a dozen Catholic priests at the dawn of independence. This fact, along with a number of actions that Jean-Jacques Dessalines took as he ascended to power, marked the beginning of the "Great Schism." His authorization of the slaughter of missionaries during the revolution, his self-designation as head of the Haitian state and Church, the liberty he took in determining parish limits and appointing former slaves as priests, and his legalization of divorce in the 1805 constitution did little to gain supporters for Dessalines in the Vatican. As a result, "[t]he Vatican refused to recognize Haiti as a republic and declined to send priests into the country, resulting in an open schism between the Haitian state and Rome which would last for fifty-six years."[67]

In spite of this official break with the Vatican, Dessalines and his successor, Henry Christophe, felt it nonetheless crucial to give the appearance of orthodoxy's legitimization of their power. "Dessalines reverted to the *Ancien Régime* custom of having his own prayer stool and armchair placed near the altar in Church. When he crowned himself emperor, the service included a *Te Deum*."[68] Likewise, Christophe's coronation was accompanied by a Mass and much Catholic religious pageantry. Christophe's efforts to achieve a rapprochement with the Holy See were more diligent than those of Dessalines, including his declaration of Catholicism as the state religion and the dispatch of a delegation of young Haitian seminarians to the Vatican. But his efforts were to no avail. As part of a diplomatic and economic isolation "imposed upon Haiti by a frightened white world,"[69] Rome would have nothing to do with independent Haiti.

Undaunted, Christophe formed an archbishopric for the city of Cap-Haïtien and bishoprics for Gonaïves, Port-au-Prince and Les Cayes; appealed for foreign clergy to come and serve the Church in Haiti; named Spanish Capuchin Corneille Brelle "Archbishop of Haiti and Grand Almoner to the King;" and took all liberties in controlling the institution in an effort to reestablish the Church in Haiti as the instrument of legitimization it had been in the past. His ambition was to prove fruitless, however, for "[d]espite the power he was prepared to exercise, in 1814 there were only three priests in northern Haiti, including Archbishop Corneille Brelle."[70]

After Dessalines, who was assassinated in 1806, and during the Northern reign of Christophe, who committed suicide in 1820, Haiti witnessed the mulatto elite gain political supremacy in the figures of Alexandre Pétion, who ruled the southern half of the republic from 1807 to 1818, and Jean-Pierre Boyer, who unified the partitioned nation and ruled from 1818 to 1843. Both of these men continued to grant Catholicism state religion status and sought an end to the schism with Rome. Desperately in need of priests, Haiti offered refuge to a number of clergy fleeing political upheaval in various parts of South America, though their impact on the religious field was minimal at best. As Desmangles notes:

> France, not wishing to counter the will of the pope, refused to send sympathetic priests to Haiti. Deprived of support from the Vatican and badly in need of young priests, the state was again forced to make new regulations regarding the church. Young Haitian men were elevated to the priesthood and were ordained by the state—a step that the Vatican would not recognize.[71]

The state of orthodoxy was one of sharp decline, as Catholicism's traditional blazing domination of the Haitian religious field waned to a mere flicker. This would have a deep and lasting effect on the religious habitus of two generations of Haitians who were educated in the absence of any significant official Catholic presence. "The long separation with Rome permitted Vodou to disseminate and anchor itself solidly within the framework of Haitian society."[72] As a consequence of orthodoxy's retreat from the field, a free market opened to the heresiarch, whose capital appealed to the religious interests of the long-suffering Haitian masses. Thus, Vodou, now unfettered by orthodoxy's assaults, and despite political measures taken to curtail its influence, emerged as the dominant religion in the field.

It must be added that Vodou underwent substantial changes at the very time it emerged as dominant in the Haitian religious field. Many scholars argue that Vodou developed as a religion during the period of schism with the Church. According to Laguerre, for instance:

> [b]ecause of the lack of organization in the official Church, Voodoo took more and more root as the religion of the masses. It lost its messianic and political orientation now that no immediate enemies confronted it. Voodoo adapted to the circumstances.[73]

Courlander agrees that over "the first sixty or more years of Haitian independence, Catholicism was weak and sporadic. Those years were crucial in preserving, crystallizing and hardening the form of Vodoun."[74] It appears that Vodou's adoption of Catholic rites and symbols *actually increased* during the period of the Great Schism, as the *pret savan* (bush priest) emerged in the field at this juncture as a hybrid religious specialist, functioning at once as the Catholic priest and the Vodou *oungan*. Hence, at this historical juncture Vodou became markedly depoliticized and gained a greater Christian veneer.

Throughout the period of schism, Haitian leaders, with the notable exception of Faustin Soulouque, maintained a posture of contempt toward Vodou. Soulouque, who crowned himself Emperor Faustin I and remained in power for twelve years (1847-1859), is one of the few presidents in Haitian history to openly embrace and promote Vodou. For obvious reasons, this resulted in the expansion of the practice of Vodou in Haiti:

> Unlike his predecessors, Soulouque revived Vodou and allowed the traditional respect for orthodoxy in Haitian society to die. He permitted ceremonies in which animals were sacrificed in the streets, and for the first time in Haitian history, state officials openly admitted their adherence to Vodou.[75]

In effect, during Soulouque's reign, "Voodoo, for a few years, became almost the established religion of the State. For it was in a world 'frequented by zombi and omens, by the marvelous and the fearful' that Soulouque was sought out to be raised to the presidency."[76]

Despite the Church's decline and the subsequent unavailability of its *legitimierende Macht* that had for so long been the primary religious interest of the dominant in Hispaniola, the political leaders of the young republic remained intent on securing orthodox religious capital in the forms of papal sanction of their power. Boyer, who ruled for a quarter century, attempted to coax Archbishop Valera to move from Santo-Domingo to Port-au-Prince in 1822, when Boyer had conquered Santo Domingo and united the entire island under his rule. Tensions between the Haitian state and the Church heightened when Valera refused. "In retaliation, Boyer promulgated a law on 24 July 1824 declaring that all ecclesial property belonged to the State, and with that, he virtually closed down the Church in Santo-Domingo."[77] The Vatican responded to these tensions by sending a series of delegations to Haiti to begin negotiations toward a concordat. The Church's decision to negotiate more earnestly with Boyer was surely in part a reaction to the Haitian state's seizure of its property. More important, however, were Boyer's overtures to Protestant missions and Freemasonry, which Rome obviously perceived as a threats to its stake in the Caribbean. In Catholicism's absence, Protestant missions (Baptist, Pentecostal, Methodist, Episcopalian, Seventh Day Adventist, etc.) multiplied in Haiti, and Freemasons—already long influential in the Haitian politics and economics—began to take over whatever remained of the Catholic Church in Haiti:

> Freemasonry became an annoyance to the Church. Not only did the Freemasons usurp parishioners, they took over Churches. Stories abound of Freemasons who invaded Churches to hold their own services. The Church did its best to block them from its doors and the country. Father Tisserant, the apostolic prefect for Haiti, tried to get a law to prohibit Masonic priests and Templars from coming to Haiti. In 1844, he was able to get a decree saying that Masons could only attend church services as observers.[78]

The fact that Father Tisserant managed to effect legislation to deal with a rising heretical movement and formidable competitor in the religious field is evidence that even during the Great Schism, despite the poor state of orthodoxy, Catholicism remained preeminently influential in Haitian affairs. The number of Catholic priests was on the rise by 1844, and there were inroads toward a concordat between Pétion and the Vatican. During the last two decades of the Great Schism the problem became less the number of Catholic priests than their quality. A passage from Father Cabon's pioneering work on Haitian religious history illuminates the state of orthodoxy's growing collective of religious specialists at this juncture:

> Priests of French origin came in passable large number during the entire period between 1815 and 1850, be they from the French Antilles, the United States, or the many bishops from France. Kicked out of their missions, they took refuge in the republic; soon the bishops in America exercised a very severe control over the new priests com-

ing from Europe and refused to recognize a great number of them; often Haiti gathered this flotsam.[79]

The unscrupulous behavior of such clergy in Haiti was a source of embarrassment for the Church. Coupled with the increase in the number of Protestant sects missionizing in Haiti, the Catholic Church had good reasons to work toward bringing the Great Schism to an end and reestablish itself as the dominant player in the Haitian religious field. While negotiations would begin under Pétion, the trials to restore official relations between the Vatican and Port-au-Prince would transcend three more Haitian governments, those of Boyer, Charles Hérard, and Fabre Nicholas Geffrard, and the papacies of Gregory XVI and Pius IX. Over the course of the 26 years of negotiations to reach an accord, Rome dispatched seven diplomatic missions to Haiti with six different men charged with leading the negotiations. Finally, on March 28, 1860, President Geffrard and papal negotiator Pierre Faubert signed the Concordat, officially ending more than half a century of schism between Haiti and Rome.

For a brief summary of the contents of the Concordat of 1860, we may turn to the following passage from Greene:

> In general, the government got more oversight authority than the Church wanted. The State would have the right to nominate bishops and clergy. According to Articles IV, the president would select the archbishops and bishops, with papal approval, and the president alone would name the priests. Bishops and clergy would swear allegiance and fidelity to the government. The clergy would receive its support from curial funds. The Church would pray for the president. According to Article I, the Church would be the religion of the majority and Article XVI specified that laws would not be passed to its detriment.[80]

From this passage, it is possible to discern the leading interests of both the Haitian state and the Church in signing the Concordat. The state would have ready access to the religious capital it so long desired, namely the ecclesial legitimation of its privilege and power, and it could effectively keep the Church in line through its license to choose bishops and priests. The Church, meanwhile, used the Concordat as the springboard to plunge back into the Haitian religious field with a remarkable vengeance and determination to monopolize once again the legitimate production and administration of religious capital.

One Hundred Years of Conflict:
From the Concordat to Vatican II

At three junctures, in 1898, 1913, and 1941-42, the Catholic hierarchy in Haiti orchestrated formal campaigns to eliminate its archrival from the religious field. Added to the immeasurable harm these "anti-superstitious" crusades brought upon Haitian society, during the hundred-year period from the Concordat to the Second Vatican Council, Haiti was also subjected to a U.S. military occupation from 1915 to 1934, which brought the return of forced black labor at the hands of whites and resulted in the deaths of thousands of Haitians. All of this had the Church's support, while Vodou proved somewhat sterile and ineffective, in comparison to 1804, offering little or nothing as a source of resistance. The hundred years following orthodoxy's return in 1860, then, were violent, both symbolically and physically, and significantly magnified the central confrontational juxtaposition between Vodou and Catholicism, the principal structural determinant of the Haitian religious field.

For orthodoxy this was a period of institutionalization and resurgence, as the Haitian Catholic Church, with its propitious rapport with the state officialized in both the *Code Noir* and the Concordat, reentered the field with renewed vigor and immediately embarked anew on its campaign for monopolistic supremacy in the Haitian religious field. As an integral element of this campaign, the postconcordial Haitian Church "took on the explicitly designed task of taking charge of the country's entire educational system,"81 thereby dominating one of the main shaping influences on the habitus of an entire people, and laying the foundation for the ideological justification for the "anti-superstitious" campaigns that it would orchestrate in the ensuing years. Orthodoxy's return to the Haitian religious field was thus marked by the Church's institutionalization, its control of the nation's educational system, and later its systematic efforts to annihilate its leading competitor, Vodou, which the Church considered to be "devil worship, a shameful cult of primitive people, a collection of archaic African superstitions to be uprooted from among the Haitian masses."[82] This attitude toward Vodou, but a single example of the supremacist posture that has characterized Christian missions globally, would have tragic consequences for these same masses.

Initially, the postconcordial Church focused on two interrelated objectives: (1) increasing the number of Catholic religious specialists in the field; and (2) establishing itself as the educator of the nation. Given the virtual absence of Catholic priests for so long a period as the Great Schism, and given the harsh living conditions and undeveloped infrastructure of late-nineteenth century Haiti, as Greene illustrates, the task of recruiting and dispatching priests throughout the country was foreboding:

> To acquire clergy for this difficult place, the bishop from Cap-Haïtien made recruiting trips abroad. His efforts were only modestly rewarded. In 1865, there were only fifty-six priests in the country. Fourteen new priests came from France between 1870 and 1871. However, due to deaths, the total number dropped to fifty-seven by the end of 1871. By 1875, the number had increased to eighty-six.[83]

The opening of *Le Grand Séminaire* in Port-au-Prince in 1873, with twenty-five enrolled seminarians, launched efforts to develop and indigenous Haitian clergy. Yet these were half-hearted efforts at best, for "by 1920, Haiti had produced only twenty priests."[84]

The postconcordial Haitian Church carried its out second objective, the establishment of a national education system, with much greater success than the first. In 1843, there were no Catholic schools among the country's sixteen educational institutions; whereas, by 1875, a mere fifteen years after the signing of the Concordat, the Catholic Church owned ninety percent of Haiti's 392 schools.[85] With such a surging control over the education of the Haitian people, or at least over that percentage of Haitians who attended schools, orthodoxy gained a position of dominance in the Haitian educational field that continues today.

Following their return into the field after the signing of the Concordat of 1860, "the [Catholic] clergy began timidly to open a propaganda campaign against Vodou…. They thought that with the education of the people and the growing urbanization, Vodou would probably eventually become extinct."[86] They were altogether mistaken. Upon discovery of the incorrectness of this assumption, orthodoxy realized that the conquest of its persistent heretical foe would demand an all out frontal assault. Over thirty years passed between the signing of the Concordat and the Church's first explicitly systematic attempt to eliminate Vodou from the Haitian religious field. Prior to 1898, the Church had "deplored its existence, denounced it from the pulpits, but hoped that with time and patience the whole population would end up Christian."[87] Yet, since no tangible signs of a mass renunciation of Vodou were apparent, the first of three "Anti-superstitious Campaigns" was unleashed against Vodou at the instigation of Monsignor Kersuzan, then bishop of Cap-Haïtien, and his League against Vodou:

> The antifetish and antisuperstition campaign began on 13 February 1898. The bishop traveled widely, speaking about it even, on occasion, at open air meetings. Conferences were held on the "lamentable moral situation" in the country. The pope gave his blessing to the effort—in 1898, Bishop Kersuzan had an audience with the pope who encouraged him in the fight against Voodoo and fetishism. The government responded by passing a decree that permitted local authorities to prohibit Voodoo dances. Newspapers picked up the theme, competing with each other in the "zeal of their arguments." They identified bocors by name and pinpointed religious sites. Bishop Jan marveled at the 'magnificent result from an alliance of religion and civil authority against fetishism.'"[88]

Despite the Church's alliance with civil authority that so impressed Bishop Jan, and although Bishop Kersuzan's "League Against Vodou" had the support of President Florvil Hyppolite, the monsignor could still complain of a lack of state and community support for the campaign, adding that "in certain places even intelligent and educated people are siding with fetishism and this is leading the common folk astray."[89] Kersuzan's complaint reflects two of the postconcordial Church's expectations regarding Vodou: (1) that the state would lend full support to the orthodoxy's quest for monopoly in the religious field; and (2) that the Church's control over the educational system would lead to mass renunciation of Vodou among the educated, who, in turn, would set an example that the illiterate masses would follow. In this case, the weapons of symbolic violence proved ultimately ineffective, as the League failed in its campaign to eradicate Vodou from the Haitian soil and soul.

Undaunted by the League's 1898 failure, Monsignor Kersuzan continued to denounce "the evils of Voodoo" and:

> threatened Voodooists with a series of sanctions. Those who took part in the ceremony were deprived of the right to communicate, *hungan* and *mambo* could not become godfathers and godmothers, and for their absolution they had to go to the diocesan bishop. In 1913, the Episcopate returned to the attack. The "monstrous mixture" became the target of a pastoral letter.[90]

Most significantly, Kersuzan recognized the interest of Vodouisants in orthodox forms of religious capital, the denial of which, he had hoped, would lead those who had wandered astray back into the monopolistic Catholic fold. He was mistaken, for "these first skirmishes were soon forgotten."[91]

The anti-superstitious campaigns, taken together, only amounted to a few years in duration, although orthodoxy's persecution and symbolic violence against Vodou has never been limited formal initiatives. At the outset of the U.S. occupation, the Haitian secretary of state announced that the government was resolved to "destroy superstition as quickly as possible," an announcement that was greeted with immediate ecclesial approval.[92] Several years later, in 1928, in an effort to keep Vodouisants from communicating at Catholic masses "the Church began to require its members to show parish cards in order to receive the sacraments, and to provide proof that they had passed a catechism exam in order to receive [*sic*] confession."[93] In addition to parish membership cards, catechisms and oaths of fidelity would become weapons of symbolic violence in the Church's virtual inquisition against the nation's popular religion.

Beginning six years after the end of the first U.S. occupation, the third and final of orthodoxy's systematic campaigns to stamp out Vodou was characterized by renewed vigor and more effective state support than the previous campaigns had enjoyed. *Operation Netoyage* (Operation Cleanup), as the most devastating of the Haitian Church's antisuperstition campaigns was called, was inaugurated in 1941 by a group of clergy under the leadership of Monsignor Paul Robert. Significantly, this group included several Haitian priests, reflecting the ironic twentieth century trend of Haitian clergy ranking among the most vehement opponents of Vodou. President Elie Lescot aided *Operation Netoyage* enormously by commissioning the army to carry out Catholic priests' orders to destroy Vodou temples. Additionally, one of the mops used in Operation Cleanup was a catechism booklet that the Haitian Church produced and distributed diffusely, which, significantly, was studied in both Catholic and public schools. The catechism of 1941 consisted of a series of questions and answers, such as:

Who is the principal slave of Satan?
The principal slave of Satan is the *hungan*.

What are the names given to Satan by the *hungan*?
The names given to Satan by the *hungan* are *loa*, angels, saints, *morts* [the dead], *marassa* [twin spirits].

Why do *hungan* give Satan the names of angels, saints, and *morts*?
Hungan call Satan after saints angels and *morts* in order to deceive us more easily.

How do men serve Satan?
In sinning, casting spells, practicing magic, giving food offerings, *manger les anges*, *manger marassa* [ceremonial food offerings for the spirits and the dead]....

Are we allowed to mingle with the slaves of Satan?
No, because they are evil-doers; like Satan himself they are liars.[94]

More emblematic of orthodoxy's campaign of symbolic violence waged against Vodouisants, the Catholic clergy demanded of all the faithful to take the "antisuperstitious oath":

I before God, stand in the Tabernacle, before the priest who represents Him and renew the promises of my baptism. With hand on the Gospels I swear never to give a food offering (*manger-loa*) of whatever kind—never to attend a Voodoo ceremony of whatever kind, never to take part in a service to *loa* in any way whatsoever. I promise to destroy or have destroyed as soon as possible all fetishes and objects of superstition, if any—on me, in my house, and in my compound.

In short I swear never to sink into any superstitious practice whatever. (For married persons) I promise moreover to bring up my children without exception in the Catholic and Roman religion, outside all superstition, submitting myself fully to the teaching of this Holy Church. And I promise that with God's help I shall abide by my oath until death.[95]

Despite the Church's insistence that all the faithful recite it, the "antisuperstitious" oath proved quite ineffective, as only a small percentage of communicants acquiesced. Members of the elite were incensed by the Church's demand, for it implied that they, too, were practicing traditions that they considered uncivilized. The upper class, normally a bastion of support for the Haitian Church:

saw in the measure nothing but humiliation and persecution.... It confirmed their suspicion that the foreign priesthood looked upon them as so many savages. Sermons, conference, reunions, home visits—nothing was neglected in the effort to make them see that the oath was necessary. But in a parish that included some 3,000 regular churchgoers, no more than a few dozen agreed to take the oath. In the whole of the diocese of Gonaïves only 3,000 were sworn in.[96]

Métraux also suggests that among those Vodouisants who did take the oath and "promised to break with the *loa*," they did so not so much out of any renunciation of Vodou as out of fear of excommunication and subsequent denial of orthodoxy's goods of salvation, "to which they attached the greatest importance."[97]

In response to yet another failure in its endeavor to expunge Vodou from the Haiti, the Church—exploiting its position of privilege and strong influence on the Haitian state rooted in both the

Code Noir and the Concordat—succeeded in its petition of the Lescot government to provide actual military support to *Operation Netoyage*. The results were catastrophic. At this point, the Catholic-Vodou confrontation that so principally structures the Haitian religious field escalated to a tragic level of physical violence and destruction. Lescot enlisted the national guard to aid the Church by way of burning hundreds of temples throughout the country and destroying thousands of instruments of Vodou ritual. In addition to effecting untold human anguish, a veritable treasury of national art was lost. With a tone of sarcasm, Métraux recalls in 1941 "seeing in the back yards of presbyteries vast pyramids of drums, painted bowls, necklaces, talismans—all waiting for the day fixed for the joyous blaze which was to symbolize the victory of the Church over Satan."[98]

Clearly, the underlying motivation of *Operation Netoyage* was to restore orthodoxy to a position of monopolistic dominance in the Haitian religious field. Such an objective necessitated the defeat of Vodou, its principal competitor in the field. The persecution, however, was not limited to Vodouisants:

> Certain members of the clergy were anxious to use the confusion created by the anti-superstition campaign as an opportunity for fighting Protestantism. Using the well known amalgam procedure, they tried to bracket Protestants with impenitent Voodooists. The bands of zealots who overran the countryside stopped at the houses of notorious Protestants and tried by threats to draw them into the bosom of the Church. Hymns composed by the curés for the special hearing of the rejectors mix violent denunciations of Voodoo with verses proclaiming: 'Protestant is the religion of Satan—doesn't lead to heaven.'[99]

The inclusion of Protestants among the persecuted shows that the Church sought total control over the field. Regarding the anti-superstition campaigns, while ostensibly aiming to free Haiti from the perils of Vodou and all its "superstition" and "Satanism," there is no mistaking the Church's ultimate ulterior motive: the total domination of the Haitian religious field over "pagan" as well as other Christian religions.

In February 1942, the Lescot government suddenly withdrew its formal support of the Church's purge of Vodou. Popular resentment for the campaign had become strong, and the campaign fell under increasing attack in the Haitian press. The elite's disdain for the meddling of a still mostly foreign clergy in Haitian affairs seemed to outweigh their disdain for Vodou, and they, also, pressured Lescot to bring the *Operation* to a close. Violence characterized *Operation Netoyage*, and, almost fittingly, an act of violence would end it. On February 22, 1942, gunshots rang out in the Church of *Notre Dame d'Altagrâce* in the Delmas section of Port-au-Prince:

> just when a priest was saying a Mass to inaugurate a new week of preaching against superstition. The Catholic newspaper let it be clearly understood that this affair was an act of government provocation—alleging that the police disguised as peasants had been sent to Delmas. The fact is that the government did immediately seize on the affair as a pretext for curbing the anti-Voodoo campaign.

One of Métraux's informants, a certain "Monsignor X," laments that "a massive swing back to superstition" occurred as a result of the suspension of *Operation Netoyage*.[100]

I have interviewed numerous Catholic priests in Haiti for this book. While most are progressive and reflect the dialogical spirit of Vatican II, some remain vehemently opposed to Vodou and seem convinced that Vodou and black magic are one and the same. One old priest who had actually participated in *Operation Netoyage* is no less persuaded today that Vodou is diabolical, apparently oblivious not only to the immeasurable psychological harm that the campaigns caused, but oblivious as well to changes in Catholicism's official stance regarding other religions. Many young Haitian priests share such convictions, moreover. For example, from the pulpit of one of Port-au-Prince's most important and vibrant churches, in 1992 on the feast day of *Notre Dame du Perpétuel Secour*, patron saint of Haiti, a young Haitian priest encouraged his flock to "resist the wicked temptations of superstition." There is no mistaking the connotation of the term "superstition" in the Haitian context: Vodou. One would, thus, be hard pressed to argue with Hurbon's judgment that among the Haitian Church hierarchy, "no true break has been made with the anti-superstitious mindset. This even now dictates the Church's stance toward Vaudou, revealing the repressive and persecutive character of the Church in Haiti."[101]

Hurbon perceptively relates the Church's attack on Vodou to its emerging domination of the educational field:

> Having become since the Concordat of 1860 the most powerful apparatus of the Haitian State, the Church oriented its activity in a double direction: the production of an elite, thanks to parochial schools serving the bourgeoisie and the petty bourgeoisie of the provinces, and the systematic persecution of the Vodou cult....[102]

To reflect upon Hurbon's point in Bourdieuean terms, the Haitian Church's systematic endeavor to rid the nation of Vodou is a clear example of orthodoxy's quest to monopolize the religious field. By, on the one hand, virtually monopolizing the educational field, orthodoxy effectively reinforced its legitimacy through the inculcation of an amicable religious and cultural habitus among educated Haitians. This resulted in the creation of an elite upon whom the Church could usually rely for political or economic capital. On the other hand, in openly attacking Vodou, orthodoxy attempted, albeit unsuccessfully, to silence the heresiarch and his/her following, in effect, to eliminate its leading competitor from the Haitian religious field.

As we have seen, in Bourdieu's sociology of religion, to turn to a crucial passage from his discussion of the structural nature of the religious field:

> the struggle for the monopoly over the legitimate exercise of religious power over the laity and the administration of the goods of salvation necessarily organizes itself around the opposition between 1) Church, which, insofar as it manages to impose the recognition of its monopoly (*extra ecclesiam nulla salus*), tends, in order to endure, to more or less completely interdict the entry into the field of new enterprises of salvation, be they sects or whatever forms of religious communities, as well as individual spiritual quests...and to thereby seize or defend a virtually total monopoly of institutional or sacramental grace..., and 2)

> Prophet (or the heresiarch) and his sect, which contests by its very existence, and, more precisely, by their very ambition to satisfy among themselves their own religious needs without the intermediary or intercession of the Church, the very existence of the Church by bringing its monopoly into question....[103]

Should we substitute here the terms "heresiarch" and "sect" with "*oungan*" and "Vodouisants," Bourdieu's general discussion of the structure of the religious field reads very precisely as an explanation of the specifically Haitian religious field, whose history and structure have been shaped to the greatest extent by the confrontation between Catholicism and Vodou. In agreement with Bourdieu, then, the investigation of any aspect of Haitian religious life must take heed of this central structural determinant and of the economic logic inherent to the field.

Papa Doc's Dominance of the Haitian Religious Field

Ironically, out of the *indigéniste* movement of Haitian intellectuals—which arose in reaction to the humiliation of the first U.S. occupation from 1915 to 1934 and which revitalized interest in Vodou as a positive source of pride and Haitian unity—emerged one of modern history's most ruthless and megalomaniacal dictators, Dr. François Duvalier, whose rule over Haiti was one of the longest and most despotic in the nation's history. Duvalier had practiced medicine and published studies in Haitian ethnography, including discussions of Vodou, before ascending to "presidency for life" and a dictatorship infamous for its widespread terror and repression. "Papa Doc's" endurance relied in no small part on his manipulation of the principal players in the Haitian religious field—Catholicism and Vodou.

"Although Voodoo has always been related to politics in Haiti," writes Laguerre, "it is the government of Duvalier, as the ultimate point of contradiction intrinsic to the Haitian political system, that has most manipulated Voodoo."[104] In recruiting *oungans* to play an integral role in the dreaded legions of the *Tonton Macoutes* (literally, "Uncle Sacks"—a reference to the Vodou spirit whom they dressed themselves to resemble), Duvalier's murderous "security force," Papa Doc managed to use the nation's popular religion to legitimate his absolutism. In this system:

> many militiamen and macoutes believe and practice Vodoun. Undoubtedly some of them belong to the Vodoun clergy. In them, politics have been amalgamated with religious faith and loyalty to a leader.... The excessive zeal of the militia is directed toward one man, Duvalier, who derives from it both political and religious strength.[105]

François Duvalier's success, measured against both other modern dictators worldwide and Haitian heads of state, laid in his cunning ability to gain the people's misrecognition of the legitimacy of his power through the manipulation of Vodou and milking it for whatever political capital it had to offer. And when that proved insufficient, brute force did the rest.

Bastien explains that François Duvalier's association with Vodou was politically practical rather than spiritually earnest:

> Not in vain did Duvalier woo Vodoun during the twenty years prior to his election. As president, he has openly espoused the popular religion, but we must consider his action a *mariage de raison* and not one of love.... The real focus of power, the rural masses, had not been exploited by the heads of state, save during the War of Independence. An effectively controlled peasantry could well outweigh the urban minority, including businesses and the Army. Vodoun was foremost among the tools required to carry out that scheme for absolute power.[106]

Along with Hoffmann, Hurbon, and others, Bastien points out the Hitler-esque echo of this scheme: For Papa Doc:

> Haiti is Black and must be ruled by Blacks. Further, its ethnic cohesion must be strengthened by a religious symbol of its own, Vodoun. Haitians must have a National Faith and a national faith calls for a national head of the church: Duvalier.[107]

Perhaps nothing so clearly illustrates the extremity of François Duvalier's self-obsession and twisted lust for power that drove him to become so commandeering of the Haitian Church than his *Le Catéchisme de la Révolution*, which is described in the following passage from Diedrich and Burt:

> But the most staggering bit of self-flattery of them all was a government printed booklet, **Le Catéchisme de la Révolution**. It contained litanies, hymns, prayers, doctrine. It substituted the Roman Catholic explanation of the Holy Trinity with a Papa Doc version.
> "(Q) Who are Dessalines, Toussaint, Christophe, Pétion, and Estimé?
> (A) ...five founders of the nation who are founded within François Duvalier..."
> There were pictures of the flag, of the President, and his First Lady, and then the 'Lord's Prayer' followed:
> "Our Doc who art in the National Palace for life, hallowed be Thy name by present and future generations. Thy will be done at Port-au-Prince and in the provinces. Give us this day our new Haiti and never forgive the trespasses of the anti-patriots who spit every day on our country; let them succumb to temptation, and under the weight of their venom, deliver them not from any evil...."[108]

Given the Catholic Church's traditional privileged position of influence and *power vis-à-vis* the Haitian state, and the fact that the Haitian Church's hierarchy was still two-thirds white when François Duvalier came to power in 1957, Papa Doc's absolutist scheme, for all its raciosupremacist nationalism, was on a collision course with orthodoxy's monopolistic posture in the religious field. In an effort to "Creolize" the Church, Duvalier deposed a number of foreign clergy and replaced them with Haitians. He made it clear that promotion in the Haitian Catholic hierarchy depended upon submission to Duvalierist absolutism:

> As early as 1959, Papa Doc staged such scenes as the beating and arrest of 60 individuals worshipping in the national Cathedral. Those present had bowed their heads in prayer for several priests who had been expelled. Duvalier

later offered the following rather extraordinary justification for the brutality: "Even Christ went into the temple and chased out the evildoers."[109]

Duvalier, in fact, made a habit of expelling from the nation any clergy who spoke out against his despotic reign of terror. It was his expulsion of Monsignor François Poirier, archbishop of Port-au-Prince, that particularly upset the Vatican. In response, Pope John XXIII excommunicated Haiti's "President for Life" in 1961.

But this was just the beginning of a stormy relationship between a megalomaniacal dictator insistent on absolute political and spiritual authority and the Catholic Church, which had grown accustomed to its position of dominance in the Haitian religious and educational fields. Duvalier's attitude toward Catholicism was, however, quite ambiguous. On the one hand, he strove to appear a good Catholic and courted the Church's legitimization of his power, while on the other, he went to extremes in efforts to humiliate the Church:

> Between 1961 and 1964, the society of Jesus, accused of conspiring in political insurrections, was expelled from Haiti; the *Grand Séminaire Théologique* was closed; and three of the four white European-born bishops in the four Haitian dioceses, as well as many foreign prelates and teachers, were exiled from the country. Papa Doc's actions merely increased Pope Paul VI's ire and caused a new, five-year schism between Haiti and the Vatican (1960-1965).[110]

One might expect, given Papa Doc's track record with the Catholic Church, that any reconciliation with Rome would demand symbolically penitential concessions on the Haitian ruler's part. Yet the exact opposite transpired, as a new Concordat between Rome and Port-au-Prince, signed in 1965, granted Duvalier his desired advantages on every important contested point. As one scholar observed, it was "[a]n amazing document all in all, and Duvalier was justly proud of it, though it must have given Paul VI some restless nights."[111] The new Concordat marked an important victory for François Duvalier, legitimizing his position of inordinate influence on the Haitian religious field.

Yet what explains the Church's capitulation to Duvalier's demands? Paul Farmer suggests that "the anti-communist hysteria, which swept the Church as well as the secular world," was the main reason. Duvalier instituted a Haitian brand of McCarthyism, and he aimed to employ the Catholic clergy in his anticommunist campaign. "The *macoutes en soutane*, as the ubiquitous priests were termed, participated in the anti-'communist' witchhunt, which continued with more arrests, beatings and executions." Priests unwilling to cooperate were summarily expelled from the country. The Jesuits, for the second time in their history in Haiti, were sent home "for plotting against the government."[112] Other entire religious orders would also later be expelled, and Archbishop Ligondé simply restructured the Church hierarchy so that more pliant clergy held positions of authority and influence.

Thus, the Haitian religious field fell under the stern will of a despot, who managed to manipulate the religious specialists of both Catholicism and Vodou and mold them into servants of his dictatorial regime. For Duvalier, Vodou was the means by which to effectively subjugate the peasantry. The long-persecuted religion would benefit to some degree, however, as the Duvalier government officially recognized its practice and guaranteed immunity to its adherents. The Catholic Church, meanwhile, also served as a key ally to Papa Doc's dictatorship, caving in to his arbitrary demands rather than taking a stance against the dictator's brutal oppression of his opponents.

In any event, François Duvalier's reign represents a critical period in the history of the Haitian religious field. The dictator's obsessive control of both the Catholic Church and Vodou, which lasted until his death in 1971, was unprecedented and would leave an indelible mark on Haitian religious life in the decades to come. For one, following the ouster of his son Jean-Claude from power in 1984, a wave of violence would crash upon certain *oungans* for the roles they played as *macoutes*. Second, Papa Doc had virtually institutionalized the conservatism and silence in the face of oppression and social injustice that has since characterized the Haitian Church (save for a significant period of sociopolitical activism in the early and mid-eighties). Third, the makeup of the Haitian Church hierarchy became largely Haitian for the first time in history. In essence, Papa Doc "established the Church in which future president Jean-Bertrand Aristide was raised"[113]—a Church whose hierarchy proved almost unanimously opposed to the young priest's populist approach to his calling; a Church whose hierarchy officially recognized the *putchist* government who overthrew him in 1991; a Church whose hierarchy remained silent during the ensuing three years of persecution and human rights abuses, sometimes committed against its own priests and nuns.

The Postconciliar Haitian Church: 180 Degrees and Back Again

After four centuries of complicity in the grave injustices that have scarred Haitian history, the Catholic Church in Haiti completed a remarkable, 180 degree turnaround by 1980. The Conference of Haitian Religious (CHR), which was formed by progressive clergy with genuine commitments to justice and human rights, released a communiqué on December 4, 1980, in which it posed a series of halting questions: "Where is God? Is he still in Haiti? Where is the Church? Does She still exist? Where are our bishops? Have they left us alone in our plight?" In what amounted to a long-overdue expression of penitent humility and sober self-examination, the CHR made a bold, reformative declaration, which, as we will see momentarily, proved to be much more than the superficial gestures that ecclesial pronunciations often in reality are. "The hour has come where we must make a choice that will bring the Haitian Church to a new turning point. The choice is clear: it is the preferential option for the poor."[114]

The CHR's pivotal 1980 communiqué further stressed that in order to make this choice to truly serve the poor, the Church hierarchy must henceforth abandon its role as "buttress of the powerful." The religious capital it must endeavor to provide for its faithful should no longer be the legitimation of social inequality; instead, it should be the inspiration and cohesion for the achievement of positive change and true justice. It was a decisive and unprecedented statement, reflective of the Church's will to realize "a break with a past infamous for its complicity with the powerful."[115]

Whereas the Haitian religious field had witnessed momentary spurts of Catholic protest against oppression (which, as with the two expulsions of the Jesuits, were usually unceremoniously squelched), never before had the Haitian Church so forcefully taken such a stance with the majority of the Haitian people—the suffering masses. It was a momentous change, one that would bear abundant fruit and prove to the world that the Church truly could effectively, as hoped at the 1968 Latin American bishop's conference at Medellín, "work for the 'liberation' or 'salvation' (words they deemed synonymous) of the poor and oppressed, whether victims of social systems, governments or individuals."[116] Such is precisely what occurred in Haiti with the ouster of Jean-Claude Duvalier in 1984.

The Haitian Church's turnaround was in large part a response to the challenges raised for the Catholic Church at the Second Vatican Council. As liberation theologians Leonardo Boff and Virgil Elizondo explain:

> The preferential option for the poor is the trademark of the Latin American church.... John XXIII, on 11 September 1962, when he announced the Second Vatican Council, gave it a clear direction, a reference point for a whole understanding of the Church: 'The Church is and wishes to be the Church of all, but principally the Church of the poor.[117]

Essentially, taking seriously the preferential option for the poor forced the Church to a critical self-examination that resulted in a radically changed sense of mission. Greene summarizes this remarkable juncture in Haitian Church history:

> The Church mission in Haiti has changed as a consequence of Vatican II (1962-1965), the indigenization of the Haitian hierarchy in 1966, and the conferences of Medellín (1968) and Puebla (1979). One Haitian bishop, who witnessed it all, described the transformation as 'spectaculaire.' The focus of Church evangelism has shifted from concern about spiritual and educational well being of the urban elite to the collective well-being of the nation, particularly its poor. Its approach to the faithful has become more egalitarian and somewhat less hierarchical. Since 1966 it has increasingly used Creole, the only language of most Haitians, and sought to incorporate Haitian culture into the liturgy.... The CEB's...are the most wide-ranging and perhaps the most important examples of the

new Church and synthesis of religious and secular work. These progressive and preponderantly female groups have become so extensive that a national committee oversees the activity of more than five thousand CEB's. As a result of its accessibility and relevance, the Church has attracted new members. Children in increasing numbers are taking communion, parents are having their babies baptized, and couples are partaking in marriage counseling. In addition, more Haitians are becoming priests.[118]

Once freed from the taxing domination of François Duvalier and, hence, finally able to respond seriously to the challenge of Vatican II, the Haitian Church simply became truly relevant to the underclass for the first time in history. In the Haitian context the option for the poor meant speaking out against more than three decades of repression under the Duvaliers and taking a stand with the poor in a serious effort to bring an end to Jean-Claude's dictatorship and to promote justice and human rights for a people to whom they have always been systematically denied.

A major spark to the Church-led movement that eventually resulted in Jean-Claude Duvalier's expulsion in February 1986 was the visit of Pope John Paul II to Port-au-Prince on March 9, 1983. Much to the chagrin of Baby Doc, who had hoped that the pontiff's visit would have a stabilizing effect for his teetering regime, the pope's speech to thousands of enthusiastic Haitians made an unmistakable plea for an end to the oppression upon which the social inequalities in Haiti have always depended. The pontiff declared that "something has to change here," words that would forever have a resounding echo for Haitians. Following is an excerpt from John Paul's Port-au-Prince speech, in which he stressed "a deep need for justice, a better distribution of goods, more equitable organization of society and more participation:"

> Christians have attested to division, injustice, excessive inequality, degradation of the quality of life, misery, hunger, fear by many, of peasants unable to live on their own land, crowded conditions, people without work, families cast out and separated in cities, victims of other frustration. Yet, they are persuaded that the solution is in solidarity. The poor have to regain hope. The Church has a

prophetic mission, inseparable from its religious mission, which demands for liberty to be accomplished.[119]

Emboldened by John Paul's rhetoric, the Haitian Church, especially progressive, courageous members of the clergy, both Haitian and foreign, like Fathers Hugo Triest, Antoine Adrien, Jean-Bertrand Aristide, Jean-Marie Vincent, and Bishop Willy Romélus, proceeded to take a leadership role in the events of late-1985/early-1986 that precipitated and ultimately resulted in Jean-Claude Duvalier's departure. The Church's role in this revolutionary moment in Haitian history cannot be underestimated:

> The Catholic Church played an important leadership role in the ouster. Numerous individuals and the CHR had key roles. Church activists led many critical events in the final six or seven months of the Jean-Claude presidency.... In part, it was inspired by a vision of a new Church envisioned by Pope John XXIII, liberation theologians and others, that would dedicate itself to the poor. As governmental authority crumbled, the Church found itself the moral conscience of the nation....
>
> Particularly in the aftermath of Vatican II, Puebla and Medellín, the Church dedicated increased attention to the service of the poor and rural Haitians, helping them establish a network of services, including CEB's, clinics, banks, and technical assistance, [which] enhanced the reputation of the Church as a caring institution, in contrast to the government. During the Jean-Claude era, the Church began to defend people who were victimized by the government...As a consequence, Haitians began to discover that they had the collective power to get the government to reverse itself and to affect public policy....[120]

The Rise, Fall, and Return of Jean-Bertrand Aristide

The Church's leadership role in the popular movement that brought an end to 33 years of the Duvaliers' dynastic rule represented a new posture for orthodoxy in the Haitian religious field, one radically different from its traditional function as the legitimizing force behind oppressive power structures. While historically there have been individuals of the clergy who have raised their voices on behalf of the marginalized masses, this marked the first instance in Haitian history where the Church as an institution acted to change the very political structures that it had supported for so long. Unfortunately, it was an initial revolutionary pulse that never realized its enormous potential for a true transformation of Haitian society. In due time the Church would once again fall silent in the face of renewed state sponsored oppression of the popular masses.

It is noteworthy that the CHR and the *Ti-Legliz* movements, rather than the episcopacy, was behind the Haitian Church's wave of political activism that lead to the events of February 7, 1986. No single individual was more instrumental in the effectiveness of the *Ti-Legliz* than Salesian priest Jean-Bertrand Aristide:

> The TKLs brought the young and the desperate back into the Church in Haiti because the community groups gave these people a new understanding of the possibility for change. In the city, Father Aristide helped initiate a number of TKLs, for young people, for students, for young women.... Aristide worked with them, but he drew his spiritual strength from—and breathed it into—a wider congregation. His Sunday sermons, full of Creole word play and biblical invective against the dictatorship, were famous in Port-au-Prince in the months and weeks before Jean-Claude Duvalier fell.... Aristide helped encourage the young people of the capital to join in the demonstrations that eventually led to Duvalier's downfall. In all this, the Church hierarchy acquiesced. In those days they saw Aristide as a spirit infuser, a useful-consciousness raiser.[121]

Yet, in due time, the Church hierarchy would revert to its traditional posture of impassivity and even outright support for illegal regimes, as oppression and violence remained widespread in the post-Duvalier years and the unjust social inequalities and persecution that characterized Haitian society during the Duvalier era continued virtually unchanged. Recognizing this, Father Aristide and other committed clergy continued the struggle in the same uncompromising spirit, while the bishops (excepting Romélus)—widely believed to have been exhorted by the Vatican to tone down the Haitian Church's political activism—now actually opposed him. Bereft of the support of the Haitian Catholic hierarchy, Aristide became the target of a number of orchestrated attacks because of his outspokenness against the abuses of the Haitian army under the series of corrupt regimes that succeeded the Duvaliers'. Among these acts of violence, the September 7, 1988 attack during Mass on Aristide's parish church, St. Jean Bosco—located in one of the capital's poorest neighborhoods, an epicenter of Ti-Legliz activities—represents "one of the most lurid crimes ever perpetrated against the church in Latin America."[122] As Aristide began to say Mass, a group of armed men in civilian dress sporting red arm bands stormed the Church. He recalls:

> While I was trying to calm the congregation and stop them from hurting one another in the panic, bullets began crisscrossing the church in front of me. One round passed just in front of me and lodged in the tabernacle.... Everyone was running, trying to find a place to hide. One man was shot in the outside courtyard, and collapsed and died in the inner courtyard, with his Bible clutched in his hand. Bullets were zinging left and right. I saw a pregnant woman screaming for help from the pews, and holding onto her stomach. A man had just speared her there, and she was bathed in blood. Another priest was trying to organize people to give the woman first aid. I saw an American journalist running up and down the aisle with torn clothes; the men with red arm bands had torn the clothing, trying to hurt the journalist. A group of young women were in the front courtyard and were attempting to resist the onslaught, attempting to resist, with our own kind of arms, the heavy weapons that the men were using against us from the street—this was a prophetic, historic resistance that we will never forget.[123]

How did the Vatican reward Aristide for his courageous stand with the Haitian poor? It appears that the more intransigent Aristide became toward the bishops' repeated insistence that he curb his political activism, the more orthodoxy deemed him a heresiarch and a threat. After he priest denied the Salesian order's demand that he submit to a transfer to a provincial parish, the Church hierarchy

decided on more drastic measures to curb their recalcitrant specialist. A mere three months after the bloody attack at St. John Bosco:

> on 8 December 1988, the press office of the Salesian Or-
> der in Rome released the final "declaration": Father Jean-
> Bertrand Aristide is dismissed from the brotherhood for
> demonstrable deviations. A more or less foreseeable un-
> raveling of a long theatrical intrigue! The "declaration"
> notes in particular:
> 1. the "choice" of life and action of Father Aristide are
> inconsistent with "*exigences communautaires*";
> 2. His "style of political engagement" is opposed to the
> will of "the Founder" and his ideological positions ("in-
> clination to hatred and violence, exaltation of class
> struggle") are opposed to the "Church magisterium";
> 3. He puts "the Eucharist and the sacraments to the ser-
> vice of political ends", thereby guilty of the "profanation
> of the liturgy" and "disqualified from the exercise of sac-
> ramental ministry"
> 4. He "disrupts the communion" with the hierarchy and
> "destabilizes (thus) the community of the faithful."[124]

Let us consider the third point the Catholic hierarchy hurled against
Aristide. By stripping Aristide of his sacramental powers of minis-
try, the Church was employing precisely the same measures of symbolic violence it always had in its efforts to defeat the heresiarch in
the struggle over the administration of religious capital: illegitimizing
the heresiarch's religious power by denying him/her authorized control over the goods of salvation. We have already seen the ways in
which the Church in Saint-Domingue reserved the sacraments for
obedient slaves while denying them to others in an effort to promote
division among the enslaved population, thereby reifying the power
structure of the colonial slave regime. Modified to suit the present
scenario, orthodoxy was using much the same strategy here. In the
hope of curbing Aristide's influence, the Church disallowed him
control of the goods of salvation. Their plan to devitalize Aristide,
however, proved a total failure. As Paul Farmer explains:

> Many thought that Aristide would be ineffective without
> his pulpit. And indeed, in the months that followed the

Salinas' decision, he seemed less present in the ongoing struggle of the Haitian poor. But Aristide was a product of the Haitian popular movement, and his persecution only enhanced his standing in the eyes of the poor majority. "Aristide himself, shorn of his church, had already become something much larger than a radical priest. White-robed, hands outstretched Christ-like as he preached, he had become pure symbol: the righteous leader in a nation shorn of them, the pure-hearted bringer of Justice."[125]

Aristide's enormous popularity culminated with his election to the Haitian presidency in December of 1989 in the first truly democratic presidential election in the history of the Haitian republic. Several attempts on his life, and his unsavory treatment at the hands of the Catholic hierarchy served only to enhance his status in the eyes of the popular masses. "As we have seen," writes Greene:

after the ouster of Duvalier, conservative forces in the Church both inside and outside the country led the institution to retreat from its activist role. Consequently, the irrepressible Aristide, with his flamboyant manner and insistence on a new social order, became a special source of irritation. On the other hand, many Haitians came to adore him. On election day, the 37 year old "Titid," or Little Aristide, as he was affectionately called by his supporters, garnered more than 60 percent of the vote.[126]

The prophet of the Haitian masses had become president.

While a detailed analysis of the Aristide's abbreviated presidency—which ran for nine months before the coup of September 1991 and 14 months after his restoration to power in October of 1994—need not occupy us here, it is clear that Aristide was perceived as a serious threat to the traditional power players in Haitian society: the economic elite, known in Haiti as the bourgeoisie, the army, the *macoutes*, and the Church hierarchy. As Farmer insightfully explains:

Although retrospective assessments often emphasize Aristide's "increasingly hard line" stances vis-à-vis the rich, the priest never had much of a honeymoon with any part of what some have called "the four-headed monster" of Haitian society. The army, the church hierarchy, the macoutes, and the wealthy may have felt constrained to temper their criticism of the intensely popular president, but their was little doubt as to their feelings on the matter. "Everyone who is anyone is against Aristide," quipped one well-to-do businessman, speaking to a reporter a couple of weeks before the coup. "Except the people." As elsewhere in Latin America, in Haiti the people are not considered to be anyone.[127]

It was of little surprise to anyone at all familiar with Haitian social and political history when Aristide was overthrown in a coup d'état, led by General Raoul Cédras with the backing of important elements of the Haitian economic elite, in September 1991. Aiming to ameliorate the lives of the masses, the priest/president deemed a weakening of the wealthy and the army a necessary prerequisite to the new social order he had envisioned. Many thought he was promoting class violence with his fiery, nuanced Creole rhetoric; yet it was more the lustful desire among the Haitian elite to maintain in tact their inordinate wealth and their intractable refusal to make any concessions for the masses, rather than any well-founded fear of their being neck-laced by the hungry, that really engendered the coup of 1991.

The rise and fall of Aristide represents a perfect example of what liberation theologian Gustavo Gutiérrez describes the "new historical situation:"

> To the extent that the exploited classes, poor peoples, and despised ethnic groups have been raising their consciousness of the oppression they have suffered for centuries, they have created a new historical situation. It is an ambivalent situation, as is everything historical. But at the same time it is a situation charged with promise—a situation that the lords of the world see rather as a menace.[128]

In September 1991 the lords of the Haitian world did away with the menace. Aristide was whisked off to exile in Washington, where he would become the target of a multifaceted character assassination. The Organization of American States and, later, the UN imposed embargoes on Haiti in an effort to secure Aristide's return. But the traditional Haitian power sectors stood their ground relatively unencumbered by the sanctions. The poor, meanwhile, took the brunt of both the economic hardship brought on by the embargo and the bloody wave of politically motivated violence unleashed by the junta against the pro-Aristide left.

What was the reaction of the Church, once so instrumental in the ouster of the very powers which Aristide countered, to the 1991 coup? "Although the Church was not an active participant in the overthrow of the president, it is unlikely to have shed many tears at the departure of its increasingly hostile Brother."[129] In fact, the Vatican would become the only nation-state in the world to recognize the *putchist* government that toppled Haiti's first truly democratically elected leader, clearly illustrating the reversal of its very short-lived commitment to the preferential option for the Haitian poor. However, as it certainly must be recognized, many brave religious in Haiti continued to speak out in the face of some of the worst oppression ever witnessed in Latin America. The Americas Watch and the National Coalition for Haitian Refugees produced a report in 1993 analyzing the post 1991 coup human rights situation in Haiti. The report details an alarming number of cases of blatant persecution of religious and lay church activists, concluding that:

> [p]riests and lay church activists have suffered unprecedented persecution since the coup.... The Haitian church's response to the continuing attacks have been muted. When priests have been arrested, their bishops have appealed directly to the provincial military commanders involved, usually obtaining their release, but have not made public protests. The Bishops Conference has criticized the OAS sponsored trade embargo of Haiti more directly than it has the harassment and violence of [*sic*] its own members.[130]

As elsewhere in Latin America, the Haitian Church is a church divided; while the hierarchy has in the main been supportive of the traditional Haitian power structure, throughout the country there are priests, nuns, and lay religious leaders who daily have willingly risked making what Jesus considered the greatest expression of friendship to the marginalized masses of Haiti; they have risked their lives.[131]

President Aristide, incidentally, would pass three years of exile in Washington before being restored to power in October 1994. While his return represents one of the most remarkable events in Haitian history, it was neither the CEB's nor Vodou that brought the Cédras junta to surrender power, but U.S. military might. The irony of Aristide's dependence on the very same power that he had so fiercely denounced form the pulpit was not lost on some observers. By 1998, three years after his abbreviated term in office closed, the one-time poor parish priest, prophet of the poor, finds himself married to an upper-class Haitian-American attorney of mulatto bourgeois stock, living in a million dollar home, the father of two children.

A Brief Conclusion

The perpetual manipulation of religious capital toward the maintenance of unjust social structures in Haitian history is perhaps most effectively portrayed and summed up through a succinct comparison of the following two passages, which give examples a quarter-millennium apart. The first is from *Les marrons du syllabaire*, Jean Fouchard's impressive discussion of literacy among colonial maroons; and the second is from *Silencing a People*, which discusses human rights abuses in Haiti from 1991 to 1993:

> *Les marrons du syllabaire*:
> The administration thus associated the Church and the teachings of Christ as instruments of domination and exploitation of the human livestock of the plantations of Saint-Domingue, and the privation of the sacraments as a check against arson, against marronage, against poisonings, and against the abortions that deprived the colonists of new slaves.[132]

> *Silencing a People*:
> In a recent incident, a priest's refusal to offer blessings to the army led to an attack. Not long after midnight on November 19, 1992, the rectory of the Catholic church in Aquin, near Les Cayes, in the south, was the target of

> heavy gunfire. At least 35 bullets struck the building, some of them shattering windows in the parish priest's bedroom. Local church people believe the attack was linked to the refusal of Father Michel Briand, a Frenchman, to offer a Te Deum mass (implying the church's blessing) on November 18, armed forces day in Haiti.[133]

The salient point is clear: in the history of the Haitian religious field, *legitimierende Macht*, or the power of legitimation, has been the most coveted form of religious capital, one upon which the dominant sectors of Haitian society have long relied and therefore insisted.

Accordingly, the Catholic Church, or orthodoxy, has provided such capital for a litany of dominating sectors and regimes, from the slave owners of the sixteenth and seventeenth centuries to the Cédras regime that overthrew Aristide's populist administration. This is the first of its two principal *raisons d'être* in Haitian society. The second is the conquest of the heresiarch, or Vodou, in an effort to secure the production and administration of legitimate religious capital. While there are some positive indications that the Haitian Catholic Church, beginning twenty years ago, has been making efforts to be more dialogical towards Vodou and to be a Church that truly reflects a "preferential option for the poor," the continued preaching of "anti-superstitious" sermons and the Vatican's recognition of the Cédras regime bode otherwise. As Greene concludes in her study of the Haitian Catholic Church, written in part during the Cédras reign:

> The Church has also reverted to the past, silent in the face of a military coup, political repression, and economic misery. There are few brave, committed Church people among the hierarchy or clergy taking the side of the people against the oppressors. *Plus ça change, plus c'est la même chose.* This old adage that the more things change, the more they stay the same, applies once again to Haiti.[134]

Lasting change, it would seem, would require something of a reconstitution of the very structures of the Haitian religious field, which, as we have seen, are not unrelated to the structures of the Haitian economic and political fields. Being that these structures are caked with 500 years of rust, it is no great surprise that the occasional progressive outburst over the centuries from a few Jesuits or Salesians, along with a comparatively late appearance of the phenomenon of base communities on Haitian Catholic soil, have managed to affect little in the way of meaningful change. In light of the Haitian Catholic Church's indissoluble links with certain sectors of Haiti's traditional power elite, such change could only emerge as part and parcel of a sweeping social transformation, which undoubtedly would demand broad-based commitment, not to mention political stability, across successive generations.

NOTES

1.   I have defined religious capital in these terms both in faithfulness to Bourdieu's definition and in sensitivity to possible Afrocentricist objections to my use of a European theorist, himself the product of a mainly European social-scientific heritage, to explain key elements of Haiti's largely African-based religious culture. While some might question whether it is appropriate, for instance, to apply such terms as "salvation" and "holiness" when discussing the ends of Haitian Vodou, once the etymology of these terms is investigated it becomes clear that not only are salvation and holiness matters of concern in Vodou, they are Vodou's raison d'être. As Catholic theologian Leonard Swidler explains, "Salvation is a term that is widespread especially in the Abrahamic Religions, but it is also one which can be used in regard to the final goal of humans in most, if not all, religions.... The term comes from the Latin *salus*, "health," whence a number of English and Romance language cognates are derived, all fundamentally referring to health: salutary, salubrious, salute, salutation. The Germanic counter part is *Heil*, "salvation," and as an adjective *heilig*, "holy," whence the English cognates health, hale, heal, whole, holy. To be "holy" means to be (w)hole. "'Salvation' ultimately means attaining, preserving or restoring a healthy, holy, whole human life—however understood." [Leonard Swidler, *The Meaning of Life at the Edge of the Third Millennium* (Mahwah, NJ: Paulist Press, 1992), p. 16.] Thus understanding the terms salvation and holiness, when we now consider with Haitian Vodou expert Karen McCarthy Brown that "healing is the *primary* business of these [African-based] religious systems" of the Americas, it emerges as altogether clear that Vodou is eminently concerned with salva-

tion and holiness. (Karen McCarthy Brown, "Afro-Caribbean Spirituality: A Haitian Case Study," in Lawrence Sullivan, (ed.), *Healing and Restoring* (New York: MacMillan, 1989), pp. 255-285, p. 257).

2. Loïc J. D. Wacquant, "Towards a Social Praxeology: The Structure and Logic of Bourdieu's Sociology," in Bourdieu and Wacquant, *An Ivitation to Reflexive Sociology*, pp. 1-59, p. 14.

3. Richard Jenkins, *Pierre Bourdieu* (London: Routledge, 1992), p. 104.

4. Bourdieu, Outline of a Theory of Practice, p. 86.

5. The 1454 papal bull *Romanus pontifex* explicitly granted the King of Portugal the right to enslave "pagans." See Valentin Y. Mudimbe, "*Romanus Pontifex* (1454) and the Expansion of Europe," in Vera Lawrence Hyatt, and Rex Nettleford, (eds.), *Race, Discourse, and the Origin of the Americas* (Washington and London: Smithsonian Institute, 1995), pp. 58-65.

6. Pierre Bourdieu, "Genèse et structure du champ religieux." *Revue française de sociologie*, vol. 12, no. 2,1971, pp. 294-334, p. 315.

7. Ibid., p. 305.

8. Pierre Bourdieu, "Legitimation and Structured Interest in Weber's Sociology of Religion," in Samuel Whimster and Scott Lash, eds., *Max Weber, Rationality, and Modernity* (London: Allen and Urwin, 1987), pp. 119-136, p. 126.

9. Ibid., p. 133.

10. Paul Farmer, *The Uses of Haiti* (Monroe, Maine: Common Courage Press, 1994), p. 60.

11. Maya Deren, *The Divine Horsemen: The Living Gods of Haiti* (London and New York: Thames and Hudson, 1953), p. 286. Regarding the distinction between Vodou's two chief rites, Deren explains, "The difference between Rada and Petro is not to be understood on a moral plane, as an opposition between good and evil, although its violence and its closeness to magic has given Petro a reputation for malevolence. The Rada deities may punish severely those who fail in their obligation toward them; and the Petro lwa, if properly propitiated, will "behave." As the Haitians put it, the Petro are 'plus raide': more hard, more tough, more stern, less tolerant and forgiving, more practical and demanding. If the Rada represent the protective, guardian powers, the Petro lwa are the patrons of aggressive action" (p. 61).

12. Most writers agree that the interchange of religious traditions that took place among the maroons was an essential contribution to Vodou's early development. The maroon communities were made

up primarily of escaped slaves and native Americans likewise fleeing European domination. For excellent insight into colonial and
revolutionary maroon communities in Hispaniola, see Jean Fouchard,
Les marrons de la liberté (Port-au-Prince: Deschamps, 1988).

13. Anne Greene, *The Catholic Church in Haiti: Political and Social
Change* (East Lansing: Michigan State University Press, 1993) p.
74.

14. Bourdieu, "Genèse et structure du champ religieux," *Revue française
de sociologie* 12, no. 2,   1971, pp. 294-334,p. 305.

15. Alfred Métraux, *Voodoo in Haiti* (New York: Schocken Books, 1972)
p. 365.

16. Greene, The Catholic Church in Haiti, p. 74.

17. Leslie G. Desmangles, *The Faces of the Gods: Vodou and Roman
Catholicism in Haiti* (Chapel Hill: University of North Carolina
Press, 1992), p. 20.

18. Bourdieu, "Legitimation and Structured Interests in Weber's Sociology of Religion," in Samuel Whimster and Scott Lash, eds., Max
Weber, Rationality, and Modernity (London: Allen and Urwin, 1987),
pp. 119-36, p. 126.

19. Laënnec Hurbon, *Dieu dans le vaudou haïtien* (Port-au-Prince:
Deschamps, 1987), p. 32.

20. Rachel Beauvoir-Dominique, *L'Ancienne cathédrale de Port-au-
Prince: Perspectives d'un vestige de carrefours* (Port-au-Prince:
Deschamps, 1987), p. 16.

21. Las Casas championed the cause of the rights of the indigenous
peoples of the Caribbean, somehow not being moved to consider the
humanity of the Africans whose enslavement he promoted. It is,
nonetheless, noteworthy that the friar would later regret his exclusion of Africans from his lofty consideration.

22. Vincent Bakpetu Thompson, *The Making of the African Diaspora
in the Americas: 1441-1900* (New York: Longman, 1987), p. 82-83.
The term which Thompson apparently coins to refer to the slave
regime, "slavocracy," is a misnomer, as literally *slave-ocracy* would
refer to a regime or state ruled by slaves themselves, rather than to a
regime that rules over slaves.

23. Bourdieu, "Genèse et structure du champ religieux," p. 278.

24. John A. Crow, *The Epic of Latin America* (Garden City: Doubleday,
1946), p. 211.

25. Desmangles, The Faces of the Gods, p. 20.

26. Ibid. "Numerous congregations were invited to send missionaries to
the island, and no doubt the clergy worked tenaciously in the performance of their often unrewarding tasks. But the heat of the scorch-

ing sun, the environmental adjustments to a new tropical habitat, and the long distances to be traveled on foot or on horseback made the priests' work extremely difficult. Yellow fever and malaria also took their toll and made the work even more discouraging. And to these difficulties can be added another: the execrable morality among the early French colonists with whom the priests had to cope."

27. Thompson, *The Making of the African Diaspora in the Americas*, p. 82.

28. Ibid.

29. Beauvoir-Dominique, L'Ancienne cathédrale de Port-au-Prince, p. 17.

30. 32. Métraux, *Voodoo in Haiti*, pp. 25-26.

31. Deren, *The Divine Horsemen*, pp. 58-59.

32. Geoffrey Parrinder, *African Traditional Religion* (London: S.P.C.K., 1962), p. 11.

33. Gabriel Setiloane, *African Theology: An Introduction* (Johannesburg: Skotaville Publishers, 1986), p. 6.

34. John S. Mbiti, *African Religions and Philosophy* (Oxford: Heinemann, 1969), p. 103.

35. Michel S. Laguerre, *Voodoo and Politics in Haiti* (New York: St. Martin's, 1981), p. 23. The question of syncretism in Haitian Vodou is further and extensively discussed in chapter five.

36. Greene, *The Catholic Church in Haiti*, p. 75.

37. Michel Hector and Claude Moïse, *Colonisation et ésclavage en Haïti: Le regime colonial français à Saint-Domingue (1625-1789)* (Port-au-Prince: Deschamps, 1990), p. 64-65.

38. Greene, The Catholic Church in Haiti, p. 75.

39. Bourdieu, "Genèse et structure du champ religieux," p. 318.

40. Laënnec Hurbon, "Esclavage et Evangelisation: Point de depart pour une méthodologie de l'histoire de l'Eglise d'Haïti," in Conférence des religieux d'Haïti (CRH), *L'Evangelisation d'Haïti, Tome I: L'Evangelisation et L'Esclavage* (Port-au-Prince: CRH, 1991), pp. 43-71, p. 50-51.

41. Thompson, *The Making of the African Diaspora in the Americas*, p. 163.

42. Hurbon, "Esclavage et Evangelisation," p. 52.

43. For a discussion of resistance to enslavement both in Africa and during the Middle Passage, see Thompson, *The Making of the African Diaspora in the Americas,* chapter four.

44. Farmer, *The Uses of Haiti*, p. 62-63.

45. Leon-François Hoffmann, *Haïti: couleurs, croyances, créole* (Montreal: CIDIHCA, 1990), p. 120.

46. Métraux, *Voodoo in Haiti*, p. 46.

47. Several writers attest that Makandal was a Muslim and fluent in Arabic. This raises the possibility that he interpreted his attacks on the colonists as a veritable *jihad*.

48. Hoffmann, *Haïti*, p. 120. In a later controversial article Hoffmann questions whether the Bois Caïman ceremony actually ever took place. See the chapter twelve of *Haïti: lettres et l'être* (Toronto: GREF, 1992).

49. The text of this sermon is taken from Laguerre, *Voodoo and Politics in Haiti*, p. 62.

50. Vittorio Lanternari, *Religions of the Oppressed* (London: MacGibbon & Kee, 1963), p. 4.

51. Ibid., p. 3.

52. Cited in Hurbon, "Esclavage et Evangelisation," p. 60-61.

53. Odette Mennesson Rigaud, "Le Role du Vaudou dans l'indépendance d'Haïti." *Présence Africaine*, 17-18, 1958, pp. 43-67, p. 43.

54. Harold Courlander and Rémy Bastien, *Religion and Politics in Haiti*, p. 42.

55. Laguerre, "The Place of Voodoo in the Social Structure of Haiti," pp. 43-44.

56. Ibid., 44.

57. Greene, *The Catholic Church in Haiti*, p. 79.

58. "Reflections sur une lettre de Mazères," 1816, as cited in Hoffmann, *Haïti*, p. 102.

59. Laguerre, "The Place of Voodoo in the Social Structure of Haiti," p. 44.

60. Hurbon, "Esclavage et Evangelisation," p. 53.

61. Greene, The Catholic Church in Haiti, p. 80.

62. Jean Price-Mars, *Ainsi parla l'oncle* (Montréal: Leméac, 1973), p. 231.

63. Hoffmann, *Haïti*, p. 125.

64. Courlander and Bastien, *Religion and Politics in Haiti*, p. 50.

65. Métraux, *Voodoo in Haiti*, p. 331.

66. Desmangles, *The Faces of the Gods*, p. 43. Métraux would agree with Desmangles assertion: The entrenchment of Voodoo in Haiti is largely due to what local historians rather pompously call 'the great Haiti schism'. Throughout the period which stretched from the proclamation of independence to the Concordat of 1860, Haiti had in fact been separated from Rome and remained outside the framework of the Church. It was only Catholic in its solemn declarations of its various constitutions. Catholic worship had fallen into unworthy hands." (*Voodoo in Haiti*, p. 50.)

67. Desmangles, *The Faces of the Gods*, p. 43.
68. Greene, *The Catholic Church in Haiti*, p. 84.
69. Robert Lawless, *Haiti's Bad Press* (Rochester, VT: Schenkman, 1992), p. 56.
70. Greene, *The Catholic Church in Haiti*, p. 85.
71. Desmangles, *The Faces of the Gods*, p. 43.
72. Ibid.
73. Laguerre, "The Place of Voodoo in the Social Structure of Haiti," pp. 46.
74. Courlander and Bastien, *Religion and Politics in Haiti*, p. 17.
75. Desmangles, *The Faces of the Gods*, p. 46.
76. Métraux, *Voodoo in Haiti*, pp. 50-51.
77. Greene, The Catholic Church in Haiti, p. 86.
78. Ibid., p. 90.
79. Adolphe Cabon, *Notes sur l'histoire religieuse d'Haïti, de la révolution au concordat: 1789-1860* (Port-au-Prince: Petit Séminaire Collège St. Martial, 1933), p. 227.
80. Greene, *The Catholic Church in Haiti*, p. 94.
81. Laënnec Hurbon, "Enjeu politique de la crise actuelle de l'église," *Chemins critiques*, vol. 1, no. 1, 1989, pp. 13-22, p. 21.
82. Hurbon, *Dieu dans le vaudou haïtien*, p. 21.
83. Greene, The Catholic Church in Haiti, p. 94.
84. Ibid., p. 103.
85. Desmangles, *The Faces of the Gods*, pp. 31-32.
86. Laguerre, "The Place of Voodoo in the Social Structure of Haiti," pp. 47.
87. Métraux, *Voodoo in Haiti*, pp. 56.
88. Greene, *The Catholic Church in Haiti*, pp. 101. "Bocors" (*bokò*) are sorcerers in some parts of Haiti. Elsewhere the term is synonymous with *oungan*.
89. Métraux, *Voodoo in Haiti*, pp. 338.
90. Ibid.
91. Ibid.
92. Jean-Marie Jan, *Collecta pour l'histoire religieuse du diocèse du Cap-Haïtien, Tome 3* (Port-au-Prince: Deschamps, 1958), p. 355.
93. Greene, *The Catholic Church in Haiti*, p. 106.
94. Cited in Métraux, *Voodoo in Haiti*, p. 337.
95. Ibid., p. 341.
96. Métraux, *Voodoo in Haiti*, pp. 341-342.
97. Ibid.
98. Ibid., p. 343.
99. Ibid., p. 351.

100. Ibid., p. 343.

101. Hurbon, *Dieu dans le vaudou haïtien*, p. 22. Written in the mid-seventies, it is possible that this is no longer Hurbon's position, or that today he would soften the tone of his assertion. In an essay written a decade later, Hurbon notes in Catholic Masses "the widespread use of the *tambour* [drum], the instrument par excellence of the Vodou cult, and the very rhythms of Vodou in the hymns. The people are little by little coming to recognize and find themselves at home in the Church, and thus no longer identifying it as a foreign institution." However, later in the same piece, Hurbon still laments "this pretension of the Catholicism to be the one and only to provide Haitian society with the basis of its identity and the coordinates of its symbolic system." *Comprendre Haïti: Essai sur l'etat, la nation, la culture* (Port-au-Prince: Deschamps, 1987), pp. 112, 120.

102. Hurbon, *Comprendre Haïti*, p. 110.

103. Bourdieu, "Genèse et structure du champ religieux," pp. 319-320.

104. Laguerre, "The Place of Voodoo in the Social Structure of Haiti," p. 48.

105. Courlander and Bastien, *Religion and Politics in Haiti*, p. 17.

106. Ibid., p. 59.

107. Ibid.

108. Bernard Diedrich and Al Burt, *Papa Doc and the Tonton Macoutes* (Port-au-Prince: Deschamps, 1986), p. 279.

109. Farmer, *The Uses of Haiti*, p. 111.

110. Desmangles, *The Faces of the Gods*, p. 54.

111. Elizabeth Abbot, *Haiti: The Duvaliers and their Legacy* (New York: McGraw-Hill, 1988), p. 140, as cited in Farmer, *The Uses of Haiti*, p. 111.

112. Farmer, *The Uses of Haiti*, p. 111.

113. Ibid, p. 112.

114. Conférence des Religieux Haïtienne, *Communiqué*, 4 December 1980. As cited in Hurbon, *Comprendre Haïti*, p. 109.

115. Ibid.

116. "Peace," #27" (Medellín document), in *The Gospel of Peace and Justice: Catholic Social Teaching since Pope John*, presented by Joseph Gremillon (Maryknoll, NY: Orbis, 1976), p. 462.

117. Leonardo Boff and Virgil Elizondo, "Editorial: Theology from the Viewpoint of the Poor," in Leonardo Boff and Virgil Elizondo, (eds.), *Concilium*, 187 (May 1986) *Option for the Poor: Challenge to the Rich Countries* (Edinburgh: T.& T. Clark, 1986. pp. ix-xii, p. ix.

118. Greene, *The Catholic Church in Haiti*, pp. 132-133.

119. Quoted in Ibid., p. 138.

120. Greene, *The Catholic Church in Haiti*, p. 191, p. 206.

121. Amy Wilentz, "Foreword," in Jean-Bertrand Aristide, *In the Parish of the Poor: Writings from Haiti* (Maryknoll: Orbis, 1990) pp. ix-xxiv, pp. xi-xii.

122. Farmer, *The Uses of Haiti*, p. 145.

123. Aristide, *In the Parish of the Poor*, pp. 53-55.

124. Franklin Midy, L'Affaire Aristide en perspective: Histoire de la formation et du rejet d'une vocation prophétique. *Chemins critiques*, vol. 1, no. 1, 1989, pp. 45-56, p. 45.

125. Farmer, *The Uses of Haiti*, p. 148.

126. Greene, The Catholic Church in Haiti, p. 246.

127. Farmer, *The Uses of Haiti*, pp. 178-9.

128. Gustavo Gutiérrez, *The Power of the Poor in History*. As cited in Farmer, *The Uses of Haiti*, p. 143.

129. Greene, The Catholic Church in Haiti, p. 246.

130. America's Watch, and National Coalition for Haitian Refugees, *Silencing a People: The Destruction of Civil Society in Haiti* (New York: Human Rights Watch, 1993), p. 79.

131. At least one priest did in fact sacrifice his life in the name of the oppressed. On August 29, 1994, Father Jean-Marie Vincent, a long-time social activist and friend of Aristide, was gunned down by paramilitary agents in broad daylight outside the residence of the Monfortain Fathers in Port-au-Prince. His killers, as with most cases of politically motivated murder in Haiti, have yet to be brought to justice. His martyrdom for the Haitian people, however, is a source of great inspiration to those who continue in the struggle for justice in Haiti. Graffiti and tee-shirts can be seen about the capital exhorting, *Pè Jean Marie: An Swiv Tras Li* ("Father Jean-Marie: Let us follow his footsteps." The word *tras* in Creole literally translates as trace, in the sense of something left behind).

132. Fouchard, *Les marrons du syllabaire*, p. 43.

133. America's Watch, and National Coalition for Haitian Refugees, *Silencing a People*, p. 43.

134. Greene, *The Catholic Church in Haiti*, p. 253.

CHAPTER THREE

THEOLOGICAL AND SOCIOLOGICAL INTERPRETATIONS OF THE VIRGIN MARY

Scriptural References to Mary

It is remarkable that one of the most important figures in the history of religion should have such scant reference in scripture. Yet such is the case with the Virgin Mary, mother of Jesus, whom the New Testament refers to by name only in two Gospels and the Book of Acts.[1] There are two kinds of discussions of Mary in these writings: (1) the infancy narratives; and (2) discourses concerning her role in Jesus' mission.

The infancy narratives, passages dealing with the miraculous birth of Jesus of Nazareth, appear only in the Gospels according to Matthew and Luke, the former giving Mary a role of far less significance than the latter. Matthew portrays Joseph, rather than Mary, in dialogue with the angel over God's divine plan, Mary represented here as a more or less passive agent in the arrangement. Moreover, Matthew offers little in the way of theological reflection on the virgin conception, one of the central tenets of Mariology. Luke's account, on the other hand, carries momentous theological and mariological import in comparison. In Luke, as notes feminist theologian Rosemary Radford Ruether, Mary is the key figure, receiving the angel's visit and actively cooperating with God in the event:

Luke makes Mary an active participant in the drama of Jesus' birth, accepting it through free consent, and meditating upon the meaning of the future mission. Thus Luke begins a tradition which transforms Mary from being merely the historical mother of Jesus into an independent agent cooperating with God in the redemption of humanity. In other words she becomes a theological agent in her own right. This is expressed especially in her obedient consent to the divine command: "And Mary said, 'Behold, I am the handmaid of the Lord; let it be to me according to your word.'"(1:38)[2]

Luke further influences the development and character of Marianism by expounding upon a continual dimension of Mary's activity in God's economy of salvation. While the virgin conception is a single historical moment, albeit with eternal consequences, Luke also gives Mary the role of intermediary on behalf of the marginalized in the stirring Magnificat, in which she proclaims the following:

> My being proclaims the greatness of the Lord,
> my spirit finds joy in God my savior,
> For he has looked upon his servant in her lowliness;
> all ages to come shall call me blessed.
> God who is mighty has done great things for me,
> holy is his name;
> His mercy is from age to age
> on those who fear him.
>
> He has shown might with his arm;
> he has confused the proud in their inmost thoughts.
> He has deposed the mighty from their thrones
> and raised the lowly to high places.
> The hungry he has given every good thing,
> while the rich he has sent empty away.
> He has upheld Israel his servant,
> ever mindful of his mercy;
> Even as he promised our fathers,
> promised Abraham and his descendants forever.
> (1:46-55)

The Catholic Church hierarchy, wittingly blind to the feminist implications in Mary's proclamation, has unfortunately muted the influence of the Magnificat on official Mariology. "As a result, for centuries Christianity has rendered the critical, liberating context of the Magnificat impotent."[3] This statement is certainly true on the level of orthodox Catholic doctrine,[4] which, in any case, hardly reflects the belief of the masses. However, the influence of the Magnificat on popular Marianism, while varying from country to country and community to community, has been considerable overall. Several Haitian lay TKL leaders whom I interviewed attest to the Magnificat being the preferred prayer for reflection in their groups. The reasons are clear, for in the Magnificat there are powerful implications of Mary's power and closeness to God in God's using her as the initial human agent in the process of salvation; her worthiness of veneration is reflected in her claim—almost exigent in tone—that "all nations shall come to call me blessed;" and her solidarity with the poor and her role in the Christian "theodicy of compensation"[5] is evident in her celebration of God's raising "the lowly to high places...while the rich he has sent empty away."

In popular Latin American Marianism, Mary's concern for the downtrodden is a crucial theme, surely one of the most powerfully attractive aspects of the symbol of Mary for the under-classes of the region, the Caribbean included. The Magnificat provides the scriptural basis for this fundamental element of popular Marianism, a theme to which we shall return later in this chapter in the context of the Mariology of Leonardo Boff and liberation theology. The key point here is that in its infancy narrative and the Magnificat, the Gospel of Luke provides the scriptural "fountainhead of Mariology."[6]

Luke's gospel, somewhat ironically however, is also the source of what has been perhaps the most troublesome biblical passage to Marian apologists. From among a crowd who had gathered to hear Jesus preach, a woman cried, "Blessed be the womb that bore you, and the breasts that you sucked!" to which Jesus retorts, "Blessed rather are those who hear the word of God and keep it!" (11:27-28). The Gospel of Mark likewise records Jesus apparently rebuffing, if not belittling, his mother and kinship group. A number of Jesus' "friends" had begun to question his psychological well being and apparently solicited his "mother and brethren" to confront him. Upon being informed of their beckoning, Jesus responds, "Who is my mother, or my brethren! For whosoever shall do the will of God, the same is my brother, and my sister, and my mother" (3:31-35). While Mariologians have attempted to confront the problems posed by these passages, official Catholic dogma, as Marina Warner notes:

> has consistently overlooked the apparent hard-heartedness in Jesus' words and stubbornly fastened on this passage as an example of the honour given Mary in the Gospels. Pope Paul VI, in his 1974 statement on the cult of the Virgin, urges all Christians to follow the woman's example in praising Mary as the mother of God, the instrument of the Incarnation. Jesus' reply does not contradict or deny the woman's accolade, but rephrases it in a loftier and more Christian way in order to emphasize the spiritual mother-hood of the Church, which is prefigured by his own mother, the Virgin.[7]

While biblical passages such as these clearly raise doubts as to whether Mary was a follower of Jesus during his lifetime, else-where scripture gives evidence that she indeed did become a dis-ciple either at the time of her son's death or during the ensuing events. In the final chapter of Luke's gospel Mary is included among the group of believers who first receive news of the vanished corpse, while Acts 1:14 portrays Mary as praying with the disciples in the upper room at Pentecost. As for the remainder of the Book of Acts, Jesus' mother plays no significant role in the early Christian com-munity, virtually disappearing from the account.

The Gospel of John—regarded by biblical scholars as the least historically accurate of the gospels—includes two discussions of Mary that are not recorded in the Synoptic Gospels. John 2:1-11 portrays Jesus' first miracle, the turning of the water into wine at Canaan, as being performed at the behest of Mary. Further paint-ing Mary in an apparently positive light, John's gospel alone places Mary at the foot of the cross (19:25). Although these passages have struck Marian apologists as indicative of Mary's influence over her son, when the stories are interpreted in the context of Johanine theology, as demonstrated by Ruether:

> the impression that they exalt Mary somewhat disappears. John's Gospel is built on the contrast between the fleshy

level of reality, where all is blindness and disbelief, and the spiritual level of redeeming insight. The Jews, Jesus' family, and even the disciples are foils of the realm of darkness and unbelief against which the drama of revelation is played out. The story of the miracle of Canaan reflects these two levels. Jesus' miracle is a sign that the old waters of purification, i.e., the Jewish law, have been superseded by the 'new wine' of the gospel. Mary's role reflects a double meaning. Belonging to the world of fleshy kinship [Mary] sees the matter literally. Jesus' harsh response to her: "O woman, what have you to do with me? (2:4) indicates her lack of understanding of the inner meaning he is about to reveal through his response to her request.[8]

Moreover, given the historical uncertainty of the fourth gospel, written by "a Jew trying to convince fellow Jews in some diaspora city...that God's wisdom had appeared in a man," one must "be wary about the use one makes of the gospel according to John."[9] This caution holds as much for Mariology as for Christology. In effect, parallel distinctions emerge in each of these two theological branches, as in Christology theologians debate the reality of Jesus the man, a low christological position, and Christ the Lord, a high christological position. Likewise in Mariology theologians examine the differences between Miriam, the poor Jewish mother of Jesus, and Mary, regal Queen of Heaven, Mother of God. The former we may, taking cue from christological parlance, refer to as a low or minimalist Mariology, while the latter is a high or maximalist Mariology. The point here is that biblical criticism demands serious consideration when raising such questions as to Mary's identity her place in Christian theology.

Extra-Christian Influences on the Development of the Cult of Mary

Passages that exalt Mary are very much the exception in the New Testament, as on the whole biblical representation of Mary is very slender and somewhat disparaging. Paul does not even mention her by name. In general Mary's position in the New Testament is subordinate, and her "significance is entirely secondary: she is the inviolate vessel for God's holy word, she bears Christ, but she is not herself a goddess. Her character, insofar as she is given one, is a model of loving obedience to something higher than herself."[10] What, then, explains the explosion of the Mary cult by the fifth century? Is it the general resemblance of popular Marian devotion to goddess worship? Given her dubious stature in scripture, how are we to understand Mary's elevation to one of the greatest religious symbols in human history? How, then, did the figure of Mary become dogmatized in the Catholic Church as perpetually virgin, Mother of God, Mother of the Church, immaculately conceived, assumed body and soul into heaven, reigning queen of heaven?

For Joseph Campbell, erudite scholar of mythology, the answer to these questions lies chiefly in Mary's inheritance "of all the names and forms, sorrows, joys, and consolation of the goddess—mother in the Western World...Seat of Wisdom...Vessel of Honour...Mystical Rose...House of Gold...Gate of Heaven...Morning Star...Refuge of Sinners...Queen of Angels...Queen of Peace."[11] It is a remarkable transition from the humble, unassuming scriptural figure of Mary to the Christian goddess. Indeed, "within 500 years of her "death" a pantheon of images enveloped her until she assumed the presence and stature of all the goddesses before her—Cybele, Aphrodite, Dmeter, Astarte, Isis, Hathor, Inanna and Ishtar. Like them, she is both virgin and mother, and like many of them, she gives birth to a half human, half divine child."[12] The development of the cult of Mary is, thus, to a great extent explicable in terms of Mary's absorption of the status, characteristics, and powers of waning and bygone goddesses of mythical tradition.

Remarkably, despite orthodoxy's persistent intention of representing Mary in a fashion amenable to its arbitrary interests and of having the laity perceive her accordingly, the fact is that on the popular level she very much represents a survival or reincarnation of the Great Mother goddess, or "the reinstatement of the devalued feminine principle."[13] Elizabeth Gould Davis goes so far as to assert that the Christian religion only survived due to the capacity for goddess worship which the symbol of Mary afforded:

> The church seemed doomed to failure, destined to go down
> to bloody death amid the bleeding corpses of its victims,
> when the people discovered Mary. And only when Mary,

> against the stern decrees of the church, was dug out of the
> oblivion which Constantine had assigned her and became
> identified with the Great Goddess was Christianity finally
> tolerated by the people.[14]

In Davis' view, then, it was the universal human religious need to
identify the Godhead as, at least in part, feminine that led to the
identification of Mary with the Mother Goddess, to the rise in the
cult of Mary, and, consequently, to the spread of Christianity.

This influence of mythical goddesses and, significantly, the reli-
gious needs to which they responded, on the evolution of popular
Marianism is poignantly discussed in Anne Baring and Jules
Cashford's impressive study *The Myth of the Goddess*:

> It had taken less than a century for Mary to take over the
> role of Isis, Cybele and Diana, the remaining goddesses,
> whose cults had dwindled with the decline of the Roman
> empire and were, in any case, often suppressed, with their
> temples closed and their teachers and priests banished. In
> fact, it looks as if the imagery of the older goddesses had
> passed directly on to the figure of Mary, inspired by the
> needs of the people and perhaps also by the understanding
> of the priests that these long-established customs of devo-
> tion had to be understood in terms of the new religion.
> Somewhere between AD 400 and 500 the Temple of Isis
> at Soissons in France was dedicated to the "Blessed Vir-
> gin Mary". Isis and Cybele had been "mother of the Gods";
> Mary was now "Mother of God".[15]

Pamela Berger, in *The Goddess Obscured*, examines one significant instance of this phenomenon, illustrating the survival of the
ancient grain goddess in the medieval conception of Mary, which
represents a victory of popular Marian devotion over orthodoxy's
efforts to both exploit and constrain the heretical association of Mary
with the ancient goddesses.[16] Numerous other examples of pagan
goddess influences on the perception and portrayal of the Virgin
Mary could be given from the history of Marian images in art
throughout the ages, yet the few references just made will, for the
sake of brevity, have to suffice, as another matter now demands our
attention. It does remain for us, however, to investigate Mary's

conflation with the original goddesses of the evangelized in the Haitian context, which shall be approached through an analysis of popular Haitian Catholic belief in subsequent chapters, exploring in particular Mary's conflation with Ezili, the African-derived female spirit of love in Vodou. Such shall represent, essentially, a study of Mary in Haiti's "religion of the people." But first an outline of Mary in the "religion of the intellectuals," to complete Gramsci's dichotomy, or the development of orthodox Marian dogma, demands attention.

The Evolution of Catholic Marian Dogma

Early Centuries
Historical record gives evidence that personal devotion to Mary was growing significantly by the third century and becoming widespread in the Church by the middle of the fourth. In particular, the earliest forms of the Mary cult were those of the Perpetual Virgin, the Mother of God, and the Queen of Heaven. Geographically, the locus of the nascent cult was in the East, from whence derives "the oldest extant prayer addressing Mary and using the term *"Theotokos"*: "Under your mercy we take refuge, *Theotokos*, do not reject our supplications in necessity but deliver us from danger."[17] Gramsci's distinction between "religion of the people" and "religion of the intellectuals" is recognizable in virtually every epoch in Christian history, as popular belief has often developed in heretical forms extraneously to orthodox dogma. Such, indeed, was the case in the early Church in the East, for popular conceptions of Mary were not always sanctioned by the teachings of the first great Christian theologians. While the Greek Fathers devoted much attention to the particulars of Mary's virginity, and for the most part esteemed her as altogether worthy of honor and veneration, it was on the popular level that the symbol of Mary rapidly developed into the Christian goddess, readily absorbing the attributes and powers of the mythical goddesses supplanted by Christianity and responding to the same religious needs as they. In *The Divine Heiress*, a fascinating study of Marianism in Christian Constantinople, Vasiliki Limberis illustrates this dichotomy between popular and official Marianism in the early Church:

> Although the early Fathers were slow to venture far from
> the gospel of Luke, Mary's life and power captured the

hearts and minds of many other faithful people. This phenomenon manifested itself during the second century in the spread of creative "popular" literature that facilitated the crystallization of special beliefs about Mary. The apocryphal stories, written around 140-160 CE, fueled the imagination of popular piety, and helped make Christianity understandable to a greater sector of Greco-Roman society. The stories about Mary formed "the real world of Christian belief."[18]

Devotion to Mary was slower to catch on in the West. It was not until the sixth century that Mary's name appears in the canon of the Mass; in the seventh century the Western Church adopted numerous Marian feasts of Eastern origin; and in the tenth, belief in the miraculous power of prayer to Mary was widespread.

On the theological level, Marianism in the West was greatly influenced by the writings of Ambrose:

> who gave Western Mariology its decisive direction. For Ambrose (d.397), Mary's physical and moral purity was necessitated by her divine motherhood, for, he says, Christ would not have chosen for his mother a woman defiled by the seed of man. Ambrose also affirmed her intimate relationship with the Church—a theme likewise developed by his disciple Augustine.[19]

The Augustinian understanding of human sexuality, as it were, would have profound influence on both the orthodox Catholic understanding of Mary, particularly the notion of her own immaculate conception, and thus on the place accorded to women in the Church in general.

The Council of Ephesus in 431 advanced the first official doctrinal promulgation regarding Mary, defining her divine Motherhood. At Ephesus, Mary's title of *"Theotokos"* ("God bearer"), became dogma. While Origen (d.230) is credited with having first coined the term for Mary, it would take the forceful influence of the person and theological arguments of Cyril of Alexandria (d.444) for it to pass into doctrine. Typifying the mariological position of the early Fathers, Cyril conceived of Mary as deserving of praise as the vehicle "through whom God becomes incarnate in Jesus, yet clearly places her in a position far subordinate to her son." Commenting on the Marian hymns that Cyril composed, Limberis writes, "even though they extol the *Theotokos* in high terms, they show that Cyril is primarily concerned with Christology and that his praise of the *Theotokos* is necessarily derivative of that Christology."[20] In effect, virtually all important conciliar discourse concerning Mary refers to her mainly in a christological context, as was the case at Ephesus. For, whether Mary is *Theotokos* or *Christotokos* would depend upon the true nature of her son, i.e., on whether he were human or divine. On the popular level, however, the christological contingency of mariological thought is usually eclipsed, and to proclaim her "Mother of God" effectively legitimized the pinning of the entire host of Goddess attributes upon Mary in the minds of the masses, for whom high-flung theological discourse was a foreign affair of little concern.

The popular masses of the city consequently greeted the Ephesus proclamation of Mary as Mother of God with enthusiastic celebration. "Ephesus was, significantly, the very place where the great temple to Artemis, or Diana as she was called in Roman times, had stood for many centuries. The cult of Artemis or Diana had been repressed in AD380 by the emperor Theodosius, and the people, deprived of their goddess, readily turned to Mary instead,"[21] in much the same way as many Haitians, in the face of centuries of the Church's repression of Vodou, would assimilate Mary with Ezili.

Among theologians two important mariological themes, Mary conceived of as the new Eve and as the Church, had already developed as early as the second century:

> For Justin...and Irenaeus...Eve's disobedience at the fall (Genesis 3:6) was counterbalanced by Mary's obedience at the conception of the Son of God (Luke 1:38). Tertullian, for his part...saw Eve's being formed from a rib of the sleeping Adam (Genesis 2:21-22), followed by his naming her the mother of all human beings (Genesis 3:20), as a figure of the Church being formed from the pierced side of the dying Christ (John 19:34). Originally, then, there were two separate parallels: one between Eve and Mary, and the other between Mary and the Church.[22]

Thus, the symbol of Mary was accorded a significant place in Catholic ecclesiology at a very early stage in Church history, one to which theologians would return again and again throughout the ages. The conception of Mary as the Mother of the Church, while controversial, has thus proven one of the most important themes in the history of Mariology.

As Marianism progressed during the first six centuries of Church history, the Virgin's humanity became increasingly transcended by her divinity. The Ephesus proclamation of Mary as *Theotokos*, as mentioned above, sanctioned for the masses the highest of mariological suppositions, in effect elevating Mary to the status of goddess. For theologians, too, the implications of the proclamation were weighty, as reflected in the title given to Mary at the Council of Chalcedon in 451: *"Aeiparthenos"* ("Ever Virgin"). Two hundred years later Pope Martin I, at the Fourth Lateran Council, reaffirmed the perpetual virginity of Mary with this title. Within the next two and a half centuries, her removal from the human condition was complete, as Catholics became convinced that Mary was simply immortal, having escaped both the stain of original sin and the pains of death. Yet despite the remarkable expansion of the cult of Mary, the proliferation of Marian feasts, and the progressively expansive deification of the Blessed Mother, orthodoxy would allow roughly more than a dozen centuries to pass before promulgating any further official dogma concerning the Mother of the Church.

Although it would not become dogma until the twentieth century, the doctrine of the Assumption, which states that Mary was assumed body and soul into heaven, originally derives from a number of ancient apocryphal stories from the East as early as the third century. Belief in the Assumption was already the inspiration for a Marian feast by the seventh century, illustrating the then popular perception of Mary as more a heavenly than an earthy being. "Pope Nicholas I (858-67) placed the Assumption on par with Christmas and Easter—tantamount to declaring Mary's translation to heaven as important as the Incarnation and the Resurrection."[23] Likewise, the other modern Catholic proclamation of Marian doctrine, the Immaculate Conception, has roots very early in Church history, back as far as Augustine.

Middle Ages

In the Middle Ages, especially between the eleventh and fifteenth centuries, the cult of Mary reached its zenith. The notion that God's wrathful judgment could be tempered by Mary, originally an eighth century idea traceable to St. Germanus (d. 733), "became one of the most popular themes of medieval Marian piety and devotion."[24] Several other unmistakably key elements of Marian piety were also introduced during this period:

> From the twelfth century the biblical Ave Maria—in the present form, with the plea for her aid at the hour of death, only from 1500—has become the most widespread form of prayer and is linked with the Our Father. The Angelus stems from the thirteenth century, [and] the Rosary from the thirteenth to the fifteenth....[25]

A number of factors influenced the medieval flourishing of the cult, perhaps none more than the Crusades, as knights rode off to the Middle East praying to Mary for success in their campaigns to wrest the Holy Land from the Muslims. Increasingly, medieval churches were consecrated to the Virgin; for example, "the extraordinary wave of adulation raised eighty cathedrals in France within a century,"[26] each of them named for the one or another Marian appellation. The Virgin thus inspired the creative soul of the medieval architect and artist, whose work in turn seemingly brought Mary closer to the believer: "The special dramatic genius of the middle ages, which could transform arid theology into vivid pictures and lively theatre, created the Virgin in the image of a human, approachable, supremely adorable woman who stood by humanity like a mother but loved it like a mistress."[27]

As for "arid theology," in the Middle Ages it, too, reached something of a zenith in the brilliance of the Scholastics, for whom Mary was a topic of considerable interest. The Scholastics developed the maximalist mariological principal that the Virgin was the irreplaceable mediatrix in the economy of salvation. "Anselm (d.1109), the father of Scholasticism, who exerted a tremendous influence on Mariology, insisted on her share in the redemption—basing his opinion on the strict parallelism between her divine motherhood and the fatherhood of God."[28] Anselm's student Eadmer (d.1124) was the first theologian to formally develop arguments for the Immaculate Conception, which had actually first been formulated by Augustine (d.430). The great Bernard of Clairvaux (d.1153) expanded Anselm's discussion of Mary's essential role in salvation, claiming that "God willed us to have everything through Mary."

Eadmer's defense of the doctrine of the Immaculate Conception did not meet with universal acceptance. The reticence of other theologians, most notably Aquinas (d.1274) and Bonaventure (d.1274), to embrace the doctrine was due to their refusal to grant Mary exemption from the consequences and universal guilt of original sin, an exemption they felt to be uniquely reserved for Christ. The crux of the matter was that if Mary had been ordinarily conceived, then she, too, would be subject to the consequences of original sin and, thus, need God's grace through Christ for redemption. For Aquinas and Bonaventure, following Peter Lombard and Pope Leo the Great, removing Mary from this human condition would be beyond theological reason.

Franciscan Scholastic Duns Scotus, "the principal architect" of the doctrine of the Immaculate Conception, approached the debate from a different angle, arguing that Mary was immune from the consequences of sin:

> in virtue of the anticipated merits of Christ. The crux of his argument was in viewing original sin as a deprivation, instead of linking it with concupiscence, as in the prevailing Augustinian view. God, therefore, could have infused grace into her soul from the very first instant.[29]

Scotus' argument would gradually overcame all detractors, for in 1476 Pope Sixtus IV approved the feast of the Immaculate Conception. Nevertheless, the doctrine's promotion to the status of official Catholic dogma would have to wait until the nineteenth century.

Further dignifying the cult of the Virgin Mary, the Scholastics also dogmatized the belief that Mary possessed greater potency than the saints and was therefore due a distinguished form of devotion. "Going beyond the veneration of the saints (*doulia*), veneration of Mary (*hyper-doulia*) was in fact distinguished theologically from the adoration (*latira*) of God."[30]

Reformation and Counter-Reformation

The doctrines of the Immaculate Conception and the Assumption proved points of controversy for the Protestant reformers. While reverent of Mary and supportive of the doctrines of her perpetual virginity, divine motherhood, and powers of intervention on the behalf of sinners, "Luther insisted on her emptiness and lowliness," while Calvin "completely rejected" the notion that Mary had any role in salvation.[31] Indeed, among other excesses in the Church against which the reformers so forcefully argued, Marianism had become rife with heresy and superstition and also stood in need of theological address. Protestants all but abandoned Marian devotion, while "[t]he Catholic tendency to go to excess in venerating Mary, which was always present in the Middle Ages, remained strong in post-Reformation times."[32]

In effect, during the Reformation the subject of devotion to Mary, to this day a stumbling block to ecumenism, became a point of theological conflict between Protestants and Catholics and had the effect of further widening the rift. Despite a rise in Marian maximalism in the post-Reformation period, later, in light of the intellectual force of the Enlightenment, "devotion to Mary appeared to be a medieval relic. The Hail Mary was dropped and the Rosary abandoned. Her feasts were reduced to a minimum and her shrines forsaken."[33]

To trace the development of any Church doctrine amounts to a fascinating study, perhaps none more so than that of the Immaculate Conception, with its lengthy history and the contribution of some of the greatest minds in Church history. Doubtless, the doctrine was used as a weapon of symbolic violence against Protestants during the Counter Reformation. Yet while embraced and promoted by the most illustrious of popes and theologians from the time of Augustine, the doctrine would not become dogma until the nineteenth century. It was a gradual elevation to such status that depended upon some significant mariological groundwork laid at the Council of Trent from 1545 to 1563, during which the Catholic Church took stock of itself in the wake of the Reformation.

Trent's actual Marian proclamations were of far less momentous import for Marianism than another conciliar decision treating a different subject. The doctrine of the Immaculate Conception was not formally proclaimed at Trent, though the Council did consider Mary to be free from the stain of original sin. Of greater significance for Mariology and the cult of Mary was the Council's promotion of unwritten Church traditions to the status of equal authority with scripture, which effectively "gave traditional beliefs, like the legends that fleshed out the shadowy Mary of Nazareth, a claim to canonical authority."[34] In effect, extra-scriptural sources for Marian beliefs were thereby sanctioned, which, when one considers with Jürgen Moltmann that already "the discrepancy between Church teaching and New Testament is nowhere as great as in Mariology,"[35] emerges as inestimably significant for both popular Marianism and formal Mariology.

Of course, biblical measures for doctrine have since the Reformation been more a concern for Protestants than for Catholics, both on the popular level and among theologians. Counter Reformation theologians Peter Canisius (d.1597), Francisco Suarez (d.1617), and Robert Bellarmine (d.1621) articulated defenses of Mary against the Reformers, highlighting in particular her role in salvation, which, as we've seen, is hardly a biblical image of Mary :

> Canisius, for example, composed a major treatise on Mary, *De Maria Virgine incomparibili*, which ran through four editions in eight years. In 1563 the first Sodality of Our Lady was established, and by 1576 this new lay movement had over thirty thousand members. In 1573 Pope Pius VI instituted the feast of the Rosary.[36]

Clearly, Catholic response to the Reformation initially amounted to a rallying of Marian apologetics, which, however, would be short-lived in light of the dawn of the Enlightenment. Soon Catholic theology would begin to display little interest in Mariology, reflective of a general downward turn for Marianism, which would last until the age of Romanticism and an increase in Marian apparitions in the nineteenth and twentieth centuries.

Modern Catholic Mariology

Due in no small part to the efforts of the Jesuits, who "applied themselves with the fierce militancy of the order to spread the belief in Mary's Immaculate Conception,"[37] the doctrine of the Immaculate Conception was eventually made dogma at Vatican I in 1854 by Pope Pius IX, the very pope who, not by coincidence, defined papal

primacy and infallibility. With the Virgin Mary thus officially proclaimed as *herself* immaculately conceived, in the very same fashion in which she had conceived her son (i.e., without the influence
of concupiscence, which was thought by Augustine to be the trans-
mitter of original sin), the Mother of God clearly encroaches upon
her Son's unique divinity. In making such a doctrinal move, the
Catholic Church thereby claimed that she is "the only human creature ever to have been preserved from all taint of original sin," which
amounts to "a mandatory belief for all those who acknowledge the
spiritual authority of Rome."[38]

Two significant theological implications of the doctrine of the
Immaculate Conception have become points of controversy among
theologians: (1) Because Mary is immaculately conceived and thus
exempt from the consequences of original sin, a position which
"clearly shows the influence of the Augustinian theory of original
sin and presupposes the traditional connection between procreation
and contamination,"[39] Mary is in a real sense separate from the rest
of humanity—"set apart from the human race in a special and separate trans-human character."[40] (2) An equally crucial theological
question arises from the fact that under the aspect of the Immaculate Conception Mary is no longer venerated in a christological context as the mother of Jesus; she alone is the object of veneration.
Warner notes that with the proclamation of the Immaculate Conception, in Catholic iconography Mary now appears alone, without
either the baby Jesus or his material corpse depicted with her. This
development in Marian imagery is significant since the Marian devotee could now gaze upon Mary alone, not merely as an instrument
in the christological drama. The theology underlying the Immaculate Conception ultimately remains, of course, christocentric, but
the effect on popular piety of iconography often overshadows the
doctrinal content that images are "supposed to" convey. "Alone,
Mary ceases to be the instrument of the Incarnation, worthy of rev-
erence because she is the *Theotokos*, the God-bearer, a creature
uniquely wonderful but only because she is the mother of the Redeemer. This had been the crux of devotion to Mary since the earliest times."[41] Yet for Protestant and Orthodox Christianity, the doctrine of the Immaculate Conception would be rejected altogether,
mainly because of the goddess-like status it implied for Mary.

It is noteworthy that popular desire for ecclesial sanction of Mary played a role in the production of Pius IX's 1854 bull *Ineffabilis Deus*, which made the Immaculate Conception official Catholic doctrine. This was also the case with the proclamation of the Assumption of Mary as dogma when Pope Pius XII—who in 1942 had already consecrated the entire human race to the immaculate heart of the Virgin—conceded in 1950 to the collective will of eight million Catholics who had signed a petition demanding that the Assumption be made dogma. The doctrine of the Assumption, which states that Mary was "taken up body and soul into heaven," was logically consequent to the Immaculate Conception, for since Mary was free form original sin she would also have been spared physical corruption in the grave, thus rendering Pius XII's controversial move theologically valid.

Just as the Immaculate Conception raised considerable theological problems regarding the implicit encroachment of Mary on the uniqueness of Christ's universal lordship, so too did the doctrine of the Assumption. In particular, the doctrine sparked debate as to whether Mary had actually died before the Assumption. To once again cite Warner's excellent study:

> The difficulty is that if Mary escaped all the penalties of the Fall, including death, she would be exalted above her son, who tasted the grave for three days. John Damascene reminded his congregation: "We do not celebrate a goddess as in the fantastic fables of the Greeks, since we proclaim her death." Hera, Athena, Aphrodite, Diana, Cybele, or Isis do not age and do not die, but Mary lived a human life that ended in a human way.[42]

Four years after the proclamation of the doctrine of the Assumption in the Marian year of 1954, "the Catholic Church proclaimed her Queen of Heaven, though notably not Queen of the Earth,"[43] thus marking the apex of the modern Marian age.

Regarding the state of Catholic Marianism in the twentieth century, Hans Küng writes:

> From the time of Pius IX...the popes have promoted Marian devotion by every means. From the nineteenth century

Marianism and papalism have gone hand in hand and given each other mutual support. The peak of this Marian age was reached in the year 1950, when Pope Pius XII, the last pope to act as an absolute ruler, against all Protestant, Orthodox, and even Catholic misgivings, defined solemnly the bodily assumption of Mary into heavenly glory at the end of her life.[44]

Yet, within a few years the Marian age would come to a abrupt halt, as the Second Vatican Council effectively addressed and attacked excesses in Marian piety, thus instilling a virtual "Mariological moratorium," and considerably lessening the importance of the cult of Mary in the Church. It is precisely to the Mariology of Vatican II, and to that of Edward Schillebeeckx, one of its principal framers and perhaps the most important Mariologian of the twentieth century Church, that our attention must now turn.

Vatican II Mariology
In a remarkable shift in direction, Catholic Mariology took on a relatively minimalist and Christocentric shape at the Second Vatican Council. The Vatican II position regarding Mary is articulated in chapter eight of the Council's crucial ecclesiological document *Lumen gentium*, entitled "The Role of the Blessed Virgin Mary, Mother of God, in the Mystery of Christ and the Church." It is highly significant that a separate document treating Mary uniquely was not promulgated by the Council Fathers, who instead chose to place their mariological exposition as a subsection within *Lumen gentium*, their document on the Church. While the Council considered, drafted, and even presented a separate discourse treating Mary alone, a slim majority of bishops saw inherent dangers of mariological maximalism lurking in the inclusion of a separate document and voted down the proposal. This decision was more significant it might appear at first glance, for placing the discussion of Mary within the document on the Church essentially brings Mary down to earth, so to speak. The move effectively emphasizes that Mary is a member of the Church in need of redemption with the rest of humanity. The intention here was clearly to discourage tendencies to elevate Mary to the level of Jesus, which infringes on his uniqueness by granting his

mother equal power in the economy of salvation, a view that has long been common in popular Catholic piety.

With the aim of casting Mary as a member of the "People of God" and not some supernatural being above the Church, the Council chose to refrain from directly using the originally medieval title "Mother of the Church" in reference to the Virgin. Whereas twice the Council documents refer to Mary as she "who is called Mother of the Church," the terms of preference employed at Vatican II were "Mother of the Redemption" and "Mother of God." Schillebeeckx, present at the Second Vatican Council as an expert theological advisor, played an influential role in the formulation of the Council's mariological position. The Dominican forcefully argued against both a separate mariological document and the use of the term "Mother of the Church," for he deemed it crucial that "Mary...not be put on the side of Jesus Christ but on the side of reception by the community of faith."[45]

The language of the eighth chapter of *Lumen gentium* reflects a great deal of revision and compromise between two conflicting mariological positions, "mariological maximalism," which emphasizes "Mary's unique connection with Christ the Redeemer," and "mariological minimalism," which stresses "her close connection with the Church and all of the redeemed."[46] Schillebeeckx refers to the former as promulgating a "Christological Mary" and putting "Mary alongside Jesus to such a degree that she—the mother of Jesus, who as Christ is head of his redeemed church is herself also called "mother of the church." The second position, mariological minimalism, for Schillebeeckx, professes a "Church-theological Mary": "Mary is our sister, an eminent and model member of church's community of faith."[47] Initially the struggle at Vatican II between the maximalist and minimalist camps was fierce and emotional, and for some time it was unclear who would prevail. Cardinal Koenig of Vienna argued the minimalist position; Cardinal Santos of Manila maintained that Mary transcended the Church because of her role as coredemptrix, hence exhorting the need for a separate document on Mary. While ostensibly concerning merely the structure of the Council's documents, the vote on whether to include a separate mariological discussion was much farther reaching, being actually a matter of the definition of the Council's Mariology. In the end, the minimalists prevailed by the slim margin of 1,114 to 1,074.

The resultant down-playing of the role of Mary in the redemption amounted to "a Mariological moratorium," as Schillebeeckx called it. For Norwegian Catholic theologian and Church historian Kari Borresen, Vatican II "marked the end of Mariology properly so called,"[48] while to Hans Küng, the Council's unmistakable condemnation of "excessive marianism" would mean that "the exaggerated Marian cult has lost its force and is no longer vital to the life of the Church."[49]

Besides its momentous decision to include the core of its mariological discourse in *Lumen gentium*, the Second Vatican Council also decided against the pronunciation of any statements promoting Marian devotions, feasts, or the rosary. This was significant in that it left the importance and place of such key elements of Marian piety to the discretion of the individual believer or local church leader. The cult of Mary, then, would be hard pressed to find in the Vatican II documents any significant theological sanction for its dearest forms of expression. Yet, to reiterate a theme to which we ineluctably return again and again in this study, orthodoxy's sanction has never been a prime concern of popular piety.

There are, nonetheless, passages in *Lumen gentium* that do laud Mary considerably, reflecting the compromise between the two positions and of concessions to the maximalist camp. While she is portrayed as the "pre-eminent" member of the community of faith, who "greatly surpasses all creatures in heaven and earth," and despite the notion that she possesses "saving influences" and "continues to win for us the fruits of salvation," she is still a "creature," "very close to us." Vatican II, then, is clear in removing Mary from a holy pedestal, where she intermingles with the trinity in activity and potency, ultimately placing her in the Church with the rest of a suffering humanity in need of God's grace through Christ for redemption. "As far as was feasible, then, Vatican II encouraged the "minimalist" line in Mariological thinking only fourteen years after the Assumption was defined."[50]

Postconciliar Mariology

Two postconciliar papal teachings on Mary appeared in the forms of Pope Paul VI's 1974 *Marialis cultus* ("For the Right Ordering and Development of Devotion to the Blessed Virgin Mary") and Pope John Paul II' encyclical *Redemptoris mater* in 1987. The former is concerned that "certain practices of piety that not long ago seemed suitable for expressing the religious sentiment of individuals and of Christian communities seem today inadequate or unsuitable because they are linked with social and cultural patterns of the past," and proceeds to outline how to effect the "right ordering and development of Marian piety."[51] John Paul's encyclical, meanwhile, expresses hope that in her absolute obedience to God Mary does offer potential for ecumenical progress. John Paul also, significantly, reflects on Mary's Magnificat and its exhortation of the Church to give preference to the poor.

Since Vatican II, several important impulses in mariological thought have emerged, notably; feminist theology, liberation theology, and positions regarding Mary as a feminine aspect of the Godhead. All three of these shall be summarily examined in the context of the discussions of the mariological thought of the following six important contemporary Catholic thinkers: Edward Schillebeeckx, Hans Küng, Leonardo Boff, Mary Daly, Rosemary Radford Ruether, and Andrew Greeley.

Schillebeeckx
There are no significant discrepancies between the Mariology of Vatican II and that of Edward Schillebeeckx, mainly because of the unparalleled influence the he had on the Council's mariological deliberations. Schillebeeckx had just finished writing what is perhaps the most important mariological treatise of the century, *Mary: Mother of the Redemption*, on the eve of the Council; the text served as a principal resource to the bishops as they formulated the Council's Mariology. As already noted, Schillebeeckx served as theological adviser to the bishops, and his influence demands recognition. Indeed, "his theology cannot be understood without the Council, just as the church's reception of the Council cannot pass over his theology."[52]

Schillebeeckx's Mariology, then, is largely consistent with that of Vatican II, though it has by no means remained stagnant during the ensuing thirty years since the close of the Council. For one, he now places greater emphasis "on the fact that we are all redeemed only through God in Jesus Christ,"[53] and that "(a)ll holiness, including that of Mary, is purely participation in the holiness of God in Christ Jesus."[54] He notes that this "removal of Mary from so-called 'objective redemption' is of course a new step in Mariology, but it is not enough."[55] Sharing the concern of Tübingen Protestant theologian Jürgen Moltmann that Mary not serve as "a melting pot for the most divergent religious needs and desires,"[56] Schillebeeckx asserts that "from the theological side a critical attitude" is "necessary even then to 'the many names' which popular devotion gives to Mary."[57] Some of these names, incidentally, also appear in Schillebeeckx's early mariological writings, but are dropped, significantly, in his more recent works.

It is fair to say, therefore, that Schillebeeckx's Mariology has been lowered during the years since the Council; i.e., that it has witnessed a diminishing of the importance and power of Mary in his theology at large. Besides his increased emphasis on the "removal of Mary from objective redemption," Schillebeeckx has actually retracted some of his former positions regarding Mary. For example, while earlier Schillebeeckx considered Mary to be the "source of all life, including that of the church," he now reserves this role for the Holy Spirit alone.[58] Here we find notable changes in direction in Schillebeeckx's mariological thought. While ever maintaining that "true veneration of Mary [to whom in 1991 he refers as "the mother of all belief" and "the mother of all believers"] is part of the essence of Christianity," Schillebeeckx is insistent on a critical Mariology "which keeps to biblical criteria,"[59] a Mariology "reactualized on the basis of the fundamental idea that the Holy Spirit is the 'mother of the church.' All further transference of pneumatological titles of honour both to the church and to Mary must be reviewed again very critically: pneumatologically and Christologically, then ecclesiologically and finally Mariologically."[60]

Here, one might question Schillebeeckx's insistence on keeping to the "biblical criteria." What, for instance, is exactly "the biblical criteria;" i.e., whose reading? In light of the biblical discussions of Mary (which are discussed above), moreover, does it follow that "veneration of Mary is part of the essence of Christianity,"[61] as Schillebeeckx claims? We shall keep this question in mind when discussing the Mariology of Hans Küng.

Küng

In relation to the maximalist position it defeated, it is accurate to refer to the Mariology of Vatican II, as well of that of Schillebeeckx, as "minimalist." However, taken in the larger context, and especially in an ecumenical context, Hans Küng is correct in labeling the Mariology of Vatican II as "moderately traditional." Therefore, I am using the Vatican II/Schillebeeckx Mariology as an example of a moderate mariological position, for the sake of comparison, contrasting it with both Küng's minimalist Mariology and the higher Mariology of Leonardo Boff.

It would be misleading to call Küng a mariologian *per se*, as he himself would, I think, agree. Yet the great breadth of his theological writing leaves virtually no stone unturned and includes in places, most notably toward the end of the third section of his classic *On Being a Christian*, outlines of his understanding of the place of Mary in Christianity, which can certainly be labeled minimalist. Küng, one of the most important Christian theologians of the twentieth century, is renown for his unrelenting insistence on rooting theology in a historically and textually criticized scriptural context. His Mariology is granted no exception to this demand, which leads Küng to a very critical stance toward both popular Marian excesses and the two papal, dogmatic Marian declarations of the modern Church: The doctrines of the Assumption and the Immaculate Conception, should be understood as "ranking very low on the hierarchy of truths," in which "no one can be obliged to believe."[62]

Given the paucity of positive scriptural references to Mary upon which to construct a high Mariology, and taking up here Küng's scripturally critical posture, one is led to a mariologically sobering conclusion:

> Mary is the mother of Jesus. She is a human and not a heavenly being. As a human being and as a mother, she is witness of his true humanity, but also of his origin from God. Hence, as a result of what was admittedly...a very problematic development both historically and objectively,

she later came to be understood as Christ-bearer and indeed as God-bearer (Mother of God). Mary is the example
and model of Christian faith. Her faith, which feels the
sword of scandal, dissension and contradiction, and is required in the face of the cross, according to Luke, is typical for all Christian faith.... There is nothing unique therefore about Mary's faith, nor has she any special insight
into the mysteries of God....[63]

Küng's reservations about the Virgin are not limited to scriptural
considerations. Long a leading thinker in the ecumenical movement, he has also raised the question of Mary in the ecumenical
context; i.e., Is not Catholic Mariology a formidable stumbling block
to serious progress toward Christian unity? In the eyes of many
Protestants, he notes, "Mariology has in fact become 'Mariolatry'—
a negative symbol of ecclesial faith" stained with "the ambiance of
papalism and triumphalism."[64]

Küng's discussions of Mary gives the impression that he would
disagree with Schillebeeckx's claim that "true veneration of Mary
is an essential part of the Christian faith." Nonetheless, Küng remains hopeful that there may be something of worth for all of Christianity in the symbol of Mary, only it must be considered in ecumenical terms, aiming "to provide a new interpretation of the figure
of Mary for our time, freeing it of clichés and rigidities and thus
smoothing the path for a genuinely ecumenical picture of Mary, the
Mother of Jesus, so that all Christian churches can once again discover the truth of Luke's words: 'All generations shall call me
blessed.'"[65]

Boff

Nowhere has the symbol of the Virgin Mary been of greater importance to the Catholic faithful than in Latin America—Haiti included.
Whether manifest in the icon of *Nuestra Señora de Guadalupe* in
Mexico, *Nossa Senhora de Conceicão* in Brazil, or *Notre Dame du
Perpétuel Secours* in Haiti, "[I]t is an undeniable fact that devotion
to Mary is the most popular, persistent and original characteristic
of Latin American Christianity."[66] And just as Latin America has
bred contemporary Catholicism's most forceful expressions of
Marianism, so too has it been the source of the most provocative

movement in post-Vatican II Catholic theology: liberation theology. A leading liberation theologian, Brazilian priest Leonardo Boff develops a Mariology that may correctly be called maximalist in comparison with those of Küng and Schillebeeckx, one rooted both in a sound understanding of the place of Mary in the Latin American Church and in a liberative interpretation of both scripture and Church history. To his credit, Boff's mariological maximalism is also rooted in a keener awareness of the place of Mary in popular Catholic piety than either Schillebeeckx's or Kung's.

Boff forcefully argues that "a prophetic liberating image of Mary is the only legitimate conclusion theology can come to against the backdrop of our situation of captivity and oppression."[67] One of liberation theology's greatest services to Catholicism is its devastating exposure of the institutional Church's complicity in Latin America's oppressive social structures, where a "tiny elite, possessed of a monopoly over the power, knowledge, and wealth needed to dictate the universal destiny...institutionalize Christianity itself, with all its symbols and concepts, and reduce it to the service of its selfish cause."[68] This, incidentally, is a prime example of Bourdieu's concept of "symbolic violence," as the symbol of the Virgin Mary, Christianity's most significant feminine religious symbol, has been an especially useful weapon of symbolic violence for this cause. Boff's penetrating analysis of this is well worth quoting at length:

> The image of Mary in popular piety has been that of the kind, sweet, pious, humble virgin mother, completely devoted to Jesus and the Holy Family. And as we know, theology has supplied this image with abundant justification" over and against the prophetic, liberative image of Mary in the Magnificat. In a law-and-order society whose masculinizing powers have received such wholehearted ideological support from Christianity, will it ever be possible for people to assimilate the ethical indignation of a Mary who prays for God to scatter the proud in the conceit of their hearts, to topple the mighty from their thrones, and to send the rich empty away, so as to be able to exalt the lowly and fill the hungry with good things? Christian ideology, always in charge here, has had a difficult time deciding between not ascribing any importance to Mary's prophetic words, superficially so male and strange-sound-

ing on the lips of a woman, and spiritualizing them—
bestowing upon them a meaning calculated to reinforce
the privileged position to Christians here, or even simply
by applying them to "the others" (Jews, pagans, or "forces
of evil"). In any event, they have not been applied to the
Church or to Christians. As a result, for centuries, Christianity has rendered the critical, liberating content of the
Magnificat impotent.[69]

To Boff, then, this historical manipulation of the symbol of Mary,
which has sapped the symbol of its liberative potential, amounts to
a challenge to the contemporary mariologian "to develop a prophetic image of Mary—an image of Mary as the strong, determined
woman, the woman committed to the messianic liberation of the
poor from the historical social injustices under which they suffer."[70]

The Magnificat, therefore, provides the scriptural foundation for
"liberation Mariology." Boff further illustrates how the Magnificat's
"prophetic, liberating image of Mary" has emerged as a central image
in popular Latin American Catholicism, particularly in the base
communities: "In the *comunidades de base* (base communities),
whenever the political dimension of the faith is discussed, a special
appreciation of Mary's role of denunciation and proclamation
(*denúncia y anúncia*) of prophecy and liberation stands out as a
key aspect of people's devotion to her."[71] Boff claims, then, that a
liberative Mariology is not merely an ideal; it already exists as an
integral, scripturally based part of popular Latin American Catholic piety.

Two important analyses of the significance of devotion to Our
Lady of Guadalupe (certainly Latin America's most important
Marian icon) lend support to Boff's assertion. Jeanette Rodriguez,
while denying that the Guadalupe icon could "be considered a source
of political activism," concludes in her recent study that "certainly
she is a source of empowerment...active and liberating,"[72] for Mexican and Mexican-American women. Likewise, Virgil Elizondo in-
terprets the "Guadaloupe event" as "the beginning of the fourfold
liberation of the people": (1) "political-economic liberation;" (2)
"liberation from sexual violation;" (3) "socio-psychological liberation;" and (4) "religious liberation."[73] We will return to the theses

of Rodriguez and Elizondo indirectly when considering our own findings about popular Haitian Marianism below.

While Boff's call for a prophetic, liberative Mariology is well stated, most welcome, and refreshing, some mariologians hesitate to fully concur, fearful of a regression into pre-Vatican II mariological maximalism. Borresen notes that "[l]iberation theology seems well suited to a particular socio-political background, but one should not forget that this makes it all the more a product of circumstances. If the actual liberator is Christ, and not Mary, I see no reason why liberation theology should not remain Christocentric."[74] On another front, Schillebeeckx is "critical of Boff's Mariological exaggerations," most especially his "seriously exaggerated" understanding of the relationship between Mary and the Holy Spirit: "He speaks of a "hypostatic union" between Mary and the Spirit of God, just as there is a hypostatic union between Jesus and the Word or the Logos of God."[75] To further illustrate the difference between Schillebeeckx's and Boff's mariological positions, it is notable that Boff regularly employs the term "Coredemptrix," a term that Schillebeeckx has long rejected for its implicit maximalist slant.

I will forego analytical commentary on the validity of these objections or on how Boff might defend himself. Suffice it instead to note that such objections are rooted in concerns with mariological maximalism, which removes Mary from the side of the Church where Vatican II placed her and returns her to the side of Jesus. In remarks such as: "Mary is the splendor of Christ"[76]..."one body, one life, one love with Christ, and this to perfection"[77]..."reigning jointly with her Son over a reconciled universe,"[78]...to whom "Christian faith confers an unequaled transcendent importance,"[79] Boff's Mariology is demonstrably maximalist, elevating Mary to a level that both Küng and Schillebeeckx would find theologically unsound, if not downright heretical.

Incidentally, Boff both anticipates and seemingly accepts, at least in qualified form, hesitations to his Mariology and the maximalist label. Whether his defense is sound is left to the reader's discretion:

> We realize, of course, that we run the risk—a risk we accept—of finding ourselves in the framework of the old, notorious Mariological maximalism. But the old maximalism is aesthetic and academic. We are maximalist

to be sure—but not in a pietistic, evasive spirit that would like to flood (but thereby contaminate) that rigorous discourse of faith that is theology. We are maximalist out of theology's legitimate, essential demand for radicalism.[80]

Those familiar with Boff's Mariology will recognize that the present summation thus far omits address of what is for Boff "the unifying core of Mariology:" the feminine. In the discussion that follows I shall analyze the theme that God's feminine side is reflected in the myth and symbol of the Virgin Mary. This notion, for Boff, responds to the simple yet demanding realization "that Mary is a woman, and that God wished to be the offspring of that woman," a realization "that can scarcely be without relevance. Theology must investigate that relevance."[81] Boff is not alone in his articulation of the provocative notion that in Mary Gods's feminine side is revealed. I have chosen here to exclude Boff from the analysis of this theme only for the sake of brevity and in an attempt to broaden the pool of thinkers referred to in this chapter. Instead, this idea, somewhat new in mariological discourse, will be discussed below in the context of the writings of Andrew Greeley and Rosemary Radford Ruether, while a brief address of feminist concerns with Mary will also invoke the thought of Mary Daly.

The Virgin Mary, Feminism, and the Feminine Side of the God

Historically, the patriarchal Church has employed the symbol of Mary to reify its definition of woman as subordinate and to "reflect and express the ideology of the patriarchal feminine."[82] Feminist theologians like Rosemary Radford Ruether and Mary Daly are especially responsible for exposing "how the appropriation of ultimate divine sovereignty as a male symbol allowed the female to appear only as the receptive and/or mediating principle of the male sovereignty.... The feminine, then, can appear in Catholic theology only as an expression of the creature, not as an aspect of God."[83]

The wealth of historical evidence contained in Warner's study of the myth and cult of the Virgin Mary corroborates the feminist critique of the extensive symbolic violence that the institutional Catholic Church has committed against women in its manipulation of the symbol of Mary. "By defining the limits of womanliness as shrinking, retiring acquiescence, and *by reinforcing that behaviour in the sex with praise*, the myth of feminine inferiority and dependence could be and was perpetrated."[84] This "inimitability of the Virgin-Mother model,"[85] in all its humility and submissiveness, has clearly served as a foundational buttress to the sexism inherent to Roman Catholicism, thus becoming an issue demanding poignant address from feminist theologians.

In light of such a formidable history of sexism with which the symbol of Mary is so inextricably associated, to approach the symbol in a quest for liberative inspiration for women amounts to a daunting enterprise. Nonetheless, Ruether and others have raised the question of Mary's relevance for female liberation:

> Is there any basis for an alternative Mariology, one that is not the expression of the male of the Church as symbolically female—that would allow us to name sexism itself as sin and point toward the liberation of women and men from the dualisms of carnal femaleness and spiritual femininity?[86]

Daly

Frequently, "Mary is rejected by feminist theologians as a possible symbolic identification figure."[87] Kari Borresen, for one, argues that Mary is "a contradiction of feminism. To make Mary a model for feminists is not only questionable but also absurd."[88] So, too, has Mary Daly "distanced herself from the symbol of Mary, convinced that she ultimately symbolizes the violation of the goddess and therefore the defeat of a society that is more oriented toward the female."[89]

Yet, it is not so much that the symbol of Mary is bereft of liberative potential that leads Daly to distance herself from this most important feminine religious symbol. On the contrary, Daly discovers "sub-intended" prophetic elements in Catholic Marian dogma (of all places in the Marian universe!) which point "toward independence for women." For Daly, once "sprung free of its Christolatrous context," Marian dogma may be perceived anew to reveal something empowering for women. "The message of independence in the Virgin symbol can itself be understood apart from the matter of sexual relationships with men. When this aspect of the symbol is sifted out from the patriarchal setting, then 'Virgin Mother' can be heard to say something about female autonomy within the context of sexual and parental relationships."[90]

Just as the doctrine of the Virgin Birth, for Daly, "the Assumption also can be seen as possessing a prophetic content interwoven with its sexist content,"[91] for in the "image of Mary 'rising'"[92] is woman's association with matter, sex, and sin challenged, if not overcome. While not pursuing these insights at great length, perhaps realizing that they are somewhat stretched, Daly has pointed to some potential for a positive feminist Mariology, one analyzing Mary as a non relational, "freewheeling symbol,"[93] free from the stranglehold of "the Christian patriarchate."[94]

Ruether

Impressed with the central tenets of liberation theology, Rosemary Radford Ruether, "one of a few feminist theologians who has consistently concerned herself with Mary,"[95] looks to the Magnificat as the basis for a "liberation Mariology." Clearly the language of the Magnificat, with its stern denunciation of unjust social relationships and its prophecy of their reversal as a necessary element of salvation, can be interpreted as protest against sexism in the Church and society. Moreover, particularly considering the Magnificat's Mariology as "symbolic ecclesiology," wherein Mary is identified with the Church, and in light of "Luke's sensitivity to women as members of the poor and the despised," there certainly is found in scripture, argues Ruether, fertile soil for a liberation Mariology:

> As a woman, specifically a woman from among the poorer class of a colonized people under the mighty empire of Rome, she represents the oppressed community that is to be lifted up and filled with good things in the messianic revolution. Mary as Church represents God's "preferential option for the poor.... If we take seriously the female personification of the Church within this perspective, then we must take the analysis of oppression and liberation a step further. If women of the oppressed classes and social groups represent the poorest of the poor, the most despised of society, then such women can become the models of faith and their liberation becomes the special locus of the

believing community. We need to move beyond the typology of Christ and the Church as dominant male and submissive female.[96]

Perhaps the most provocative advance in twentieth century Mariology is the notion that the symbol of the Virgin Mary represents an expression of God's feminine side.[97] Ruether, one of the leading exponents of this approach to understanding the significance of Mary, traces the history of Marianism and feminine religious symbols to show that—despite the efforts of a male-dominated Church to reserve God for maleness, and to limit the feminine role in Catholicism to one exemplified by a creaturely, passive, obedient virgin—the basic human insights into the divinity which affirm a certain inherent femininity are so powerful that in Catholic history they reemerged in the face of formidable ecclesial resistance and pinned themselves upon Mary. It appears then that Mary's initial rise in popularity was due more to her absorption of "pagan" religious symbolism pertaining to the Mother goddess and other feminine deities of mythic tradition than to any deeply mystical relationship with the Mother of Jesus that the early Christian believers may have experienced.[98] As Ruether concludes, "Mariology consists in focusing these symbols in the person of Mary."[99]

For Ruether, notwithstanding her regret that it is the mother of Jesus, and not Mary Magdalene, who becomes the central female symbol in Christianity, Mary represents the femininity of God. As Catholic theologian Leonard Swidler and others have demonstrated, the Hebraic "tradition often speaks of God in masculine—and feminine—images...."[100] Feminine symbols in Judaism—Israel as Yahweh's spouse, humanity as emergent from Yahweh's womb, Yahweh as nursing and comforting mother, etc.—were readily adapted by the early Christians: "At first they were adapted and developed in the New Israel quite independent of teaching about Mary. Later as Mariology developed, they were drawn in and absorbed by it."[101] Hence the reemergence of pre-Christian feminine imagery for the Godhead, especially considering the "pagan" soil from which the Hebraic tradition culled them, illustrates, for Ruether, the timeless human insight into the femininity of God which surfaces in the symbol of Mary, in spite of centuries of resistant patriarchal/orthodox symbolic violence.

Greeley

As such an expression of God's femininity, the symbol of the Virgin Mary in effect acts as to counterbalance "a dreadfully masculinized conception of the godhead,"[102] as the great Theilhard de Chardin once put it, offering the Christian believer a fuller vision of God. Another Catholic thinker to explore this notion is Andrew Greeley, who does so from a sociological and historical perspective. Stepping far outside of the domain of doctrine, which for centuries has imprisoned orthodox Mariology in so much traditionalism and hence limited our understanding of one of humanity's most important religious symbols, Greeley asserts that a careful study of religious history allows the mariologian "to see Mary as a reflection of the femininity of God."[103]

Greeley's approach in *The Mary Myth* employs the "language theology" of Catholic theologian David Tracy, particularly Tracy's insights into the phenomenon of "limit experiences" and the "limit language" that attempts to communicate them. Greeley's position is that religious symbols arise out of limit experiences in which the finitude of our existence is revealed to us in such an awfully halting way that we may glimpse the infinite beyond. "In such an experience the thing-turned-symbol shatters the old structures of our perception and organizes them into new and different constellations in which we see things more clearly, more profoundly, more penetratingly."[104] The religious symbols that emerge from limit experiences, which themselves are to some degree triggered by deep existential need, signify both the experience and the insight or glimpse of the beyond which they afford.

Applying this theory of the emergence and function of religious symbols to Mary, Greeley posits that the symbol of Mary is rooted in the limit experience of sexual differentiation. There are many forms of this limit experience; Greeley outlines four of them, viewing them as the formative limit experiences that have spawned the four major forms of the symbol of Mary: Virgo, Sponsa, Pieta, and Madonna. A brief illustration may here serve to summarize Greeley's development of one of these: The Pieta manifestation of the Mary symbol is rooted in the limit experience of our mortality, since we emerge from "woman as source of who lives only to die," and in our existential need of repose in the maternal arms of the Pieta. In the emergent Marian symbol of the Pieta (exemplified artistically best, for Greeley, in Michelangelo's masterpiece) is expressed God's warm comfort of the fearful and tender acceptance of the fallen, evoking characteristics of God's feminine side. Hence the symbol of Mary permits the believer to envision God as Mother, and thus arrive at an understanding of God that is truer and more whole.

The brevity of the present summary does not do justice to Greeley's trenchant "four-celled paradigm," which attempts to illustrate the relationship between deep human limit experience and the emergence of Marian symbols. It is hoped, nevertheless, that it provides the reader with a practicable view of one of the most provocative sociological interpretations of *The Mary Myth* yet to be expounded. The sociology of religion, as it were, has greatly neglected the analysis of what is in fact one of history's most important religious phenomena: Marian devotion. In any case, the key point is, for Greeley, that Mary reveals the feminine side of God: She is "the Catholic symbol which reveals to us that the Ultimate is androgynous, that God is both male and female,...passionately tender, seductively attractive, irresistibly inspiring, and graciously healing."[105]

In sum, I have surveyed the history and development of Catholic Marian doctrine and the mariological positions of several leading twentieth century Catholic thinkers with the aim of providing a contextual background for our analysis of Haitian Marianism. This was the intention of chapter two as well. To examine Haitian Marianism in a vacuum would be to run many risks, for Haiti, despite periods of relative economic isolation and ecclesial dislocation from Rome, possesses a culture that, for all its uniqueness, is intimately related to other cultures of the world. Moreover, to understand what Mary means in Haitian religious life demands recognition of the facts that, however heretically she may be manifest, Mary is, though not exclusively, very much a Catholic symbol, and that most Haitians consider themselves members of the "one holy Roman and apostolic Church."

NOTES

1. New Testament references to Mary appear in the following passages, some of which are indirect and of little moment: Mk.3:19-21,31-45,6:3; Mt.1:2,12:46-50; Lk.1:5-2:52,8:19-21,11:27-28; Jn.2:1-11,19:25-27; Acts 1; Gal 4:4. Maurice Hamington, *Hail Mary?: The Struggle for Ultimate Womanhood in Catholicism* (New York & London: Routledge, 1995), p. 183.

2. Rosemary Radford Ruether, *Mary: the Feminine Face of the Church* (New York: Harper and Row, 1987), p. 189.

3. Leonardo Boff, *The Maternal Face of God: The Feminine and Religious Experience* (New York: Harper and Row, 1987), p. 189.

4. One notable exception is Pope Paul IV's 1974 apostolic exhortation *Marias cultus* ("For the Right Ordering and Development of Devotion to the Blessed Virgin Mary"), which explains that "Far from being a timidly submissive woman...she was a woman who did not hesitate to proclaim that God vindicates the humble and the oppressed, and removes the powerful people of this world from their privileged positions (cf. Luke 1:51-53 n.37)." As cited in Richard P. McBrien, *Catholicism* (San Francisco: Harper, 1994), p. 1098.

5. Weber identifies this "need for just compensation, envisaged in various ways but always involving reward for one's own good deeds and punishment for the unrighteousness of others," as a, if not the, principal religious need of the subjugated, "the most widely diffused form of mass religion all over the world" (*The Sociology of Religion*, p. 108). It is, therefore, logical to argue that as CEB's reclaimed certain scriptural teachings that had long been transmuted by the Church, such as the Magnificat—passages with socially revolutionary implications became particularly popular among the poor —since they respond to their need for the assurance of compensation. Indeed, Boff notes that "recently" in such communities, "another form of Marian piety is developing," one centered precisely on the liberative dimension of the Magnificat (*The Maternal Face of God*, p. 188).

6. Ruether, *Mary*, p. 34.

7. Marina Warner, *Alone of All Her Sex: The Myth and Cult of the Virgin Mary* (New York: Knopf, 1976), p. 15.

8. Ruether, *Mary*, p. 39.

9. Gerard Sloyan, *Jesus in Focus* (Mystic, CT: Twenty-Third, 1983), p. 80.

10. Anne Baring and Jules Cashford, *The Myth of the Goddess: Evolution of an Image* (London: Penguin, 1993), p. 551.

11. Joseph Campbell, *The Masks of God: Occidental Mythology* (Harmondsworth: Penguin, 1976), p. 45.
12. Baring and Cashford, *The Myth of the Goddess*, p. 548.
13. Ibid., p. 556.
14. Elizabeth Gould Davis, *The First Sex* (New York: G.P. Putnam's Sons, 1971), pp. 243-244.
15. Baring and Cashford, *The Myth of the Goddess*, p. 551.
16. Pamela Berger, *The Goddess Obscured: The Transformation of the Grain Protectress from Goddess to Saint* (Boston: Beacon, 1985). As Mary Daly notes, one reason for the Church's failure to shield the Virgin Mary from syncretism with pagan goddesses was that "[a]lthough the converts were taught that Mary 'is only human, and not divine, their subliminal perception and identification of Mary with the Goddesses were used to seduce them into the Christian church." [*Pure Lust: Elemental Feminist Philosophy* (San Francisco: Harper, 1984), p. 76].
17. Vasiliki Limberis, *The Divine Heiress: The Virgin Mary and the Creation of Christian Constantinople* (London: Routledge, 1994), p. 104.
18. Ibid., p. 102.
19. Thomas Bokenkotter, *Essential Catholicism: Dynamics of Faith and Belief* (New York: Image, 1986) p. 127.
20. Limberis, *The Divine Heiress*, p. 106.
21. Baring and Cashford, *The Myth of the Goddess*, p. 551.
22. Kari Borresen, "Mary in Catholic Theology," in Hans Küng, and Jürgen Moltmann, (eds.), *Mary in the Churches, Concilium*, 168 (New York: Seabury, 1983), pp. 48-56, p. 50.
23. Warner, *Alone of All Her Sex*, p. 88.
24. McBrien, *Catholicism*, p. 1085.
25. Hans Küng, *On Being a Christian* (New York: Doubleday, 1984), p. 461.
26. Warner, *Alone of All Her Sex*, p. 115.
27. Ibid., p. 155.
28. Bokenkotter, *Essential Catholicism*, p. 128.
29. Ibid.
30. Küng, *On Being a Christian*, p. 461.
31. Bokenkotter, *Essential Catholicism*, p. 130.
32. Ibid.
33. Ibid., p. 131.
34. Warner, *Alone of All Her Sex*, p. 245-246.
35. Jürgen Moltmann, "Editorial: Can there be an Ecumenical Mariology?" in Küng, and Moltmann, (eds.), *Mary in the Churches*,

pp. xii-xv, p. xii.
36. McBrien, *Catholicism*, p. 1089.
37. Warner, *Alone of All Her Sex*, p. 247.
38. Ibid., p. 236.
39. Borresen, "Mary in Catholic Theology," p. 52.
40. Warner, *Alone of All Her Sex*, p. 247.
41. Ibid., p. 251
42. Ibid., 252.
43. Baring and Cashford, *The Myth of the Goddess*, p. 553.
44. Küng, *On Being a Christian*, p. 461.
45. Edward Schillebeeckx, "Mariology: Yesterday, Today, Tomorrow," in Edward Schillebeeckx, and Catharina Halkes, (eds.), *Mary: Yesterday, Today, Tomorrow* (New York: Crossroads, 1994), pp. 12-42, p. 18.
46. Avery Dulles, fn. 256, p. 85, in Walter M. Abbot, ed., *The Documents of Vatican II* (New York: Guild, 1966).
47. Schillebeeckx, "Mariology: Yesterday, Today, Tomorrow," p. 16.
48. Borresen, "Mary in Catholic Theology," p. 52.
49. Küng, *On Being a Christian*, p. 462. Whether Küng is correct in asserting that Marianism "has lost its force and is no longer vital to the life of the Church," is open to question. The findings of the present study would seem to indicate that in Haitian Catholicism the opposite is true. In Haiti, on the contrary, one could go so far as to argue that Mary is most vital to the life of the Church. Moreover, I would suspect that the Haitian case is not at all unique, as in Mexico, Poland, and especially in other poor countries, Catholicism seems to consist largely in Marian devotion, as much today as ever.
50. Borresen, "Mary in Catholic Theology," p. 53.
51. As cited in McBrien, *Catholicism*, p. 1097.
52. Marianne Merkx, "Introduction," in Schillebeeckx, and Halkes, (eds.), *Mary*, pp. 1-11, p. 3.
53. Schillebeeckx, "Mariology: Yesterday, Today, Tomorrow," p. 18.
54. Ibid., p. 23.
55. Ibid., p. 19.
56. Moltmann, "Editorial: Can there be an Ecumenical Mariology?" p. xiv.
57. Schillebeeckx, "Mariology: Yesterday, Today, Tomorrow," p. 18.
58. Ibid., p. 28.
59. Ibid., p. 42.
60. Ibid., p. 29.
61. Ibid., 42.
62. Küng, *On Being a Christian*, p. 461.

63. Ibid., p. 459.
64. Hans Küng, "Editorial: Mary in the Churches," in Küng, and Moltmann, (eds.), *Mary in the Churches*, pp. vii-xi, p. vii.
65. Ibid., p. xi. For a recent compelling contribution towards an ecumenical Mariology, see John Macquarie, *Mary for All Christians* (Grand Rapids: Wm. B. Eerdmans, 1990). Oxford theologian Macquarie has since 1970 been a member of the Ecumenical Society of the Blessed Virgin Mary, which was founded in Brussels in 1966. The society's history, aims, and various publications are discussed in Alberic Stacpoole's foreword to the text.
66. Virgil Elizondo, "Mary and the Poor: A Model of Evangelizing Ecumenism," in Küng, and Moltmann, (eds.), *Mary in the Churches*, pp. 59-65, p. 59.
67. Boff, *The Maternal Face of God*, p. 189.
68. Ibid., p. 191.
69. Ibid., pp. 188-89.
70. Ibid., p. 189.
71. Ibid. p. 188.
72. Jeanette Rodriguez, *Our Lady of Guadalupe: Faith and Empowerment among Mexican-American Women* (Austin: The University of Texas Press, 1994), pp. xxi, xviii.
73. Elizondo, "Mary and the Poor," pp. 62-63.
74. Borresen, "Mary in Catholic Theology," p. 54.
75. Schillebeeckx, "Mariology: Yesterday, Today, Tomorrow," p. 28.
76. Boff, *The Maternal Face of God*, p. 189.
77. Ibid., p. 15.
78. Ibid., p. 17.
79. Ibid., p. 9.
80. Ibid., p. 21.
81. Ibid., p. 19.
82. Rosemary Radford Ruether, *Sexism and God-Talk: Toward a Feminist Theology* (Boston: Beacon, 1983), p. 149.
83. Ibid., p. 139.
84. Warner, *Alone of All Her Sex*, p. 191, emphasis added. One of Bourdieu's definitions of symbolic violence resonates well with Warner's explanation, especially that part which I italicized: "that gentle, invisible violence, unrecognized as such, chosen as much as undergone, that of trust, obligation, personal loyalty, hospitality, gifts, debts, piety, in a word, all of the virtues honoured by the ethic o honour" *The Logic of Practice* (Cambridge: Polity, 1990), p. 127.
85. Mary Daly, *Beyond God the Father: Toward a Philosophy of Women's Liberation* (Boston: Beacon, 1973), p. 81.

86. Ruether, *Sexism and God-Talk*, p. 152.
87. Catharina Halkes, "Mary and Women," in Küng, and Moltmann, (eds.), *Mary in the Churches*, pp. 66-73, p. 66.
88. Borresen, "Mary in Catholic Theology," p. 54.
89. Halkes, "Mary and Women," p. 69. Lest we give the impression that Daly is somewhat uncritical in her feminist interpretation of the Virgin, in her later work Daly argues that Mary is the "model rape victim": "Believing that, through her own fault, a male has succeeded in degrading her, she concludes that only a male can save her. This is one reason for the hold of christian myth on women's raped psyche's. The myth itself, of course, reinforces the self-blame of victimized women." *Pure Lust: Elemental Feminist Philosophy* (San Francisco: Harper, 1984), pp. 105-106.
90. Daly, *Beyond God the Father*, p. 85.
91. Ibid., p. 87.
92. Ibid., p. 89.
93. Ibid., p. 87.
94. Halkes, "Mary and Women," p. 69.
95. Ibid.
96. Ruether, *Sexism and God-Talk*, pp. 156-57.
97. Ruether, *Mary*, p. 43.
98. For a detailed and well-researched analysis of this phenomenon, see Stephen Benko, *The Virgin Goddess: Studies in the Pagan and Christian Roots of Mariology* (Leiden and New York: E.J. Brill, 1993).
99. Ruether, *Mary*, p. 43.
100. Leonard Swidler, *Biblical Affirmations of Woman* (Philadelphia: Westminster, 1979), p. 21.
101. Ruether, *Mary*, p. 43.
102. In a footnote, Andrew Greeley comments: "Perhaps the greatest weakness of most of the current Catholic theology about Mary is that the authors are unwilling to take the step that the history of religions enables them to take and see Mary as a reflection of the femininity of God. Still, one theologian saw such a step over a half century ago. Pierre Theilhard de Chardin spoke of the 'biopsychological necessity of [Marianism] to counterbalance the masculinity of Yahweh.' He argued that the cult of Mary corrects a 'dreadfully masculinized conception of the godhead.'" Andrew Greeley, *The Mary Myth* (New York: Seabury, 1977), p. 15.
103. Greeley, *The Mary Myth*, p. 13.
104. Ibid., p. 211.
105. Ibid., p. 11.

CHAPTER FOUR

THE HISTORY OF HAITIAN MARIANISM

Iberian Catholicism and the Importation of Marianism to New Spain

The Virgin Mary was first transported to the Americas from Europe across the Atlantic on a ship that bore her name. Columbus, although complaining that her namesake, the Santa María, was a "cumbersome" vessel ill suited for discovery, was nonetheless a man possessed of the deep Marian piety that remains typical of Italian and Spanish Catholicism:

> Mediterranean scholars...have always noted that the Mary cult seems to be a distinct feature of the Latin Catholic countries, primarily Italy and Spain, that border the northern edge of the Mediterranean. Even Catholic commentators like Laurentin, more concerned with theology than with anthropology, have noted that Marian devotion in Italy and Spain seems especially noteworthy—a phenomenon often mentioned in studies of local religion in these areas.[1]

Doubtless, the Italian Columbus and his mostly Spanish crew said many Ave Marias while trying to fathom their direction and destiny. The Virgin Mary's long-standing status in European Catholicism as ruler over the seas (*Stella Maris;* Our Lady of the Navigators) made her the logical choice for guiding spiritual force of Spain's maritime exploration and subsequent "New World" conquests. "The Virgin's governance of the oceans was adapted to a practical purpose: she was prayed to by the missionaries who set out across the Atlantic and other oceans to conquer new territories for Christ."[2] It was under the guidance of the Blessed Virgin Mary in early December of 1492 that the Columbus expedition stumbled upon the northwest corner of what is today Haiti, named the island Hispaniola, and claimed it for the Spanish crown. It is noteworthy that the Genoan explorer named the first specific locale on the island in honor of the Virgin. Although Puerto Maria has long since become La Baie de Mole, we may pinpoint Columbus' christening of this bay as the point of origin of Marianism in the Haitian religious field.

Shortly thereafter, the explorers chanced upon another bay a bit further to the east. They also named this one after the Virgin— Puerto de la Concepción. Puerto de la Concepción would later have its named changed by the French to La-Baie-des-Moustiques (Mosquito Bay), in reference to a much more worldly reality. In all, Columbus would name no fewer than eight locations in the Caribbean after the Virgin Mary, one of them Santa María, Hispaniola's first Spanish settlement. The most significant among these is the island of Guadeloupe, named for the manifestation of the Virgin that is most popular in the Estremadura region of Spain whence came most of the explorers and conquistadors.

Thus the cult of the Virgin Mary first entered the Haitian religious field with the Columbus expedition and the ensuing waves of Spanish conquistadors, settlers, and missionaries. Jacques Lafaye, in his excellent study of Marianism in Mexican culture, points out the main reasons for the initial proliferation of the cult of Mary in the Americas:

> The development of the Marian cult in the Americas appears to have several causes. Doubtless the first historical reason is the widespread cult of Mary among the leaders of the conquering expeditions, who came from Estremadura or other Iberian provinces.... The first Catholic images given the Indians were St. James, who appeared to them as a formidable god of war and of thunder, and the Virgin Mary, whose appearance, by contrast, must have

consoled the vanquished. This introduction of the Marian
cult into the Indies was soon reinforced by the arrival of
the first missionaries, especially the Franciscan religious,
who were especially devoted to the Virgin.[3]

Clearly, therefore, gaining insight into the original form of Marianism
in the Americas, demands a brief analysis of sixteenth and seventeenth century Iberian Catholicism. Three qualities characterized
Catholicism in Spain in this period: Marianism, millenarianism, and
militancy, all of which would converge to furnish theological
legitimization of the Spanish exploits in the New World. Throughout Spain, and especially intense in Estremadura, devotion to Our
Lady of Guadeloupe, "Protectress of Iberian Christianity," was
among the most popular forms of Catholic piety. According to a
Spanish tradition which dates back at least to the fourteenth century, "Our Lady, the Virgin Mary, appeared to a shepherd as he
watched his flock and ordered him to go home, call the priest and
other people, and return to dig at the place where she was, where
they would find a statue of the Virgin."[4] Sure enough, upon returning with "the priest and other people," the statue was found, and the
site was thus transformed into a Marian sanctuary that would attract millions of pilgrims and miracle seekers in the ensuing ages.

Beliefs surrounding Our Lady of Guadalupe, though not unique
to Iberian Marianism, are reflected in a fifteenth-century account of
one dialogue that took place between the shepherd and Virgin, who
incidentally was a dark-skinned woman in the shepherd's vision,
and another which took place between him and his wife:

> She said: "Have no fear, for I am the Mother of God,
> through whom all mankind will be redeemed."... The Shep-
> herd came home, found his wife in tears, and said to her,
> "Why do you weep?" She replied, "Your son is dead,"
> and he said: "have no care, for I dedicate him to the Holy
> Mary of Guadalupe, that she may bring him back to life
> and health."... Immediately the young man rose up sound
> and well.[5]

Evident in this brief story are several key Marian beliefs: that Mary
protects those who pray to her; that humanity shall be redeemed
through Mary; and that Mary possesses miraculous powers of heal-

ing. Later we will show the extent to which and the forms in which these beliefs, along with the phenomenon of pilgrimage, remain fundamental to Haitian Marianism. For now, the point to be emphasized is that the cult of the Virgin Mary, particularly of Our Lady of Guadalupe, was central to the Catholic faith of the earliest Spanish explorers, conquistadors, and missionaries in Hispaniola. Hence, it is clear that Catholicism in the Haitian religious field has always been characterized by deep Marian piety.

Besides Guadalupe, also ranking among the most important Marian cults of Spanish Catholicism in the colonial age was that of Our Lady of the Immaculate Conception. It was Queen Isabella's particular devotion to the Immaculate Conception that inspired her to insist that the first Catholic church in the "New World" be consecrated to her. "In 1503, under the order of her Majesty, the Most Catholic Isabella of Castilla, Queen of Spain and the New World, Nicolas Ovando built in the paradisiacal fields along the banks of the Guayamouco the first church in the Americas, dedicated to the Immaculate Conception."[6]

Consecrating the first church in the Americas in Mary's honor had a two-fold purpose: on the one hand, a sincere expression of devotion to the Virgin Mary, invoking her guidance and protection over Spain's mercantilist and evangelical enterprises; on the other hand, the Marian legitimization of Spanish domination and deculturalization of the island's indigenous population and, somewhat later, imported African slaves. That the Spanish employed the symbol of the Virgin from the very outset of colonial exploitation as a weapon of symbolic violence, manipulated to lend a glaze of ecclesial sanction over this brutal chapter in the history of European imperialist domination, is strikingly illustrated in the following passage from Haitian historian Thomas Madiou, who depicts Nicolas Ovando, the above-mentioned church builder and governor general of the colony, in action:

> Ovando subjected three hundred Haitian chiefs, vassals to the queen, to torture. It was during their torment that they certified having conspired [against the Spanish]. They were then burned alive. After the extermination of the better part of the population of Xaragua, Ovando founded

a town which he named Sainte-Marie-de-la-Paix [St. Mary
of Peace!], near present-day Leogâne.[7]

Besides the conquerors' quest for spiritual legitimation of their plunder and their militant perception of the Virgin, the millenarianism
characteristic of Counter-Reformation Iberian Catholicism also influenced the early development of Marianism in Hispaniola.
Counter-Reformation Catholicism, especially in Spain and the New
World, was "a religion on the defensive which had exhausted its
creative energy."[8] Out of this defensive posture emerged significant
trends of millenarianism, which would lend theological force to arguments that the New World's conquest was urgent, for too many
pagan souls would perish in the aftermath of the imminent apoca-
lypse if not soon converted. In essence, this "millenarian hope thus
implied a certain vision of the discovery of the New World and of
the providential mission of its Spanish conquistadors."[9] Lafaye
illustrates how "the identification of Mary with the Woman of Revelation," certainly among the most important images in Christian
eschatology, effected a fusion of millenarianism and Mariology,
thereby inclining the "New World" cult of Mary to represent "the
announcement of the last times, or at least the end of the church of
Christ, to be replaced by the church of Mary, the church of the last
days."[10]

Later in his study, Lafaye concludes that because of the defensive climate of Counter-Reformation Catholicism and the
eschatological dimensions of the cult of Mary, "the Mother of Christ
came to signify the salvation of the New World, a world chosen to
be the site of a renewed Christendom"[11]—a world certainly worth
fighting for; and fight for it they did, with religious-ized capitalistic
zeal.

Thus "the warlike and combative nature of Iberian Catholicism"[12]
became intensified and extraordinarily manifest in the Spanish conquest of the New World. Projecting its millenarian vision onto New
Spain, the Catholic Church elevated Mary to a position of lordship
over the Americas, a point that Gebara and Bingemer make clear in
their study of Latin American Marianism:

> The conquest was regarded as the work of the Virgin, the
> powerful and yet tender lady, who was concerned about

protecting the Spanish and Portuguese believers and converting the Indians to faith in her divine Son. So it was
customary to say, as did Fray Antonio Maria, "No one can
doubt that the conquest was successful because of the great
Queen of the Angels."[13]

Notably, the Marianism of Fray Antonio and the other "Spanish
and Portuguese believers" drew little or no inspiration from the
Magnificat. Their celebration of the conquest, on the contrary, involved exactly that which the Magnificat denounces—the subjugation of the poor at the hands of the mighty.

Marian Appropriation and Political Liberation in Colonial Latin America

In due time, however, the subjugated of Latin America would recognize Mary's liberative potential reflected in the Magnificat, seizing and appropriating the symbol for their own interests. This appropriation of Mary usually involved some degree of syncretism
with indigenous or, as in the Haitian case, imported African feminine religious symbols. The resulting scenario was remarkable, as
sometimes different icons and perceptions of Mary represented spiritual forces for opposing factions on the very same battlefield, as in
the example below, which is clearly an extreme manifestation of
contested uses of the same religious symbol. Thus, the militant
dimension of the symbol of Mary has since its introduction in the
field proven malleable to either orthodox/status quo or heterodox/
under-class interests, which, as we shall see, is a central theme in
the history of Haitian Marianism.

The militant elements of Iberian Catholicism and the mingling
of Mariology and eschatology are in significant part responsible for
the deep connection between Marianism and militant nationalism
witnessed in a number of Latin American countries, most notably in
Mexico but also in Haiti. The symbol of Mary, as illustrated by
Warner, had a long history on the battlefields of Europe and the
Middle East prior to her appearance on behalf of military factions,
nationalist or other, in the New World. "The Virgin played her part,
putting in a judicious appearance to hearten her champions, or intervening with an earthquake or similar prodigy to help them to

victory."[14] The point I am stressing is that this militant aspect of the symbol of Mary was not lost over the course of centuries of transference and assimilation to other ages and cultures. What is remarkable in the Americas is how Mary's guardianship was eventually preempted from crown and papacy and placed over Indian and slave. For the downtrodden of Latin America, she now became the guarantor of victory and compensation, "the protectress of various liberation movements, including those of slaves."[15]

The case of Fathers Miguel Hidalgo y Castilla and Jose Maria Morelos y Pavon and their "Guadeloupes" liberation movement in Mexico (1810-15) forcefully illustrates this phenomenon of politically revolutionary Marian adaptation, as Enrique Dussel here describes:

> The oppressed class, the indigenous peoples, and later the creoles, found in the Virgin, the object of popular devotion, first support for the creation of national Mexican consciousness and later the flag of emancipation struggles. In 1800 a group of patriots called themselves the "Guadeloupes." The priest Hidalgo used the flag and the colours of the Virgin of Guadeloupe for his army, as did Morelos, while the Spaniards grouped themselves under the banner of Perpetual Succour, which Cortes had saved from the Aztecs in the "sad night."[16]

This most striking example—where adversarial warring factions *on the very same battlefield*, with diametrically opposed interests and ideologies, each used the symbol of Mary as a legitimizing and inspirational force—is explicable in terms of the convergence of millenarianism, militancy, and Marianism in the Iberian style of Catholicism first introduced to the region. For Hidalgo and company, it was especially the appropriation of Old World Marianism's militant and protective dimensions that allowed Mary to become their symbol of resistance and, eventually, of post-independence Mexican nationalism.

In light of the example of Hidalgo and Morelos, I would fully agree with Gebara and Bingemer that "religious cultural assimilation becomes a 'weapon' through which" the oppressed "can reassert their worth despite the fact that the presence of the colonizers is a fait accompli."[17] Unlike the "weapon of symbolic violence" into which the colonizer turned the symbol of Mary, for the oppressed the same symbol became a weapon in the struggle for liberation and the reversal of an unjust social order. Haitian history provides another impressive example of such Marian appropriation in the revolutionary figure of Romaine-la-Prophétesse. Discussion of this extraordinary personage follows below, but first a brief summary of the growth of Marianism in Saint-Domingue is requisite.

Marianism in French Saint-Domingue

While the Spanish were responsible for the introduction of the cult of the Virgin Mary in Hispaniola, their missionary activities were, by all accounts, quite limited, and true conversions to Queen Isabella's faith were few. It is not unreasonable to speculate, thus, that the visual introduction of the symbol of Mary, in the absence of an effective catechism, to the Indians and enslaved Africans permitted a substantial degree of syncretism to characterize the cult's early development. "It seems logical to assume that when the missionaries evangelized the slaves during the colonial period," writes Leslie Desmangles, "they related the stories of the Virgin's life and made instructional use of the Catholic symbols connected with her, but that the slaves responded to such instruction by transfiguring these symbols in African terms."[18] Historical research reveals that Desmangles' assumption is correct, as we will see later in this chapter.

The first waves of French missionaries, mainly Dominicans and Capuchins, were only marginally more successful than the Spanish. Writing in 1665, Father Breton remarks that "During six months of peace, they [the Dominicans] catechized to many, baptized a few, but in the end only one woman preserved...."[19] Another priest, Father Jean-Baptiste DuTerte, wrote of the futility of preaching to potential converts among the Caribs who "just a quarter-hour later would reflect no more" on the principles of their new religion. However, in the same passage DuTerte makes a remark that is richly suggestive: "[t]here are many among them who are enough instructed in the mysteries of our faith, and hence a number of them wear the rosary around their neck and know how to pray to God."[20] It is impossible to say with any certainty whether the Caribs actually employed the rosary as an instrument of Marian devotion. Probably so, Father DuTerte must have thought. It is more likely that the Carib's religious habitus, like that of the enslaved Africans later, predisposed them to esteem the rosary as spiritually charged and worthy of qualified incorporation into their own disrupted system of symbols and ritual. This adaptation was encouraged not only by the religious habitus of the slaves, but also by the missionaries' inability to communicate with them effectively. According to several accounts, the language barrier was paramount among the difficulties that the Spanish and French Catholic missionaries of the colonial period encountered, which explains in part the limits of their success. "Conscious of this obstacle, the missionaries seem to have privileged the wearing of certain 'ways': images, medals, rosary beads, crosses."[21] As one frustrated priest put it, "[A]n image or a medal sometimes serves better than a long discourse."[22] For the missionaries to offer religious symbols and trinkets to the "pagan" targets of their evangelization, while lacking the capacity to communicate clearly their meaning and function, represented a most fortuitous religious environment for syncretism to flourish.

While earlier missionaries labored with marginal success to teach the slaves French first and the Gospel second, the Jesuits actually took up the study of African languages. As one Jesuit attested, "One has even translated into their languages the Our Father, the Hail Mary, the Apostles' Creed, and the commandments of God."[23] How the slaves interpreted these prayers is, of course, open to question. Thus, the introduction of the Virgin Mary and other Catholic symbols, first to the Indians and then to the displaced Africans, was marred from orthodoxy's standpoint by its specialists' inability to communicate the symbol's meaning and hence to employ the symbol to monopolize control of the laity. The Jesuits, both through greater achievements than their predecessors in teaching the slaves French and through their own study of African languages, improved this situation and consequently considerably expanded the Catholic mission in Hispaniola. The development of a less-syncretized form of Marian piety among the enslaved masses, while ephemeral, was likely fundamental to this expansion.

In any event, like the Spanish before them, the French employed the symbol of the Virgin Mary to legitimize their colonialist agenda in the Americas. "The crowned Virgin, sublime symbol of the feudal European order, in effect was consecrated patron saint of France by Louis XIII...king of France from 1601 to 1643, as much the father of slavery as promoter of the cult of *Notre Dame de l'Assomption*." Thus, the Spanish understanding of their colonization of the New World as a Marian drama was shared by the French, as "from the time of the Spanish colony [and throughout the period of French rule from 1697 to 1804], the lands along the Gulf of Gonâve took the Holy Virgin as patron."[24]

Instability and discord characterized the seventeenth- and eighteenth-century Church in Hispaniola. "The apparent weakness of the Church was spawned in part by her internal division and the ferocious struggle which unfolded between different monastic orders for the monopolization of the evangelization of the island."[25] Nonetheless, the cult of Mary suffered apparently little because of this conflict, save perhaps for a lack of uniformity, as it developed freely throughout the colony—perhaps too freely for orthodoxy's taste.

In order to illustrate the importance of the cult it suffices alone to cite the principal colonial churches placed under her patronage:

> **under the name of l'Assomption**—Cap, Port-au-Prince, Cayes, Petit-Goave, Ouanaminthe;
> **under the name of l'Immaculée Conception**—Port-de-Paix, Petit Anse;
> **under the name of la Nativité**—l'Acul du Nord, Verrettes, Terre-Neuve;
> **under other names**—Gros Morne, Saut-d'Eau, Croix-des-Bouquets, Pignon, Camp Coq....[26]

Indeed, this list could easily be lengthened. The particular image of the Virgin to patronize a church or parish was determined usually by the Marian affinities of the order responsible for its foundation and in most cases involved the benediction and placing of the icon in question. The above list demonstrates how under the French, *Notre Dame de l'Assomption* eclipsed the colony's earlier Spanish choices of Guadeloupe and Immaculate Conception as the dominant Marian icon, for the three most important churches of Saint Domingue, those of Port-au-Prince, Cap-Haïtien, and Les Cayes, were dedicated *to Notre Dame de l'Assomption.*

Regarding the emergence of *Notre Dame de l'Assomption* as patroness of Saint-Domingue in the second half of the seventeenth century, Rachel Beauvoir-Dominique finds it ironic that "the establishment of the slave regime should be patronized by such a figure," rightly concluding that religious symbols are adapted to the political and religious needs of social groups:

> The symbol of the bodily ascension of the Virgin, the purity of this carnal representation would seem fundamentally opposed to the physical violence committed against thousands of enslaved men and women. All the same, one what one wants of signs and symbols; they are manipulated, diluted, and adapted to needs. And, among the various representations in which she has been experienced from the very beginning of Christianity, the figure of Notre Dame most monopolized by the first colonists would be that of the crowned Virgin, the immediate and logical development of the Assumption.[27]

Most of the earliest churches throughout Saint-Domingue, not surprisingly, were dedicated to the Virgin Mary. In Port-au-Prince, part of a large sugar refinery was converted into a chapel in 1743, which served provisionally as the city's first church. "As such, the refinery became a parish under the patronage of *Notre Dame de l'Assomption*."[28] Remarkably, this church was established in the proximity of Bel-Air, which, a century and a half later, would be the site of the most significant event in the history of Haitian Marianism.

The Jesuits and the Daughters of Notre Dame

The Jesuits, arguably the most popular religious order among the subjugated of Saint-Domingue, distinguished themselves from the other Catholic missionaries with their language and educational skills and a more genuine openness to the slaves. That the Jesuits had greater financial resources also helped. Replacing the Capuchins, who were themselves French Catholicism's first missionaries in the Haitian religious field beginning in 1681, "around 1704, the Jesuit order undertook the responsibility for church building, education and the slaves in the colony. By 1725, they were working with approximately half the slaves, which numbered around fifty thousand, and they were also trying to convert the maroons, or escaped slaves."[29]   Given the Jesuits' affinity for Mary—it was they (as mentioned in chapter three) who forcefully promoted Counter Reformation maximalist Mariology—along with their popularity among the colony's disenfranchised and the expansive breadth of their mission, it is highly probable that they had a significant influence on the development of popular Marianism in eighteenth century Hispaniola.

Reflective of the Jesuits' deep Marian piety, by late 1718, there had been enough progress made on the construction of Cap-Haïtien's cathedral for them to dedicate it to *Notre Dame de l'Assomption* on December 18, 1718. The city square already bore her name, *Place de Notre Dame* (tellingly, the square is also known as *La Place des Armes*!). Ten years earlier a Jesuit named Champaing "imported a painting of the Nativity of the Virgin, thus establishing under which invocation the parish should be dedicated"[30] in the nearby village of Limonade.

To Monsignor Jean-Marie Jan, one of the principal historians of the Haitian Church, "it is notable that the blacks had a marked attachment for the so-called Jesuits…this mutual affection was so strong and so public that it more than once alarmed the spirit."[31] In 1713, a quarter-century into the Jesuit mission in Saint-Domingue, the first group of French nuns of the *Compagnie de Notre Dame* (Daughters of Notre Dame) arrived in the north; they soon became the object of similar affection among the slaves. According to their Mother Superior, writing in 1745, "the devotion to the Mother of God was the principal form of devotion"[32] of the nuns. So similar were they to the Jesuits in ritual, practice, and emphases (among which the Marian emphasis was paramount) that the Daughters became known as the *Jesuitines*. Their popularity among the slaves was especially evident whenever one of the nuns passed away: a slave escorted the funeral procession "from one end of the city to another," all the while announcing in harmony with the funeral bells, *"Bon blanch' mouri, mauvais rete"* ("A good white has died, the bad remain")![33]

Besides their evangelical tasks, the Daughters of Notre Dame served in the hospital and fed upwards to eighty families daily in Cap-Haïtien. In 1733, a Jesuit priest wrote, "one admired with reason the courage of these holy girls who appear mature well beyond their age...in remarkable shape and of a ripe age."[34] Even more impressed were the city's poor and enslaved, especially women, "who were particularly moved [by]...[and] very attached to the nuns." An interesting prayer for the nuns entered the devotions of under-class women who had lost their mothers and evidently adopted the Daughters as replacement mothers: *"Bon Die, Menagez Mamans pitites"* ("Good God, care for the mothers of children").[35]

Among the courageous and dedicated Daughters of Notre Dame, the name Suzanne de Fontenille is particularly noteworthy. Typifying the profound Marian piety of her order, Mother Suzanne's:

> devotion to the Mother of God was at once the most tender and most solid. She only ever spoke with the most glorious respect for the incomparable Virgin; her sweetest desire was to hear her praised, and to entirely pattern her life after hers.[36]

With the Daughters, Mother Suzanne served the sick and dying in Cap-Haïtien's hospital, where she gained some renown for "the creation of remedies," perhaps having acquired knowledge of herbalism through her contact with the slaves.

One quality in particular made Mother Suzanne stand out among an order that, like the Jesuits, was probably mistrusted by Saint-Domingue's elite sectors. Mother Suzanne "acquired a sovereign influence over the privileged classes of the colony, knowing well how to interest them in the lot of the poor."[37] Somewhat precursory of liberation theology, more than 200 years before the Church proclaimed its "preferential option for the poor," Mother Suzanne asked whether "the hate of some wasn't too often explicable in terms of the selfishness of others."[38] The young French nun found in "the image of Jesus Christ, the suffering and the poor," and in "the image of the Holy Spirit that is love the thread that unites the rich and the poor; she was this thread."[39]

Missionaries like Mother Suzanne and the Daughters of Notre Dame, along with the Jesuit Fathers were particularly responsible for the promotion and development of the cult of the Virgin Mary in eighteenth century Saint-Domingue, and in they established a positive rapport with the colony's under-class. From such a position of popularity, the Jesuits and the Daughters were able to promote effectively Marian devotion on the popular level.

Letters written by the Jesuits and Daughters in the eighteenth century provide some insight into the nature of Marian piety in Saint-Domingue. For devout colonists and slaves, who, in the mind of at least one priest, "are very touched by God...and live much more Christianly in their condition than many of the French,"[40] Marian devotion ostensibly took the form of novenas, recitations of the rosary, and the regular celebration of Marian feast days, which often included processions. It is possible that some free Marian devotees were also making pilgrimage to the shrine of *Nuestra Señora de Altagracia* at Higuey in the Spanish part of the island during this period, though the earliest concrete evidence of this dates from the period of island unification under Boyer (1821-43). I have found no accounts of Marian apparitions in Saint-Domingue prior to the revolution, though it is perfectly reasonable to speculate that some had indeed occurred.

A letter written by one of the Daughters illustrates how slaves made supplicative prayers to the Virgin, employing votive candles in an act of touching devotion.[41] Describing her church, the nun writes, "The statue of the Holy Virgin is altogether beautiful. Eight candles burn continually before her; such is the devotion of the blacks."[42] Whether the candles and accompanying supplications were in fact directed through the symbol of Mary ultimately to Ezili, the Vodou spirit of love, is an important question. Consider and compare the following scene from the cathedral in Port-au-Prince described by a foreign writer visiting Haiti in 1993:

> Often I saw a crowd of wailing women round the Madonna. Many would prostrate themselves in supplication, lying prone with faces pressed against the floor, clutching in one hand a lighted candle, a rosary in the other. Some curious votive offerings had been placed at the Madonna's plaster feet: a small mirror, a white silk handkerchief, empty bottles of Cinzano and Madeira. These were objects left in honour of Erzulie Freda, an African divinity of Dahomean origin who is mirrored in Catholicism by the Virgin Mary.[43]

It is not impossible that somewhere between the late eighteenth century and 1993, orthodox religious specialist suspended efforts to proscribe the entry of things like Cinzano bottles and mirrors, not to mention chickens, into "their" churches, resigned to the irreversible fact that for many if not most Haitians these orthodox Catholic symbols are integral to Vodou's ritualistic and symbolic systems, and that Vodouisants consider themselves Catholic and Catholic churches as important shrines of the *lwas*. This would in part explain the differences in the two above-quoted accounts, which, though separated by two hundred years, describe the same ritual performance.

Doubtless, Marian syncretism on the popular level occurred from the time of the very entry of the Virgin symbol into the religious field, but was probably less prevalent during the first Jesuit mission than from 1804 to 1860, the period of the "great schism." The relative absence of quality Catholic religious specialists like the Jesuits and Daughters of Notre Dame, who obviously had a significant influence on the religious habitus of the masses, marked this period of schism with the Vatican, as previously discussed in chapter two.

As for the fate of our heroic missionaries, Mother Suzanne died of yellow fever in 1734; the Jesuits were expelled from the colony in 1762; and the Daughters of Notre Dame, who remained in the face of mounting danger and despite all petitions that they leave, were slaughtered by Haitian revolutionary hero Biassou and his rebels in 1793.[44]

Marian Appropriation and Political Power

Whatever the interests that European imperialism intended to promote through the symbol of the Virgin Mary in the colony, religiously heretical or politically resistant groups have long appropriated the symbol toward their own ends. Various and contested interpretations of Mary have developed in the Haitian religious field, each emerging from specific class-determined religious and political interests. A Creole expression reflects this colorfully: "*Jipon Lavyej, plen koukouy*" ("The Virgin's slip is full of fireflies").[45] This section of the chapter carefully analyzes three remarkable events in the history of Haitian Marianism. In each case there is seen an attempt among either dominant or subjugated sectors to appropriate the symbol of the Virgin Mary and to employ it in the pursuit of political or military advantage. The example of Romaine-la-Prophétesse is the most radical representation of the revolutionary potential of Marian appropriation in Haitian religious history, one clearly "in active opposition" to the European hegemonic worldview supported by orthodox Catholic Mariology since the dawn of colonial exploitation. Romaine effectively transformed the Mother of Jesus from a legitimizing force for the slave regime into an oppositional form of religious capital that met under-class religious needs and served under-class political interests. Less than a quarter-century later, in the internal military struggle for political supremacy between Christophe and Pétion over a newly independent, though divided and largely unstable, republic, the symbol of the Virgin was once again appropriated and employed for strategic advantage. And still another quarter century later, the Soulouque administration, in an effort to legitimate his military excursions into the Dominican Republic and to solidify its power and justify his coronation as Emperor, seized upon widespread credence given Marian apparitions at Champs-de-Mars and Saut-d'Eau. Thus, while certain Catholic religious in Haitian history, like the Jesuits and the Daughters of Notre Dame, seem to have employed the symbol of Mary toward apolitical and sincerely apostolic ends, in the political realm the symbol's religious dimension has often been overshadowed by its *legitimierende Macht* for political factions.

Romaine-la-Prophétesse

Chapter two argues that Vodou played a vital role as an inspirational and unifying force for the slaves in the Haitian Revolution. This argument, while popular, is not universally accepted. Some writers, like Micial Neréstant, feel that in general "Haitian historians and ethnographers, disciples of Jean Price-Mars, have overestimated the role of Vodou in the acquisition of independence in Haiti."[46] Similarly, Carolyn Fick, in her assiduously researched study of the Haitian Revolution "from below," concludes that: "In the South, curiously, there seems to be no evidence at all of Vodou as an organizational vehicle...."[47] Nevertheless, while some have overstated the influence of Vodou on history's only successful slave revolt, and while historical accounts supportive of such exaggerated positions are undoubtedly tinged with some measure of legend, it is irrefutable that Vodou was to some degree instrumental in the overthrow of French colonial power in Saint-Domingue.

Boukman heads a long list of Vodou priests and/or Vodouisants who used "the spiritual power of Vodou on the battlefield...a tremendous inner force, a force by which to make a mockery of death in the face of Leclerc's army or Rochambeau's firing squads, one that certainly contributed to and reinforced the determination of the blacks in their armed struggles for freedom."[48] Romaine-la-Prophétesse, an obscure religious visionary who, from September 1991 to March 1992, inspired his band of thousands of freed slaves to wreak torturous havoc against the whites of Leogâne and Jacmel, is usually counted among these Vodou leaders of the Haitian Revolution. However, a more critical analysis of the style and content of Romaine's religious ritual and practice, as indicated by Fick, raises the question as to whether Romaine actually practiced Vodou at all. We will return to this question below.

There is very little information available concerning Romaine-la-Prophétesse's, background, and contradictions abound from one account to another. For our purposes, what is important is that Romaine used the symbol of the Virgin Mary very much in "active opposition" to the orthodox worldview that served as theological legitimization for plantation slavery. Nineteenth-century Haitian historian Thomas Madiou, who is the most commonly cited, and often the lone, source for contemporary discussions of this intriguing historical figure, explains that Romaine:

> called himself the godchild of the Virgin Mary. He dominated through superstition the bands of slaves whom he'd led into the mountains. He said Mass, brought all kinds of torture upon the whites and pretended that this was according to the orders of the Virgin.[49]

Here, once again, the militant aspect of the Virgin Mary was manifest and represented an inspirational force for warriors. This time the warriors happened to be slaves.

Perhaps nowhere is there a clearer example of how a "religious symbol becomes a force for change and the basis for liberation"[50] than in the figure of Romaine-la-Prophétesse and his radical appropriation of the symbol of Mary. Like Hidalgo and Morelos, Romaine took the Virgin as protectress and inspiration for a violent liberation struggle against the European colonizer. Yet, one of the things that separates Romaine so clearly from history's other military leaders under Mary's patronage, besides his claim to being the Virgin's godson, is that Romaine also claimed that the Virgin instructed him and his band of maroons to rape, pillage, and burn beyond the borders of the battlefield. Romaine understood the Virgin to be insistent that he bring unspeakable torture against all whites, not just his opponents in warfare. "The messages of this Virgin adapted to the times of war seem to have been particularly radical since the violence and the fervor of Romaine have remained notorious."[51]

What led Romaine to such an extreme interpretation of Mary? The lack of historical detail concerning his background disallows any definitive response to this question. However, pieces of information exist that do permit cautious speculation. It appears certain that George Eaton Simpson is incorrect in calling Romaine a "Spaniard."[52] It is more likely that Romaine was either a mulatto or free black originally hailing from the Spanish side of the island and was perhaps associated with the infamous Bahoruco maroon community there. While it is unclear whether he was ever himself a slave, it does appear that Romaine was a landowner. His true name was Romaine Rivière, and he was married to a mulatress with whom he had and raised two children. Contemporary Haitian historian Jean Fouchard offers some intriguing evidence suggesting that Romaine was well educated and that he corresponded regularly with certain French priests active in *Les Amis des Noirs* (Friends of Blacks—a French abolitionist society), one of whom appears to have served Romaine as an "adviser."[53] Given his level of education and regular correspondence with a French Catholic priest sympathetic to the slaves' cause, it is at least possible that Romaine was familiar with the Magnificat, from which he may have taken scriptural inspiration for his excessively violent campaigns. To "depose the mighty from their thrones" and to raise "the lowly to high places" was, after all, certainly fundamental to Romaine's ideology.

Romaine "was often possessed by the mysteries"[54] and actually claimed to be in direct communication with the Virgin Mary, his "godmother," who commanded him not only to a series of victories in battle but to the torture of white civilians. It is not unreasonable to venture that Romaine was possessed the Virgin. Significantly, in an impressive instance of what Desmangles labels "symbiosis by ecology,"[55] Romaine established his headquarters in an abandoned Catholic church in Trou Coffy, in the mountains above the western port city of Leogâne. There he regularly said Mass, usually dedicated to his men, and personally communicated with the Virgin. Evidently, this act was the focal element of his strange religious ceremonies, as many of his followers probably waited in anxious anticipation for the Virgin's latest oracle before returning to the battle or raid. "Seen upon the altar was a tabernacle, into which he would place his head to consult with the supernatural. The Virgin Mary responded to him in writing and the response would be found in the tabernacle."[56]

A few other details lend further insight into the nature of Romaine's theology and ritual. Romaine had amassed an assortment of religious "ornaments and cult objects,"[57] some apparently stolen from other churches, which he used to adorn his own church at Trou Coffy, indicative of the great value he and his followers placed on such things; i.e., on such forms of religious capital. The extreme nature of Romaine's appropriation of religious symbols is evident in the fact that "he preached mass before an inverted cross with a sabre in his hand."[58] This remarkable image is particularly telling, as it reveals not only a radical appropriation of Catholic symbolism "in active opposition" to the dominant worldview but also a radical attempt to reverse both the social and religious order.

The strong conviction that he was a prophet was central to Romaine's theology and success as both a religious and military leader. Why he chose to call himself *Prophétesse* (feminine) rather than *Prophète* (masculine) is a mystery. Several commentators accuse him of fanaticism. That he suffered from some degree of megalomania is likely, for he instructed his followers to inform the slaves whom they freed from the plantations that "the king" had freed them. "One source even claimed that his real intention, once the whites were defeated, was to become king of Santo Domingo."[59] While Fick prefers to call Romaine a "shaman" rather than a "prophet," without bothering to define either term, the key point is that he and his followers fully believed him to be in communication with the Virgin, guarantor of their imminent victory, whose messages were for them the source of conviction and inspiration that led them to act out Romaine's "theodicy of compensation."[60]

Some of the Virgin's messages to Romaine were similar to beliefs preached by other religious leaders of the Haitian Revolution who are more clearly identifiable as *oungans* or Vodouisants. For instance, Romaine "instructed the slaves that God was black and that all whites had to be killed."[61] He also preached that "those who would die during the war would return to Guinea where they would enjoy eternal bliss,"[62] and "promised his followers...immunity against bullets."[63] Yet, other than these divine, inspirational messages, did Romaine have anything ritualistic or theological substantially in common with the likes of Boukman, Hyacinthe, Biassou, or other decidedly Vodouisant revolutionary leaders? Can we accurately label Romaine-la-Prophétesse an *oungan*, or is Fick correct in denying that he practiced Vodou at all?

> A self-styled prophet who also practiced herbal medicine, he no doubt was seen in the eyes of many a slave to be empowered with some sort of supernatural power. Yet in all of the documentation surrounding these events, not one reference to this leader can be found that even vaguely suggests genuine African Vodou practices, unless his were in some way peculiar to cults in the Spanish colonies. It is possible that he adopted a shamanistic pretense to reinforce his influence and augment his numbers.[64]

Fick's argument is provocative, yet flawed by an anachronistic conception of Vodou and some degree of oversight.[65] The fact that Romaine "practiced herbal medicine," an important element of Haitian Vodou, certainly more than "vaguely suggests" that he practiced Vodou. Furthermore, Milo Rigaud writes that Romaine "went to combat mocking bullets and bayonets—an empowered cock (*coq rangé*) on his saddletree."[66] The belief in spiritual and sacrificial powers embodied in the cock is common in Haitian Vodou. Moreover, were any of Romaine's contemporaries on the island then practicing "genuine African Vodou," for that matter? In light of the historical evidence of the great variety of Vodou traditions during the revolutionary period, this term is a misnomer.

Drexel Woodson points to Fick's spurious argument as illustrative of the surrealism commonly committed by those who write about Haitian culture solely in terms of dichotomies:

> A particularly disappointing example of surrealism is Fick's interpretation of a dichotomy which, judging from textual evidence, she established without much support from her sources or their subjects: "genuine voodoo practices"/"bizarre and dubious [Dominguoise or Creole] cults." The first term refers to the religious-cum-political conduct of "voodoo priests" who became rebel slave leaders, such as Boukman Dutty.... The second term refers to the conduct of rebel slave leaders such as Romaine Rivière (aka Romaine-la-Prophétesse).... Romaine's amazingly syncretic cult was, she admits, subversive.... Yet the cult relied too heavily, it seems, on systematically inverted Catholic ritual paraphernalia and symbolism to suit Fick's taste for genuine Africana. Thus, she alleges, Romaine's cult was "bizarre," and he/she was merely a shaman (i.e., of lower ritual status and lesser authority than a priest) and a political opportunist.[67]

In part, since there is no evidence to support the claims of Beauvoir-Dominique and Serge Larose that Romaine practiced rituals common in Vodou's Petro cult,[68] and while it would be somewhat uncritical to list him without reservation among the Vodouisant leaders of the Haitian revolution, as Métraux and most other writers have, I am, nonetheless, inclined with Woodson to disagree with Fick's assertion that Romaine was neither an *oungan* per se nor a religious leader who practiced what one could reasonably label Vodou. That Romaine's religious practice and rituals differed from those of Boukman, Biassou and others is evident. It would be fallacious, however, to conclude that he was therefore not practicing Vodou, for during the revolutionary period, as Laguerre and others demonstrate, there was more variety than uniformity among Vodou cults. "The various Voodoo traditions that developed in the colony were not standardized. Reciprocal acculturation and syncretism occurred; yet each Voodoo cult had its own traditions."[69] Historical sources clearly suggest that Romaine took part in such "reciprocal acculturation," taking interest in forms of religious capital recognizable even today as Vodouisant, which he effectively employed, is suggested by the. Whether this interest was genuinely religious or merely to strengthen his sway over his followers, most of whom certainly were dedicated to the *lwas*, is open to speculation. In any case, and here Fick is correct, "it is true that as a leader of slave resistance, his influence over his following was as undisputed as any Vodou leader using the rallying powers of religion for political ends."[70]

One issue of paramount importance to the sociology of religion is the influence of politically effective religious leaders like Romaine, and inevitably the researcher is drawn to Max Weber's notion of charisma in exploring the matter. Weber's discussion of prophecy and charisma in his classic *The Sociology of Religion* might be employed as a useful paradigm for the analysis of revolutionary religious leaders such as Romaine-la-Prophétesse. But, in my judgment, a truer understanding of Romaine's popularity and effectiveness is wrought through modifying Weber's definitions of prophet and charisma in light of Bourdieu's criticism. Bourdieu's sociology of religion is itself very much an extension of Weber's, though with different emphases and refined terminology. One of Bourdieu's most insightful critiques of Weber on religion concerns weaknesses in Weber's discussion of charisma. The emergent view of prophecy is well suited to an analysis not only of Romaine but of the role of religious leaders in any period of social change.

Weber defines the prophet as "the purely individual bearer of charisma, who by virtue of his mission proclaims a religious doctrine or divine commandment."[71] Furthermore, "the prophet's claim is based on personal revelation and charisma." There are, for Weber, two kinds of charisma; one that is "wholly merited, based purely on personal calling, and another that lies dormant in the prophet and is "produced artificially...through some extraordinary means."[72] Often the two types merge, though, in any case, charisma "cannot be acquired by any means." "Charisma is a gift that inheres in an object or person simply by virtue of natural endowments"[73]—either the prophet has it or not, case closed.

Concerned primarily with "religion as a source of the dynamics of social change,"[74] Weber further develops the notions of prophet, charisma, and breakthrough (the sudden prophet-provoked shift in a religion's development) to understand "the effect of religious views upon the conduct of life."[75] It is the prophet, thus naturally endowed with charisma, who produces such an effect. "The essential criterion of prophecy for Weber is whether or not the message is a call to break with an established order."[76] Doubtless, such a break was a key element to Romaine's agenda. Furthermore, the prophet, in order to activate the break or stir his/her following into belief, must appeal to some source of accepted moral authority in order to legitimate the break. In Romaine's case, the Virgin Mary embodied that moral authority. Put simply, not just any one is able to effect such a break. S/he who does inspire a "breakthrough," for Weber, is able to do so by virtue of his/her charisma. "In contrast to the ordinary layman," such a person "is permanently endowed with charisma."[77]

On the surface, it might appear satisfactory to conclude positively that Romaine-la-Prophétesse may be called a prophet in Weber's understanding of the term. However, there is something deceptively facile in this conclusion that, thus accepted, would limit the insights one might otherwise gain into Romaine and the nature of his religious activities and popularity. Such a position would ineluctably lead the researcher to determine that since Romaine was naturally endowed with a great deal of charisma, he became an important religious leader of the Haitian revolution. This would be a gross oversimplification.

There is, therefore, a hazardous weakness lurking in Weber's definition of charisma, and hence of prophet, which, once applied uncritically, can give rise to a series of unsatisfactory conclusions about the socioreligious climate of the prophet and the social dialectic that unfold between message, moral authority, prophet, and laity. Bourdieu realizes this and attacks Weber's notion of prophet. "Max Weber never produces anything other than a psycho-sociological theory of charisma, a theory that regards it as the lived relation of a public to the charismatic personality."[78] Bourdieu is critical of such a definition of "charisma as a property attaching to the nature of a single individual"[79] because it ignores the structures of the religious field and the relationships between these structures and the religious habitus of the laity, which, for Bourdieu, must be the primary object of analysis for the sociology of religion. "Weber consistently fails to establish a distinction between (1) direct interactions and (2) the objective structure of the relations that become established between religious agencies."[80] For Bourdieu, "The latter is crucial...[since] it controls the form that interactions may take...."[81] While sharing Weber's insistence that a condition of true prophecy is its capacity to produce effective religious and/or social change, Bourdieu goes on to argue that "[p]rophecy can play such a role only because it has as its own generative and unifying principle a habitus objectively attuned to that of its addressees."[82] Charisma, then, exists in the ability to cultivate a message preexistent in the religious and political interests of the laity, not in nature. Charisma, as it were, exists within the prophet, but as *vox populi* and not *vox dei*.

Consideration of Bourdieu's critique of the Weberian notion of charisma leads to an understanding of Romaine's success as being explicable in terms of the religious and political needs and aspirations of his followers being articulated for them in the Virgin's messages through Romaine. The renegade slaves were thus socially predisposed to respond positively to Romaine's prophecy. Romaine's religious power, then, is not the product of nature, but rather "the product of a transaction" between the "religious agent," Romaine, and "the lay people," in which their religious interests are reflected and satisfied. Bourdieu further elaborates this argument:

> All the power that the various religious agents hold over the lay people and all the authority they possess... can be explained in terms of the structure of relations.... The prophet's power rests upon the force of the group he can mobilize. This depends on his authority to give symbolic expression—in an exemplary form of conduct and/or in a (quasi) systematic discourse—to the specifically religious interests of lay people occupying a determinate position in the social structure.[83]

I would argue that Romaine's religious power is to be understood precisely in this light.

This is a suggestive conclusion. For on the one hand, it raises new questions as to the nature of the role which religion played in the Haitian revolution. Chapter two illustrates how the potency of the general message of Makandal, Boukman, and other resistance prophets depended largely upon the religious needs and interests of

their audience, in this case one of history's most oppressed peoples—
the enslaved of African descent in the New World. As Weber notes,
and Bourdieu agrees, in addition to their basic religious need for
alleviation from their suffering, subjugated classes often have "a
need for just compensation,"[84] which "serves as a device for compensating a conscious or unconscious desire for vengeance."[85] Moreover, the theodicy of compensation, or of "the disprivileged," reflected in both Boukman's sermon and Romaine's theology—that
God is black and the tides are to be turned—was essential to the
prophecy of each Boukman and Romaine. If, for the sake of argument, Romaine were not an *oungan* but a self-styled prophet syn-
cretizing capital from various religious traditions, and since his
impact and success were at least as great as those of Boukman's,
one might venture that it is precisely in the expression of such a
"theodicy of compensation," keeping in mind the transaction between religious agent and laity discussed above by Bourdieu, wherein
lies the fundamental explanation of religion's positive role in the
Haitian Revolution. It was not so much out of Vodou that 1804
issued, but out of the transaction between religious agents, such as
Boukman and Romaine, and the laity around the slaves' desire for
revenge and compensation, as much as their desire for freedom.
While other elements, such as the promise of immortality in Africa
and immunity against bullets, certainly played a role, the essence of
religion's effectiveness in the revolution was the theodicy of compensation. The prophets served to rally the masses of slaves and
maroons around the vision of this theodicy realized. The rest is
history.

Another conclusion, significant for our broader purposes of understanding the development of Haitian Marianism, may be drawn
through analyzing Romaine's movement in light of Bourdieu's modi-
fication of Weber's notion of charisma. For Bourdieu, the primary
weakness of Weber's understanding of charisma lies in its rooting
in nature—the idea that the prophet is naturally charismatic. On the
contrary, charisma is better understood as being socially grounded.
The prophet's success, or popularity, is, in the main, due to his/her
articulation of the laity's religious and/or political needs, which may
have previously been unconscious and mute. Thus, in the case of
Romaine-la-Prophétesse, it becomes apparent that freed slaves and
maroons of late-eighteenth-century Saint Domingue already lent

substantial credence to the Virgin Mary as religious symbol and moral authority. Otherwise, Romaine's message would have lacked the legitimating foundation that was prerequisite to its success. In other words, at the latest, the Virgin Mary had become an important religious symbol on a wide scale for the subjugated masses, mainly slaves, of Saint Domingue by the late eighteenth century. Romaine, either through spiritual revelation, fortuitous happenstance, or calculating design, expressed the symbol's previously dormant liberative, revolutionary content. Such is the function of the prophet's charisma for his followers.

La Vierge Bosquette: The Spy in Drag

An electrifying comet streaked across the Haitian skies one night around the end of 1811 and again during one of the first evenings of 1812. To the fascinated peasants, the comet's return must have been interpreted as a sign from the spirits that something earth-shattering was about to happen. We may speculate that divination took place to fathom the spirits' celestial sign, and that some *mambos*, *oungans*, or devotees were possessed by certain *lwas*, who offered explanations for the astronomical oracle. For nineteenth-century Haitian historian Alexis Beaubrun Ardouin, the comet's appearance and reappearance ripened the peasants' for religious fervor and revival: "[T]he weak spirits were predisposed for superstition."[86] The condescending tone of his suggestion aside, Ardouin is likely correct in referring to the comet as a spiritually charged conductor that hot-wired the Haitian religious field for one of the most remarkable events in its history.

Shortly after the revolution was won, Haiti became divided into two states: Henry Christophe—or King Henry I, as he preferred to be called—ruled the north, while Alexandre Pétion controlled Port-au-Prince and the south. As noted in chapter two, each of these leaders promulgated legislation against Vodou, although neither was opposed to making certain concessions on this point for political gain. Such was the case as 1811 turned into 1812, when Christophe was planning an attack on Port-au-Prince. Concerned that the peasants would offer resistance, Christophe employed the services of the area's *mambos* and *oungans* in preparation for the invasion, "winning them to his cause, through the persuasion of money." In effect, the Vodou priests sold out to Christophe's scheme and "in their Vodou ceremonies announced to the believers that a great army, sent from heaven, would soon penetrate the region, and those who opposed or resisted would incur the total wrath of God."[87]

Having thus succeeded in proliferating the fabricated divine message through Vodou's religious specialists, it remained for Christophe to fortify his plan through the employment of Catholic religious sanction, which, as illustrated in chapter two, Vodouisants highly esteem. One moonlit night in early January, a spy from Christophe's camp named Bosquette dressed himself up to resemble the Virgin Mary and climbed to the top of a tall tree somewhere near Croix-des-Bouquets. Evidently told of the Virgin's imminent apparition by the Vodou priests who had sold out to Christophe, the peasants flocked to the scene and "La Vierge Bosquette" became "an object of worship for the better part of the population."[88] Not surprisingly, according to Ardouin's account, the Virgin's message to the peasants to whom she appeared, mainly women was precisely that which the *lwas* had spoken through the *oungans* and *mambos*: "A mighty army shall soon descend upon the plain, and it should not be resisted, for to do so would be to disobey God."[89] With that, the Virgin vanished into heaven, and the tree in which she appeared was transformed into a shrine, attracting pilgrims from throughout the surrounding area and from Port-au-Prince. For a short while, anyway.

At least as calculating and shrewd as his adversary, Pétion immediately saw through the apparition and fought back with his own religious assault. In an effort "to destroy through religious ceremony, namely Christian and Catholic ceremony, the distressing moral effect that this affair had produced upon the superstitious masses,"[90] as Madiou puts it, Pétion enlisted the services of Port-au-Prince curate Abbé Gaspard to visit the celebrated tree and, through a purposely extravagant display of orthodox Catholic ritual, expose the hoax in a manner convincing to the peasants. Ardouin's account of the great religious pomp accompanying the Abbé's visit to the tree is worth quoting here in full:

> The priest arrived on the scene, in effect, with the cross and the banner of the Church, escorted by precentors, a children's choir, and above all the devout. There he encountered a great crowd. After having blessed with holy

water the tree alleged to have served as the Virgin's refuge, he broke out into singing the ritual chants and made
a brief address to his attentive audience. He then declared
that it was necessary to recognize whether it was really
the Holy Virgin who had momentarily appeared: if so, then
the mapu tree actually participated in the holiness of the
event and would resist the effects of the fire that he was
igniting. But the sticks gathered about the tree caught flame
as well as might otherwise be expected, and shortly the
fire spread from the trunk to the branches. The experi-
ment was conclusive, and the amazed spectators condemned the supposed Virgin as an impostor.[91]

Madiou's version ends on a slightly different note: "The crowd dis-
persed, somewhat dismayed over the sacrilege that had just been
committed, but nonetheless pretty much convinced that they had
been fooled by a false Virgin."[92]

Needless to say, Christophe failed in his efforts to dupe the masses
into acceptance of his invasion, and the territory remained under
Pétion's control. "As for Bosquette, Christophe, unhappy with his
mission that had not fully succeeded,"[93] had him executed. Abbé
Gaspard, who, interestingly, had never been ordained, returned to
Port-au-Prince and published an epistle addressed to his parishioners in the newspaper L'Echo, "warning them against lending credence to false doctors of boorish sects of fetishism, one of whom
had just been believed to have taken the form of the Virgin."[94]

Before turning our attention to another episode in the history of
Haitian Marianism, it behooves us first to briefly note what the
story of La Vierge Bosquette reveals about the state of the Mary
cult in Haiti during the early nineteenth century. Although this is
the earliest historical account of a Marian apparition in Haiti—
albeit a false one—that my research has discovered, the immediacy
with which Catholics and Vodouisants flocked to the Virgin's tree,
let alone the fact that Christophe contrived of the hoax in the first
place, suggests that Marian apparitions had occurred previously in
Haiti and were given credence by Catholics and Vodouisants alike.
That women were predominant among the initial seers of the Vierge
Bosquette, or, as Madiou explains, that convincing women of the
divine might of Christophe's army was the intent of the scheme, is

significant, at least for the sole reason that elsewhere women and children are usually the witnesses of Marian apparitions. Also, the effectiveness of the prediction of the Virgin's apparition by Vodou religious specialists indicates that the Virgin's importance in Vodou was firmly established before Haitian independence.

The Emperor and the Virgin

While nowhere as shrewd as Christophe and Pétion before him, Faustin Soulouque, who ruled Haiti from 1847 to 1859, also recognized in the Haitian people's Marian devotion a potential source for the legitimation of his power and for the promotion of his political and military agenda. After the death of President-for-Life Jean-Pierre Boyer, who had succeeded in uniting the entire island under his rule, the Dominican Republic regained its independence from Haiti in 1844. Soulouque, an illiterate, power-hungry despot, was intent on recapturing the eastern two-thirds of the island. His troops were routed in their attempt to do so in the spring of 1849. So:

> Soulouque decided to strengthen his authority at home. Searching for excuses to name himself emperor, Soulouque found an opportunity when a rumor that the Holy Virgin had appeared in a palm tree on the property of one Debarine in the Champs-de-Mars began circulating in Port-au-Prince.[95]

It is not unreasonable to suggest that the apparitions were, as in Christophe's case, merely dramas staged by Soulouque's supporters.

Whether real or false, Soulouque seized upon the apparitions to promote his elevation to emperor. The Virgin's message, probably not coincidentally, was that God had sanctioned Soulouque's coronation as Emperor Faustin I. Soulouque also used the occasion to invoke Mary's name in the inscription and inspiration of his troops to retake the Dominican Republic. Father Adolphe Cabon records the account of one witness to the events surrounding the 1849 Champs-de-Mars apparitions, translated in part as follows:

> Around the beginning of the month of July in 1849...the easily exploited public gullibility was witness to miracu-

lous occurrences in a majestic palm tree. The Holy Virgin with the divine child in her arms made frequent apparitions, but only to the elect. One day it was permitted to everyone to see the Holy Virgin. A dry leaf detached itself from the tree, falling for the unbelievers to see the portrait of the Mother of God. The leaf was taken up most respectfully and brought to the palace. A painter who was called in to trace the contours of the image declared that nothing was distinguishable. A second, a mystifier, who wanted not in the least to get on the president's bad side, followed some water marks and drew on the stains, outlining the general form of the Virgin as drawn by nature, then the coat and finally the crown.... In such a fashion did heaven bequeath a crown to Soulouque.[96]

A few days after the Champs-de-Mars apparitions, the Virgin appeared again, this time in a mapu or palm tree by a waterfalls near the provincial village of Ville-Bonheur, now more commonly referred to as Saut-d'Eau. Judging these events as possessing enormous political potential, Soulouque sent an investigative commission comprised of members of his cabinet to Saut-d'Eau. They returned to the capital and presented a positive report to Soulouque, who proceeded to promulgate a decree that a church be constructed in Saut-d'Eau, consecrated, of course, to the Virgin Mary, in this case, to Our Lady of Mount Carmel, the image in which the Virgin had appeared. This move, as Micial Neréstant insightfully explains:

> appeased the widespread discontent of the peasantry at a time when the society was divided into two factions: the peasantry bore the weight of the elite class and the coercive system installed by the rural code of 1826; the religions, far from being a source of resistance against the dictatorial regime, were an instrument of the established power.[97]

We will return to Saut-d'Eau in greater detail below.

Expectant worshippers continued visiting the Virgin's palm tree at Champs-de-Mars for months following the July apparitions, hoping for the Holy Mother's return. This was not entirely in vain: "On Monday, 23 November 1849, with another rumor circulating that the Holy Virgin had again appeared in the Champs-de-Mars, the emperor's wife went to see the event. Her visit strengthened popular and national belief in the veracity of the apparitions."[98]

Given the mutually stabilizing relationship between the Haitian church and state, as analyzed in chapter two, it was both logical and expected that Soulouque should court ecclesial sanction of the 1849 apparitions. Cabon illustrates, however, that orthodoxy's recognition of the apparitions as authentic was universal neither among the clergy nor among perceptive laypersons. "Abbé Cessens later recounted how Abbé Pisano, the curate of Petion-Ville, declared the apparitions to be authentic; on the contrary, Cessens was very much opposed to this position, thereby gaining as much the esteem of honest citizens as the wrath of the government."[99]

In the case of the 1849 apparitions, Soulouque's manipulation of popular religious sentiment for his political gain employed several diverse elements: the spreading of rumors, the leaf and the painter, the investigative commission, the decree for the Saut-d'Eau church, Abbé Pisano's affirmation, and Madame Soulouque's visit to Mary's palm tree. Unlike Christophe before him, Soulouque in effect succeeded marvelously in using the symbol of the Virgin Mary as a weapon of symbolic violence, thereby buttressing his dictatorial regime with spiritual legitimacy.

In each of these three remarkable chapters in the history of Haitian Marianism we see how Haitian leaders have manipulated and adapted the symbol of the Virgin Mary in the service of their political and/or military interests. Among them, Romaine-la-Prophétesse is unique, for instead of using the Virgin Mary for the support of the status quo and de facto authority, Romaine was a revolutionary who employed the symbol of Mary "in active opposition" to orthodoxy's conception of the Mother of God. Pétion, Christophe, and Soulouque, on the other hand, each employed the symbol of Mary as a weapon of symbolic violence in an effort to legitimize their power, strengthen its foundation, while weakening opposition through religious means—much as would the Cédras junta from 1991 to 1994.

Saut-d'Eau and Marian Pilgrimage

While sometimes not considered a Latin American country, Haitian history shares much of importance with that of Spanish- and Portuguese-speaking countries of the Americas, and thus social scientists and historians should expect parallels between Haiti and other nations of Latin America and the Caribbean. Paul Farmer argues that Haiti, being "in many respects the most representative of the Latin American republics," is "best understood in a general Latin American context."[100] While there should be greater caution used in applying this maxim to religious studies than to other areas of research (since Haiti arguably demonstrates the strongest African religious influences in the Americas), certain key elements of Haitian religious life are typical of most Latin American countries: the popularity of the cult of Mary and pilgrimage are two such elements. Insofar as there is for Haitians a national pilgrimage, for both Catholics and Vodouisants—often one and the same—Haiti participates in a common Latin American religious trend. "Most Latin American countries have their own national and religious shrines, and pilgrimages have special social functions among the peasant population. In these countries every year at certain periods, pilgrims travel to shrines—often far from their homes—to fulfill vows and accomplish their objectives."[101] Indeed, there are examples of this in virtually every country south of the Rio Grande and Florida.

For Haitians, pilgrimage has retained an extraordinary appeal, unlike elsewhere in Latin America, where, as Daniel H. Levine explains, pilgrimage and other long-standing popular forms of Catholic devotion are on an appreciable decline:

> But as a general matter, viewing the saints as lawyers or agents has fallen into disfavor and appears to be of dubious orthodoxy to most [popular church] group members. Excessive attention to saints is also felt to turn one's eyes away from God.... As prevailing views of saints begin to change, traditional practices like pilgrimage or the making of specific promises (to bind the saints to their word) have also lost popularity. Concern for orthodoxy and greater access to regular religious practice at home remove much of the clientele such devotion once enjoyed.

> Why go to a distant shrine, incurring the costs of travel,
> lodging, fighting crowds, and running the notable risks of
> robbery or accident when the same thing is now available
> close at hand?[102]

There is no indication that a similar change is occurring in Haiti, nor can one be expected soon, for the cults of the saints for Haitians, on the contrary, remain as vibrant as ever, and attendance at pilgrimages and feast day Masses is enormous, ranking among the most important forms of devotion in Haitian Catholicism. This is perhaps explicable in terms of Haiti's total lack of progress in the struggle against poverty and illiteracy, which remain the highest in all of Latin America (Levine finds a causal connection between the rise in literacy and the decline of pilgrimage in Latin America). Moreover, as we will demonstrate in detail in chapter six, many poor Haitians deem prayer to the Virgin Mary as more effective than direct petition to Jesus Christ or to God *precisely because of her role as an "attorney."*

For all its importance to Haitian religious life, Saut-d'Eau is only one of many important annual pilgrimages for Haitians both in Haiti and of the Diaspora. Marian feasts also attract throngs of pilgrims to other destinations throughout Haiti, like Fonds-Verettes, Dame Marie, and Bizoton, while a Port-au-Prince travel agency finds it lucrative enough to organize annual bus trips to Higuey in the Dominican Republic for the feast of Our Lady of Altagracia there, and package deals to Caracas for yet another popular Marian pilgrimage. Furthermore, it would be misleading to give the impression that the Virgin Mary is the focus of all Haitian pilgrimages. On the contrary, the attraction of the feast celebrations of other saints at sometimes distant churches that bear their names is very strong for Haitian pilgrims, as with, for example, the feast of St. François in the northwestern town of Bombardopolis and the feast of St. Jacques in La Plaine du Nord.

In the Haitian Diaspora, which consists of approximately a million people concentrated mostly in New York, Miami, Boston, and Montreal, distance from the homeland has not in the least weakened the vibrancy of Marian pilgrimage. "Many Haitians living in New York," notes Hurbon, "try to recreate the fervor of pilgrimage in Haiti by traveling to the great pilgrimage centers of Canada."[103]

Other notable substitutes for Saut-d'Eau and Bel-Air for Diasporan Haitians include the shrine of Our Lady of Czestochowa in Pennsylvania, which attracts bus-loads of Haitian pilgrims from New York, New Jersey, and Boston annually, and a circuit of New York City churches consecrated to Our Lady of Mount Carmel. This circuit includes the Church of Our Lady of Mount Carmel on 115th Street in Harlem, the focus of Robert Anthony Orsi's excellent sociomariological study *The Madonna of 115th Street*. In a later article, Orsi explains that "there is a church dedicated to Our Lady of Mount Carmel in Greenpoint-Williamsburg (founded as an off-shoot of the church on 115th St.) and another in the Belmont section of the North Bronx, and at first Haitian pilgrims traveled around the city visiting each representation of the Madonna of Mount Carmel, who," Orsi mistakenly adds, "is also the Patroness of Haiti."[104] As for the 115th Street feast of Our Lady of Mount Carmel in Harlem, Orsi notes that many Haitians arrive from Brooklyn and Queens in chartered buses.

By Orsi's account, Haitians have come to be an integral part of the landscape of the once exclusively Italian Marian life on 115th St. and are openly accepted by the long-standing Italian community because of the deep devotion they bring to the feasts. "The powerful and evident piety of the Haitian pilgrims, furthermore, which was there for everyone to see in the aisles of the church and in the streets of the neighborhoods, deeply impressed and moved the Italian Americans, who openly expressed respect for Haitian spirituality during the event."[105] Indeed, Haitians have become so essential a part of the 115th St. church that "Haitian altar boys participate in the official ceremonies of the *festa*; the Haitian national anthem is played (along with the Italian and the American) at the start of the processions of the Madonna, and the Haitian flag is carried in the street."[106]

Back in Haiti, meanwhile, each year in mid-July—on the same day of the 115th St. *festa*—thousands of Haitians flock to the village of Saut-d'Eau. The village sits a couple of miles down the mountain from the fabulous waterfalls whose mystical powers had already been attracting Vodouisants prior to the mid-eighteenth-century Marian apparitions that turned it into a national shrine. During the twenty-year period when the entire island was under Haitian rule, Haitian faithful developed the tradition of making an annual pilgrimage to the Dominican village of Higuey, site of a shrine *to Nuestra Señora de Altagracia*, patron saint of the Dominican Republic. Cabon informs us that "the Saut-d'Eau, or Ville-Bonheur, pilgrimage was instituted from the time of the separation of the Eastern Part in 1844, as a replacement for the pilgrimage to Higuey, to which Haitians could no longer go."[107] It is, thus, likely that Marian apparitions occurred near Ville-Bonheur prior to the celebrated 1849 apparitions, hence making Saut-d'Eau a pilgrimage site for devotees of Mary as well as the *lwas*, often one and the same.

Between 1844 and 1849, however, pilgrimage to Saut-d'Eau was of a limited scale compared to what it would become and remains. It would take the remarkable events surrounding the July 1849 apparitions there and at Champs-de-Mars to turn Saut-d'Eau into a national pilgrimage center attracting thousands of Haitians and some foreigners annually, most of them seeking healing and/or purification. As already mentioned, the Saut-d'Eau apparitions occurred just days after the first apparitions at Champs-de-Mars. The date was July 16. Laguerre has translated the following narrative recounted to him by an old Saut-d'Eau villager explaining the event:

> During the regime of Faustin Soulouque, in 1849, a young man, Fortune Morose, looked one morning for his horse which he had left in his garden the night before. In search of this animal, he penetrated a bush area not too far from the place where the village of Saut-d'Eau is now located. Once he pushed his way in, a strange noise made by the rubbing of leaves attracted his attention. Great was his surprise to see a young lady inviting him to look at her. Despite the solicitations of this beautiful young lady, Morose was taken by fear and went to report the event to the nearest police station. A policeman was delegated to accompany Morose to be a witness to the event. Unhappily, the unknown lady did not show up when they arrived or they did not see her. A little bit later, they were still looking for her everywhere when the policeman turned his look toward the palm tree. Surprise. He saw a great and beautiful animated picture on a palm leaf. He invited Morose to take a look at the picture. Morose identified it as the picture of the lady that he had seen previously. Immediately they went and announced the news to anyone

they could meet in the region. From this time on, the people of the surrounding area came from time to time to see if the picture was still there and waited patiently until the leaf fell to observe it more closely. After about a month, the leaf fell and the picture was not on it. But the same picture was reproduced on another leaf. The news of the apparitions of the Holy Virgin raced throughout the country. The place where the palm trees on which the Holy Virgin appeared is known as Nan Palm. It has become since then a holy place, and every 16 July, pilgrims make a trip to Saut-d'Eau.[108]

The apparition of Mary at a Vodou pilgrimage site was, not surprisingly, interpreted in a variety of ways by different groups. Given Vodou's syncretic nature and its "seizure" of Catholic symbols, it would be expected that among Vodouisants an oral tradition should develop "that Ezili appeared to a crowd as the Blessed Virgin Mary, in the branches of a palm tree near the waterfalls."[109] Some scholars assert that "[f]or the peasants, the apparition of the Virgin Mary was none other than Erzulie Freda, the goddess of love, and her presence was less a miracle than an expected blessing that only added to the reputation of the sacred waterfall."[110]

Accounts regarding the Catholic clergy's reaction to the apparition vary considerably. According to Desmangles, immediately following the apparitions the people "summoned the white Catholic vicar of the nearby Ville-Bonheur parish to come and witness the apparition and to pray with them, but when he arrived he could not see the Virgin, although everyone else could. He then accused the people of blasphemy and ordered the area closed."[111] Convinced that the affair was some superstitious hallucination, the vicar directed the police to shoot into the trees at the apparition, which, to the eyes of the believers, darted from branch to branch in deft avoidance of the bullets. Undeterred, the priest ordered the tree cut down. This was a bad mistake, for "as the Catholic priest returned home, word came that the presbytery had burned down and nothing had been saved. He is reported to have died soon after from a sudden paralytic stroke."[112]

Following Desmangles' account further, the police captain, who had collaborated with the parish vicar, also suffered divine retribution for having, among other things, lined the area with guards to prohibit the pilgrims' progress:

> The captain's fate was not as disastrous as that of the priest, for he was merely afflicted with a temporary madness that caused him to wander aimlessly throughout Ville-Bonheur and its surrounding area. He was healed soon after the incident, and returned to the place of the apparition to ask the Virgin's pardon. Fire subsequently burned the Ville-Bonheur church, a fire said to have been caused by the powerful anger of Ezili Danto. The area of the apparition remained closed for a while, but when the nation's police chief in Port-au-Prince heard of the Virgin's anger and the fates of both the vicar and the captain, he ordered the area to be reopened.[113]

Word of these events, however tinged with legend and hyperbole, spread and further enhanced popular belief in both the apparitions and the holy waters of Saut-d'Eau.

The priest and the captain were not the only detractors to suffer divine retribution for their efforts to impede the intercourse between the spirits, the Virgin, and the pilgrims. Reminiscent of the spiritually charged courage of the under-armed Haitian freedom fighters in the Revolution, "during the occupation of Haiti by U.S. marines (1915-1934), Haitian guerrillas used the name of the Holy Virgin of Saut-d'Eau to incite peasant struggle against them.... Despite their lack of weapons—trusting only the scapulars they wore,"[114] they mounted some formidable resistance against the foreign occupying force. "The U.S. was aware of the political use made of the apparitions by the guerrillas—this was one of the reasons why a marine posted in Mirebalais ordered one of the palm trees of Saut-d'Eau cut down, for this palm tree was an object of veneration to the peasants. A few days later, the marine became sick and was sent back to the US...."[115] That the marine fell sick only added to Saut-d'Eau lore and deepened belief in the mystical power of the place. This story is also significant since it represents yet another in a series of examples of Marian apparitions used as an inspirational source for battle, both against foreign and internal enemies. In addition to the example of Romaine-la-Prophétesse, Soulouque had exploited belief in the Saut-d'Eau apparitions to recruit and inspire troops for a series of failed attempt to reconquer the Spanish half of the island. And, much later, in 1994, as *putchist* general Raoul Cédras finally realized that a U.S. invasion of Haiti was inevitable, he could be seen saluting his troops from the balcony of military headquarters above a large icon of *Notre Dame du Perpétuel Secours*.

Today Saut-d'Eau attracts more visitors than ever, though my impression is that a considerable percentage of the thousands who descend on the provincial village in mid-July are hardly sincere pilgrims. Gamblers, hustlers, hookers, beggars, merchants, chauffeurs, partyers, thieves, guides, journalists, anthropologists, curious expatriates, and adventure seekers of all sorts are quite numerous among the pilgrims. Some enterprising Haitian has built a night club near the entrance to the village and reportedly makes a fortune during pilgrimage season. It is a maddening spectacle—Saut-d'Eau during what the villagers refer to as "Holy Week." Cots line the walkway leading up to the church. Some of them are for rent, others serve as the temporary homes for a few of the multitude of beggars who wait around the church for charity. Just beyond the church gate are the gambling tables, spread amid the peddlers of religious trinkets. One may purchase lithographs depicting every Catholic saint commonly known in Haiti (I collected eight different Marian images in a single sweep).

The Church of Our Lady of Mount Carmel provides something of a refuge from the bustle of the dirty village streets. There is only problem: It is often impossible to find a way in, especially during Mass. The style of Mass is not considerably different from that of Marian feast days elsewhere in Haiti: There are the standard Marian hymns that the whole nation has memorized; a sermon celebrating the Virgin's miraculous concern for Haiti; and an attentive, packed congregation of mostly poor women, arms outstretched, hands grasping beads, candles, icons, or photographs. Their demeanor appears to be one of sincere supplication. Between Masses, the style of worship becomes less formal, almost familial. I have been deeply touched by the personal, sisterly fashion in which under-class Haitian women address Mary, especially when unencumbered by liturgical obligations. This point is further discussed in chapter six.

One especially interesting element of devotion at Saut-d'Eau are the colorful ropes pilgrims' wear around the waist or head while entering the church. These are everywhere for sale in the village. Several of my informants simply explained that they wear them "in order to look beautiful for the Virgin." Yet there is much more to it than this. When the pilgrims leave the church and make the tiresome trek to the mystical waterfalls, they bring the ropes along and tie them around trees at the base of the falls. The ropes are the mark of the pilgrim in Haiti, worn not just at Saut-d'Eau but everywhere that pilgrims venture (though most popularly, it seems, on Mount Carmel's feast day). They are left behind at the falls as a mark of having been there, shed as a symbol of having been purified or of having reestablished harmony with the spirits. An intriguing question (one to which I have found no satisfactory answer) is: Why are the ropes left on trees by the falls rather than on pews in the Ville-de-Bonheur church? I suspect that underlying this choice is some arcane reason rooted in Vodouisant belief and ritual.

The Saut-d'Eau pilgrimage is unparalleled in the Haitian religious field. From my discussions with dozens of pilgrims, it is apparently a time of purification and an occasion to summons the aid of the spirits in what is for most Haitians a very difficult life. Thus, "[t]he Vodou ceremonies at the falls and near the palm trees, as well as the Catholic masses in honor of the Virgin at the Ville-Bonheur parish, occupy an important place in the complex rites and liturgical calendars of the Haitian church and off Vodou."[116] As such, the Saut-d'Eau pilgrimage is one of the most striking expressions of Marian piety in Haitian religion; for many pilgrims it is the most opportune time and place to have one's prayers heard and answered by the Mother of God.

Among scholarly analyses of pilgrimage, many provocative theories are indebted to Mircea Eliade's discourse on space in his classic *The Sacred and the Profane*, which conceives of the pilgrim as one who ventures toward the center of his/her religious world, or *axis mundi*. Differentiating the tourist or adventurer from the pilgrim illustrates this point well:

> A tourist moves from the center of his existence, his home, to the periphery, in order to vacation. A pilgrim, however, moves from the periphery to the center of his world. Perhaps the best definition of center was given by religious historian Mircea Eliade, who wrote that the center

is where the "axis mundi" (the center axis of meaning) penetrates the earthly sphere.[117]

For many Haitian Catholics and Vodouisants, Saut-d'Eau represents something of an *axis mundi*. Explaining the Saut-d'Eau pilgrimage in precisely these terms, Laguerre elaborates that "because they live in a peripheral situation (not necessarily a geographical, but a spiritual periphery), pilgrims initiate their journeys to shrines to be part of a spiritual center. This might be done as a rite of reaffirmation of their faith and purification."[118] From my discussions with several dozen pilgrims at Saut-d'Eau, I would agree that this explanation accurately reflects the nature of pilgrimage in Haiti, only adding that many Haitians understand this reaffirmation of faith as a reharmonizing of their relationship with the spirits. When this is in balance, good things happen; when it is not, one can expect calamity. As one woman who traveled from Cap-Haïtien to Saut-d'Eau told me, "I could pray to the Virgin anywhere, but it is here and now that she is most open to me." When I asked her about the *lwas*, she replied, "Yes, them too; I am here to settle my account with them" ("*Mwen la pou regle zafe'm ak yo*").

**Miracles, Monsignors, Presidents,
and *Notre Dame du Perpétuel Secours***

One of the most pervasive religious symbols in Haiti, where religious symbols are more visible than in most other countries, the Marian icon of *Notre Dame du Perpétuel Secours* was unknown to Haitians until late in the nineteenth century. Today *Perpétuel Secours* is Haiti's patron saint, as she has formally been since 1942, though on a popular level her supersession of *Notre Dame de l'Assomption* was complete long before. As with Guadeloupe for Mexicans, *Notre Dame du Perpétuel Secours* eclipses God, the Holy Spirit, Jesus Christ, and the community of saints in popular Haitian Catholic consciousness, is considered accessible for miraculous intervention in the people's daily lives, and plays a leading role in the guardianship of the nation. As such, *Notre Dame du Perpétuel Secours* is the most often addressed spiritual being in the Catholic pantheon in Haitian religion, both popular and intellectual, petitioned constantly and widely in the supplicative prayers of Haitians of all social strata.

A detailed summary of the illustrious history of this Byzantine-style icon need not distract us here—a few words will instead suffice. The artwork inspiring the cult of *Perpétuel Secours* appears to date from very early in Marian history, becoming the center of an important cult in Crete. Popular legend attributes the painting to the mythic figure of St. Luke. Centuries later, the fifteenth-century Turk invasion of Crete drove many of the islanders to mainland exile. "One of them," according to a French Canadian novena manual widely circulated in Haiti, "took the holy image and embarked with the treasure for Italy, settling finally in Rome."[119] Another version notes that the image was stolen, not taken, and that the thief paid for his crime with his life, victim of some sort of divine justice. In any event, once in Rome, *Perpétuel Secours* was recognized in numerous apparitions, during which "the Holy Virgin made it known that she wished to be honored in the city under the title of *Notre Dame du Perpétuel Secours* and that the center of her cult should be the Church of San Matteo."[120] When, on June 3, 1798, this church was destroyed, one of thirty Roman churches crushed by Napoleon's forces, the icon disappeared, only to be rediscovered in 1863 "under manifestly providential circumstances."[121] Thereafter, in December 1865, "the Sovereign Pope Pius IX thus wished that the Holy Virgin, under this beautiful name, be honored in the church of the Redemptorist Fathers, located in the precise location of the church of San Matteo." This is the Roman Church of San Alfonso.

The following year, the first recorded of the many miraculous cures attributed to *Perpétuel Secours* occurred. On January 19, 1866, "[a]s Father Michel Marchi was carrying the image during a procession to the Church of San Alfonso, two women appeared before the image with their families in search of healing.... Their children were thus healed."[122] Two months later, the pope exhorted the Redemptorist Fathers to propagate the cult of *Perpétuel Secours* around the globe.

Against a golden background that typifies Byzantine icons, and flanked by the archangels Gabriel and Michael, the serene, yet subtly stern-faced Virgin, crowned and draped in a dark blue cloak, holds the child Jesus, also crowned, in a delicate caress.[123] Jesus, appearing at least several years old, clasps both his hands around his mother's right thumb. Five groups of Greek letters surround the icon's four figures. As Beauvoir-Dominique points out, to most

Haitians— long accustomed to *veves* (symbols of Vodou spirits) and masonic symbolism— these letters appear as "cabalistic signs."[124] In reality, they merely spell out the names of the four figures: Mother of God, Jesus Christ, Archangel Gabriel, and Archangel Michael.

One intriguing aspect of the icon is Jesus' right sandal, which dangles by a single strand. The Canadian novena manual explains that Jesus, "his head turned toward some object which has put the look of fear on his sweet face...throws himself so quickly toward her that the little sandal falls off his right foot, held suspended only by one strap."[125] Underlying this explanation is the notion that Marian devotees may, in times of fear and tribulation, throw themselves into the comforting arms of the *Notre Dame du Perpétuel Secours.*

A second supersedure of the Haitian religious field's dominant Marian image took place following the miraculous events in Port-au-Prince early in 1882. Just as *Notre Dame de l'Assomption*, on the coattails of the emergence of French over Spanish political and, more gradually, religious power late in the seventeenth century would replace *Nuestras Señoras de Guadeloupe* and *la Concepción, Notre Dame du Perpétuel Secours* would usurp the French-introduced *Notre Dame de l'Assomption* as patroness of Haiti roughly two centuries later. The cause of this second eclipse of one Marian icon over another was ostensibly of a much more spiritual nature than that of the first; i.e., the purging of Port-au-Prince from the small pox epidemic of 1882.

A small pox plague ravaged Haiti's urban centers were from December 1881 to March 1882. At its zenith "the scourge" was claiming more than sixty victims daily in Port-au-Prince and a dozen or so more in Gonaïve. These were just the reported deaths; the actual daily toll was probably much higher. Special hospices and graveyards were created in haste by religious orders to deal with the crisis, though the scale of the epidemic was so overwhelming that most simply died and were buried at home. By March 1882, when the pandemic spread was halted by what many Haitians would attribute to *Perpétuel Secours'* miraculous intervention, more than 100,000 people, by one estimation, had died.

Many believed the epidemic to be divine punishment for Haiti's sins. Early in 1882, Monsignor Belouino exploited such popular belief to attack the heresiarch, preaching, "Let us hate the sin that has engendered this.... No more shameful superstition."[126] Belouino thus seized the occasion to blame Vodou for the epidemic and thereby gain advantage for orthodoxy in the struggle for monopoly in the religious field. The monsignor's logic is telling: Eliminate Vodou and the plague shall cease. While others would perceive the epidemic in religiously far more tolerant terms, penitence and prayer were widely believed to be the key to eradicating the scourge. "The pious faith constantly demanded new public prayers to end the epidemic."[127] On January 16, there was "a procession of penitence from the Cathedral to St. Joseph and St. Anne."[128] Still the epidemic raged on unabated.

"Around this time a pious lady arrived, bringing with her from Paris, where she'd fortuitously found it, a painting of the Holy Virgin under the name of *Perpétuel Secours*. This devotion had been [theretofore] entirely unknown in Port-au-Prince."[129] She offered the painting to the cathedral's curate, Monsignor Kersuzan, who placed it in a corner of his room. Suddenly it occurred to the curate that there would be nothing to lose by testing the new icon's miraculous powers against he surging epidemic. Having shared the notion with Monsignor Guilloux, archbishop of Port-au-Prince and one of the dominant figures in Haitian Church history, who "favorably welcomed" the idea, Kersuzan scheduled a Mass for *Perpétuel Secours*'s "introduction to the faithful and her formal invocation to end the plague."[130]

On Saturday, February 5, 1882, the faithful were summoned to the church of St. François in Bel-Air. "All Port-au-Prince still healthy transported itself in groups and in prayers to the hill." They came "like the archbishop...reciting the rosary,"[131] many accompanying a large group of religious in a penitential procession from the cathedral, to take part in the elaborate ceremonies:

> The archbishop, before the united faithful, spoke of the necessity of resorting to God in times of public calamity, recounted the history of the miraculous image of *Perpétuel Secours*, and blessed the painting, which was paraded around the church inside and out before being placed on its designated altar. At the curate's request, the prelate exited with the holy image just outside the door, and from the top of the hill traced with it the sign of the cross over

the capital. The participants carried the conviction that their prayers for the city's health were answered; they continued them for the following eight days....[132]

Halfway through this collective novena to *Notre Dame du Perpétuel Secours*, the skies opened and heavy rains brought an end to an unusually long drought, which had exacerbated the epidemic. The two-day downpour, which "came to wash and purify Port-au-Prince, was judged an indispensable condition for the disappearance of the scourge. From that moment on, there was not a single new case of small pox."[133] Indeed, the death-by-small pox rate in Port-au-Prince tapered off dramatically in the ensuing weeks: From 243 to 200, then to 168 and 83, and finally to 47.[134]

In October of the same year, Monsignor Guilloux, accordingly, would consecrate the Church of St. François Xavier in Bel-Air to *Notre Dame du Perpétuel Secours*, invoking "all the blessed of the sanctifying Holy Spirit, purifying the altar, the walls, and the floor of the temple,"[135] with a great display of Catholic religious pomp. "In sum, it was with a thousand such mysterious elaborations apt to make a strong impression that Msg. Guilloux consecrated the chapel at Bel-Air."[136] Evidently Guilloux and his eventual successor Kersuzan would go to considerable lengths to promote the cult of *Notre Dame du Perpétuel Secours*, in part, no doubt, to revitalize the struggling postconcordial church and further orthodoxy's quest for dominance in the Haitian religious field.

Two questions arise regarding the monsignors' agenda: (1) Were their efforts in themselves essential to the cult's development, or would popular belief in the miracles attributed to *Perpétuel Secours* have sufficed alone to elevate the icon to a preeminent place in Haitian Marianism? (2) Could the introduction of a new Catholic religious symbol be at all instrumental in orthodoxy's struggle against the heresiarch, or did it ultimately represent yet another opportunity for Vodouisants to adapt and syncretize the Virgin with some manifestation of Ezili? As for the first question, this much at least is certain: had Guilloux and Kersuzan never organized the February 5, 1882 Mass, the rains that fell five days later would not have been attributed to the miraculous intervention of *Notre Dame du Perpétuel Secours*, most likely leaving her a minor figure in Haitian Marianism. Yet, once belief spread that the miracles were the work of *Notre*

Dame du Perpétuel Secours, orthodox sacerdotal influence on the cult's development became tangential. The Haitian people had been fervently praying and hoping for a miracle to deliver them from desperate circumstances. Moreover, as Beauvoir-Dominique correctly points out, the material conditions in which the cult took root, such as "the beginning of the widespread migrations, the development of squalid urban slums, the formation of an increasingly threatened proletariat and sub-proletariat" were also instrumental to the development in Haiti of the "cult of this mediatrix, comforter of the afflicted...."[137]

In response to the second question, it is possible that since Kersuzan was distressed by forms of syncretism and other Vodouisant adaptations of the known Marian images in Haiti, mainly Assumption, Immaculate Conception, and Mount Carmel, he thus devised the promulgation of a new Marian cult to counter such deviation. In other words, the introduction and proliferation of a theretofore unknown image of the Virgin, one free of course of any trace of *le mélange*, might have occurred to Kersuzan as a means to recuperating a wayward laity and gathering them in the orthodox fold. Pedro A. Ribiero de Oliveira, writing about the struggle between orthodox and popular Catholicism in Brazilian history, provides a good example of just such underlying motives to the introduction of *Notre Dame du Perpétuel Secours* in Brazil:

> Let's take for example the devotion to Notre-Dame-du-Rosaire, which was quite widespread. Its devotees formed a confraternity for the maintenance of the cult, the promotion of its feast, the guidance of the recitation of the rosary, etc. This confraternity was controlled by the laity.... When a "Romanized" (*romanisé*) priest, a German Redemptorist, for example, took charge of the parish, he immediately pitted himself against the confraternity, itself zealous in devotion to Notre-Dame, but lax in regards to the sacraments and Mass attendance. To thwart the confraternity, the Redemptorist encouraged devotion to Notre-Dame-du-Perpetuel-Secours, whom he presented as a miraculous saint. As he managed to have the new devotion take hold, he endeavored to solemnly introduce its image in the church, to celebrate its feasts, and to form a new confraternity of devotees of Notre-Dame-du-Perpétuel-

Secours, whereas Notre-Dame-du-Rosaire was little by little relegated to the sacristy and oblivion. At the same time, the Redemptorist proceeds to preach that the sacraments are the best means for obtaining the favors of Notre-Dame-du-Perpetuel-Secours and of the saints in general. Thus did he manage to regather the faithful into the parochial fold.[138]

In Haiti, the combination of the increasingly difficult social conditions, the epidemic, and the widespread yearning for miraculous intervention to end "the scourge" were the central underlying causes of the *Perpétuel Secours'* initial propagation. The cult's flourishing was also in part due to Kersuzan's campaign to promote it nationwide, a campaign that doubtless had designs similar to those of the German Redemptorist in the above example from Brazil.

The cynosure of the cult of *Notre Dame du Perpétuel Secours*, both on the popular level and in Guilloux and Kersuzan's systematic promotion of the cult, was the symbol's miraculous healing power. Over the course of several decades following the small pox epidemic, there were reports of a series of miracles attributed to *Perpétuel Secours* involving Guilloux and Kersuzan, which Kersuzan, in particular, went to great lengths to publicize. The first of these transpired shortly after the cessation of the 1881-82 epidemic. A yellow fever epidemic erupted, affecting primarily foreigners, particularly religious:

> Father Taragnat, superior of the Petit Séminaire Collège, was stricken and abandoned his doctors, who had exhausted their science. The patient was conferred to *Notre Dame du Perpétuel Secours* by Monsignor Kersuzan, Monsignor Ribault.... The next day, 30 September, all danger had disappeared and the Father was convalescent and very rapidly regained his force.[139]

The following year "a terrible fire" broke out in downtown Port-au-Prince. A strong west wind thrust the blaze toward the cathedral, which, along with the archbishopric, the presbytery, and the school "seemed irredeemably condemned. Suddenly the wind direction changed to south-east, toward the already charred quarters."[140] The winds were believed to have heeded the divine command of *Notre*

Dame du Perpétuel Secours, whom Monsignor Guilloux had just implored for the cathedral's deliverance.

Notre Dame du Perpétuel Secours, some years later, would intervene once again to spare church property from a raging blaze, this time at the request of Guilloux's protégé Monsignor Kersuzan, to whom *Perpétuel Secours*'s torch was relayed. While on sabbatical at Mont-des-Oiseaux in 1912, "Kersuzan placed his residence under the protection of Notre Dame, seeing to the publication of this deed in *The Holy Family*." The woods surrounding the home caught fire, which violently raged toward the monsignor's quarters; "the flames pushed on by the mistral, already licking the edges of the edifice, before stopping as if obedient to some superior command."[141]

Kersuzan's Marian devotion was as profound as his infamous disdain for Vodou; he was, after all, the leader of the second antisuperstitious campaign in 1896.[142] For Kersuzan, like his colleague Monsignor Hillion, writing in 1894, in all these miraculous happenings, the Virgin Mary "has shown herself to be an empowered weapon in the battle that has shattered heresy and the enemies of God."[143] The monsignor was equally energetic in his promotion of the cult of Mary, which, undoubtedly, he saw as a means to combat the heresiarch. "At the cathedral of Port-au-Prince Monsignor Kersuzan was the promoter of devotion to *Notre Dame du Perpétuel Secours*, to whom he had dedicated an altar in the St. François chapel at Bel-Air, and whose image he had placed in his coat of arms when he was named bishop, along with the motto of his faith: *Spes Nostra*."[144]

Increasingly satisfied with the cult's impressive development in Port-au-Prince, Kersuzan took it upon himself to propagate this new form of Marian devotion in Cap-Haïtien, long a stronghold of *Notre Dame de l'Assomption*, Cap's patroness. To orthodoxy's religious specialist, it seemed that "devotion toward the Most Holy Virgin was the most sincere expression of love among the Cap faithful,"[145] who "loved to celebrate Mary's feast days and month...their preferred prayer was the rosary, and at every meeting her name was invoked and everyone called tenderly upon his mother."[146] The longstanding tradition of Marian piety in Cap-Haïtien is noteworthy: Cap-Haïtien was the epicenter of the missions of the Jesuits and the Daughters of Notre Dame, who played a fundamental role in the cult's development throughout the colony, especially in the north around Cap-Haïtien. Further evidence of the cult's strength is that two Marian associations had been established in the Cap parish years prior to Kersuzan's arrival. *La Confrérie du Saint Rosaire* counted around 400 members, who, according to Monsignor Hillion, all "gathered the first Sunday of each month to recite the rosary."[147] Members of *La Congregation des Enfants de Marie* distinguished themselves by wearing "a special costume at processions and, at all of their meetings, a medal hung around the neck by a blue ribbon. This pious association certainly forewarned a good number of young people against the dangers of the world."[148]

Clearly, Marian devotion was the most popular form of Catholic piety in Cap-Haïtien when Monsignor Kersuzan arrived in April 1883 "to propagate a devotion that was most dear to him." Toward this end, "he decided to offer to the public cult, in the cathedral, a painting of *Notre Dame du Perpétuel Secours*."[149] In a moving sermon, the monsignor exhorted the Cap faithful to adopt *Notre Dame du Perpétuel Secours* and make a special place for her in their devotions:

> We want that *Notre Dame du Perpétuel Secours* be received and reign in the city of Cap-Haïtien and that her entry amid you be an explosive triumph. This is why we are inviting you, in the most solemn way, to the great feast we shall initiate in her honor on April 30, to be continued through the entire month of May.[150]

The April 30 mass—with its elaborate processions, enormous crowd, and Kersuzan's mystical gestures, Latin utterances, and emotional sermon—must certainly have made an indelible impression. Jan's description is worth including here:

> Benediction of the painting at 4:00, followed by a procession to the chapel of St. Joseph and back to the cathedral. All the fraternities were aligned around their banners, with *Les Enfants de Marie*, dressed in white, carrying the precious painting. On the church steps the painting stopped, with Monsignor positioning himself adjacent to it, facing the people amassed on the square, while the cathedral curate asks blessings for himself, for his people and for the

country, with the phrase *Iube, Domine, benedicere*. The
bishop responded: *Nos cum prole pia benedicat Virgo
Maria*. In church Monsignor lets his heart speak in a touching allocution, falling to his knees before the image of
Perpétuel Secours and repeating the prayer that ended his
pastoral instruction and consecrated his person and diocese to *Notre Dame du Perpétuel Secours*.[151]

Kersuzan would devote a great part of his clerical career to two
different, but not unrelated, goals: the development of the cult of
Notre Dame du Perpétuel Secours, and the eradication of Vodou
from Haitian society. That he considered the former instrumental in
the accomplishment of the latter is evident, though he was greatly
mistaken. For Haitians, Mary had already long been identified with
Ezili, the Vodou spirit of love, and the introduction of another Marian
icon only provided new avenues for Marian syncretism with Ezili.
Perhaps aware of the supernatural importance that Vodouisants at-
tach to their dreams and hoping to strike a chord in their religious
habitus, Kersuzan shared his own dream with his parishioners in an
eloquent discourse in 1915:

> Do you know of what I have dreamt? Of an image of *Notre
> Dame du Perpétuel Secours* upon one of the heights loom-
> ing over our city; we have no *tuf* (volcanic hill), but we
> have no shortage of mountain heights. I would want a
> basilica there to house the holy icon, but would be content
> with a chapel, provided it were beautiful. Next to it I would
> place a bell, a beautiful and valiant bell whose bronze voice
> would be heard afar: that would be the voice of Notre Dame,
> of Our Mother calling her children to prayer. I tell you,
> there would not be a single unbeliever disobeying that
> voice.[152]

Reflective of his dream, Kersuzan made a vow that same year: "to
erect a church, as far as I am able, at the foot of the mountain upon
which shall be erected my little hermitage, which I shall call
Kermaria, resting place of Mary."[153] While Kersuzan succeeded in
introducing the image of *Perpétuel Secours* to many, his dream of a
basilica and hermitage devoted to Mary, like his desire to see *Notre
Dame* defeat Vodou, would never be realized.

While numerous other icons would remain or become the objects of Marian cults in Haiti (Assumption, Altagracia, Immaculate Conception, Fatima, Lourdes, Mount Carmel, Monte Calvaro, Czestochowa, Caridad, Nativity, Wisdom, Rosary, Victories), by the late-nineteenth century *Notre Dame du Perpétuel Secours* would attain a place of unparalleled prominence in Haitian Marianism, culminating with her official promotion to patron saint of Haiti in 1942. The privileged place of *Perpétuel Secours* in Haitian religious life, as well as the almost universal belief among Haitian Catholics of her particular concern for the nation, was galvanized in significant fashion both in 1932 and 1942, when Church and state sanction were united in the cult's promotion. A brief summary of these spectacular events is in order.

Monsignor Joseph Legouaze, then Archbishop of Port-au-Prince, declared three days of national prayer for December 15, 16, and 17, 1932 to mark the fiftieth anniversary of the 1882 miracle attributed to Notre Dame du *Perpétuel Secours*. The three days of prayer, which were precipitated by a national novena, were inaugurated by Father Manise of the Redemptorist order—the order that, as noted above, Pope Pius IX in 1864 had charged with the propagation of the cult of *Perpétuel Secours*.

The 1882 miracle's silver anniversary culminated with a remarkable procession and solemn High Mass on December 18, 1932, with President Estenio Vincent in attendance. The president "wanted to enhance with his presence both the splendor of the ceremony and (to legitimize) the members of his own government."[154] Haitian journalist and Church historian Gerard Maisonneuve describes the procession that brought the painting of *Perpétuel Secours* from its home in the church at Bel-Air to the Cathedral for the December 18 Mass:

> The palace musicians played rich selections of religious music from its repertoire: *Ste. Cecile, La Fete Dieu, Ste. Anne, Notre Dame du Perpétuel Secours Sauvez Haïti, etc....* Cadets from the military academy were posted to civilly keep perfect order. Fathers Bettenberg and Nio filled their roles as masters of ceremonies. In front of the cathedral, on the steps above the courtyard, the Archbishop of Port-au-Prince speaks before a crowd estimated at 40,000—a powerful voice, to which the crowd listens with

a pious attention that would touch the spirit of all faithful.
To close the beautiful ceremony, the consecration of the
sacrament is performed by Monsignor Julien Conan,
former Archbishop of Port-au-Prince, above the
esplanade...after which all the bishops gather to give their
collective blessings and ask that divine graces descend upon
the nation.[155]

While the fiftieth, rather than the sixtieth, anniversary of the 1882
miracle might seem a most appropriate occasion for the elevation of
Notre Dame du Perpétuel Secours to national patroness status, for
whatever reason, such a notion was never acted upon in 1932, if
indeed it was ever advanced. Ten years later it would be, by
Redemptorist Father Paul de Landheer. Given his function as confessor to President Elie Lescot, de Landheer was ideally positioned
to solicit of the president "'a vow' to take measures to consecrate
the beautiful country of Haiti *to Notre Dame du Perpétuel
Secours.*"[156] In turn, Lescot charged the archbishopric with the responsibility of carrying out the initiative. For his part, Lescot drafted
a letter calling for national support of the project, which was signed
by the nation's bishops and "read in every church and chapel in the
country,"[157] inviting all Haitians to share in the December 8 Mass
to celebrate the inauguration of *Perpétuel Secours*' national patronage.

Like the 1932 celebration, there was a declaration of three days
of preparatory national prayer, although it is unclear whether there
was also a nation-wide novena prayed leading up to December 8.
The most significant difference between the 1932 and 1942 celebrations, besides, of course, the issue of consecrating the nation to the
Perpétuel Secours, was the location, as well as the date. As if to
emphasize the state's sanction of the event, the December 8, 1942
Mass took place outdoors at the national palace. The choice of
December 8, the feast day of Our Lady of the Immaculate Conception, was perhaps made to drive home the point that *Perpétuel
Secours* had eclipsed other Marian icons in importance. The palace
was adorned with an immense icon of *Perpétuel Secours*, some seven
meters in height, hung directly above the stairs, from upon which
the archbishop said Mass before an enormous crowd. "Monsignor
Legouaze's sermon proclaimed the act of consecration of *Notre Dame*

du Perpétuel Secours before all the Haitian bishops, President Lescot, members of his government, and a crowd estimated at 60,000—all to the sounds of bells and canons."[158]

What were the underlying motives of Lescot in staging such a spectacle and consecrating the nation to *Notre Dame du Perpétuel Secours*? Beauvoir-Dominique suggests that, for one:

> the idea was to abolish once and for all the absolute [and long-standing] power of the clergy from Brittany, taking advantage of circumstances favorable to such a venture that were brought on by World War II, with Haiti now leaning firmly on its powerful allies, especially the United States. Thus with the consecration of Haiti came the Oblates Order of Immaculate Mary, a [largely] American Catholic rite, along with other religious orders that would supplant the long standing monopoly of a European clergy.[159]

Lescot's intention to weaken the influence of the European clergy was motivated by his conviction that they were inspiring subversive sentiment against his regime among the popular masses.

Of even greater influence over both Lescot and the Church in the elevation of *Perpétuel Secours* to national patroness, moreover was orthodoxy's quest to suppress Vodou. 1942, as noted in chapter two, marked the height of the last antisuperstition campaign, in the service of which "Lescot ordered the army to cooperate with the cures in their hunting-down of all objects having to do with the Voodoo cult."[160] Monsignor Legouaze, for his part, was one of the principal authors of *l'Apostolat de 80 Ans*, in which it is declared that the Church must "establish an effective barrage against the intrusion of paganism into Catholic religious practice."[161] Lescot, who claims to have taken the initiative for Haiti's consecration to *Perpétuel Secours*—seemingly forgetful of his confessor's instigation—was unambiguous that the event was designed to represent a major blow against Vodou:

> On this occasion occurred the most imposing spectacle in our religious annals, along with the ceremonies that remain vivid in the memory of all who served as the most vivid retort to all the nation's detractors known and un-

known, to those who would have our country appear a
community weaned upon the most base superstitions. Such
a manifestation of Catholic faith is re-comforting and is a
good sign for the future of our country. [162]

Lescot was even more direct in his letter soliciting support for "his"
initiative, where he explained that his chief reason for placing Haiti
under the patronage of *Perpétuel Secours* was to combat Haiti's
image abroad as "the land of predilection...for the most repugnant
paganism."[163] Thus Lescot, like Kersuzan and Guilloux half a century before him, promoted the cult of *Notre Dame du Perpétuel
Secours* toward the triumph of orthodox Catholicism over Vodou.
Hence, it is evident how the Haitian Church-state alliance was re-
vived in the promotion of the cult of *Perpétuel Secours* with the aim
of bolstering their domination over both the political and religious
fields. The symbol of the Virgin, now in the new (to Haitians) form
of *Perpétuel Secours*, was thus once again transformed into a weapon
of symbolic violence and employed on a grand scale in the acculturation of the people to domination. Given repeated instances in
the religious history of the "New World" of this very phenomenon,
it would be no exaggeration to call this one of the principal themes
in the history of Marianism in the Americas.

While to some degree such moves by orthodoxy as the consecration of the Haitian nation to *Notre Dame du Perpétuel Secours* did
serve to concretize Haitians' devotion to this particular Marian image, on another level, the cult's development has depended mainly
upon popular belief in her miraculous powers and her particular
concern for the Haitian people, on whose behalf she may intervene.
Popular piety, along with some degree of Marian syncretism with
Ezili, has fueled the cult of *Perpétuel Secours* far more than any
dogmatic ecclesial proclamations or gestures.

The Feast of *Notre Dame du Perpétuel Secours*: June 27

June 27 is the feast day of *Notre Dame du Perpétuel Secours*. Each
year on this day, the church at Bel-Air attracts thousands of worshippers. By 5:00 a.m., one can no longer find a seat. By 6:00, the
aisles and doorways are so packed with bodies that entrance into
the church demands a great deal of physical persistence and, for

some, downright rudeness. Scores of beggars line the sidewalks around the church, while a few wealthy Haitians say their prayers from within their expensive, air-conditioned four-wheel-drive vehicles double and triple parked in the street. There is an assortment of religious trinkets, from every imaginable Marian lithograph and plastic rosary beads, to shawls and medals, available for purchase from any number of merchants about the premises. Interestingly, without a single exception on the five occasions I visited Bel-Air on June 27, all the vendors of these items were women.

One would describe the Church of *Notre Dame du Perpétuel Secours* as of average size for a Catholic church in Port-au-Prince, and, like most Haitian Catholic churches, neither exceedingly ornate nor awfully beautiful. The altar is dominated by the large icon of *Perpétuel Secours*, above which loom three long stain glass windows, each depicting female Catholic saints other than Mary. To the right of the altar is a white statue of Our Lady of the Immaculate Conception, which is usually surrounded by votive candles and flowers left by devotees. Affixed to the wall to her left are several dozen plaques dedicated to *Perpétuel Secours* by Haitians in thanks for prayers that she has answered. Most of these are linoleum signs, the kind normally found on office doors. The higher ones, much older, are of marble. A typical plaque reads, "*Merci, Notre Dame du Perpétuel Secours*, for having answered my prayers. M.M.J. 6/7/82." One plaque is a collective expression of thanks from three Haitian banks, which, apparently and somewhat ironically, chipped in on one together. Such plaques hang in many Haitian Catholic churches.

Women make up a slight, but by no means dominant, majority of those present for any of the several Masses during the day. Virtually every strata of Haitian society is represented in the congregation, and remarkably in percentages roughly proportional to the greater societal makeup; i.e., a small percentage of the worshippers are from the elite, another small percentage from the middle class, while clearly the poor make up the better part of the faithful. There are few empty hands, as many of the faithful carry or display plastic rosaries, devotional manuals, lighted and unlighted candles, lithographs, icons, and photographs of sick or deceased loved ones. Most are worshipfully attentive to the sermon and prayers. Some weep.

To the right of the church and in front of the convent is a walled courtyard that protects a stone grotto[164] from the outside tension, poverty, and madness that characterize twentieth-century Port-au-Prince. A statue of Our Lady of the Immaculate Conception stands in the grotto; before it several women sway in deep meditative prayer. The courtyard is also quite full of worshippers who listen to the sermons and prayers emanating from within the church with the aid of a speaker hung on high. A strong smell of urine is unmistakable, and several homeless people sleep in shady corners, one just beside the door of the Center for the Diffusion of Devotion to *N.D. du Perpétuel Secours*. There is one disturbing scene, unnoticed by many, of several boisterous adolescent males sniffing glue, gambling, and viciously mocking a handicapped boy.

Above all of this courtyard clamor and devotion drift the priest's Creole words: "Notre Dame has often miraculously intervened on behalf of the Haitian people since the great cure of 1882." His sermon is carefully subtle in political content: "Mary delivered us from the shackles of slavery. Let us pray to Mary that we may never be enslaved again.... Whether you are bourgeois, whether you are people (*pèp*), we all must seek the will of God through his mother." It seems the priest is concerned not to allow Notre Dame's feast day to become a highly charged political display as it did the two years prior. In 1993, a great panic broke out after a number of prodemocracy activists disrupted the Mass with chants of "*Viv Aristide!!*" and calls for the ouster of the military junta. A Haitian press account describes the ensuing events: "Numerous persons, including some senior citizens, were manhandled when soldiers and armed civilians invaded the Church of *Perpétuel Secours* in Bel-Air, a poor neighborhood of Port-au-Prince. The soldiers made ten arrests, including that of Nicksonn Desrosiers, a member of a popular organization, and a young boy, Roosevelt Remy, upon his arrival home."[165]

A year later, the military regime remained defiantly in power, thanks in part to a stunning failure in international diplomacy, with its trade sanctions, leaky embargoes, loud bark, and weak bite. By the summer of 1994, it was apparent that the Clinton administration had painted itself into a corner with no option but to invade Haiti. Aware of this, the junta sounded the battle call, enlisting every means necessary to give the impression that the U.S. troops would encounter six million angrily defiant citizens ready to defend Haiti's "national sovereignty" with their lives. Anyone familiar with Haitian political and religious history was not surprised, then, when the junta's puppet president, Emile Jonassaint, showed up at the Church of *Perpétuel Secours* on June 27, 1994 for a Mass said, fortuitously, by an ardent Duvalerist priest, Father Salomon Jean-Baptiste. The Haitian Press Agency's account reads as follows:

> On the occasion of the patronal feast of *Perpétuel Secours*, a Mass is celebrated by Father Jean-Baptiste Salomon in the presence of Maitre Jonassaint, members of his government and members of the high command of the army. The priest invokes Notre Dame that she deliver Haiti from "a new small pox epidemic sui generis," which he never identifies in any specific fashion.[166]

These events illustrate clearly that the symbol of the Virgin Mary and the Haitian people's Marian devotion continue to be manipulated by political forces for the legitimization and promotion of their agendas and power. In 1993, prodemocratic activists attempted to stir resistance amid the nation's most important Marian celebrations, and soldiers broke up the Mass to arrest them; in 1994, the de facto regime invoked *Notre Dame* both to legitimize its power and to rally largely unarmed Haitians to combat the most powerful army the world has ever known, to whom the projunta priest referred as the "slave master"; and in 1995, the priest's subtle plea that Mary never permit the Haitian people to be "enslaved" again was to many ears a word of thanks to *Perpétuel Secours* for delivering the Haitian people from the bloody repression that they had suffered for three years under the Cédras military junta.

The Crying Virgin of the Sistine Chapel

A block from the sea, in Port-au-Prince's once-majestic Bicentennaire quarter, sits a small, somewhat unkempt basilica, a frail attempt at a miniature replica of Rome's St. Peter's called by Haitians "the Sistine Chapel." To the right of the chapel's small altar stands a statue of Our lady of Fatima. On any given day a small group of worshippers can be found standing of kneeling before her, praying the rosary or meditating. On May 13, 1976, the anniversary of the Fatima apparitions in Portugal, a first-year medical student by the name of Marie-Flor Thélus came to the chapel to pray to the Virgin Mary. Under considerable stress during exam week, Thélus was moved to ask Fatima to help her pass her exams. Around noon, she said her prayers and placed a small piece of paper under a lamp near the statue. The paper read, "Remember, Our Lady of Fatima, your dear child Marie-Flor Thélus." She asked specifically for help passing an exam scheduled for the following day and promised to return.

Having fared very well, Thélus returned to the chapel to thank Fatima on May 15, only to find the doors locked. Somewhat negligent of her promise to Fatima, the young woman allowed a week pass before finally visiting the chapel again, only once inside she forgot to thank Fatima in her prayers for helping her pass her exams. Noticing that the paper she had left for the Virgin was missing, she asked the chapel custodian if he had seen it, but no such paper had been found.

A few days later, while running some errands, Thélus passed the chapel, but did not bother to pay a visit to the Virgin. Thereafter, she was overcome by a host of strange emotions. A journalist to whom Thélus would later accord an interview writes: "Returning from the bank, she experienced a sensation of no longer being herself: she has no hold of herself, feeling very distant. This impression would last through to the 25th; despite her promise that she return to the chapel, she did not go at all."[167]

Finally honoring her promise, Thélus returned to the Sistine Chapel on May 30, 1976. At the doorway she was seized by a tremendous feeling of joy unlike any she had ever known. She then proceeded to the cross, where she said a short prayer, before making her way to the Virgin, before whom knelt a half-dozen women in silent prayer. Standing, Thélus began to pray, when suddenly she heard a compelling voice commanding her to "lower your head and get on your knees to pray." Aghast, she quickly knelt before the statue and begged forgiveness for having forgotten her promise, repeating in meditative concentration, "I trust in you—I trust in you." Overcome by uncertainty and guilt, Thélus demanded of Fatima, "Notre Dame, Notre Dame, if you are going to answer my plea, you must smile at me as if to say yes." Minutes later, "she sees a smile born, she sees this smile grow, she sees the cheeks turn pink, and she sees a tear fragilely suspended upon the lashes, about to flow. And flow it did." The women kneeling in silent prayer, suddenly alarmed, ran to the statue to witness the same. As for Marie-Flor, "she was pouring tears, unable to control herself, carrying on as if in another world."[168]

The women ran into the street crying *"La Vyej ap crie! La Vyej ap Crie!"* ("The Virgin is crying! The Virgin is crying!"), creating a great deal of commotion. "The church was immediately packed. Cars stopped, their passengers running to the church. Public offices and even banks were bereft of their functionaries in a flash."[169] It was a remarkable day in Port-au-Prince, one not soon to be forgotten in Haitian lore, but one that would bear little fruit for the future of Haiti's Mary cult. While a couple of my informants go to the chapel with the faint hope of seeing the Virgin cry once again, the event has been relegated to a place of relatively minor importance in Haitian Marianism, and Fatima's cult has only marginally profited from the Virgin's tears. Considering the development of Medjugorje as a major international pilgrimage center, or the large crowds which visit the homes of seers of Mary in places like Marlboro, New Jersey and Brooklyn, New York, the Sistine Chapel events have proven quite impotent. An exploration of reasons for this need not detain us here, though the fact that the lone message accompanying the tears was entirely personal—calling a single young Haitian woman to fall to her knees in prayer—while elsewhere messages of universal or wider importance are received by Marian seers, may represent at least a partial explanation. The Virgin transmitted nothing to Thélus in the way of the "popular apocalyptic ideology" that characterizes modern Marian apparitions, as demonstrated by Sandra Zimdars-Swartz.[170]

As for Marie-Flor Thélus, she sank into depression immediately following her experience, at one point requiring medication. She would come to understand the Virgin's tears to be tears of sadness. "The Virgin cried because I did not keep my promise to thank her." Suffering from insomnia one night, and sedated on tranquilizers, Thélus finally managed to cry herself to sleep, eventually having the Virgin appear to her in a dream. "She saw in this dream an object falling before her: it was the Virgin standing in her grotto. She walked toward the Virgin and hugged her, hugged her as hard as she could. Then, she awoke, unable to sleep again."[171]

Marie-Flor Thélus reported a continuation of the same vague, distant feeling that began to haunt her between her initial promise to give thanks to the Virgin and her vision of the crying statue. For some time thereafter, "she stayed at home, overcome with uncertainty and vague chagrin."[172] The statue of Our Lady of Fatima remains in the very same spot. If she has cried or smiled again in the ensuing twenty years, either no one noticed or no one said anything.

Popular Marianism as a Force Against the Duvalier Regime

The introduction to this study cites Leonardo Boff regarding the importance of Marian devotion to members of base communities, who demonstrate "a special appreciation of Mary's role of denunciation and proclamation (*denuncía y anuncía*), of prophecy and liberation."[173] Similarly, in the view of Haitian Catholic priest Yves Voltaire, in Haiti's *Tilegliz* movement has been noted the Virgin's appeal to base community members as a force of resistance to domination:

> Another locus of popular resistance is found undoubtedly in popular Catholic piety. Victims of a violent Christianization that was an accomplice to the slave system and to neocolonialism, subjected to a sacramentalization devoid of catechetical guidance, the poor created their own religious and symbolic universe, where they reinterpret official religion.... The TKL's respect this popular piety, from which they take spiritual energy and which they themselves influence. Mary, the mother of the poor, *Notre Dame du Perpétuel Secours*, plays therein a predominant role, in whom the TKL's discover a model of guidance in the faith after that of Jesus, and a revelation of the maternal face of God, hidden by a generally very patriarchal presentation of God.[174]

As noted by numerous commentators—and as seen in chapter two— the role played by the TKL movement played an indispensable role in the ouster of the Duvalier regime. The syllogism thus forms itself: since Mary is for *Tilegliz* a key motivational force for resistance, and since *Tilegliz* played a leading role in the collapse of the Duvalier dictatorship, it may be deduced that devotion to Mary contributed to this remarkable revolution.

The common perception is that Pope John Paul II's visit to Haiti in 1983 sparked the Church-led movement that eventually brought down the Duvalier regime. As chapter six will demonstrate, many poor Haitians saw both the pope's 1983 visit and the eventual departure of Baby Doc in 1986 as the work of the Virgin Mary. Two factors, it may be argued, helped to solidify this belief: (1) The fact that the pope's visit was in the context of a Eucharistic and Marian conference; and (2) although such a visit had not been slated in John Paul's itinerary, at Archbishop Ligondé's request a decision was made to visit briefly the Church of *Notre Dame du Perpétuel Secours* in Bel-Air. The nuns at Bel-Air were apparently aware that the archbishop would make such a request of the pope and were praying to *Perpétuel Secours* to sway the Holy Father into acquiescence. Their prayers were answered, as the pope arrived and held a brief meeting with the sisters inside the church, after which he proceeded to the front of the church and blessed the city with the historic miraculous icon in much the same way as Guilloux had done a century prior. There is little doubt, then, that the association of the pope's visit with the explosion of popular Catholic resistance to the dictatorship would be seen by many as guided by the hand of the Virgin, who, after all, brought the pope to Haiti in the first place.

The texts of both a 1985 youth prayer vigil of protest and the Haitian bishops' Christmas message of the same year suggest that this deduction is accurate. After denouncing the army's November 1985 murder of three school boys in Gonaïves, as well as blaming outright "(t)his small group that keeps the people enslaved," the youth vigil ended by posing the question, "Are we not the brothers of Jesus, children of Marie.?"[175] The bishops' Christmas message, while never openly attacking the Duvalier regime, did implicitly cry out against the dictatorship—as well as other sectors of Haitian society equally responsible for the misery of the masses—denouncing "dishonesty," "servitude," "selfishness," "torture," "violence," and "hate." The bishops end by encouraging the Haitian people to find strength in "praying to Mary, Queen of peace."[176]

The considerable risks that popular church leaders took in openly protesting against the Duvalier regime certainly demanded a great deal of strength, and several TKL members have attested to me that they found such strength in Mary. Novenas broadcast over Radio Soley dispensed this empowerment. One woman described to me the omnipresence of the repetitious prayers:

> Everywhere you went you could hear the novenas on the radio. Everywhere! This unified us and gave us courage to stand up to the motherless Duvalier and his army." Another woman explained that certain Marian hymns, also regularly broadcast over Radio Soley, took on subversive import for the resistance. "Even when they closed Radio Soley a month and a half before Jean-Claude left, many people continued to sing the hymns to the Virgin in the streets. It was remarkable, really. The army could shut down Radio Soley, but it could not keep the songs from being heard.

The hymns themselves became, as it were, an expression of defiance.

Even in the absence of Radio Soley, TKL activists still managed to organize one last novena before Duvalier left on February 7, 1986. The novena ended, remarkably, on the eve of Baby-Doc's departure. As one lay leader of a TKL group explained, "We had already prayed many novenas in an effort to topple the dictator, yet with this one you could just feel the power and you just knew that it would be the one that finally worked. And it did—the day after the last hail Mary, Duvalier left."

While it is clear that devotion to Mary did play a role in the *Tilegliz* movement's effective and unparalleled contribution to the ouster of the Duvalier regime, it would be an exaggeration to label this role as predominant. The popular masses were bolstered through their unity in faith and structured their resistance around a number of themes. The Virgin Mary's concern for the Haitian people was but one of them. Yet the leading voice of popular Church resistance against political oppression, Jean-Bertrand Aristide, had the greatest influence over the TKL without apparently ever making the Virgin a central or regular theme in his sermons. This example illustrates that while popular Mariology was fundamental to the Church's role in the extraordinary drama of February 1986, it was not indispensable to the resistance movement. While some TKL's, like *Les Ambassadeurs* and *Groupe Chrismatique Virgo Maria*, are especially devoted to Mary, most of them, according to one priest with close ties to the *Tilegliz* movement since its genesis in the early eighties, "are in fact very christocentric." In his view, for those TKLs with a mariocentric theology, the Virgin was, indeed, the force that overthrew Duvalier, but for the majority, this was simply not the case. In any event, therefore, it would seem that the most important dimension of popular Marian piety in this context was it ability to strengthen the faithful in the face of the grave danger that their resistance entailed.

This dimension of popular Marian piety, as chapter six demonstrates, would be remanifest in the form of protest against the Cédras regime just five years later. This is not to suggest that Mary's provenance of courage to engage in political activism was dormant during the period between the ouster of Jean-Claude Duvalier in 1986 and the Cédras coup d'état in 1991 and the ensuing three year junta. In her dissertation "The Transformation of the Catholic Church in Haiti," Suze Marie Mathieu describes the events of November 7, 1986, when Radio Soley organized a procession from the Radio station to the Church of *Perpétuel Secours* in honor of Catholic literacy activist Charlot Jacquelin, who was arrested without a warrant and never heard from again. The army, now under the command of de facto head of state General Henri Namphy, intervened to break up the procession, reflecting the state's recognition of the subversive potential of popular Marianism:

> I asked someone where the procession was being organized and they said "Inside the [radio station] grounds," so I tried to get inside quickly. As I pushed my way through the crowd of half-dressed barefoot men and a few women standing at the gate with rocks in their hands and cheering on the man with the helmet, I heard shooting. It was the army shooting at the radio station.[177]

In concert with the procession, the novena broadcast over Radio Soley served as a vehicle of popular protest. Mathieu recounts:

> For nine days before the march the Catholic Church had
> organized prayers [a novena] for this young man [Charlot
> Jacquelin] that were broadcast over Radio Soley. Anyone
> living in Port-au-Prince at the time could go about their
> daily activities and follow the novena as it seemed that
> every radio in every home, taxi, bus, hospital and place of
> business was tuned to it.[178]

It seems evident, therefore, that for the popular masses, Marianism's role as a cohesive force, as a strengthener, and as a motivator for protest has been especially manifest in times of heightened political crisis. The degree to which the crisis worsens is proportionate to the deepening of the fervor in praying to the Virgin for the realization of a solution salubrious to the poor.

Conclusion

Understanding the history and character of Haitian Marianism demands focus on the structures of the Haitian religious field and their relationship to the religious habitus, in its various forms, of the Haitian people. Since, to a large degree, conflicting ideological forces shape these structures, analysis of both these forces and the religious needs born of suffering and poverty shared by the vast majority of the Haitian people are requisite to any attempt to penetrate the meaning of the Marian cult's development in Haiti and, for that matter, elsewhere in Latin America.

Counter Reformation Iberian Catholicism, itself characterized by Marianism, militancy, and millenarianism, religiously legitimized the initial Spanish conquest of Hispaniola. While these three elements merged to transform the Virgin Mary into the patroness of Spanish and, later, French colonial endeavors and concomitantly the slave trade, they also laid a lasting foundation for the development of Haitian Marianism in its various contemporary manifestations. Their influence remains, indeed, quite marked on the cult in Haiti today. Though it has taken on diverse forms throughout Haitian religious history, it must be stressed that originally Mariology ranked among the colonizers' most powerful weapons of symbolic violence, employed to engender the misrecognition as legitimate the arbitrary social structures established for the expansion of crown and church. The deep social rift of contemporary Haitian society is, in fact, rooted in these very colonial structures.

The oppression wrought by the transatlantic slave trade is perhaps unsurpassed in human history. For the enslaved Africans and Creoles of Saint-Domingue, this existential condition clearly had a deep influence on their religious needs and consequently on those forms of religious practice and belief that emerged as characteristic of Vodou and, to a somewhat lesser and consequent extent, popular Haitian Catholicism. As discussed in chapter two in the context of our summary of Vittorio Lanternari's analysis of the religions of the oppressed, the use of symbols and rituals among the subjugated often represents a form of resistance against deculturalization. In situations where the oppressed's religious traditions are under attack, as in colonial Hispaniola, elements of the dominant religion are often adopted, adapted, and syncretized with corresponding features of the jeopardized or proscribed religion both to surreptitiously preserve the endangered traditions and, at times, to oppose political domination. Romaine-la-Prophétesse represents perhaps the most radical single example of this in Haitian religious history, with his extreme appropriation of the Virgin Mary as the guardian of his violent rebellion against the white slave regime of Saint-Domingue.

Romaine is something of a unique example in the politico-religious history of Haitian Marianism, however, of the symbol of the Virgin Mary being employed to motivate outright and aggressive resistance against political domination. For the most part, it has been quite the contrary: the nation's political, economic, and religious elites have exploitatively manipulated the symbol of the Virgin and popular Haitian Marian devotion to legitimize and augment their power and render dissension impotent. On the political level, Pétion, Christophe, Soulouque, Lescot, Jonassaint, and Cédras illustrate this clearly. On the religious level, we may not only point to the efforts of Guilloux, Kersuzan, and Leguoaze but also to the following Creole hymn that demonstrates just the kind of effect the Haitian Church hierarchy—or at least those with influence over hymn composition and selection—has intended for Marian devotion to have among their flock:

> In our chagrin and misery
> The Virgin shall help us

Always granting us succor
If we on the earth pray to her
Each time we are suffering
Each time we are sick
If we pray to Mary
And have trust.[179]

As Micial Neréstant, himself a Haitian priest, remarks:

Here is discovered an accent on evasion and resignation.
Resignation seems to be recommended to atone for one's
sins and prepare oneself for eternal life. This depoliticized
attitude played to the advantage of the Duvalierist regime,
and in part explains the long duration of the regime."[180]

This, then, is a clear example of the employment of popular Marian
devotion by the dominant to engender passivity in the masses.

Thus, ideological forces, most especially the socially stifling
agendas of the Haitian religious, economic, and political elites, have
had a deep and lasting influence on the structure of the Haitian
religious field and on the development and characteristics of Haitian Marianism. An opposing form of ideology is likewise
discernable in popular Haitian Mariology, which at times in Haitian
history, most notably in Romaine-la-Prophétesse's movement, has
transformed itself into an inspirational force for protest or insurgence. These ideological forces, in addition to the religious needs
and dispositions of the both the minority economic elite and the
subjugated masses, thus emerge as two of the chief determinants of
Haitian Marianism.

NOTES

1. Michael P. Carroll, *The Cult of the Virgin Mary: Psychological Origins* (Princeton: Princeton University Press, 1986), p. 10.
2. Marina Warner, *Alone of All Her Sex: The Myth and Cult of the
   Virgin Mary* (New York: Knopf, 1976), p. 267.
3. Jacques Lafaye, *Quetzacóatl and Guadaloupe: The Formation of
   Mexican National Consciousness, 1531-1813* (Chicago: The University of Chicago Press, 1976), p. 226. It is noteworthy that these

remain the most important saint cults in Haitian Catholicism. And just as Mary would be assimilated with Ezili, so would St. Jacques, who appears in Catholic hagiography as a sword-wielding soldier on horseback, be conflated with Ogun, the spirit of iron and warfare.

4. Ibid., p. 218.
5. Ibid., p. 219.
6. Jean-Marie Kyss, "La nouvelle cathédrale de l'Immaculée Conception de Hinche." *Le Nouvelliste*, 15 November 1995.
7. Thomas Madiou, *Histoire d'Haïti, Tome I: 1492-1799* (Port-au-Prince: Deschamps, 1989) p. 15.
8. Octavio Paz, "Foreword: The Flight of Quetzacóatl and the Quest for Legitimacy," in Lafaye, *Quetzacóatl and Guadaloupe*, pp. ix-xxii, p. xv.
9. Lafaye, *Quetzacóatl and Guadaloupe*, p. 34. In their excellent study of the dubious political history of Catholic Marianism, Nicholas Perry and Loreto Echeverría draw the conclusion that: "Indeed, we can say that Hispanic colonization was Marian colonization." *Under the Heel of Mary* (New York: Routledge, 1988), p. 31.
10. Ibid., p. 88. It should be noted that, as Ruether points out, although the woman depicted in the Book of Revelations is commonly assumed to be the Virgin Mary, this is simply not the case: "there is no evidence that the author of the book linked the image of the woman to Jesus' historical mother. The woman here in Revelation is a symbol of the church in the time of persecution that is "pregnant" and in birth pangs with a Messianic king who is to come at some time in the future (i.e., the Second Coming of Christ)." *Mary: The Feminine Face of the Church*, p. 31.
11. Lafaye, *Quetzacóatl and Guadalupe*, p. 227.
12. Ivone Gebara and Maria Clara Bingemer, *Mary: Mother of God, Mother of the Poor* (New York: Orbis, 1987), p. 129.
13. Ibid. In *Under the Heel of Mary* (London & New York: Routledge, 1988), Nicholas Perry and Loreto Echeverría conclude that "Hispanic colonization was Marian colonization." P. 31.
14. Warner, *Alone of All Her Sex*, p. 304.
15. Gebara and Bingemer, *Mary*, p. 134.
16. Enrique Dussel, "Popular Religion as Oppression and Liberation: Hypothesis on its Past and Present in Latin America," in Norbert Greinacher and Norbert Mette, (eds.), *Popular Religion, Concilium*, 186, August 1986, pp. 82-94, p. 88.
17. Gebara and Bingemer, *Mary: Mother of God, Mother of the Poor*, p. 149.

18. Leslie G. Desmangles, *The Faces of the Gods* (Chapel Hill: The University of North Carolina Press, 1992), p. 143. It is important to consider in this regard the case of slaves from the kingdom of the Kongo, where Catholicism had been first adopted *freely* by Kongolese early in the sixteenth century, and where devotion to the Virgin Mary was very popular. For these slaves, then, the Virgin Mary was nothing new, and their devotion was, thus, an extension of Kongolese Marianism.

19. R. P. Breton, "Relations de l'île de la Guadaloupe," as cited by Gérard Lafleur, "L'Église dans la societé du XVIIe siècle aux Antilles," in Laënnec Hurbon, (ed.), *Le phénomène religieux dans la Caraïbe* (Montréal: CIDIHCA, 1989), pp. 23-56, p. 28.

20. Jean-Baptiste DuTerte, *Histoire générale des Antilles*, as cited by Liliane Chauleau, "Le baptême á la Martinique au XVIIe siècle," in Hurbon, (ed.), *Le phénomène religieux dans la Caraïbe*, pp. 23-56, p. 28.

21. Chauleau, "Le baptême á la Martinique au XVIIe siècle," in Hurbon, (ed.), *Le phénomène religieux dans la Caraïbe*, pp. 57-71, p. 68

22. Pierre Pelleprat, "Relations des missions des P.P. de la Compaignie de Jésus dans les îles et dans la Terre-Ferme de l'Amérique méridionale," as cited in Chauleau, "Le baptême á la Martinique au XVIIe siècle," p. 68.

23. Ibid.

24. Rachel Beauvoir-Dominique, *L'Ancienne cathédrale de Port-au-Prince* (Port-au-Prince: Editions Henri Deschamps, 1991), p. 14.

25. Gérard Lafleur, "L'Église dans la societé du XVIIe siècle aux Antilles, in Hurbon, (ed.), *Le phénomène religieux dans la Caraïbe*, pp. 21-40, p. 24.

26. Beauvoir-Dominique, *L'Ancienne cathédrale de Port-au-Prince*, p. 14.

27. Ibid., pp. 27-28.

28. Ibid., p. 20.

29. Anne Greene, *The Catholic Church in Haiti: Social and Political Change* (East Lansing: Michigan State University Press, 1993), p. 76.

30. Jean-Marie Jan, *Les congregations religieuses au Cap-Français, Saint-Domingue: 1681-1793* (Port-au-Prince, Editions Henri Deschamps, 1951), p. 80.

31. Ibid., p. 130. Jan does not specify what it is exaclty that was "alarming."

32. Letter from Sister Thèrese de Saint-Ange, Mother Superior of *La Compagnie de Notre Dame*, 1745, as cited in ibid., p. 197.

33. Jan, *Les congregations religieuses au Cap-Français, Saint-Domingue*, p. 193.
34. Ibid., p. 80.
35. Ibid., p. 194.
36. Ibid.
37. Ibid., p. 195.
38. Ibid.
39. Ibid.
40. Citation is from DuTerte letter, as cited in Chauleau, "Le baptême á la Martinique au XVIIe siècle," p. 67.
41. This form of devotion remains especially popular in Haitian Marianism.
42. Jan, *Les congregations religieuses au Cap-Français, Saint-Domingue*, p. 226.
43. Ian Thomson, "A devil may care voodoo society" [!] *Financial Times*, 26 February 1993.
44. Jan explains that despite being "imploringly solicited to return to their families," the Daughters "would remain, unable to part company with the poor black girls, whom they continued to teach and to console." Ironically, some of these "poor black girls," as Jan suggests, may have had a hand in the nuns' slaughter. Jan, *Les congregations religieuses au Cap-Français, Saint-Domingue*, p. 225.
45. This expression is cited in Beauvoir-Dominique, *L'Ancienne cathédrale de Port-au-Prince*, p. 24.
46. Neréstant, *Religions et politique en Haïti*, p. 80.
47. Carolyn E. Fick, *The Making of Haiti: The Saint-Domingue Revolution from Below* (Knoxville: The University of Tennessee Press, 1990), p. 244.
48. Ibid., p. 244.
49. Thomas Madiou, *Histoire d'Haïti, Tome I: 1492-1799*, p. 127.
50. Dussel, Enrique. "Popular Religion as Oppression and Liberation: Hypothesis on its Past and Present in Latin America," in Greinacher, Norbert, and Norbert Metz (eds.), *Popular Religion, Concilium*, 186, pp. 82-94, p. 88.
51. Beauvoir-Dominique, *L'Ancienne cathédrale de Port-au-Prince*, pp. 64-65.
52. George Eaton Simpson, *Religious Cults of the Caribbean: Trinidad, Jamaica, and Haïti*, Caribbean Monograph Series, 15 (San Juan: University of Puerto Rico, 1965), p. 235. Most mention of Romaine in scholarly literature is brief and refers merely to Madiou's short discussion, where he refers to Romaine as a "*grif espagnol*" (a Spanish quadroon). Simpson evidently takes this literally and assumes

that Romaine was truly a Spaniard. However, it is common in Haiti to hear any native Spanish speaker referred to as "a Spaniard." In Creole, in fact, a Dominican is simply called *panyòl,* which is the Creole mutation of the French *espagnol,* or Spaniard. It is thus likely that Madiou's reference to Romaine as a Spaniard indicates that he was originally from the Spanish side of the island and hence a native Spanish speaker, one commonly referred to as a Spaniard.

53. Fouchard's *Les marrons du syllabaire* includes several plates depicting letters written by Romaine-la-Prophétesse to a French priest. They are practically legible in these reproductions. The letters are written in a tone of almost pompous respect for *"Monsieur l'Abbé,"* and usually thank him for his advice, request further advice, and/or inform him of Romaine's most recent and next move. Each letter is closed in the same fashion: "Your most humble and most obedient servant, Romaine riviere, *La Prophétesse, Comandant Générale.*" One can only wonder what *"Monsieur l'Abbé"* made of Romaine's predilection for calling himself *Prophétesse,* a title hardly reflective of Christian humility, and one that reflects either grammatical or sexual confusion. Equally intriguing is the question as to whether he was aware of Romaine's radical appropriation of the symbol of the Virgin Mary.

54. Milo Rigaud, *La tradition vaudou et vaudou Haïtien: Son temple, ses mystères, sa magie* (Paris: Niclaus, 1953), p. 66.

55. *"Symbiosis by ecology* refers to Roger Bastide's notion of syncretism in mosaic, which manifests itself in two paradigms: on the one hand, in the spatial juxtaposition of Vodou (or diverse African-derived) elements and Catholic symbols in the ounfò.... [T]he geographical proximity of a church to a ounfò constitutes the spatial juxtaposition of the two traditions." *The Faces of the Gods,* p. 8.

56. Garran-Coulon, as cited in Beauvoir-Dominique, *L'Ancienne cathédrale de Port-au-Prince,* p. 64.

57. Henock Trouillot, *Introduction à une histoire du Vaudou* (Port-au-Prince: Fardin, 1983), p. 64.

58. Fick, *The Making of Haiti,* p. 127.

59. Ibid., p. 138.

60. "Theodicy of compensation" is Weber's term for what he sees as a key component of the "religion of non-privileged classes," a category into which Romaine's followers obviously fit. "Resentment is a concomitant of that particular ethic of the disprivileged which, in the sense expanded by Nietzsche and *in direct inversion* of the ancient belief, teaches that the unequal distribution of mundane goods is caused by the sinfulness and illegality of the privileged, and sooner

or later God's wrath will overtake them" [my italics]. Max Weber, *The Sociology of Religion*, p. 110.

61. Fick, *The Making of Haiti*, p. 127.
62. Serge Larose, "The Meaning of Africa in Haitian Vodu," in I. M. Lewis, ed., *Symbols and Sentiments* (New York: Academic Press, 1977), pp. 85-116, pp. 111-12.
63. Métraux, *Voodoo in Haïti*, p. 47.
64. Fick, *The Making of Haiti*, p. 128.
65. I credit and thank Drexel Woodson for first pointing out to me the weakness in Fick's conception of Vodou. See note 67 below.
66. Rigaud, *La tradition vaudou et le vaudou Haïtien*, p. 66. Laguerre informs his brief mention of Romaine with Rigaud's. His translation of Rigaud's term *"coq rangé"* is, however, incorrect and misleading. Laguerre states that Romaine "always carried on his saddlehorse a *rangé* chicken (one having magical powers)," whereas *coq* should be translated as "cock" or "rooster," and certainly not as "chicken." The difference is significant, for in Vodou the cock is the embodiment of power and virility; whereas the chicken, as far as I know, is far less evocative. The powerful symbolism of the cock was not lost on Jean-Bertrand Aristide, who effectively employed it as the emblem of his political party FNCD (*Front Nationale pour le Changement et la Démocratie*) during Haiti's 1990 presidential election, which Aristide won by a landslide.
67. Drexel G. Woodson, "Which Beginning Should be Hindmost?: Surrealism in Appropriations of Facts About Haitian "Contact Culture." Unpublished manuscript, cited with author's permission, pp. 47-48.
68. See Larose, "The Meaning of Africa in Haitian Vodu," p. 111, and Beauvoir-Dominique, *L'Ancienne cathédrale de Port-au-Prince*, p. 64.
69. Laguerre, *Voodoo and Politics in Haïti*, p. 34.
70. Fick, *The Making of Haiti*, p. 128.
71. Weber, *The Sociology of Religion*, p. 46.
72. Ibid., p. 2
73. Ibid.
74. Talcott Parsons, "Introduction," in Weber, *The Sociology of Religion*, pp. xix-lxvii, p. xxx.
75. Weber, *The Sociology of Religion*, p. 9.
76. Parsons, "Introduction," p. xxxiii.
77. Weber, *The Sociology of Religion*, p. 2.
78. Bourdieu, "Legitimation and Structured Interest in Weber's Sociology of Religion," p. 129.

79. Ibid., p. 131.
80. Ibid., p. 126.
81. Ibid.
82. Ibid., p. 131.
83. Ibid., p. 129.
84. Weber, *The Sociology of Religion*, p. 2.
85. Ibid., p. 110.
86. Alexis Beaubrun Ardouin, *Etudes sur l'histoire d'Haïti, tome septième* (Port-au-Prince, Dalencour, 1958), p. 111.
87. Madiou, *Histoire d'Haïti, Tome V: 1811-1818*, p. 111.
88. Ibid.,
89. Ardouin, p. 111.
90. Madiou, *Histoire d'Haïti, Tome V: 1811-1818*, p. 112.
91. Ardouin, p. 111.
92. Ibid., p. 112.
93. Ibid.
94. Ibid. Ardouin's account indicates that it was not only the unlettered masses who lent credence to the false apparitions. Significantly, members of the urban elite were also noted among those who flocked to Mary's tree prior o the exposure of the fraud.
95. Laguerre, *Voodoo and Politics in Haïti*, p. 87.
96. Adolphe Cabon, *Notes sur l'histoire religieuse d'Haïti, de la révolution au concordat, 1789-1860.* (Port-au-Prince: Petit Séminaire Collège St. Martial, 1933), pp. 271-72.
97. Neréstant, *Religions et politique en Haïti*, p. 97.
98. Laguerre, *Voodoo and Politics in Haïti*, p. 87.
99. Cabon, *Notes sur l'histoire religieuse d'Haïti*, p. 99.
100. Farmer, *The Uses of Haiti*, pp. 51-52.
101. Laguerre, *Voodoo and Politics in Haïti*, p. 83.
102. Daniel H. Levine, *Popular Voices in Latin-American Catholicism* (Princeton: Princeton University Press, 1992), p. 171.
103. Hurbon, *Dieu dans le vaudou Haïtien*, p. 104.
104. Robert Orsi, "The Religious Boundaries of an Inbetween People: Street *Feste* and the Problem of the Dark-Skinned Other in Italian Harlem, 1920-1990." *American Quarterly*, vol. 44, no. 3 (September 1992) pp. 313-347, p. 331.
105. Ibid., p. 332.
106. Ibid.
107. Cabon, *Notes sur l'histoire religieuse d'Haïti*, p. 406. Cabon indicates that pilgrimage to Saut-d'Eau actually began in 1844, some five years prior to the Marian apparitions that are assumed to have initially sparked pilgrims' interest in going there. Cabon points

this out, in fact: "[P]eople today only remember the false apparitions of the Holy Virgin in a group of palm trees in 1849." This
leads me to believe that Marian apparitions in Saut-d'Eau had actually taken place as early as 1844, if not earlier, for what else could
explain Haitian pilgrims adopting it as a replacement destination
for Higuey in 1844, which is only one year after the waterfalls was
created by a massive earthquake? Something involving the Virgin
Mary must have occurred at Saut-d'Eau either prior to or in 1844.
Following this train of thought, if the waterfalls—which by most
accounts are deemed by Vodouisants as embodying mystical powers
and being the home of certain *lwas*—was the center of Vodou pilgrimage, this tradition could not, then, predate 1843, whereas at
least a trickle of Marian pilgrims could have been coming to Saut-
d'Eau earlier than the creation of the falls. The falls in themselves
would not be an essential ingredient to apparitions of Mary. They
are, however, the essential ingredient to Vodouisant pilgrimage at
Saut-d'Eau. Could it thus be that Marian pilgrimage, on a minor
scale, to Saut-d'Eau predates Vodouisant pilgrimage there, contrary
to common assumptions?

108. Laguerre, *Voodoo and Politics in Haïti*, pp. 88-89.
109. Desmangles, *The Faces of the Gods*, p. 135.
110. Wade Davis, *The Serpent and the Rainbow* (New York: Warner,
1987), p. 205. The facility with which scholars make such statements as this in reference to the complex question of the assimilation of Catholic saints with Vodou spirits in Haitian religious culture will be taken to task in the following chapter.
111. Desmangles, *The Faces of the Gods*, p. 135.
112. Ibid.
113. Ibid.
114. Laguerre, *Voodoo and Politics in Haïti*, p. 97.
115. Ibid.
116. Desmangles, *The Faces of the Gods*, p. 135.
117. Rebecca Lee, "The Jerusalem Syndrome." *The Atlantic Monthly*,
May 1995.
118. Laguerre, *Voodoo and Politics in Haïti*, p. 82.
119. Anonymous, *Supplique et Neuvaine à Notre Dame du Perpétuel
Secours* (Quebec: Librarie de la Bonne Sainte Anne, 1963), p. 27.
120. Ibid.
121. Ibid.
122. Lig Notre Dam Pepetyèl Sekou, *An'n chante Manman Pepetyèl:
Koze, lapriyè ak chan pou Mari Patwon e Rèn Dayiti* (Port-au-Prince:
Le Natal, 1992), p. 7.

123. The *Perpétuel Secours* image is one of a host of Byzantine Madonnas, collectively referred to in Greek as *Odiguitria* (Guide).
124. Beauvoir-Dominique, *L'Ancienne cathédrale de Port-au-Prince*, p. 121.
125. *Supplique et Neuvaine à Notre Dame du Perpétuel Secours*, p. 27.
126. Cited in Cabon, *Notes sur l'histoire religieuse d'Haïti*, p. 431.
127. Ibid., p. 432.
128. Ibid.
129. Ibid, p. 433.
130. Ibid.
131. Jean-Marie Jan, *Collecta pour l'histoire du diocèse du Cap-Haïtien, tome 3* (Port-au-Prince: Deschamps, 1958), p. 123.
132. Cabon, *Notes sur l'histoire religieuse d'Haïti*, pp. 433-434.
133. Jan, *Collecta pour l'histoire du diocèse du Cap-Haïtien, tome 3*, 123.
134. Cabon, *Notes sur l'histoire religieuse d'Haïti*, pp. 434.
135. Jean-Marie Jan, *Documents pour l'histoire religieuse d'Haiti* (Port-au-Prince: Deschamps, 1956), p. 127.
136. Beauvoir-Dominique, *L'Ancienne cathédrale de Port-au-Prince*, p. 118. At both the February and October 1882 Bel-Air ceremonies, the Catholic clergy employed an impressive array of ritualistic gestures in an effort to overwhelm the faithful with the mystical importance of the new Virgin, from displaying the icon in a blessing over each of the four directions over the capital, to blessing the very walls of the church which would house it. To the Vodouisant religious habitus, these elaborations were familiar, as similar rituals are often performed by *oungans* in Vodou temples. Thus, while the introduction of *Perpétuel Secours* to the Haitian people was intended in part as a blow to the Vodou-saturated Marys of the Haitian religious field, the ritualistic flamboyance at these ceremonies probably very much backfired and painted *Perpétuel Secours* in Vodouisant colors from the beginning.
137. Ibid., p. 119.
138. Pedro A. Ribeiro de Oliveira, "Catholicisme populaire et hégémonie bourgeoise au Brésil." *Archives des sciences sociales des religions*, 24, 1979, pp. 53-79, p. 70.
139. Jan, *Collecta pour l'histoire du diocèse du Cap-Haïtien, Tome 3*, p. 124.
140. Ibid.
141. Ibid.
142. For further insight into Kersuzan's attitude toward Vodou, we may refer to his pastoral letter of 29 January 1896, in which he writes,

"Those who pretend to be Christian receive the sacraments and yet are not afraid to participate in pagan practices, as if they could at once serve Jesus Christ and the devil. Shame on these wretched ones." As Neréstant remarks, "The term 'devil' which Kersuzan uses to define his position in regards to Vaudou is most significant." Kersuzan letter cited in Neréstant, *Religions et politique en Haiti*, p. 124.

143. 1894 letter from Mgr. Hillion, as cited in Jan, *Collecta pour l'histoire du diocèse du Cap-Haïtien, Tome 1*, p. 152.

144. Jan, *Collecta pour l'histoire du diocèse du Cap-Haïtien, Tome 3*, p. 11.

145. Ibid.

146. Ibid.

147. Jan, *Collecta pour l'histoire du diocèse du Cap-Haïtien, Tome 1*, p. 283.

148. Ibid., 284. Marian associations are diffuse in Haitian Catholicism. At the feast day of *Notre Dame de l'Assomption* in 1995, I counted approximately twenty of them, each carrying the association's banner during the procession. I suspect that in Port-au-Prince alone there are dozens more. The largest of these is the Legion of Mary, whose center sits adjacent to the national cathedral. Most of these associations, unlike the Legion, could be considered more or less CEB's, while a few are conservative and comprised mainly of upper-class members.

149. Jan, *Collecta pour l'histoire du diocèse du Cap-Haïtien, Tome 3*, p. 11.

150. Ibid.

151. Ibid., pp. 11-12.

152. Ibid., p. 112.

153. Ibid.

154. Gerard Maisonneuve, "Notre Dame du Perpétuel Secours," *Le Nouvelliste*, 6 December 1992.

155. Ibid.

156. Ibid.

157. Ibid.

158. Ibid.

159. Beauvoir-Dominique, *L'Ancienne cathédrale de Port-au-Prince*, p. 135.

160. Métraux, *Voodoo in Haïti*, p. 342.

161. Cited in Bien-Aimé, *Eglise pour changer* (Port-au-Prince: St. Gérard, 1987), p. 83.

162. Elie Lescot, *Avant l'oubli: Christianisme et paganisme en Haïti et autres lieux* (Port-au-Prince: Deschamps, 1974), p. 453.

163. Ibid., p. 459.

164. Grotto-centered devotion is quite pronounced in Haitian Marianism. I have discovered more than a dozen grottoes around Port-au-Prince, approximately half of them physically independent from church property. Some are in private yards or parks; one is in the General Hospital. Most notable among the Port-au-Prince grottoes is the one housing *Notre Dame de l'Imaculée Conception* in Haut-Turgeau, which attracts a regular group of faithful each Saturday. Some of the women in this group also belong to *Le Foyer de Notre Dame*, a mariocentric TKL, which, although not centered in a grotto, has its own statue of the Virgin. Once a month, the statue is removed from its pedestal to pass a week in the home of one of the group members. I have learned in hazy detail about a series of visions of the Virgin Mary reported in a natural grotto near the sea in the South-East Department, not far from Jacmel. As one informant explained to me, the grotto began to attract a great deal of attention, eventually causing the development of a marketplace. The local Catholic priest soon decided to put a stop to it, declaring to the deluded that the apparitions were false. One may speculate that the long history of Vodouisant fascination with caves and grottoes might have had something to do with the priest's decision. In any case, these events demand further research.

165. Agence Haïtien de Presse, *1993 au quotidien* (Port-au-Prince: Editions AHP, 1994), p. 74.

166. Agence Haïtien de Presse, *1994 au quotidien* (Port-au-Prince: Editions AHP, 1995), p. 81.

167. Frantz Bataille, "Marie-Flor Thélus nous raconte," *Le Nouvelliste*, 30 May 1976. My rendition of this story is entirely dependent on Bataille's article.

168. Ibid.

169. Ibid.

170. Sandra L. Zidmars-Swartz, *Encountering Mary* (New York: Avon, 1992), p. 245. Zidmars-Swartz indicates that "the immediacy of the initial religious experience and the personal meanings attached to these experiences by the seers and by other early participants in these apparition dramas have usually been understood in terms of some much more comprehensive structures of meaning.... Most apparition devotees have understood recent apparitions as part of a pattern of divine activity in the 'last days' immediately preceding the Second Coming of Christ.... In fact, something like a single,

transcultural, apocalyptic ideology based on apparition messages has grown up in recent years around the edges of mainline Roman Catholic institutions..."(pp. 245 ff.).

171. Bataille, "Marie-Flor Thélus nous raconte."

172. Ibid.

173. Boff, *The Maternal Face of God*, p. 188.

174. Yves Voltaire, "Existe-t-il une Eglise des pauvres en Haïti?" in CHR, *Evangelisation d'Haïti, 1492-1992, Tome 3: Les TKL et la nouvelle évangelisation*, pp. 15-99 (Port-au-Prince: Le Natal, 1993), p. 53.

175. As cited in Martin-Luc Bonnardot et Gilles Danroc, eds., *La chute de la maison Duvalier: Textes pour l'histoire* (Paris: Karthala, 1989), p. 83.

176. Ibid., p. 87.

177. Suze Marie Mathieu, "The Transformation of the Catholic Church in Haiti" (Ph.D. diss: University of Indiana, 1991), p. 97.

178. Ibid.

179. Neréstant, *Religions et politique en Haiti*, p. 194. The hymn is recorded by Neréstant on same page.

180. Ibid.

CHAPTER FIVE

THE PROMISCUOUS VIRGIN:
THE SYMBIOSIS OF MARY AND EZILI

Lithographs depicting Catholic saints have been one of the most effective conduits of Catholic/African assimilation in Haitian religion, with saints widely taken to be reflections, manifestations, or associates of particular *lwas*. Indeed, most writers agree that this phenomenon of visual identification and cross-religious relating of symbols is central to the syncretism (or symbiosis) of Catholic and African religious elements in Haitian Vodou. It is usually superficial visual symbolic identification, rather than any popular theological reconciliation between the saints and *lwas*, that determines this form of symbolic conflation, as will be demonstrated below. Thus, while Catholic and Vodouisant representations perceived in images may be thoroughly syncretized, it does not necessarily follow that the spiritual beings behind the representations are themselves subjected to the same conflation of identity. In other words, although it may be common for Haitians to see *lwas* implied in Catholic hagiography, they do not as a matter of fact perceive automatically of spirits and saints as being one and the same. We will return to this point below. In the case of the Virgin Mary with few minor exceptions, it is Ezili with whom the mother of Jesus Christ is identified.[1] Upon first glance, it might appear indeed that in Haitian Vodou "Mary is Ezili, the Vodou love spirit."[2] But the issue is far more complex than this, and the question remains, what is the nature of the assimilation of these two religious symbols? To what degree can they be said to be truly syncretized? Does the syncretism of visual images and symbols necessarily imply a correspondent syncretism of the spiritual beings or forces they represent? With these questions in mind, in this chapter we analyze the function of Ezili for Vodouisants and the nature of her assimilation with the Virgin Mary.

Ezili: Origins, Characteristics, and Function

The origins of many Vodou spirits, especially those of the *rada* pantheon, are readily traceable to West and Central Africa, and such is the case of Ezili, Vodou's spirit of love, sensuality, and romance. Cults centered around Ezili are still vibrant in parts of West Africa, namely in Benin, Nigeria, and Senegal, where the Haitian counterpart originated. Yet, as with many displaced African spirits, Ezili has undergone something of a personality transformation due to the tremendous upheaval to which she and her devotees in the Americas have been subjected since being torn from the mother continent. Desmangles, in the following passage, discusses the origins of the Ezili spirits and illustrates briefly how Haiti's Ezili differs from her African counterpart. This passage is also of interest to us for its reference to Marian hagiography:

> Ezili in Haiti derives from diverse African ethnic religious traditions, the most notable of which are the Mami Water spirits found in various regions along the western coast of the continent. But most striking are the resemblances between the personae of Ezili in Haiti and those of Oshun in Nigeria and Ezili in Whydah, Benin. In comparing the personae of Oshun and Mary, one notes extraordinary similarities both in the symbols employed and in the significance of those symbols. These resemblances can be seen in the color blue and in the symbolic significance of jewelry—necklaces, bracelets, earrings, and crown—for both the Fon's Ezili and Yoruba's Oshun. The dagger, too, occurs in the depiction of both Oshun and Mary, although its symbolic significance differs. It is these similarities between the Catholic symbols connected with Mary and those of Oshun and Ezili that have caused Vodouisants to identify Mary with Ezili.[3]

As with many Vodou spirits, Ezili is not limited to a single representation, but has numerous and varied manifestations. Some of these manifestations can appear quite the opposite of others. Métraux lists nine Ezilis altogether, most of them rarer *petro* manifestations of minor importance in the Vodou pantheon. Primarily, the cult of Ezili is focused on just two of the *lwas* who bear her name: Ezili Freda-Dahomey, or Maitresse Ezili, and Ezili Danto, or Ezili Ze Rouj (Red Eyes). Ezili Freda "is a member of the *rada* pantheon. Most of these gods are *racine* or root *loa*; i.e., most of them can be easily traced to their African counterparts."[4]

Freda, being the spirit of love, of lovers, and "the goddess of the sensuous,"[5] is one of the most popular *lwas* in Haitian Vodou. She is characterized as a wealthy mulatto woman of radiant beauty, superfluous flamboyance, and extravagant taste. Her devotees are often under considerable economic and spiritual pressure to secure and provide the gifts that Freda so taxingly demands: fine French perfumes and wines, expensive jewelry, satin, and lace. As Karen McCarthy Brown explains, these idiosyncrasies are most palpable during Vodou ceremonies when Ezili possesses her devotees:

> A person who is possessed by Ezili has her (or his) body drenched in perfume, covered with powder, draped in satin and lace. Maitresse Ezili is as extravagant in passing out affection as she is in amassing finery. At a Vodou ceremony, the goddess goes about the temple kissing, greeting, touching, hugging, embracing, and generally reaching out to everyone in sight.... So, affection, love, and approval are the hungers inside Maitresse Erzulie and she searches endlessly for gratification.[6]

Insatiable in her hunger for love and affection, Ezili's countless love affairs with a host of spirits and mortals are among the most colorful tales in Vodou mythology. The copiousness of her desire transcends the chasm between the world of spirits and the world of humans, which actually is a narrower rift in Vodou than in most religions. Many Ezilian devotees, be they married, *plasay* (common law partners), or single, male or female, enter into conjugal relationships with Ezili. Often this involves a wedding ceremony between devotee and spirit, complete with marriage contract and nuptial vows. A kind of asceticism features in these relationships, as one night a week the devotee must sleep apart from his or her worldly partner to await Maitresse Ezili. It is not uncommon for Ezili's human lovers to keep a bed or even a room solely for her weekly nocturnal visits. I know of one wealthy Haitian man who actually purchased, furnished, and maintained a large house for years in upscale Pétion-ville, sleeping there only on Thursday nights, which were reserved for Ezili.

When attempting to understand the assimilation of Ezili with Mary, one question immediately arises, as puzzling as it is obvious: How does such a promiscuous, materialistic figure such as Ezili Freda come to be identified with the seemingly entirely opposite symbol of the Virgin Mary? Perhaps equally intriguing are the differences between the two leading manifestations of Ezili themselves, especially Freda and Danto. To the former question we will return momentarily. To address the latter demands first an introduction to Ezili Danto, the leading *petro* manifestation among the Ezili.

Brown describes the *petro* pantheon as "a fierce and powerful group of deities associated through a variety of symbols—fire, gunpowder, whips, and whistles—from the New World slavery experience."[7] Unlike Freda, Danto is married and rarely enters into relationships with men. She is renown for her capacity for violent anger and militant protectiveness of her children and devotees. Freda, antithetically, is childless, or, by some accounts, has only one child:

> Thus, Maitresse is the lover of all, Danto is the protectress of the chosen few. Where Maitresse tends to self-destruction, Danto is more tempted by infanticide. Where Maitresse demands sexual fidelity, Danto demands familiar loyalty. While Maitresse Ezili is loving above all else, Ezili Danto maintains her integrity above all else. While the exuberance of Maitresse can easily turn into greed, so the honor of Danto can seem rigid and repressive.[8]

Yet in spite of, and perhaps because of, these marked differences, the Ezili form a mosaic that, on a theological level, might be considered Vodou's expression of the divine feminine principle. This, indeed, is the approach of Maya Deren and Leslie Desmangles to understanding Ezili. "Ezili represents the cosmic womb in which the divinity and humanity are conceived," writes Desmangles. "She is the symbol of fecundity, the mother of the world who participates with the masculine forces in the creation and maintenance of the universe."[9]

Describing the Vodou spirits as a representation of the forces of creation, with the *lwas* each playing various roles in the cosmological drama, is certainly valid on one level. However, this perspective is limited, especially if not linked to a careful analysis of the material conditions in which Vodou has developed and is practiced. The validity and relevance of Deren's and Desmangles's cosmological understanding of Ezili can be readily measured through an exploration of the question as to whether Haitians in general really conceive of Ezili in these terms. I suspect there are actually very few who do. However divine they may be, no religion's spirits, symbols, rituals, and ethics are monolithic; the spirits especially usually reflect the lifestyles, sufferings, joys, and aspirations of the people who serve them.

This is one point that Brown forcefully illustrates in her writings on Vodou, which renders her understanding of Ezili sounder than that of either Deren and Desmangles. "Vodou spirits," she writes, "present the world to those who serve them. They present it through all its representative types, male and female, empowered and disempowered."[10] The spirits, in essence, articulate the quotidian options that many Haitians face, and people petition them for guidance in what is for many an onerous existence beset by abject poverty. For most Haitians, life is a struggle for survival with little margin for error. Like Bourdieu, I believe that the sociological study of religion must preference the analysis of the structures of the religious field and their relationship to the religious habiti of agents; therefore, in the Haitian context, this poverty and struggle must be taken into account if we are to understand Vodou and its spirits (or Haitian popular Catholicism and its saints, for that matter) and how they function in Haitians' lives. "Vodou is a religion of survival," notes Brown, "and it counsels what it must to ensure survival."[11]

Thus, it is to the religious needs born of enslavement and poverty that the Vodou spirits respond. Paramount among these is the need for a *bourad* (Creole: "a push") to the next meal, to making the next rent or tuition payment, to placating a lover. Indeed, Vodou is essentially not a religion of high-flung cosmology, but of practical assistance in getting by in this world as best one can. Yet this world is not entirely distinct from that of the spirits, which is precisely what allows the *lwas* to so routinely intervene in the lives of humans, fortifying them in the struggle to survive. "A Vodou spirit is not a deus ex machina but a catalyst who mobilizes the will and energy of human beings."[12] Such is Ezili. Such, for Haitians, is the Virgin Mary as well.

Brown's elucidation of Ezili's function in the lives of Haitian women is an insightful contribution to the understanding of Haitian Vodou, especially of the spirits and their value and relationship to believers. Among the bastion of Vodou spirits, who together, in Brown's view, represent "a language of personality types, clarifying and demarcating styles of life,"[13] Ezili Freda and Ezili Danto are particularly important to Haitian women. In Freda and Danto are reflected two approaches to life that confront Haitian women as existential possibilities, and each serves as a consultative model and as a source of fortitude for their female devotees in their confrontation and negotiation of these possibilities. As such, the Ezili speak to Haitians, and are read by them, as a language:

> The discovery or creation (both are true) of the names of the gods is the discovery and/or creation of a very special sort of language, one especially well suited to handle existential situations, to describe behavior, to understand and judge human action, to build self-awareness and integrity (in both the moral and non-moral senses of the term), to understand oneself and others in the past, and to plan for the future. In short, the gods provide the categories of thought that make people and the situations that arise between them thinkable.[14]

Having served as the mistress to spirits and men (and women) of means, Ezili Freda has reaped a considerable harvest of material reward. She has successfully bartered with her sexuality and thereby wrought for herself a seemingly desirable collection of luxurious things. Yet, the pitfalls of such a lifestyle are evident when Freda breaks into her characteristic inconsolable weeping. Despite all the gifts that men (and women) shower upon her, Ezili Freda remains ultimately unfulfilled. As Deren puts it, "her pain is not only great, but perhaps even eternal…. The wound of Ezili is perpetual."[15] The myths of Ezili and, for that matter, all Vodou spirits thus represents a lesson to Haitians as they square themselves before the existential options that life offers them. For Haitian women, this offering is not entirely free, often demanding some compromise of their sexuality. Such proposals can be hazardous and warrant heedful calculation. As Brown explains, "Ezili Freda drapes herself in romance, wealth and social status and at the same time reminds Haitians how precarious and superficial such things are."[16]

Yet how far does Ezili's pedagogic aspect go in explaining her unsurpassed popularity in Haitian Vodou? Certainly not the entire distance. Deren offers another, perhaps more satisfactory, explanation for the appeal of such a wealthy figure among such poor worshippers:

> Even though (or perhaps precisely because) it is so difficult for him [the Vodouisant] to acquire even those things that are requisite for daily life, he is almost obsessed with the vision of life which would transcend these, a dream of luxury in which even the essentials of life are refined to appear as indulgences. The lady of that sublime luxury is Erzulie. In her character is reflected all the *élan*, all the excessive pitch with which the dreams of men soar, when, momentarily, they can shake loose the flat weight, the dreary, reiterative demands of necessity; and the details with which the serviteur has surrounded her image reflect the poignant, fantastic misconceptions of luxury which a man who has only known poverty could cherish.[17]

Deren's argument is consistent with one of the important conclusions of I.M. Lewis' classic study *Ecstatic Religion*. Lewis highlights the relationship between economic oppression and spirit possession, which is the central religious experience in the cult of Ezili. Briefly stated, Lewis' argument is that cults such as this "appeal most strongly to the subordinate segments of society. To these they offer a consummate religious experience, lifting downtrodden men and women to heights of exaltation which, whatever else they do, certainly serve to underscore the lowly secular position of the possessed devotee."[18] Elsewhere he writes, "possession is concerned essentially with the enhancement of status…to enable people who lack other means of protection and self-promotion to advance their interests and improve their lot by escaping, if only temporarily, from the confining bonds of their allotted stations in society."[19] In Haiti, these bonds are especially confining, and becoming Ezili clearly offers an escape, however fleeting.

In essence Brown's and Deren's discussions of Ezili each represent partial explanations of the goddess' popularity and function; taken together, they suggest that Ezili's function in the lives of her devotees is two-fold. On the one hand, as Freda, she offers to the poor Haitian a flight of fancy, a momentary grasp of otherwise unattainable luxury and ease, an opiate, to use Marx's famous metaphor. On the other hand, Ezili's various manifestations reflect the lives of Haitian women, the paths likeliest to present themselves to these women as existential possibilities, and warning signs about potential pitfalls along these paths. As a goddess who possesses all, yet is consumed by eternal longing and sadness, Ezili's message is universal, somewhat reflective of that of Jesus regarding the fleetingness of worldly possessions. Thus, Ezili functions for Haitians as both an escape from a painful existence and as a guide in the negotiation of this existence. Like the other spirits with whom she shares the Vodou pantheon, like the Virgin Mary as well, Ezili represents a driving force in the struggle for survival.

Theories on Syncretism in African-Based Religions of the Americas

How is it that such a promiscuous, materialistic figure as Ezili, with her rapacious sexuality and insatiable desire for worldly luxury, comes to be identified with the humble, submissive, virginal handmaid of the Lord, Mary, Mother of Jesus? Before discussing this specific example of syncretism between Ezili and the Virgin Mary, it behooves us here to summarize some of the leading arguments on the assimilation of African and Catholic religious beliefs and traditions in the Americas. Indeed, it would be impossible to understand clearly Haitian religious culture without doing so.

As preface to the following discussion, I wish to acknowledge the validity to questioning the question itself. Desmangles, for example, believes that exploring the African and Catholic elements of Haitian Vodou can have the effect of obscuring the "Creoleness" of this belief system, while Hurbon cautions that, "in truth, the use of the concept of syncretism belies a rejection of Vaudou as an original culture and living religion."[20] Hurbon, moreover, reminds us that Catholicism is itself a syncretic religion, implying that in the use of the term syncretism lurks an assumption that Vodou is somehow impure and hence inferior.[21] It is safe to say that "no religion is an island," and therefore that all religions are to some degree syncretic. To acknowledge this is to free the term syncretism of those negative connotations that it has carried as long as it has been employed in reference to religions—usually in reference to the religions of the victims of colonization, as it were. Hence to explore the syncretic nature—the various interreligious strands and intersections inherent to all religions—should be an objective contribution to the research and understanding of any religious tradition. That, in any case, is my intention in the present discussion.

There are basically three theories, expressed in various forms, advanced in the effort to gauge the degree of African and Catholic influences in African-derived religions of the Caribbean and South America. What follows is a survey of each of these theories as found in the writings of several important scholars of neo-African cultures, intertwined with brief illustrations of the suggestive relevance of Bourdieu's theory of practice to the question at hand.

Five writers who have devoted considerable attention to the question of the *Africanité* and Catholicity of African-based religions of the Americas are Métraux, Desmangles, Melville J. Herskovits, Roger Bastide, and Raoul Canizares. Expressed in different ways, their writings embody the three leading theories discussed here: (1) The synthesis theory—which holds that the two religious systems are so genuinely and thoroughly "fused" together so as to form a third distinct religion; (2) the symbiosis theory—which holds that African and Catholic elements exist and function side by side as part of a total mosaic, without any truly substantial fusion occurring; and (3) the theory of dissimulation—which holds that Catholic elements of ritual and symbolism were merely draped over the African in efforts to conceal the latter in an environment that was hostile to their survival.

Métraux's understanding of Vodou is representative of the synthesis theory, viewing Vodou as a "fusion" of traditional African and Catholic beliefs, liturgy, and ritual. His very definition of Vodou reflects this: "a new syncretic religion"[22] characterized by "a very syncretic quality by which it blends together, in almost equal proportions, African rites and Catholic observances."[23] Métraux's approach to the question is mainly historical, highlighting the effects of the periods of physical disconnection with official Catholicism in Haitian history, as discussed above in chapter two. There is some agreement among scholars that the crystallization of Haitian Vodou occurred roughly between 1760 and 1860. As we have seen, the second half of this period witnessed a virtual void of "official" Catholicism in Haiti. It strikes Métraux as remarkable that Vodou, with all its Catholic embellishments, developed during this absence of orthodox Catholicism. Hence, he believes that the phenomenon of African survivals in Haitian Vodou is exceeded in noteworthiness by the fact that Haitians with little or no formal Catholic religious instruction, free of the imposing supervision of orthodox religious specialists, took it upon themselves to continue saying and attending Mass and performing other Catholic rituals, which they incorporated into the Vodouisant religious system. In effect, they saw Catholic religious capital as effective, hence "the rapid intermingling of so many Catholic elements that were greedily adopted,"[24] by the popular masses. Métraux refers to "this veritable seizure of Catholicism by Vodou"[25] as "the root"[26] of "*le mélange.*"

An application of certain Bourdieuean concepts begets an expansion of Métraux's argument for the synthesis theory. The largely West African religious habitus of most Haitians during Vodou's formative period, even those several generations removed from Africa, predisposed the formulators of Vodou to assess certain foreign forms of religious capital, both European and newly discovered African forms, out of their original contexts, as valid. Thus, in the absence of orthodoxy's religious specialists—who normally would otherwise have carried out a vigorous campaign to control religious capital, especially "the goods of salvation," or sacraments—the African and Creole religious consumers in Saint-Domingue were free to adopt, translate, and administer Catholic symbols and rituals to suit their own express religious needs and interests. As Father Lecum, one of the half dozen or so Catholic priests remaining in Haiti in 1804, observed, "In most parishes, Negroes took pieces of holy ornaments and sacred vessels, and though they don't know how to read, they administered all the sacraments and even celebrated Masses."[27]

The assertion I am here making, that "this veritable seizure of Catholicism by Vodou" in Saint-Domingue is explicable by reference to an interest in alien forms of religious capital characteristic of a definitively African religious habitus, is supported by the fact that similar phenomena occurred in Africa, where early missionaries complained of the "theft" of holy water and other orthodox sacred objects. Wyatt MacGaffey provides analogous evidence among the Kongo, who were first exposed to Christianity by Portuguese missionaries early in the sixteenth century. The Portuguese mission was soon thereafter abandoned, and a second wave of Capuchin missionaries sent by Rome in the late seventeenth century "were hailed as *banganga za n'kisi* (magicians) of Nzambi Mpungu (God)." A ritual sack hung around the neck of the traditional Kongo king contained, among other charms, "a bull from pope Urban VIII authorizing the coronation." In yet another example, "the governing (Kongo) class made use of the missionaries at times to keep the population in subjection by threats of mystical penalties,"[28] a tactic that would have been neither effective nor concocted were it not for the popular estimation of Catholic religious capital among the seventeenth century Kongolese, a population who would make up over 50 percent of slave imports to Saint-Domingue in the three decades prior to the Haitian Revolution. A capacity to synthesize foreign forms of religious capital is, therefore, demonstrable as a chief characteristic of the African religious habitus.

To return to the discussion of the nature of religious syncretism in African-American cultures, Herskovits, like Métraux, holds to the synthesis theory, arguing that practitioners of hybrid forms of African religions in the New World found elements of Catholic ritual and liturgy as religiously powerful. Hence the birth of "a new syncretic religion." As with most scholars who address this question in the Haitian context, Herskovits points to the conflation of Catholic saints as depicted in popular chromolithographs with Vodou *lwas*. Catholic missionaries widely distributed these lithographs throughout Haiti in the late nineteenth and early twentieth centuries. Whether originally symbolic or not, certain images accompanying the saints depicted in the lithographs came to be identified with the characteristics of Vodou spirits, thus effecting a conflation of saints and *lwas*.

For example, St. Patrick is depicted as standing over a number of the serpents that he allegedly expelled from Ireland; thus, in Vodou he came to be identified with Damballah, the originally Fon snake spirit.

Unlike Métraux, who dismissed such visual identification as ultimately insignificant and tangential to Vodou, Herskovits asserts this phenomenon to be "the most vivid evidence of the intermingling of Catholic and Vodou elements at the heart of Haitian Vodou."[29] Despite this point of contention, Herskovits and Métraux are in accord in believing some degree of genuine "fusion" between Catholic and traditional African elements to have taken place in Vodou's formative development.

Roger Bastide, writing about African cultural survivals in Brazil, offers an analysis markedly more sophisticated than that of Herskovits. Like Métraux, Bastide emphasizes the historical context of the meeting of the different religious systems and concludes that the first incidents to occur between them was what he terms "syncretism in mosaic."[30] This is the first of three forms of syncretism outlined by Bastide. Along with Bastide's second form, "syncretism in correspondence,"[31] it is the most important form of syncretism, representing clearly the symbiosis theory, wherein elements of each system exist side by side as pieces of the same mosaic without any significant interpenetration transpiring.

It is Bastide's contention that the earliest phases of any syncretism were forced upon the collective worldview of the enslaved African and Creole peoples by the physical displacement of transatlantic slavery. For instance, African spirits were removed from their traditional harvest cycles that had largely determined the schedule and types of rituals with which they were associated. Consequently, in Brazil, as in Haiti, Catholic holy days became feasts for African spirits in the Americas. Bastide refers to this kind of syncretism as "syncretism in mosaic."

Among the three forms of syncretism outlined by Bastide, the second, "syncretism in correspondence," he claims, is "the most widespread and most often studied."[32] Syncretism in correspondence, exemplified by the lithograph phenomenon in Haiti, is the identification of an African religious symbol with a Catholic one on the basis of visual association. Unlike Métraux, however, who sees this as a superficial association, Bastide holds that the syncretism in correspondence seen in the conflation of Catholic saints with African spirits reflects the understanding in African based New World religions that "the saints are taken to be co-mediaries with the African spirits, both operative in the intermediary realm on behalf of those in the material world."[33] Bastide correctly points out how the compatibility of the Catholic and African pantheons readily facilitated this kind of syncretism. Generally speaking, the traditional African conception is of a single high creator God, Nzambe Mpungu for the Bakongo, for example, who is so remote as to be unapproachable. Hence Africans traditionally address their petitions and prayers to the lesser intermediary spirits. Likewise, Catholics often beseech Mary and other saints to pray to the one God the Father on their behalf.

"Syncretisme en reinterpretation," or of "collective conscious,"[34] Bastide's third category of syncretism, approaches the synthesis theory in meaning. Syncretism in reinterpretation occurs when, for example, biblical myths are taken and appropriated, interpreted in a manner rooted in the distinct experience of the interpreters, who, in the case of Bastide's and our analysis, are the enslaved African and Creole peoples of the Americas. Also, in rare instances when a Catholic saint is actually transformed into a Vodou *lwa*, as in the case of St. James the Greater becoming *Sen Jak Majeur*, syncretism in reinterpretation is evident.

In any case, predominant in Bastide's discussion, taking his three notions as a single argument, is the theory of symbiosis: the African and the Catholic elements of belief, liturgy, and symbolism exist side by side, even in the spiritual world, where Catholic saints and African spirits function on behalf of their material world devotees, without any profound interpenetration transpiring between the two. The religious mosaics of Vodou in Haiti, Santería in Cuba, and Candomblé and Umbanda in Brazil all emerged in this manner.

Desmangles's discussion of the degree of formative African and Catholic influence in Haitian Vodou reads as little more than a rehashing of Bastide's, with Desmangles's "symbiosis by ecology"[35] and "symbiosis by identification"[36] corresponding exactly to Bastide's syncretism in mosaic and syncretism in correspondence respectively. Desmangles, like Hurbon, does raise an important reason for pause regarding the study of syncretism, adding a provocative example to the entire debate. Echoing Hurbon's concern that the kind of investigation under discussion might function as a negation of Vodou's genuine originality, Desmangles expresses regret that the search for Vodou's African and Catholic roots usually breeds oversight of the fact that Vodou is a religious expression of the Creole people, who are neither African nor European. He prefers "to describe Vodou as a *tertium quid*; part of which is a Creole phenomenon that owes little to Africa or Europe but is indigenous to Haiti, born out of the difficulties and oppressive conditions of slavery and the necessary adaptation to a new environment."[37]

Without exception, those who address this subject include reference to the chromolithographs in their discussions. Some, like Métraux, privilege the analysis of ritual. Desmangles adds to these references a significant object of analysis in the form of a person, the *pret savan* (literally "bush priest"), who represents "the symbolic embodiment of the contact between Catholicism and Vodou."[38] The *pret savan*, "whose function is to invoke the benediction of the Christian deity on the Vodou ceremony,"[39] possesses far less sacramental power than the *oungan* or *mambo*, but is nonetheless an important sacerdotal figure in Haitian Vodou. The *pret savan's* main task in certain Vodou ceremonies (baptism for example) is to recite the litany of Catholic hymns, prayers, and chants, and to manipulate the Catholic symbols that usually open such ceremonies. Once he finishes, the *pret savan* steps aside and the *oungan* or *mambo* takes over and continues with the decidedly African-based elements of the ritual at hand.

For Desmangles, this juxtaposition of *pret savan* and *oungan* offers clear evidence of Vodou's symbiotic nature:

> Vodouisants have learned to separate the functions of each of these persons as well as their use of ritual paraphernalia in Vodou ceremonies. The Vodou and the Catholic objects possess their own power related to different aspects of reality: those of the church represent the power of the Godhead, and those of the oungan, the power of the Gods of Africa.[40]

In Bourdieuean terms, the *pret savan* may thus be conceived of as a religious specialist operative in a heterodox subfield in a fashion quasi-representative of the dominant orthodoxy, or of Catholicism.

His role in Vodou is explained by the access he is believed to have to orthodox forms of religious capital, particularly the benediction of the supreme Godhead, who is popularly conceived of as more accessible through Catholicism than through Vodou. As Desmangles demonstrates:

> Because the church does not approve of Vodou and has attempted so often in the past to control it, Vodouisants feel the need for some symbol of the church's sanction of their religious activities in order to create an overt similarity between the two religious systems. They therefore have attempted to provide, within the structure of their rituals, what they consider to be desirable in Catholicism.[41]

Given the consistency with which Bourdieu employs economic metaphors in his theory of practice, it would be neither exaggerated nor inappropriate to refer to the *pret savan* as a sort of unlicensed black market peddler of orthodox religious capital. His function is determined by the laws of supply and demand in the Vodou subfield. Vodouisants' religious habiti predispose them to deem as desirable and efficacious certain forms of Catholic religious capital, their religious interest thus representing the supply side of the equation, which renders relevant the *pret savan's* function as independent supplier of orthodox religious capital.

Both the synthesis and symbiosis theories are supportive of my argument that the incorporation of Catholic fragments into the mainly African-derived religious system of Haitian Vodou is explicable in terms of a characteristic tolerance traceable to the African religious habitus, which predisposed African and Creole slaves, and later juridically free Haitians, to esteem certain forms of orthodox Catholic symbolism and ritual as powerful and effective, and hence worthy of consumption. This is the main reason why certain Catholic traits became elemental to Haitian Vodou, and is clearly a major force behind Mary's popularity in Haitian religion.

There remains a third theory, the theory of dissimulation, that stands in direct contention to the argument I am making here, to which our attention must now turn. Writing about Cuban Santería, Raoul Canizares argues that enslaved Africans originally used Catholic symbols and rituals merely to mask African traditions that were illegal in all New World plantation colonies.[42]   According to Canizares' theory of "dissimulation," slaves adopted Catholic symbols, feast days, and rituals in colonial Cuba not for any effective religious value that they were thought to possess, but as instruments of concealment in attempts to mask and thereby perpetuate otherwise threatened African traditions.

While interesting and supported by concrete examples, Canizares' theory is underdeveloped and, in one sense, fallacious. From the single fact that particular examples are evidence of a masking that did occur, one cannot deduce a lack of genuine interest in orthodox Catholic ritual and symbolism among the enslaved population in Cuba. Canizares commits a fallacy of generalization in offering a partial explanation as the comprehensive one. Moreover, the general impression he gives is that Catholicism is not a significant part of Santería, contrary to Vodou, where Vodouisants have, as illustrated above, lent great credence to Catholic religious capital in its own right, hence the popular Creole expression, "*pou sevi lwa yo se pou'w bon katolik*" ("to serve the *lwas*, one must be a good Catholic"). It would remain for Canizares to explain why—if Santería's debt to Catholicism is indeed different—enslaved Africans in Cuba, coming from the very same parts of Africa as their Haitian counterparts, with virtually the same religious habitus, were not similarly impressed with Catholicism.

All of the writers represented here do, in fact, acknowledge that the need to conceal African religious practices did play some role in *le mélange*, and I by no means intend to argue to the contrary. Yet few would go so far as Canizares to suggest that this is the central explanation of how Catholic and African elements merged to form the African-derived religions of the Americas. It is far more reasonable to assert that those victimized by the transatlantic slave trade very naturally sought means of dealing with their plight in the new religions encountered along their tragic way. I fully agree, then, with Métraux where he writes, "In giving a Catholic cachet to ceremonies which are not Catholic, Voodooists are in no way trying to pull the wool over the eyes of authorities or the Church: rather it is that *they are convinced of the efficacy of Catholic liturgy and therefore wish their own religion to benefit from it.*"[43]

I have expounded on this debate at considerable length for several reasons. For one, we may now proceed to analyze the specific case of syncretism between Ezili and Mary in an intelligent, informed fashion. Furthermore, my argument in chapter two was that the historical structure of the Haitian religious field, and therefore the background and context of Haitian Marianism, was largely shaped in an atmosphere of competitive struggle between Vodou and Catholicism. This detailed summary of the leading theories on the syncretism inherent to Haitian Vodou and—to a lesser degree especially since Vatican II—to popular Haitian Catholicism further clarifies this struggle. While I would favor something of a compromise between the synthesis and the symbiosis theories, with a functionalist bent—one stressing the merging of different religions evident in Vodou as functioning "as a manner of overcoming ethnic or cultural contradictions, and as such a new synthesis that will serve as a basis of cohesion"[44]—it must be stressed that whatever theory is adopted, scholars are clearly in agreement that Haitian Vodou is decidedly far more African in essence than Catholic, being "in structure and spirit...essentially Dahomean."[45]

To reiterate the salient point, once the absorbent nature of African religious traditions is taken into account, a functionalist perspective on syncretism in Haitian religion emerges as appropriate. Again, Bosal (African-born) and Creole slaves perceived Catholic religious symbols as altogether functional, since those who were employing them, namely the whites, were powerful beyond imagination. It is thus likely that religious syncretism occurred from the very moment that Catholic symbols were introduced to those with an African religious habitus (the religious habitus of many of the thousands of Kongolese brought to the colony, moreover, was already Catholicized prior to enslavement). The Virgin Mary, certainly one of the first and most emphasized of these Catholic symbols, was immediately identified with the leading feminine religious symbols of the displaced African religions in Hispaniola. Ezili, as it turned out, was prevalent among these.

Pre-Lithograph Syncretism in Haitian Religion

Evidence abounds in the historical accounts of early French travelers and missionaries of the slaves' affinity for Catholic ritual paraphernalia. We have already cited a few.[46] In reality, reference to this phenomenon amounts to historical evidence of expansionist religious adaptation rather than genuine conversion to the Catholic faith. As one of the first and most promoted of Catholic symbols by both the French and the Spanish, it is reasonable to argue that Mary has undergone a longer, more extensive process of assimilation than any other Catholic symbol in the Haitian religious field, save perhaps the cross. Whether this implies that there have been different stages of Marian syncretism in Haitian religious history is difficult to say, though it is possible, as argued in chapter four, that during the first Jesuit mission in the eighteenth century a decline in Marian syncretism and a proportionate rise in orthodox Marian devotion may have occurred. A significant development in the degree and complexity of syncretism, in any case, definitely took place with the late-nineteenth century introduction to Haitians of lithographs depicting Catholic saints. Marian inculturation would thereafter emerge as the most complicated example of interreligious assimilation in the field, as the proliferation of various icons of Mary encouraged heterogeneous syncretism with the different manifestations of Ezili. The nature and forms of syncretism before the introduction of the lithographs, however, is much less clear.

Prior to the proliferation of the lithographs in the Haitian religious field, images of Mary were limited to devotional manuals, medals, and church art. A striking example of the latter is the wall carving in the cathedral at Cap-Haïtien, described here by one admiring nineteenth-century French priest:

> on the wall itself is sculpted in plaster an Assumption of the Holy Virgin, among three apostles, two of whom are looking at an empty tomb, the third contemplating Mary being lifted into heaven upon a cloud, while two angels pose a crown upon her head.[47]

How must this elaborate sculpture have appeared to someone whose religious habitus was decidedly African or Vodouisant? It is quite probable that instances like this of pre-lithograph Marian syncretism was, like the lithograph-based forms of syncretism, also superficial and characterized almost wholly by the visual identification of images and symbols, with no dependence whatsoever on the stories and teachings behind the Catholic figures. Vodou mythology, on the other hand, played a major role in determining the assimilation between saints and *lwas*. Damballah, for instance, is identified with St. Patrick because of the snakes at Patrick's feet; knowledge of Patrick's expulsion of the snakes from Ireland is unimportant here. Thus the woman on the wall of the Cap cathedral must have been identified with Ezili mainly and simply because she was a woman. Her crown must also have immediately been seen as another of Ezili's luxurious accouterments. The fact that Our Lady of the Assumption is the object of attention and is offered a gift in this sculpture could also have been interpreted clearly as Ezilian. Furthermore, the angels may very well have been taken to be Ezili Danto's children, as they would be later in Vodouisants' perception of several Marian icons depicted in lithographs.

In the historical accounts, however, there is no direct reference to the identification of Mary with any African spirit among the slaves, though it is reasonable to suspect that indeed they must initially have perceived the Virgin to be some peculiar manifestation of the goddesses of the homeland. The missionaries were surely aware of this, as, as seen in chapter three, historically the Catholic clergy has attempted to eradicate the worship of "pagan" goddesses by eclipsing them with Mary, although on the popular level:

> In fact, it looks as if the imagery of the older goddesses had passed directly onto Mary, inspired by the needs of the people and perhaps also by the understanding of the priests that these long-established customs of devotion had to be understood in terms of the new religion. Sometime between AD 400 and 500 the Temple of Isis at Soissons in France was dedicated to the "Blessed Virgin Mary." Isis and Cybele had been "Mother of the Gods"; Mary was now "Mother of God."[48]

There is every reason to believe that by the Catholic clergy in the "New World" took a similar attitude regarding the feminine deities of the people whom they evangelized:

> Those evangelizing at that time were always preoccupied with replacing the deity of the mother-goddess with Our Lady in order to prevent, as they saw it, the continuation of idolatry. . .Nevertheless, one can say there was a syncretist

integration of the great deities of the Indians (and later of the blacks)....[49]

In Haitian religious history, the case of Romaine-la-Prophétesse is the first clear example of the appropriation of the symbol of Mary among the subjugated, though it is anything but evident that Romaine identified the Virgin Mary with any particular African goddess. While less definitive, there is another historical account from the revolutionary period that suggests Marian appropriation among the under-classes, this one from the north. A French priest, describing the tumultuous events in Cap-Haitïen during the very same period of Romaine's campaign in the south, laments the waywardness of one of his best students as he writes the following intriguing passage:

> An ex-student, among the most intelligent, became the leader of an Amazon gang and would be known in history as Princess Amesythe. Initiated in the sect of Ghioux or Vaudoux, a sort of religious and dancing Freemasonry...introduced by the *Rada* women to Saint-Domingue, she dragged a fair number of her colleagues into the sect.[50]

Princess Amesythe's "Amazon gang" must have been especially troublesome to the Jesuits and Daughters of Notre Dame since its membership seems to have been comprised of their own students, who otherwise carried on as if devout Catholics. "Their piety seemed not at all diminished, since the sectarians permitted the adoration of Our Savior, devotions to Mary, the wearing of the scapular, and even denounced the blasphemies against Our Savior."[51] Yet these same young women could be seen and heard at night in the streets and on the outskirts of town dancing and singing:

> *Eh Ehe Bomba*
> *Canga bafio te*
> *Canga Mousse Canga do ki la*
> *Canga li.*[52]

—all the while wearing their trademark red kerchiefs. Jan's account suggests that these very "sectarians" took part in the slaughter of the Daughters of Notre Dame two years later.

The historical researcher working with indirect textual references such as these runs the risk of over-extending the implications of the passage at hand. Aware of this, I would nonetheless venture that the above account is suggestive of a symbiotic appropriation of Mary in revolutionary-era Haitian Vodou. That the followers of Princess Amesythe, who herself was probably a *mambo*, continued with their Marian devotions in a fashion satisfactory to the Jesuits implies that ostensibly Mary was venerated in a separate time and place than the *lwas*. Moreover, that the "Amazon gang" "denounced blasphemy against Our Savior" indicates that they were probably sincere in their Catholic practice despite their nocturnal apostasy. Catholic by day in the Jesuit-influenced mission environment; Vodouisant by night in the streets and forests. What could more clearly evince the symbiotic nature of *le mélange* than this?

It would thus seem, from this account, that in the late-eighteenth century Haitian religious field the nature of the assimilation between Mary and Ezili was symbiotic—specifically an example of "symbiosis by identification," to adopt Desmangles's terminology: "a system of identification or transfiguration by which, on the basis of the similarities between African and Catholic myths and symbols the saints were identified with African gods."[53] While during the slave era this identification may have in part served to mask the forbidden service of African spirits, the adoption of Mary by Vodouisants is more correctly understandable in functionalist terms—the Virgin is a functional religious symbol, therefore, she is adopted. Mary thus becomes, for Haitians, a leading member of the spirit world, which consists of both African gods and Catholic saints. Her identification with Ezili, in my judgment, is superficial and of far less weight than most writers on Vodou would be willing to admit. In several hundred interviews, very few of my informants have expressly identified Ezili and Mary as one and the same. For most of those who admitted to revering both, my impression is that each operates as distinct in their belief system—as parts of a mosaic consisting of Catholic and African spirits, each invoked for their miraculous interventionist powers to aid the believer in the struggle of life. This insight is consistent with Bastide's position quoted above: "the saints are taken to be co-mediaries with the African spirits, both operative in the intermediary realm on behalf of those in the material world."

Desmangles's field research, nearly two centuries removed from Princess Amesythe's movement, also demonstrates that the assimilation of Mary and Ezili is quite symbiotic, rather than syncretic. At Saut-d'Eau, Desmangles was struck by:

> a marked change in the religious attitude of devotees as they traversed from the Vodou site to the village and vice versa: in the countryside, they "served" the *lwas* by loud singing and violent possessions, while at the church they showed more subdued devotion by quietly praying before the statues of the saints. During the entire period of the Fete, there were no Vodou ceremonies in the village. The devotees attended the numerous masses during the day of the Fete, received communion, and lit their votive candles to the Virgin and to the other saints that adorn the church's sanctuary.[54]

My own observations at Saut-d'Eau, for the most part, corroborate Desmangles's findings, though I did observe one Vodou ceremony in the village itself. Moreover, the Marian devotion he describes is apparently that which takes place between Masses, which is indeed most solemn. The Eucharistic celebrations at Saut-d'Eau, hardly characterized by "quiet praying," were the liveliest I have witnessed in Haiti, though this cannot be taken as an indication of Vodouisant worship in the church itself. For the most part, the nature of the Marian devotions in and around the Church of Our Lady of Mount Carmel in Ville-Bonheur during pilgrimage season differed in no significant way from that at the Church of *Notre Dame du Perpétuel Secours* in Bel-Air, the Church of Our Lady of Mount Carmel at Bizoton, or other Marian pilgrimage sites in Haiti on feast days.

A significant conclusion may be drawn from these observations: the identification of Mary and Ezili in Haitian religion is symbiotic rather than syncretic. In other words, the assimilation of Mary and Ezili in popular Haitian Catholicism and Vodou is a prime example of symbiosis by identification, or, to use Bastide's more original term, syncretism in correspondence, where each symbol has its specific time and place, each offering certain levels of recourse and power, while maintaining her individuality surprisingly in tact. Mary and Ezili are identified visually and superficially primarily because they are women. Such was probably the case as much before as after the introduction of the lithographs into the field, which did, of course, complicate the nature of syncretism considerably. On the level of meaning and internal theological characteristics, the assimilation of saints and *lwas* is altogether weak and ambiguous, bearing little if any weight on their devotees' belief systems, and does practically nothing to generate wholesale syncretism. The visual identification of symbols in Catholic iconography with symbols in Vodouisant mythology and popular Haitian religious imagination performs an almost exclusive function in this regard. This conclusion—that in the main the identification of Mary and Ezili in Haitian popular religion is merely visual and emotive and does not fully penetrate to a cognitive level—will be fortified in chapters six and seven through a more thorough process of verification against the findings of my field research.

August 15: Symbiosis by Ecology

That the invocation and celebration of Mary has long sparked religious fervor in both Catholic and Vodou circles is evidenced by the following testimony of a school teacher, who describes here the festivities surrounding the celebration of the feast of *Notre Dame de l'Assomption* in Cap-Haïtien in 1840:

> From the morning Angelus on Saturday August 15, all the bells tolled, announcing to the faithful the great solemnity of this day, Feast of *Notre Dame de l'Assomption, Fête Paroissiale*. At two in the afternoon, at the beginning of vespers, the procession of the Virgin began, with a great crowd, brilliance, and majesty.... Every city quarter was decorated with superb ribbons of light. The church entrance was most tastefully illumined with glass bulbs of various colors.... In the *Place d'Armes* there were public dances that lasted through to the following morning. For the entire day, after the [formal] religious ceremonies, there was great public rejoicing. Without confronting the least

disorder, one could see the joy painted on all faces, as the frankest gaiety animated everyone.[55]

The dancing continued for the next two nights in the city square, although Mary's feast day was technically over. These celebrations attracted people from afar, as "five or six societies from the plain came to the city, their flags flying with their different decorations, and danced to the beat of their tom-tom, continuing like this for several days their noisy dances."[56]

What should we make of this remarkable account? It is evident that in 1840 Mary was a forceful religious symbol for the under-class masses. Yet, were the "noisy dances" that continued for days after the feast of the Assumption of Mary actually celebrations of Mary at all? Tom-toms (or "*tambours,*" as they are called in both French and Haitian Creole), themselves a sacramental feature of Vodou, have only been incorporated into Catholic worship in Haiti since Vatican II. The boisterousness, public dancing, and flights of ecstasy described here are hardly typical of congregational Haitian Marian piety, which, on the contrary, is usually characterized by reserved solemnity and penitent supplication. In reality, the danc-ing masses in the city square were participating in a Vodou celebra-tion of particular importance: the feast of "Mambo Inan," primal mother of 101 Vodou spirits. Beauvoir-Dominique explains that some Vodouisants believe Mambo Inan to be the mother of all the *lwas* of Vodou's Kongo pantheon, 101 in all. The occasion of the August 15 feast of the Assumption of Mary has simply been adopted by Vodouisants as that of Mambo Inan, a clear example of symbio-sis by ecology, or syncretism in mosaic. That some refer to Inan "Queen Mother" suggests that symbiosis by identification has also occurred between this *lwa* and Our Lady of the Assumption. In an interview with leaders of the Nan Soukri Vodou sanctuary in Gonaïves, supposedly the repository of the "purest and most royal" form of Kongo religious expression in Haiti, Beauvoir-Dominique was informed of the conflation of Mambo Inan with *Notre Dame de l'Assomption*:

> On August 15, under the pretext of the Assumption is cel-ebrated Mambo Inan. Mambo Inan is represented as you see her in the image [of the Assumption]. Look there,

surrounded...by who do you think? ("The little angels, so
they say...") Oh no! Those are not angels at all! Those
are her children....[57]

Another ubiquitous reason underlying the dancers' energetic festivities in Cap-Haïtien's city square was the anniversary of the August 14, 1791 ceremony at Bois Caïman, discussed in chapter two,
which many credit as having sparked the Haitian Revolution, ultimately resulting in the emancipation of the enslaved. Beauvoir-
Dominique's interesting discussion of the Vodouisants' association
of Notre Dame de l'Assomption with Cecile Fatima, the old woman
who is said to have sacrificed the pig at Bois Caïman, is worth
quoting here at length:

> For the descendants of the rebel slaves, the dogma of the
> Assumption as understood by Christians constitutes proof
> of misunderstanding: it is obvious (for Vodouisdants) that
> a body could never be materially assumed into heaven.
> The truth, according to them, is that Cecile Fatima (the
> old woman) remained possessed by Ezili Je-wouj (femi-
> nine *petro* divinity) during the entire night of the 14th,
> that is, through to the 15th, and it was not until this date
> that the divinity departed. This much is perfectly com-
> prehensible in the cultural context. "But the body remained
> there!! What do you expect?! It is the *lwa* that departed."
> Thus, the feast of Notre Dame of August, or the so called
> Assumption, is as much a celebration of Bois Caïman....[58]

Adding further to the nationalist mysticism surrounding the dates
August 14th and 15th and *Notre Dame de l'Assomption*, on August
14, 1934, the American flag was lowered and the Haitian flag flew
once again over the nation, ending nineteen years of brutal foreign
occupation. It is likely that many Haitian Vodouisants understood
the departure of the U.S. Marines as an event arranged by *Notre
Dame de l'Assomption*.[59] Hence, the confluence of certain momentous events in Haitian history that occurred on either the 14th or
15th of August with the feast day of *Notre Dame de l'Assomption*
has served to fuse Haitian Marianism and nationalism, amounting
to a rehashing of a similar nationalist Marian fusion in the original
form of Marianism brought to the island by the Spanish. It is thus

evident why *Notre Dame de l'Assomption* is popularly referred to in Haiti as *Notre Dame d'Août* (Our Lady of August).[60]

In light of the connection between Mary, Boukman, and the departure of the white occupying forces in 1934, it is not surprising that Mary was invoked once again in 1994 to inspire resistance against a foreign invasion, albeit this time an invasion that most Haitians would welcome enthusiastically. The summer of 1994 often witnessed General Cédras (a Protestant!) and the high command of the *putchist* army on the balcony of military headquarters in Port-au-Prince standing just above a large icon of *Perpétuel Secours*, saluting their troops and recent civilian recruits (or forced inscriptions) on the eve of the imminent U.S. military intervention to oust them from power and to return democratically-elected President Jean-Bertrand Aristide to the majestic national palace on the Champ-de-Mars.61 Equally unsurprising were the murals that appeared in Port-au-Prince slums, after Aristide's return, of the priest/president replacing the child Jesus in the arms of *Notre Dame du Perpétuel Secours*, as oppressed Catholics throughout Latin America have over and again reclaimed the Virgin for their own cause, cleansing her of her complicity in the injustice against which they struggle. These two images reflect two recurrent tendencies in the history of Haitian Marianism: (1) The tendency of for certain dominant sectors, like the slave regime and the Cédras junta, to re-adapt the symbol of the Virgin Mary to legitimize repressive social structures; and (2) the tendency of the underclass to see through their oppressors' twisted manipulation of the Virgin and re-appropriate Mary as a force of strength in their own opposition to social inequality and to resistance against subjugation.

Lithograph-Based Marian/Ezilian Symbiosis: The Example of Czestochowa/Danto

With the proliferation of the lithographs depicting Catholic saints and the concomitant introduction of images of Mary different from those already known in the Haitian religious field, extraordinary developments unfolded in the synthesis of the saints and *lwas*. Since, as has been seen, Ezili is embodied in a variety of manifestations, it would strike Vodouisants as only logical that so too should the Virgin Mary appear in so many different icons. "Although these litho-

graphs, used by the Church in the past mainly for religious instruction, ostensibly to represent the Virgin Mary in her various roles as
they are depicted in the New Testament, in Catholic hagiography,
and in Catholic oral tradition, are nevertheless interpreted by
Vodouisants as representations of the various personages of Ezili."[62]
Which particular Marian icon would ultimately come to be conflated
with which particular Ezili was determined primarily, if not exclusively, by the visual association of aspects of the figures in the lithographs with characteristics of the *lwas* expressed in Vodou mythology or possession experiences. Métraux provides insightful commentary on this process. "Often it is a mere detail, to our eyes an
unimportant one, though important in the context of Vodou mythology, for a poster to be selected as a representation of this or that
African divinity."[63] Although arguing that when Vodouisants perceive these images, especially when on the wall of the *ounfò* (Vodou
temple), the identity of the *lwa* eclipses that of the saint, Métraux
admits that "we cannot really talk of a true assimilation of *lwa* and
saints...."[64] Métraux never directly poses, however, the question as
to whether the same image in the Catholic setting undergoes the
same process of transformation in the perception of the Vodouisant.

   Perhaps to Haitians the most striking image of Mary that the
lithographs introduce is Mater Salvatoris, familiar to Haitians primarily in the form of Our Lady of Czestochowa, the Polish black
Virgin. This is "the chromolithograph Haitians most often use to
represent Ezili Danto."[65] In this icon Mary, with halo and jeweled
crown framing her shrouded head, casts a stern, confident stare
directly at the viewer. She holds her right hand against her chest,
while the child Jesus, also adorned with crown and halo, sits in her
left arm. The child appears the personification of sacred wisdom,
seated squarely and erect, a closed book held on his lap by his left
hand, while his right hand reaches toward his mother's face in a
pedagogic, almost admonishing gesture. Beauvoir-Dominique feels
the book is an example of one of those details described above by
Métraux as "to our eyes unimportant," though meaningful to the
Vodouisant. "What is this book? No doubt it is a "magic book,"
according to popular belief, wherein are held all her recipes, the
source of her power, of all that which renders the figure awesome."[66]

   The more obviously compelling features of this icon are the two
vertical scars on the Virgin Mother's right cheek, which "corre-

spond, in Vodou mythology, to a story of a fight between Ezili Freda, Ezili Danto and Ogun (St. Jacques).... The image thus reinforces the legend that this Black Virgin is especially powerful."[67] Desmangles posits that the scars "symbolize her (Danto's) occasional *Petro* anger when she is said to tear the flesh of recalcitrant devotees."[68] One of Brown's informants, meanwhile, expressed the belief that the scars were gotten while Ezili fought on behalf of the enslaved in the Haitian Revolution.[69]

I am inclined to disagree with Brown's assertion that in the Czestochowa icon, "[t]he child is the most important iconographic detail, for Ezili Danto is above all else the mother, the one who bears children. This explains why certain white Virgins depicted with children, especially Our Lady of Lourdes and Our Lady of Mount Carmel are also said to be Ezili Danto."[70] This explanation is questionable because of the simple fact that the leading figure of Mary in the Haitian religious field, *Notre Dame du Perpétuel Secours*, also holds a child but is identified by many Haitians with Freda, while by others as Danto.[71] Czestochowa's scars or her dark skin, it would appear, are of greater influence on her assimilation with Danto than is the presence of the child.

Yet, perhaps such explanations as these assume an inherent logic in the syncretism of *lwas* and saints that simply does not exist. For example, in the chromolithograph depicting *Maria Dolorosa de Monte Calvaro*, a sword penetrates the heart of the Virgin, a decidedly violent image that one would expect to lead to association with Danto or some other *petro* Ezili. Instead, "Haitians recognize this image as Ezili Freda."[72] In the final analysis, these observations instruct that pause is warranted before attempting to draw conclusions about the underlying reasons for a particular saint's conflation with a particular *lwa*. In other words, there are no clear-cut, comprehensive explanations for this important phenomenon in Haitian religion.

On The Worth of Reconciling Virginity and Promiscuity

In spite of seemingly clear ambiguities in the assimilation of certain Marian icons with Ezili Freda or Ezili Danto, it is plain that at least since the lithographs became widespread in the Haitian religious field that this synthesis is explicable mainly in terms of the visual association of symbols and characteristics. The details of the rich cult traditions out of which emerge the various Marian icons are for the most part unknown to Haitians. This ignorance, however, has never represented a void, as Vodou's own replete mythology has provided the background for understanding the imported images of holy women whom Catholic religious specialists and their laity traditionally call Mother of God.

To the outsider, the identification of Mary with Ezili would at first glance seem puzzling, heterodox, and rife with contradictions, especially in regards to sexuality and humility. Such an impression is perfectly reasonable. Some Vodou apologists, namely Deren and Desmangles, have attempted to explain away these apparent contradictions; however, the soundness of their arguments is at best questionable:

> Deren:
> The concept of Erzulie as virgin is not intended as a physical analysis. To call her virgin is to say that she is of another world, another reality, and that her heart, like the secret insulated heart of Mary Magdalene, is innocent of the flesh, is inaccessible to its delights and its corruptions. To say that she is virgin is to say that she is Goddess of the Heart, not of the body....[73]

> Desmangles:
> For a devotee to call Ezili (or Mary) a "Virgin" is to say that "she is of another world, another reality," and that her life transcends her devotees' financial and existential problems. To assert Ezili's virginity, then, is to say that she is untouched by the corruptions of the living. Vodouisants do not see promiscuity as a sign of corruption, for plasay is commonplace in Haitian society. The mythology that depicts Ezili's persona mirrors the realities of Haitian life. Thus, the identification of Ezili with Mary is not based upon Mary's virginity, but upon her physical beauty and her persona.[74]

These essentially identical arguments, while admirable for their eloquence and sensitivity, are so highly speculative and transparently "new age" that they fall well outside the pale of even a soft science

like the sociology of religion. It is palpably obvious that "the identification of Ezili and Mary is not based upon Mary's virginity"—
this much we need not be told. Furthermore, the deduction that this
identification is based upon Mary's "physical beauty and persona"
is clearly fallacious. I would venture that the main explanation for
this identification has nothing in the least to do with virginity or
with beauty, but everything to do, quite simply, with womanhood!
Moreover, it seems to occur neither to Deren nor Desmangles to
raise the question as to whether their discourses on virginity are at
all rooted in popular Haitian thought or are just so much empty
speculation. Here, again, as with their cosmological explanations
of the place of Ezili in Haitian Vodou, the soundness of their arguments is highly suspect. Regarding Deren's claim that calling Ezili
"a virgin is to say that she is Goddess of the heart, not of the body,"
it must be asked, for how many Haitian Vodouisants is this the case?
How many Haitians, for that matter, are so plagued by the question
as to be compelled to intellectually reconcile Ezili's lustful promis-
cuity with Mary's eternal virginity?

In contrast with Deren's and Desmangles's embroidered attempts
to negotiate this contradiction, Brown's approach to the matter is
refreshing and far more satisfactory:

> Lasyrenn, Ezili Danto, and Ezili Freda are each conflated
> with particular manifestations of the Virgin Mary: Nuestra
> Señora de la Caridad del Cobre, Mater Salvatoris, and
> Maria Dolorosa. But unlike the Mary of mainstream Ca-
> tholicism, who offers an impossible ideal of perfectly sub-
> missive (and virginal) motherhood for emulation, the Ezili
> are much closer to the human drama [and not "of another
> world" as Deren and Desmangles would have us believe!].
> In addition to providing examples of love, care, and hard
> work, they model anger—righteous and raging—power
> and affectivity, sensuality, sexuality, fear, frustration, need,
> and loneliness. In doing so, they become mirrors that give
> objective reality to what would otherwise remain, as it does
> in so many other cultures, women's silent pain and un-
> honored power.[75]

This passage is rich in implications. For one, it raises the question
as to whether Mary's popularity in Haitian religion is primarily

influenced by her conflation with Ezili. In other words, is it only by stripping Mary of the qualities of purity, virginity, and submission, which for so long have been manipulated by the Church to relegate women to inferior status, or at least by negating them through synthesis, that Mary becomes truly relevant for Haitians? As shown in chapter two, history provides witness that Mary's absorption of the feminine religious symbols of the cultures in which she has taken root often explains her emergent popularity, thus it should be expected that the same should have occurred in Haiti. Or perhaps the symbiotic assimilation of Mary and Ezili strikes for Haitians a functional balance that either figure in and of herself could neither achieve nor offer.

Provocative is Brown's claim, discussed above, that in mirroring the lives of Haitian women and offering themselves as realistic and instructional models, the Ezilis give voice to "what otherwise would remain, as it does in so many other cultures, women's silent pain and unhonored power." In this respect, Ezili resembles the Mary of the Magnificat and could perhaps serve Haitian Catholics in the rediscovery of this largely forgotten New Testament female role model. In speaking out on behalf of women and serving women as a source of empowerment, it would seem that Ezili plays a role in Haitian women's religious lives that the Virgin Mary cannot, unless of course the Magnificat's Mary should indeed finally emerge to occupy a place of primacy in Haitian Marianism.

Some feminist theologians argue that the Christian faithful have been effectively robbed of another feminine role model in the biblical figure of Mary Magdalene, whose potential to serve women especially in positive, liberative ways—as Ezili does—remains untapped. Rosemary Radford Ruether believes that this has been a regrettable loss for women:

> The suppression of the role of Mary Magdalene in the official church tradition may have something to do with the desire of the church to assign subordinate and conventional roles to women. Whatever her sexual history, Mary Magdalene is clearly an unconventional woman. Here is an independent woman whose close relations with Jesus are borne out by her faithfulness at the cross and her primacy in the resurrection experience. She represents a role

model for women that later church leaders probably preferred to neglect.[76]

In suppressing Magdalene, Ruether argues, the Church has not only
effectively dislocated believers from a potentially powerful feminine role model, but also has diminished greatly the relevance of the
Catholic system of symbols for women. The Catholic hierarchy's
adamant misogynist manipulation of the symbol of Virgin Mary
has effectively limited her relevance for Haitian women, as it has
for Catholic women of other cultures, since Mary is relegated by
orthodox Mariology to otherworldly status—an inimitable figure
who may intervene miraculously in the lives of men and women in
the material world. Despite the sisterly fashion in which Haitians
tend to address the Virgin, she does not, unlike Freda and Danto,
clearly mirror their lives, and, in the final analysis, therefore is not
a figure with whom Haitians may truly identify, save perhaps on the
level of suffering motherhood. As such, Mary functions quite differently than Ezili Freda and Ezili Danto:

> These two Erzulies, Erzulie Danto and Maitresse Erzulie,
> are both conflated with the Christian Mary, and articu-
> late, through their opposition to one another, a series of
> existential options that Haitian women face. One has only
> to look at the two Marys of Christianity, the Virgin Mary
> and Mary Magdalene, to see that different cultures view
> these fundamental options in different ways.[77]

The Ezilis speak out on behalf of Haitian women in ways that the
Virgin Mary cannot—perhaps because she speaks alone, without
the balancing voice of Magdalene—thus explaining, it may be argued, why it is that "Vodou empowers women to a larger extent
than the great majority of religious traditions."[78] In this light, feminist theologians who aim to recast the Virgin Mary in "the struggle
for ultimate womanhood in Catholicism,"[79] might profit more from
an analysis of the role Ezili plays in the lives of Haitian women than
from any attempt to portray Magdalene as a model for the liberation of women. As Warner cautions, such an attempt is dubious:

> Together, the Virgin and the Magdalene form a diptych of
> Christian patriarchy's idea of woman. There is no place

in the conceptual architecture of Christian society for a
single woman who is neither a virgin nor a whore.... The
Church venerates two ideals of the feminine—consecrated
chastity in the Virgin Mary and renegade sexuality in the
Magdalene. Populous as the Catholic pantheon is, it is
nevertheless so impoverished that it cannot conceive of a
single female saint independently of her relations (or lack
of relations) with men.[80]

It merits suggesting, therefore, that Mariology has something to
learn from the relationship between the Ezilis and Haitian women.
That such a step has yet to be taken is but a single culturally specific example of what is, according to Greeley, "[p]erhaps the greatest
weakness of current Catholic theology about Mary...to take the step
that the history of religion enables them to take and see Mary as a
reflection of the femininity of God."[81]

In conclusion, to claim that when Haitians venerate the Virgin
Mary they are actually worshipping Ezili is a facile overstatement.
For one, the question of gender demands careful consideration here;
i.e., what are the differences in the ways in which Haitian men and
Haitian women venerate or worship the Virgin Mary? Are these
differences negated in devotion to Ezili, where either men or women
can marry the Vodou spirit? Class considerations, as we'll see, would
likewise reveal greater complexities to the issue than such an uncritical claim would reflect. Moreover, the very fact that each Mary
and Ezili presents herself in different ways—not that each is different—would seem to preclude this kind of assimilation; i.e., the sen-
sibly tangible presence of Mary, who, as far as I am aware, never
actively possesses devotees in Vodou ceremonies, is limited to stat-
ues, pictorial images, and rare apparitions. This is nothing at all
like the presence of Ezili, who appears regularly in embraceable
human form in the body of her possessed devotee. While the image
of the Virgin, especially when perceived in a Vodou environment,
might conjure up notions of Ezili in any of her many manifestations, this identification is, in the final analysis, highly superficial.
For very few Haitians, I would argue, Mary and Ezili are one and
the same, understanding oneness and sameness to mean precisely
that. Instead, historical and contemporary anthropological research
reveals that Mary has been adopted and welcomed by Haitians as

an important spiritual force, operating side-by-side with Ezili—each functioning in a complex mosaic among the many *lwas* and saints who may be invoked in the daily struggle to survive and the quest for health and the fullness of life.

NOTES

1. Deren, citing Herskovits, informs us that the Virgin Mary, as *Notre Dame de Grâce*, is sometimes assimilated with "La Siren." [*The Divine Horsemen: The Living Gods of Haiti* (London and New York: Thames and Hudson, 1953), p. 308]. While this might be taken as an indication that Mary is conflated with Vodou spirits other than the Ezili, Brown suggests otherwise, adding "Lasyrenn...the mermaid who links ancient African senses of woman power and water power," among the Ezili group. Karen McCarthy Brown, *Mama Lola: A Vodou Priestess in Brooklyn* (Berkeley: University of California Press, 1991), p. 220.
2. Brown, *Mama Lola*, p. 3.
3. Leslie G. Desmangles, *The Faces of the Gods: Vodou and Roman Catholicism in Haiti* (Chapel Hill: The University of North Carolina Press, 1992), p. 143.
4. Karen McCarthy Brown, "Olina and Erzulie: A Woman and a Goddess in Haitian Vodou." *Anima*, 5 (Spring 1979), pp. 110-116, p. 111.
5. Ibid.
6. Ibid.
7. Ibid., p. 112.
8. Ibid., p. 113.
9. Desmangles, *The Faces of the Gods*, p. 131.
10. Brown, *Mama Lola*, p. 254.
11. Ibid.
12. Ibid.
13. Brown, "Olina and Erzulie," p. 110.
14. Ibid., p. 110.
15. Deren, *The Divine Horsemen*, p. 145.
16. Brown, *Mama Lola*, p. 250.
17. Deren, *The Divine Horsemen*, p. 138.
18. I.M. Lewis, *Ecstatic Religion: An Anthropological Study of Spirit Possession and Shamanism* (Harmondsworth: Penguin, 1974), p. 104.

19. Ibid., p. 127.
20. Laënnec Hurbon, *Dieu dans le vaudou haïtien* (Paris: Payot, 1972), p. 101.
21. For excellent insight into the history of the term syncretism and relevant contemporary debates, see J. Gort, H. Vroom, R. Fernhort, and A. Wessels, eds., *Dialogue and Syncretism: An Interdisciplinary Approach*, Grand Rapids, MI: Wm. B. Eerdmans Publishing Co., 1989; also C. Stewart and R. Shwan, *Syncretism and Anti-Syncretism: The Politics of Religious Synthesis* (London and New York: Routledge, 1994).
22. Alfred Métraux, *Voodoo in Haiti* (New York: Schocken Books, 1972), p. 29.
23. Ibid., p. 324.
24. Ibid., p. 34.
25. Ibid., p. 331.
26. Ibid., p. 35.
27. Cited in Michel Laguerre, "The Place of Voodoo in The Social Structure of Haiti," *Caribbean Quarterly*, vol. 19, no. 3, 1973, pp. 10-24, p. 45.
28. Wyatt MacGaffey, *Religion and Society in Central Africa* (Chicago: The University of Chicago Press, 1986), pp. 203-204.
29. Melville J. Herskovits, *Life in a Haitian Valley* (New York: Doubleday, 1971), pp. 281-282. Elsewhere Herskovits' discussion seems more reflective of the theory of symbiosis, especially where he writes that in "Haitian religion" "the forces of the universe are under dual control," and that any true synthesis occurs on the personal "psychological" level: "His reconciliation he keeps to himself, and in his everyday life both the African beliefs and those of the Church have their place." p. 288.
30. Roger Bastide, *Les amériques noires: les civilisations africaines dans le Nouveau monde* (Paris: Payot, 1967), p. 159, 167.
31. Ibid. p. 167.
32. Ibid., p. 160.
33. Ibid.
34. Ibid.
35. Desmangles, *The Faces of the Gods*, p. 8.
36. Ibid., p. 10-11.
37. Ibid., p. 15.
38. Ibid., p. 9.
39. Deren, *The Divine Horsemen*, p. 54.
40. Desmangles, *The Faces of the Gods*, p. 10.
41. Ibid., p. 89.

42. Raoul Canizares, *Walking with the Night: The Afro-Cuban World of Santería* (Rochester VT: Destiny Books, 1993).

43. Métraux, *Voodoo in Haiti*, p. 328, emphasis added.

44. André Droogers, "Syncretism: The Problem of Definition, The Definition of the Problem," in J. Gort, et. al., (eds.), *Dialogue and Syncretism*, pp. 13-27, p. 17.

45. Métraux, *Voodoo in Haiti*, p. 29

46. And for one more colorful example, C.L.R. James writes, "(a)bout the middle of the eighteenth century one of them (the Catholic priests) used to baptize the same Negroes seven or eight times, for the ceremony amused the slaves, and they were willing to pay a small sum for each baptism. As late as 1790 another was competing with the Negro obeah-men for the coppers of slaves, by selling charms against illness and talismans to insure the success of their ventures." *The Black Jacobins: Toussaint Louverture and the Saint-Domingue Revolution* (New York: Vintage Books, 1963), p. 32.

47. As cited in Jean-Marie Jan, *Collecta pour l'histoire religieuse d'Haïti, Tome 1* (Port-au-Prince: Deschamps, 1958), p. 270.

48. Anne Baring and Jules Cashford, *The Myth of the Goddess: Evolution of an Image* (London: Penguin Books, 1993), p. 551.

49. Ivone Gebara and Maria Clara Bingemer, *Mary: Mother of God, Mother of the Poor* (Maryknoll: Orbis, 1989), pp. 131-132, emphasis added.

50. Jean-Marie Jan, *Les congregations religieuses du Cap-Français, Saint-Domingue* (Port-au-Prince: Deschamps, 1951), p. 225.

51. Ibid.

52. Ibid. Fick provides a translation of this "sacramental voodoo hymn:"
    "Eh! eh! Rainbow spirit, eh! eh! [rainbow spirit = serpent]
    Tie up the BaFioto [a coastal African slave-trading people]
    Tie up the whites [i.e., Europeans]
    Tie up the witches
    Tie them." [*The Making of Haiti* (Knoxville: the University of Tennessee Press, 1990), p. 58, 266].

53. Desmangles, *The Faces of the Gods*, p. 10.

54. Ibid, p. 136.

55. This passage is a description by a teacher named M. Cliquot in 1844, as cited in Jan, *Collecta pour l'histoire religieuse d'Haïti, Tome 1*, pp. 53-54.

56. Ibid.

57. Beauvoir-Dominique, *L'Ancienne cathédrale de Port-au-Prince*, p. 42.

58. Ibid., p. 44.

59. Indicative of the transmutability of the Virgin Mary's ideological functions, less than sixty years later thousands of Haitians were praying to the Virgin to bring the American marines back to Haiti, this time to oust General Raoul Cédras and his brutal military junta.

60. My discussion here is indebted to Beauvoir-Dominique, *L'Ancienne cathédrale de Port-au-Prince*, pp. 41-46.

61. At the same time, in a futile, somewhat pathetic effort to use Vodou to inspire the masses to support the very structures responsible for the exacerbation of their suffering, a group of pro-putchist neo-Duvalierists staged a commemorative celebration at Bois-Caïman on the anniversary of Boukman's legendary evening of spark.

62. Desmangles, *The Faces of the Gods*, p. 138.

63. Métraux, *Voodoo in Haiti*, p. 324.

64. Ibid., p. 326.

65. Brown, *Mama Lola*, p. 228.

66. Beauvoir-Dominique, *L'Ancienne cathédrale de Port-au-Prince*, p. 121.

67. Ibid.

68. Desmangles, *The Faces of the Gods*, p. 144.

69. Brown, *Mama Lola*, p. 229. This Marian icon may have entered the Haitian religious field at an earlier date than the introduction of the lithographs, as the Polish presence in Haiti dates to the colonial era. Some of Napoleon's Polish inscriptions deserted in Saint-Domingue and fought for the rebels, so it possible that Czestochowa's banner actually flew above he slaves in their struggle for liberty, which is perhaps the origin of the belief that her scars were gotten in the revolution. The icon's circulation, however, was probably very limited prior to the proliferation of the lithographs about 100 years later.

70. Ibid., 228.

71. Beauvoir-Dominique notes a popular association in Haitian religion between *Perpétuel Secours* and Czestochowa that renders *Perpétuel Secours* correspondent to Ezili Danto. There are certain similarities between the two icons which could indeed trigger such an association: the figures are positioned alike; in each icon both Mary and Jesus are crowned; the child Jesus rests in his Mother's left arm; Mary glares at the viewer, while Jesus looks away, etc. While an association of Czestochowa and *Perpétuel Secours* is thus a reality, it does not necessarily follow that *Perpétuel Secours* is universally identified with Danto. Many of my informants, on the contrary, clearly stated that to them *Perpétuel Secours* represented Freda, while for fewer she was assimilated with Danto. The luster of her jewels

would seem to promote her identification with Freda, as it were. On that note, two women explained to me that the determination of Perpétuel Secours' syncretism depended upon which version of the icon was in question. There are, indeed, two slightly different portrayals of *Notre Dame du Perpétuel Secours* in circulation in the Haitian religious field: in the more common one, Mary's robe is blue; in the other it is black. One woman told me that the blue-robed Madonna is Ezili Freda, and the black-robed Madonna is Ezili Danto. Another, meanwhile, explained that the first is not at all identifiable with Ezili, while the black-robed Virgin is Ezili Freda. All of this serves as testimony to the fact that in Vodou, there is little that is uniform, and exceptions are something of a norm.

72. Brown, *Mama Lola*, p. 246. Brown suggests that the differences between Freda and Danto amount to an attempt to understand or portray through mythology class, gender, and racial strife in Haitian society: "In the tension between Freda and Danto, Haitians explore questions of race, as well as those of class and gender. Freda is a white woman and, as a result, a privileged woman who has the power to draw to herself both men and wealth. She marries, and her status as wife and partner is legal and public. It has financial and social solidity. Danto is black, "black, black, black," and, as a result, she is poor and must work hard. Danto does not marry. The men in her life are as poor as she is, and they cannot be counted on. But Danto is fertile. Her best hope for security and care in her old age lies with her children, especially her girl children." *Mama Lola*, p. 256.

73. Deren, *The Divine Horsemen*, p. 144.

74. Desmangles, *The Faces of the Gods*, p. 138.

75. Brown, *Mama Lola*, p. 221.

76. Ruether, *Mary: The Feminine Face of the Church*, p. 40.

77. Brown, "Olina and Erzulie," p. 116.

78. Brown, *Mama Lola*, p. 220.

79. This term is adopted from the subtitle of Maurice Hamington's *Hail Mary? The Struggle for Ultimate Womanhood in Catholicism* (London and New York: Routledge, 1995).

80. Marina Warner, *Alone of All Her Sex: The Myth and the Cult of the Virgin Mary* (New York: Knopf, 1976), p. 235.

81. Greeley, *The Mary Myth: On the Femininity of God* (New York: Seabury, 1977), p. 15.

CHAPTER SIX

THE MARIANISM OF THE HAITIAN POOR

The five preceding chapters provide an informed methodological, theological (mariological), and historical background against which to confront forthrightly the central questions that this study now endeavors to address: What are the differences between the Marian devotion of the Haitian poor and that of the Haitian rich, and what explains these differences? We will approach these questions in this and the next chapter, which discuss respectively under-class and elite Haitian Marianism. These two chapters are structured alike. First, they review relevant and provocative social theories concerning religion and class; second, elements from these theories are used to shape the questions to be raised and to answer them; and third, data generated by hundreds of interviews and questionnaires,[1] along with one detailed case study from each socioeconomic class, are analyzed in light of the theories discussed.

An obvious and vital prerequisite to proceeding with the task at hand is to define, as simply and directly as possible, the categories of analysis. Few nations demonstrate so radical a division between rich and poor as Haiti.[2] The squalor and abject poverty of Port-au-Prince's seaside slums stand as the greatest contrast imaginable to the extravagant luxury and hillside mansions of the Haitian elite. Of course, class structure in Haiti is far more complex than the haves/have-nots dichotomy, and some will cry foul at the sight of my admitted over-simplification of the matter. Yet, all subjects of analysis, especially large-scale sociological analysis such as the present study, must be delimited somewhere. This accounts for the exclusion of the Haitian middle-class from consideration in this study. There are several reasons for this. First, as an overarching focus of this study is the relationship between religion and power, the Haitian middle-class is somewhat irrelevant since it lacks both the economic power of the elite and the power-in-numbers of the poor masses. Second, there is much less cultural uniformity among members of the Haitian middle-class than among members of either the elite or the under-class, making the Haitian middle-class a potentially problematic object of ethnological analysis. Some middle-class Haitians are recently arrived from the under-class and remain basically possessed of a habitus reflective of an economically impoverished background, while others have recently fallen from the upper-class and still maintain the basic values and dispositions of the elite, though without the economic power. In other words, the Haitian middle-class is demographically fickle.[3] Finally, excluding the middle-class from this study permits greater focus and more thorough direct analysis of the main adversaries in Haiti's class struggle.

Sidney Mintz lucidly characterizes this formidable division of class in Haitian society:

> The bulk of the Haitian people are rural (though less now than ever before), agricultural (though agriculture has been declining for at least half a century), and illiterate. Their language is Creole, which is unintelligible with French and, until the last twenty years or so, was rarely written (and never read). Their religion is a form of ancestral cult, though they view themselves as being Catholic (as well, rather than instead); these days, a growing number of people in the towns are Protestant, usually in nonecumenical denominations. A modest minority—no more than ten percent—speaks and reads some French and has twelve or more years of education, lives in cities, works in professions, service trades, and the government, and attends Catholic (and Protestant) services. They will probably be somewhat disdainful of vodoun; they may refer condescendingly (or quite venomously) to the poor; and they feign disinterest in questions of cultural origin— that is, what is or might be "African." Often the gap be-

tween such people and other Haitians seems absolutely unbridgeable; in certain ways, it is.[4]

It is with each of these elements of Haitian society that the present study concerns itself, with perhaps a disproportionate representation of the urban poor over the rural peasantry.

To the outsider unfamiliar with Haiti, such differences might seem to suggest that Haiti is a nation of two different peoples or castes. Some writers, most notably American anthropologist Richard Leyburn[5] have distinctly argued that the term "caste" is appropriate for discussing Haitian society. Mintz, however, cautions against such a view:

> At the same time, though, Haitian culture is a more clearly definable system, top to bottom, than is American culture. There are no real ethnic divisions in Haiti; everybody understands and speaks Creole; everybody eats the same kind of food; everybody dances the same way (or knows how to). Hence the content of "being Haitian" is widely shared, even if the life and fate of Haitians vary (as it does) from quite rarefied luxury to terrible misery and suffering.... Haiti is divided by economics, language, education, religion, and ideological awareness.[6]

Haitian anthropologist Michel-Rolph Trouillot agrees with Mintz's point. While admitting firmly that "Haiti is undeniably a society split into two,"[7] Trouillot rejects the "dualist approach typified by Leyburn," as it "neglect[s] the dialectics of social reproduction,"[8] specifically the seepage of elements of peasant cultural expressions and worldview into the habitus of the dominant or urban elite. In Trouillot's view, the cultural relationship between the upper and lower-classes in Haiti is analogous to "guerrilla warfare," in which popular Haitian culture "cannot be said to be victorious [over the Eurocentric cultural preferences of the elite]...but it has an implicitly acknowledged presence" in elite culture. In the religious field, one of the outcomes of this interclass, cultural guerrilla warfare is that "substantial tenets of the same philosophy and a number of the basic beliefs are held by most Haitians."[9] Trouillot further elaborates this point: "even when practices vary—as of course they do—they often take root in the same underlying values. The crux of the matter is that these underlying values are differently acknowledged, and carry a different symbolic weight in different class presentations."[10]

Trouillot's provocative claim may be measured against the data produced by our fieldwork among both poor and wealthy Haitians concerning their Marian beliefs and practices. In other words, Trouillot inspires the question as to whether elite Haitian Marianism indeed takes root in "the same underlying values" as under-class Haitian Marianism. We will address this question below. Meanwhile, the immediate tasks at hand rank as paramount among the objectives of this study: a survey of key sociological conceptions of the relationship between poverty and religion, and a critical, analytical portrayal of the place of the symbol of the Virgin Mary in the religious life of the poor Haitian masses.

Religion and Poverty: Marxist and Gramscian Perspectives

In seeking to understand the Marian devotion of the Haitian poor or, for that matter, any form of religious expression of oppressed peoples, the researcher is ineluctably confronted with Marx's assertion that popular religion amounts to an illusory and alienating anesthetic. "Indeed, the classical Marxist definition of religion as the 'opium of the people' is the ever-present background to any sociological analysis of popular religion."[11] Therefore, from the very outset there is one question that must be addressed forthrightly: How alienating is popular Haitian Marianism?

Discussions of Marx's view of religion usually begin with, and are sometimes limited to, his (in)famous metaphor from the introduction to the "Critique of Hegel's Philosophy of Right;" Religion "is the *opium* of the people."[12] Tied to Marx's notions that "[m]an makes religion, religion does not make man,"[13] that "[t]he ruling ideas of any age are the ideas of the ruling elite,"[14] and that "true happiness is the abolition of illusory happiness [religion],"[15] a wholly negative view of religion emerges in orthodox Marxism.[16] This view understands religion to be little more than an instrument of domination that is, in Bourdieu's terms, a multifaceted weapon of symbolic violence employed to have the popular masses misrecognize the social order as legitimate, despite its inequalities, injustice, and arbitrariness. In this view, popular religion is, thus, merely a pale reflection of the religion of the dominant, who, after all, are the producers of society's dominant ideas, religious ideas included. As such, religion represents a formidable obstacle on the path toward the true liberation at the heart of the Marxist agenda and must therefore be abolished.

This ostensibly negative and antithetical view is generally considered the classical or orthodox Marxist statement on religion. However, a certain positive nuance in *Marx's* writings on religion is ignored here, belied by the overall adversarial bent of the classical Marxist attitude toward religion. The citation of Marx's opium metaphor is often in isolation from other equally rich and far-reaching comments in the very same passage. Marx also writes that "religion is the sigh of the oppressed creature,"[17] implying that the oppressed, through their religious expression, might recognize that they are in fact oppressed, and not merely suffering by fate. More suggestive still, Marx adds, "religion is a protest against real suffering."[18] The implication is not only that religion might bring the subjugated to recognize their suffering as caused by injustice, but also that religion could even become a motivational and cohesive force promotive of revolutionary praxis. Protest, it would seem, is a first and irreplaceable step toward sociopolitical revolution.

However, as Hans Küng explains, although Marx did affirm that religion:

> is not only a consequence [of] but also…a protest against inhuman social conditions…this protest of religion remains ineffectual and helpless, since religion diverts attention from the present world and its transformation and puts us off with a promise of the hereafter. Thus religion, in the end, simply has the effect of a sedative or a narcotic, producing illusory instead of real happiness.[19]

It is puzzling that Marx, at least in his writings, never drew out the seemingly obvious implications of his definition of religion as protest; that beyond its negative alienating aspect, popular religion itself might play a positive role in the quest for the human transcendence that is Marxism's ultimate aim. The development of this idea would be left for other socialist thinkers, like Friedrich Engels and, later, especially Antonio Gramsci.

Gramsci agreed with Marx's central tenets in *The Communist Manifesto*, in particular that "the history of all hitherto existing societies is the history of class struggles."[20] Yet Gramsci was dissatisfied with the exaggerated degree of economic reductionism that he found in Marx's writing, believing instead that culture, rather than being largely shaped by the dynamics of the economic sphere, has itself some important degree of autonomy for self-determination and functions in a dialectical, co-determinate relationship with economic forces. It is this departure in emphasis from classical Marxism that renders possible and worthwhile a Gramscian sociological analysis of religion and other forms of cultural expression. As Dwight Billings explains:

> A Marxist sociology that reduces ideas, including religion, to a 'direct' reflection of economic forces is not conducive to the sociology of religion. But Gramsci's version of Marxism, which repudiated all such 'linear' and 'mechanistic' thinking, views culture as a semiautonomous sphere of society that plays an important mediating role in the totality of social life.[21]

Thus, in the Gramscian perspective, the notion that class struggle also unfolds outside the boundaries of the economic field is further developed than in the Marxian view, and is not as limited to a conflict between owners versus producers, capitalists versus laborers, or the bourgeoisie versus the proletariat locked in a struggle over the means of production. This perspective actively conceives of class struggle playing out in decisive ways in the cultural sphere, including the religious field, beyond the purely economic realm. This form of struggle is the cynosure of Gramsci's sociology of religion, in much the way it is of Bourdieu's.

As Lucia Chiavola Brinbaum notes in her interesting study *Black Madonnas*, it is not insignificant that feelings of physical and social difference and outsiderhood tempered Gramsci's own life experience, perhaps engendering in him a certain sensitivity to the cultural richness and originality of "folklore," or of subjugated or "subaltern" cultural expression:

Antonio Gramsci may best be understood if one remembers that he was a Sardinian dwarf, and a hunchback. His bodily sense of difference gave him an immediate consciousness of subordinate cultures and the marginality of others. Folklore was scarcely a dilettante amusement for Gramsci; he called it a vernacular *concezione del mondo e della vita*, a conception of life that challenged the hegemony of the educated classes.[22]

To Gramsci, popular religion, or the religion of the people, being an integral part of "folklore," can in itself represent a threat to the dominant culture and as such can indeed make a positive contribution to revolutionary praxis. Far more than the ineffectual protest that it remained in Marx's writings, popular religion, in the Gramscian perspective, can take the form of active challenge to hegemonic culture and the unjust social structures of which it is both a product and legitimizing pillar.

There is no attempt here to give the impression that Gramsci romanticized about popular religion or that he admired it as anything more than a "significant social fact." Given his rural background, Gramsci was fully exposed to the "magical" and "superstitious" dimensions of peasant religiosity, which he personally detested. While there are those who believe that Gramsci converted to Catholicism on his deathbed, the overall tone of his scattered writings on religion are unmistakably atheistic and adversarial. Nowhere is this more clearly demonstrated than in his blunt claim—which resoundingly echoes Marx—that "modern man can and should live without the help of religion,"[23] and without "the imbecile illusion of immortality."[24] Like Marx, Gramsci ultimately sees religion as a product of human despair:

> Religion is a need of the spirit. People feel so lost in the vastness of the world, so thrown about by the forces they do not understand; and the complex of historical forces, artful and subtle as they are, so escapes the common sense that in the moments that matter only the person who has substituted religion with some other moral force succeeds in saving the self from disaster.[25]

This negative posture aside, the key difference between Marx and Gramsci on popular religion, as already suggested, has far reaching consequences. For Gramsci, the religious ideas and practices of subjugated peoples are not merely passively and dully reflected versions of the dominant religion imposed upon them by the powerful, but are rather active and creative productions of meaning and cultural expression that are at least potentially revolutionary. What this amounts to, in Gramsci's view, is an ensemble of different religions within an ostensibly unified single religion like Catholicism:

> Every religion, even the Catholic (in fact, especially the Catholic, precisely because of its effort to remain united superficially, and not split up into national churches and into various social strata) is in reality a multiplicity of distinct and often contradictory religions: there is a Catholicism of the *petit bourgeoisie* and city workers, a women's Catholicism, and intellectual's Catholicism equally varied and disconnected.[26]

It is this realization that permitted Gramsci both to perceive the creativity of popular religion and to elucidate the class struggle that unfolds in the religious field. It is plausible, as John Fulton points out, that Gramsci's training as a linguist influenced his notion of the creativity involved in the interpretive transformation of dominant religion that is elemental to the religious perception of popular classes. The linguist understands that any statement's meaning is neither monolithic nor universally understandable with uniform intelligibility, but is interpreted differently by different addressees, filtered through their own points of view, backgrounds, and personalities; through the perceivers, habiti, as it were. It is likewise with orthodox religious beliefs, rituals, and symbols. Rather than being passively absorbed by subjugated agents and re-expressed in muted, semi-literate form, they are actively appropriated to meet their own needs and serve their own interests. Through this process, the under-class transforms orthodox religious beliefs and symbols to represent what amounts to "an active conception of the world" that stands "in opposition" both to the dominant, hegemonic worldview and the arbitrary, unequal social order that it legitimizes.[27]

Gramsci's contribution to the sociological study of religion, therefore, ultimately lies in his ability to "identify in the religion of the people a revolutionary capacity."[28] As Fulton explains, it was Gramsci's keen insight into the cultural creativity of the popular sector, and his belief that "every man is a philosopher," that permitted him to arrive ultimately at this provocative conclusion: "Gramsci took a major step forward in respect to Engels and the Marxian tradition as a whole by taking seriously, as a source of power, the self-understanding of religious groups and the interpretation of the world in which these groups actualize their existence."[29]

A Gramscian Analysis of Haitian Marianism

Gramsci discusses several significant historical examples that demonstrate the revolutionary capacity of popular religion.[30] There are other good examples in Lanternari's *The Religions of the Oppressed*, already discussed briefly in chapter two. Lanternari, as we mentioned, goes so far as to assert that all "third-world" revolutionary movements have popular religious roots. There is arguably no greater example of this than the Haitian Revolution, during which, as shown in chapter four, Romaine-la-Prophétesse radically appropriated the symbol of the Virgin Mary—the patroness of European colonial endeavor—to crystallize the slaves' revolutionary praxis. At at least two other junctures in Haitian history the Virgin Mary has taken on subversive meaning for the oppressed: (1) During the U.S. occupation early this century, when insurgents took her as their inspiration and protectress; (2) prior to the ouster of Jean-Claude Duvalier, when mass novenas followed on the radio and processions amounted to forms of protest against the Duvalier regime's mounting abuses against political activists. Clearly, then, the revolutionary capacity of popular Marianism has been actualized at certain junctures in Haitian history, albeit infrequently.

A crucial question—one we will return to below—thus arises: To what degree does the symbol of Mary maintain this revolutionary capacity today? Of course, depending upon the "historical moment" this capacity may or may not be discernible as outwardly threatening to the dominant. In an article exploring dimensions of protest in Chilean popular religion, Christian Parker makes this point aptly:

> The religion of subordinate classes, whose articulation depends on other sociocultural representations corresponding to the situation of each class, may have various social functions. These sometimes appear exclusively, sometimes in parallel and they may even co-exist in a contradictory manner within popular culture. Factor of alienation, factor of popular identity and symbolic opposition to the official religion and culture, finally an ethical reinforcement for an attempt at social advancement or an attempt to transform society: popular religion may or may not be either of these depending on the social and historical situation.[31]

In many cases, then, the revolutionary capacity of popular religion is unseen, perhaps even dormant or latent, thus demanding that the researcher perform some degree of what George E. Marcus refers to as "ethnographical midwifery,"[32] in order to uncover it. This approach, characterized by an attempt to reveal hidden or latent forms of protest in the cultural expression of the oppressed, while criticized by Ernst Gellner and others,[33] has become routine for a growing number of anthropologists and sociologists. Following Clifford Geertz, many thinkers now readily accept that "anthropological writings are themselves interpretations."[34] In regards to the social scientific study of religion in particular, Geertz's "two stage operation" is reflective of this understanding and, to a limited degree and in modified form, will guide the following analysis of the data that my fieldwork produced: "first, analysis of the systems of meanings embodied in the symbol which make up the religion proper, and second, the relating of these systems to social structure and psychological processes."[35]

The various positions outlined here are basically in agreement with Paul Willis' claim that "the role of ethnography is to give voice to the cultural viewpoint of the oppressed, to lend expression to their hidden knowledges and resistances."[36] This sums up well what I consider to be one of the primary objectives of this chapter: to expose and articulate the revolutionary capacity of contemporary popular Haitian Marianism. Yet, before proceeding with this endeavor, it would be worthwhile to sharpen our analytical approach further by turning our attention to some of the fruitful concepts that James Scott develops in his analysis of the often unintelligible ways in which popular protest is manifest.

Hidden Transcripts and Ideological Negation

Specifically, there are two concepts outlined by Scott in *Domination and the Arts of Resistance* that are useful for our analysis of popular Haitian Marianism: "hidden transcript" and "ideological negation." The hidden transcript is an underground means and arena of social discourse created by and for the oppressed to express their critiques of or protests against the dominant. These expression are usually coded in ways intelligible only to the oppressed. The hidden transcript is, thus, quite distinct from the public transcript, which is the whole of accepted forms of inter-class communication and interaction, involving speech, gestures, and a host of other sometimes subtle forms of expression. To understand the public transcript is both to know one's place, i.e., "to have a feel for the game," or, to quote a Haitian exhortation, to "remain within your role" (*"rete na wòl ou"*). Being largely the creation of the dominant, the public transcript is designed to preserve their positions of power and privilege. In contrast, being the creation of the oppressed, the hidden transcript contains the seeds of revolutionary praxis, which of course is the key ingredient in any struggle against social domination.

Scott enumerates a number of elements that make up the hidden transcript, which "does not contain only speech acts but a whole range of practices,"[37] ranging from defiant gestures and outright insurgence, to tax evasion and pilfering. In the religious field, spirit possession and the appropriation of symbols, ritual, and doctrine also represent constructive elements of the hidden transcript. As an example of this, Scott cites Albert Raboteau's discussion of the difference between the themes of Christianity preached to slaves in the open by the white American masters (obedience, subservience, faith in a heavenly kingdom and recompense in the afterlife for having patiently endured suffering in the material world) and those themes that were prominent in the slaves' "underground" Christianity, outside the gaze of the master (redemption, this worldly liberation from bondage, the evils of wealth, etc.).[38] It is in this underground form that religion operates as a functional part of the hidden transcript.

Spirit possession is another form of religious expression that is elemental to the hidden transcript of the oppressed. Scott's discussion of possession is entirely dependent upon several significant conclusions made by I.M. Lewis in *Ecstatic Religion*, which form he backbone of Scott's discussion. For one, Lewis makes a decisive connection between the tendency for the occurrence of possession and economic or social deprivation, observing that "the accumulation of pressures experienced in situations of oppression is an essential condition for the development of spirit possession."[39] His comparative analysis reveals that it is almost exclusively the subjugated of any society, namely women and members of the underclass, who exhibit "the greatest tendency toward spirit possession."[40] Interestingly, these same groups seem to exhibit the greatest tendency for deep Marian piety.[41]

For Scott, spirit possession—since it is the spirit doing the possessing, rather than the possessed, who is perceived as the speaker—affords the oppressed, otherwise voiceless masses a certain liberative anonymity, which permits them to express their grievances and critiques of elite culture without fear of retribution. As such, possession is a single weapon at their disposal in "an arsenal of techniques that tend to shield their identity while facilitating criticism."[42]

Because the Virgin Mary rarely, if ever, possesses her Haitian devotees in the same manner the *lwas*,[43] the relevance of Lewis' and Scott's treatment of spirit possession to the present study might reasonably be questioned. I would argue that insofar as Mary is identified—however superficially—with Ezili, the idiosyncrasies and characteristics of Ezili, which Vodouisants know mainly through the experience of spirit possession, have "rubbed off" somewhat on Mary, influencing to some degree the manner in which many Haitians appropriate and perceive the Virgin. Even though, as argued in chapter five, Mary remains *essentially* distinct from Ezili, she does not emerge wholly unscathed from the experience of symbiosis with the Vodou love spirit. Instead she emerges as a "Haitian-ized" Mary, having absorbed some of Ezili's traits. This would explain why a number of my informants spoke of Mary as becoming jealous if they ever prayed to other saints. One wealthy woman, herself quite opposed to Vodou (albeit somewhat ignorant of it), described for me her reluctance to pray to any other Virgin besides *Caridad del Cobre* for fear of sparking in *Caridad* a jealous rage that could trigger disastrous retribution. "This Virgin is very jealous and possessive," she recounted. "She can do all sorts of miraculous things for you, but once you make a vow to be faithful to her, you must never venerate another Virgin." This type of fiery anger and possessive jealousy is characteristic of certain *lwas*, Ezili included. Thus, since it is through the experience of spirit possession that the *lwas* are known, and since the *lwas*'s characteristics influence the way many Haitians perceive of Mary and other Catholic saints, spirit possession can thus be said to have an indirect influence on Haitian Marianism, especially on, but not limited to, the popular level.

As we saw in chapter four, Romaine-la-Prophétesse made cogent use of spirit possession to promote slave rebellion. We may recall how all that Romaine commanded of his band of renegade slaves and maroons was at the behest of the Virgin Mary. Furthermore, Romaine received the Virgin's messages through either spirit possession or some similar channel. As such, Romaine attempted to transfer the ultimate responsibility for his actions to the Holy Mother. His contorted brand of Marianism, moreover, was essential to the rebels' use of religion as a hidden transcript, as it changed not only the style but also, quite radically, the content of orthodox Mariology.

Another of Scott's useful concepts is that of "ideological negation," which might be described as a kind of philosophical and ritualistic assault on bourgeois hegemony. In the above-cited example that Scott takes from Raboteau, autonomous slave religion represented not only a negation of the style of official religion, it contradicted its content as well. Insofar as it did, autonomous slave Christianity amounted to ideological negation; a "counterideology" or "resistance to ideological domination."[44] Throughout Haitian religious history the under-class has engaged in the ideological negation of Catholic symbols, doctrine and ritual. Vodou, of course, is rife with examples of this, while the case of Romaine-la-Prophétesse represents an obviously politically effective example of the ideological negation of the symbol of the Virgin Mary. Scott's discussion inspires the question, thus: Does contemporary popular Haitian Marianism reflect any such ideological negation?

We have explored key elements from the discussions of popular religion in Marx, Gramsci, Lewis, Scott, and Bourdieu with the conviction that, taken together, they form a trenchant paradigm for the analysis of popular Haitian Marianism. Later still, we will discuss certain theories of Weber to further refine the emerging paradigm. For now, our analysis of the meaning of under-class Haitian's Marian devotion may be guided by several direct questions that are the framework of this paradigm:

1. *To what extent does their Marian devotion serve poor Haitians as an "opiate," providing them with consolation from the pains of suffering? Does this devotion thus serve to alienate the Haitian poor, inspire in them fatalistic resignation to their lot, and represent an obstacle to political empowerment for social change?*

2. *What role does the symbol of the Virgin Mary play in explaining to under-class Haitians the meaning of their world and their place in it?*

3. *Insofar as the Marian piety of the Haitian under-class differs from that of the elite, to what extent may we understand their Marianism to be a cohesive "factor of popular identity," or as an instrument in the development of (revolutionary) class-consciousness?*[45]

4. *In popular Haitian Mariology, are there expressions, however oblique or couched, of protest against domination and suffering? Does the poor's appropriation of Mary demonstrate any degree of ideological negation?*

5. *What are the discernible religious interests and needs among the Haitian under-class to which the symbol of the Virgin Mary responds? How do these interests and needs influence the forms and style of Marian devotion preferred or created by the poor?*

6. *What conclusions, if any, can we reach regarding the identification of Mary and Ezili in the religious views of our lower-class informants?*

The Case of Guertha

That the insecurity and existential needs that characterize poverty shape to a large extent the religious habitus of severely economically deprived or oppressed agents is a conscious assumption that the present study makes. The majority of the popular Haitian masses are in fact victims of what John Galtung, in *The True Worlds*, refers to as the "crisis of misery...where much of the population is still underfed and underclad, lacks adequate shelter, suffers ill health, and has scant or no education...."[46] The commonly dehumanizing effects of impoverished Haitians' crisis of misery were markedly exacerbated by the virulent "crisis of repression"[47] to which they were subjected by the Cédras military regime from the time of its overthrow of President Aristide in September 1991 until the U.S. military intervention that reinstalled Aristide three years later.[48] Violently deprived "of all human rights relating to freedom and the opportunity to take part in politics—to participate in governing oneself,"[49] Haiti's popular sector—almost unanimously pro-Aristide and prodemocracy—found itself confronting persecution unsurpassed even in their nation's turbulent, often bloody 200-year history. Their religious needs—such as their need for protection from adversaries, for consolation for pains, for hope for survival, for strength for perseverance, and for inspiration for solidarity and activism—were doubtless greatly amplified as their crisis of misery was compounded with the crisis of repression during the three years of junta rule.

The case of Guertha, a 34 year-old street merchant, "*mawon*" ("exiled")[50] in Port-au-Prince because of the political persecution in her rural hometown in the north, is hardly atypical among victims of political persecution and human rights abuses that the Cédras regime committed.[51] The effects of poverty had long influenced Guertha's religious needs in general and her devotion to Mary in particular. Indeed, her religious habitus was that of a poor Haitian peasant woman. Her religious needs, however, would change dramatically during a series of unspeakable tragedies that occurred in her life over a two-year period. What became evident over the course of our interviews was that as her suffering increased through political persecution, her religious needs expanded and consequently her devotion to the Virgin Mary intensified, Mary thus taking on new roles in Guertha's religious life. The following discussion outlines Guertha's crises and their effects on her religious belief and practice, at the center of which emerges the symbol of the Virgin Mary. The deepening of Guertha's Marian piety in proportion to the worsening of her compounded misery/repression crisis will be soundly theorized below through Andrew Greeley's "four-celled paradigm"[52] in conjunction with theoretical insight from Gramsci, Bourdieu, Weber, and Scott.

Born of a rural family in the northern Haitian mountains, Guertha experienced a childhood of poverty and struggle typical of Haiti's peasant masses. Her family's scant economic resources afforded her with a aggregate of only three sporadic years of formal education, hence like most of the Haitian poor, Guertha embarked on life's way with the social disadvantage of illiteracy.

Guertha's peasant upbringing also imbued in her a Vodouisant religious habitus, featuring what Bastide refers to as "*la dialectisation du social.*" As Hurbon explains, Haiti's popular religion furnishes its practitioners with the "[d]ialectization of the social in the sense that Vodou is the language which permits the Vaudousiant not only to experience his circumstances as objective facts, but also to give him a sense of control over and orientation toward them."[53] Yet, what occurs when a Vodouisant experiences a brutal and tragic uprooting of the unfamiliar severity of Guertha's? Might not the dialectization of the social breakdown, the circumstances suddenly appearing totally beyond control, and a process of disorientation thus occur? This, I would argue, is precisely what happened to Guertha, beginning in December 1992, when a group of paramilitary thugs (*attachés*) stormed her home, beat and raped her, abducted her husband, and roughed up her children. They then burned her house to cinders. They had targeted her husband because of his pro-Aristide activism. Several days after the raid, his body was discovered on a hillside, half-eaten by dogs. Fearing ensuing attacks, Guertha sent her oldest two children to stay with relatives in a nearby village, while she and their younger three siblings fled to the anonymity and dubious economic prospects of Port-au-Prince.

Guertha and her three youngest children, ages one, four, and seven, arrived in the capital virtually penniless, with the address of a cousin she had not seen since childhood. After several nights on the strange, dark, and dangerous streets of Port-au-Prince, Guertha finally managed to locate her cousin's house. The small, two-room dwelling was located in the lower-class neighborhood of Bel-Air, a quarter long known for its progressive political fervor and for its miraculous church, the Church of *Notre Dame du Perpétuel Secours*. The fact that the house was already overcrowded with seven occupants—three adults and four children—was beside the point, and Guertha and her three children were graciously invited to move in.

Ira Lowenthal's dissertation on the sexuality and "conjugal contract" of rural Haitian peasants illustrates how women's sexual services represent a form of economic capital readily marketable in exchange for either financial reward, material goods, or men's labor either in agriculture or construction.[54] Within a month of her arrival in Bel-Air, Guertha had entered into such conjugal contracts with two men, through which she had garnered enough cash to set afoot a small-scale business pedaling plastic ware in the streets. The slight improvement in her family's living conditions that this effected, however, was short-lived. Six months into her stay in Bel-Air, attachés ransacked her new-found home under the pretext that her cousin was a pro-Aristide activist in possession of a cachet of arms. He, the household's principal breadwinner, was abducted and never heard from again.

Having lost her savings and much of her merchandise in the attack, Guertha was hard-pressed to reestablish herself as a street merchant. Worse still, the more generous of her two *menaj* (lovers), by whom Guertha was now pregnant, was also the victim of a severe beating and arbitrary arrest by the army. Fearful for his life, and unjustly rejected by the U.S. Immigration and Naturalization Service in his request for political asylum, he was forced to flee to the relatively safe haven of a distant provincial village.

After six more months of hardship, deprivation, and an almost total lack of financial resources, Guertha, her three children, and the other remaining six members of the household were evicted. Neighbors and friends were too frightened to harbor them, leaving Guertha, by now very pregnant, and her children once again in the streets.

This ill-fated series of calamitous events and the devastating confluence of the crises of misery and repression plunged Guertha into abstruse despair. The "language" of rural Vodou, which might have provided her with some empowerment in the face of less formidable, more familiar adversity, was now unintelligible.[55] Guertha's darkening situation was entirely out of her control. While ever-respectful of the *lwas*, her distrust of the few Vodou priests and priestesses whom she had met in Port-au-Prince, along with the utter gravity of her quandary, resulted in feelings of spiritual angst and powerlessness that she had never before known. Guertha suddenly felt abandoned by the *lwas*.

The intention here is not to suggest that Vodou functions best in the rural world of the Haitian peasant, for, as Karen McCarthy Brown demonstrates, "it would be a mistake to see Vodou as an agrarian religion that is precarious when transported to the city."[56] The point is specific to Guertha's case, where the spiraling descent of her crises, along with the hostility of the strange urban environment and her distrust of the Port-au-Prince Vodou circles in which she had dabbled, left her religious needs, now amplified, unmet. The Virgin Mary would ultimately fill this void, particularly in the guise of *Notre Dame du Perpétuel Secours*, "*sel moun ki kap ranje zafe'm le kriz la ap kraze'm*" ("the only person who can work things out for me in times of crushing crisis").

Prior to Guertha's exile in Port-au-Prince, the Virgin Mary already had a place of importance in her religious life, though nothing like the place of primacy she would later occupy. "I used to pray to her, in front of her statue after every Sunday mass. I prayed to Mary [then] for my family, my husband's business ventures, for our fields, and for general security." To Guertha, Mary was one of a host of spiritual beings—both Catholic saints and Vodou *lwas*—to whom she could turn to meet her religious needs, helping her confront her life of struggle with courage and resilience. One of my few informants who spoke, as far as I could tell, with total openness regarding her Vodou practice, Guertha revealed to me that she understood the Ezili spirits to be, in her words, "the same" as the Virgin Mary, only subordinate—almost as if her servants. "The Virgin makes them do the things that she herself does not want to do."

Beside Ezili Freda, to whom she was once very devoted, though never married, Guertha was especially reverent of Kouzen Zak, Vodou's agricultural spirit. This stands to reason, given her family's long-standing dependence upon the harvest for survival. In the north, Guertha regularly attended Vodou ceremonies, especially those favorable to the presence of Ezili or Zak. In times of need, such as when she doubted her husband's fidelity or when heavy rains up rooted her entire bean harvest, she would normally consult Vodou's religious specialists.

Thus, Guertha had always believed in the intercessory powers of the Vodou *lwas*, as well as *lemò* (the dead) and, like most Vodouisants, saw no inherent contradiction in praying to Mary and serving the *lwas* concurrently. She explained this rather philosophically: "Just as all people are people, all spirits are spirits." Spirits, like persons (dead or alive), serve different functions, quite simply.

The Virgin's function in Guertha's belief system was originally supplemental to that of the *lwas* and other saints, consisting mainly in the provision of support, consolation, and the affectionate sisterly identification offered especially to women. There is nothing particularly Haitian in this aspect of Guertha's Marian piety. Robert Anthony Orsi, in *The Madonna of 115th Street*, could just have well been writing about Haitian peasant women as Italian immigrant women in New York City, where he notes that, "[t]he Madonna to whom these women were so attached was not a distant, asexual figure, but a woman like themselves who had suffered for and with her child."[57] Unlike the Italian women of Harlem, however, for Guertha, devotion to Mary was not the centerpiece of her religious life, but an integral part of a mosaic system of symbols and saints—both Catholic and Vodou. Besides the Virgin Mary, Guertha could also turn to Ezili for this sympathetic maternal identification with a powerful intercessory spiritual being who herself knows suffering.

Yet, for reasons enumerated above, the Virgin would come to eclipse Ezili in Guertha's religious life, beginning late in 1992 when she lost a home and a husband and was forced into exile in a hostile and unfamiliar urban environment. It was here that Guertha's devotion to the Virgin Mary, represented forcefully in the image of *Perpétuel Secours*, intensified. In a real sense, her worsening plight contributed to this, just as it did for Orsi's Italian-American informants:

> When their sufferings as mothers and wives were most intense, as these women tell their stories, when they felt that no one else could understand their particular agonies, they turned to the one who long ago had appealed to the

masses of Europe because of her evident participation in humanity's trials.[58]

Like Guertha, the Italian women of Harlem turned to "the only person who can work things out...in times of crushing crisis."

Several approaches might be taken to assess the differences between Guertha's Marianism and that of Orsi's informants. An Afrocentric perspective, for instance, might be developed. Afrocentricists, I realize, might object to the comparisons as misguided, since Guertha is of an African-based culture and Orsi's women are straight out of Italy. I admit that there is a degree of validity to this objection, but none so forceful as to negate what is a real commonality between both the early Italian immigrant women of Harlem and Guertha—in a word, oppression. In a real sense, then, Guertha threw herself upon *Notre Dame du Perpétuel Secours* for much the same reason that the Italian women of Harlem—themselves, as Orsi is careful to point out, victims of serious oppression—turned to the Madonna of 115th Street: "As all accounts of graces reveal, women turned to the Madonna out of an awareness of the severe limitations of their power and a sense of desperation over their powerlessness."[59] Similarly, Guertha's sense of oppression and powerlessness are only too evident. Furthermore, a careful analysis of sociomariological literature reveals that the religious needs rooted in oppression, especially the oppression of women— which lie far beneath the ways different cultures may adorn the Virgin or color her skin—are virtually universal in popular Marianism. Yet, for Guertha, unlike the women of Orsi's study, the intensification of Marian devotion after 1992 was fueled not only by despair in the face of a cascade of tragedies, but also by a sense of failure or inaccessibility of other traditional sources of religious succor and empowerment.

Guertha explained to me that she came to understand that it was the Virgin who had saved her and her children and brought them to Bel-Air. This dawned upon her during her first visit to the Church of *Perpétuel Secours*, located within short walking distance from her cousin's home. She had heard that this was a miraculous church and that *Perpétuel Secours* was the patron saint of Haiti who had performed countless miracles for the Haitian people. It was as much through logical reflection as spiritual intuition that Guertha concluded that she should both implore *Perpétuel Secours* to perform a miracle for her and her family, and that she owed *Perpétuel Secours* a great deal of thanks. Guertha undertook both of these endeavors immediately by making daily visits to the church, sometimes to pray the rosary, and at other times—when affordable—to leave a candle before the altar, but always to talk to Mary.

With rare exception, every morning for more than two years Guertha would awake before dawn and walk to the Church of *Perpétuel Secours*. Most days she brought a candle and a grue-some photograph of her husband's half-devoured corpse. On sev-eral occasions I accompanied Guertha to observe her ritual—she very much welcomed my presence. Crossing herself upon entering the church, Guertha walked directly to the altar and stopped just before the railing. Then she began to pray. Always standing, with arms outstretched, lighted candle in one hand, her worshipful eyes attentively fixed on the miraculous painting of *Notre Dame du Perpétuel Secours* hung centrally on the wall behind the altar,[60] Guertha would recite three Ave Marias, as if to invoke the Virgin's presence,[61] before breaking out into a litany of requests and suppli-cations. These were expressed informally, as if to a sister, but with imploring intensity. Like many poor Haitians, Guertha prayed aloud before the Virgin Mary:

> *Mami Cherie*, I salute you and thank you for all that you have done for me and my children, but all is still not well. They killed my husband [showing photograph to the icon], two of my children are far from me, and my business has been crushed. Soon we shall be evicted from our house, and already we have nothing to eat. Really, *Mami Cherie*, I fear that I can no longer carry on. Please, *Mami Cherie*, I implore you to do something for me and my children. Please take care of my husband [showing photograph to the icon]. Look what the motherless macoutes did to him. Please take care of him. I know that he is with you.

Reflective of her keen awareness of the ultimate causes of her suf-fering, Guertha's daily prayers also had a strong political content: "*Mami Cherie*, I pray to you to bring the American soldiers to Haiti to oust the forces of darkness who are crushing the people. Make the Americans come and return Titid to power so that we can live again." Guertha once explained to me that she firmly believed that only *Perpétuel Secours* could force Cédras from power and restore the democratically elected Aristide to the presidential palace. The very same day, tellingly, I witnessed General Cédras addressing his troops on the eve of the US military intervention, standing on the balcony at military headquarters, a large banner draped before him depicting none other than the same *Notre Dame du Perpétuel Secours* to whom Guertha and thousands of other oppressed Haitians were praying for deliverance from his regime! It immediately struck me that on a symbolic level, the war was already long-underway.

At the root of the recent flowering of Guertha's Marian devotion was a gripping sense of despair and powerlessness, but also an unshakable faith in *Perpétuel Recourse's* miraculous intercessory powers. Convinced that *Perpétuel Secours* was her protectress and sole hope, Guertha made vows, prayed the rosary and occasionally novenas, and even went on pilgrimage to Saut-d'Eau in the summer of 1994, a relatively costly sojourn in light of her meager financial means. This trip, she explained, was "to thank the Virgin for all she has done for me and to ask her forgiveness for my sins. Above all, to ask for her strength and to ask her to make the American soldiers come to Haiti."

That a sense of powerlessness brought Guertha to such a firm devotion to the Virgin suggests reference to Andrew Greeley's "four-celled paradigm" in understanding the meaning of her devotion. In Greeley's theoretical analysis of the development and function of Marian symbols, the "Mary myth" emerges from human "limit experiences" of the kind that Guertha endured in extreme form, and responds to the pronounced "existential needs" of the kind she experienced:

> We can not always help those we love, and there will come a time when they will not be able to help us. Life is finite, and within the boundaries of life our own particular existence is hemmed in on all sides by physiological, biological, psychological, and sociological limitations. We may be pilgrims of the absolute, we may hunger for the infinite, but the being that we experience in our daily lives is all too fragile, all too finite.... Such experiences are "ru-

mors of angels," "signals of the transcendent," or, in David Tracy's more metaphysical words, "disclosive of a final, a fundamental meaningfulness [which] bears a religious character."[62]

For Greeley, "[t]hese 'disclosive' experiences reveal to us a world of meaning beyond the everyday, and this world is that through which religious symbols come."[63] While Guertha, obviously, did not play a role in the creation of the symbol of Mary, this symbol's re-creation is an ever-occurring phenomenon wherever and whenever Guertha or anyone else cries out to the Virgin Mary. Guertha's own very glaring limit experiences are precisely what disclosed to her the power of the symbol of the Mother of God.

Admittedly, we are disregarding somewhat Greeley's notion that it is especially out of the limit experiences of "sexual differentiation" that the Mary myth emerges oversimplifies his theory. Many of Guertha's problems were indeed those typically experienced by poor women rather than men, like, for instance, sexual exploitation, pregnancy without spousal support, rape, single parenthood, etc. While it would be possible to apply further his theory of sexual differentiation in an analysis of Guertha's Marianism, of greater relevance here is Greeley's definition of those existential needs to which the "four aspects of Mary" (Madonna, Virgo, Sponsa, and Pieta) respond: "Discouragement, despair"; "Weariness"; "Aloneness, isolation, restriction, inhibition"; "Futility of life, separation."[64] Although this list might be expanded or reworded, these are more or less precisely the very emotions rooted in Guertha's existential needs during her exile, to which we may point in explaining the intensification of her devotion to *Notre Dame du Perpétuel Secours*.

Before turning our attention to the survey, and by way of conclusion to our discussion of Guertha's Marian devotion, we may first gain insight into the matter at hand through a discussion of the several questions outlined above in regards to her case.

1. *To what extent does Guertha's Marian devotion function as an opiate? Does her Marianism promote any degree of fatalistic resignation to the material conditions of her existence?*

There is little question that Guertha found a great deal of consolation in the Virgin Mary, making her suffering less painful. In this sense, then, her Marian devotion was therapeutic, indeed, like a drug. However, this anesthetic effect amounted neither to the fatalism nor to the kind of alienation against which Marx so forcefully argued. Throughout her crises, Guertha remained politically active as a member of a clandestine popular organization with a pro-Aristide agenda. Far from numbing her into submission to her fate, which, after all, was largely determined by political circumstances, Guertha's feeling of closeness with Mary gave her the courage to take the great risks that her political activism entailed. "They can kill my body," she once said, "but the Virgin is watching over my soul and will keep it forever alive."

2. *What role does the symbol of the Virgin Mary play in explaining to Guertha the meaning of her world and her place in it?*

During her exile in Port-au-Prince, Guertha came to understand that she was to serve the Virgin Mary in realizing her divine plan for the restoration of democracy in Haiti. Often she would speak of herself as the Virgin's *"domestik,"* or maid. This consideration gave Guertha a real sense of purpose and meaning, despite circumstances that could easily have brought her to view life as meaningless.

3. *To what extent can we understand the symbol of Mary be to be a "factor of popular identity," or as an instrument in the crystallization of class consciousness?*

While this question would be better addressed in a class-wide survey, rather than in an individual case study, it did strike me that Guertha was aware of the fact that her prayers to Mary for the return of Aristide were common among the popular masses. Her identity as one among an entire population whose lot was at stake in the unfolding political drama might be seen, thus, as having gained some definition through her Marianism.

Class consciousness is very strong in Haiti, and it would be misleading to point to any single symbol as responsible for its development. Nonetheless, because the *Tilegliz* movement since the early eighties has played an important role in the crystallization of revolutionary class consciousness in Haiti, and since, as demonstrated in chapter four, Mary's place in *Tilegliz* is an important one, we thus may conclude that popular Marianism played some role in unifying the masses in recognition of their common plight and political objectives.

4. *In Guertha's Marianism are there expressions, however oblique or couched, of protest against domination or suffering? Is her use of the symbol of Mary an example of ideological negation?*

In praying (often aloud and in public) to Mary to topple the Cédras regime, and in being empowered by Mary to courageously engage in the resistance movement, Guertha's Marianism clearly took the form of overt and active protest not only against domination and suffering, but against the very political forces responsible for them. This is a good example of ideological negation, since Guertha saw through the junta's use of the symbol of Mary as a weapon of symbolic violence employed to legitimize their power, and since she negated this ideology by perceiving of Mary as both opposed to the military regime and directive of the resistance movement. As Scott writes, "resistance to ideological domination requires a counterideology—a negation."[65] Guertha's Marianism amounted precisely to this.

5. *To which of Guertha's religious needs does the symbol of the Virgin Mary respond? How do these needs influence the forms of Marian devotion that she prefers or creates?*

The need for consolation and courage ranked paramount among Guertha's religious needs, especially during her period of exile in Port-au-Prince. Her concern for her own sanctification was rarely, if ever, perceptible, and may thus be ranked very low among her religious interests. This would support Weber's claim regarding the "situation of the disprivileged," in the sense that "(t)hey do not always experience this need for salvation in a religious form."[66] Another of the oppressed's leading religious needs, notes Weber, is "the need for just compensation…involving rewards for one's own good deeds and punishment for the unrighteousness of others."[67] Guertha felt assured that those who were responsible for her plight would, as she put it in Magnificat-esque language, "be brought before the Great Master by the Virgin for judgment."[68] Clearly, therefore, Mary responded to Guertha's need for the assurance of compensation.

These needs seem to have brought Guertha to prefer informal, familiar address to the Virgin over the recitation of standard prayers and other ritualistic observances. Only three times had she ever prayed the novena. Although the rosary did occupy her about once a week, she admits to rarely finishing the entire prayer cycle and to substituting personalized requests for repetition. Her principal needs for consolation and empowerment greatly surpassed her needs for the forgiveness of sins or the assurance of eternal life. Arguably, these needs were more readily met through speaking to Mary as a close sister and comrade, rather than as a distant supernatural mediatrix swayed by the repetition of formal prayers.

6. What is the degree and nature of the identification of Mary with Ezili in Guertha's belief system?

"When I pray in the Church of *Perpétuel Secours*, it is to Mary that I pray. Ezili has no place there. When I need Ezili or when she needs me, I go to an *ounfò* (Vodou temple)" Therein, Guertha recognized spatial delineations between the places where each, the Virgin and Ezili, is formally venerated or communed with. This is suggestive of an essential difference between the two. Guertha's apparent contradiction in saying that Mary and Ezili were indeed "the same," though approached differently and in different places, seemed not in the least to trouble her. Theological speculation was of little interest to Guertha; she knew what worked, and this, almost alone, guided her religious considerations and behavior.

With the worsening of her circumstances, including her uprooting from the rural world to which she was accustomed—indeed, the only world that she knew until 1992—Guertha's religious needs, as has been demonstrated, intensified, and she turned almost exclusively now to Mary, whom she long considered possessed of greater powers than Ezili. For Guertha, another difference between Mary and Ezili, one understood by many of my poor informants, was that Mary's graces came "without a price," whereas Ezili's services were more conditional, demanding a taxing, "unfair" devotional exchange on the devotee's part.

Under-class Survey: Results and Analysis

A total of nearly 500 questionnaires were either distributed or employed to structure interviews, with 300 selected as representative of the Haitian under-class. In the majority of these cases, respondents were impoverished and illiterate, thus necessitating oral interviews. The socioeconomic class of respondents was sometimes difficult left unarticulated, so a combination of factors were taken into account to make this determination. For instance, anyone with a monthly income of less that the equivalent of US$166 was included in the pool of lower-class respondents. In the absence of knowledge of respondents' level of income, we took other factors, such as trade or profession, or unemployment, neighborhood of residence, and schools attended as indicators of class. All "border line" or clearly middle-class cases were omitted from the survey.

Of lower-class respondents, 62 percent either resided in rural localities or were recent immigrants from the provinces to Port-au-Prince. Twenty-eight percent were either native to or long-standing residents of Port-au-Prince. The remaining 10 percent were from other cities; mainly from Les Cayes, Jacmel, and Cap-Haïtien. Thus the survey achieved a wide geographical representation in the pool of lower-class respondents.

As concerns employment, 37 percent could be defined as peasant farmers and 43 percent as unemployed. Twenty-four percent claimed to be employed as either wage laborers or in private, small-scale business enterprises (of the informal sector) such as Guertha's marketing of plastic ware in the streets.

In regard to age, ten percent of lower-class respondents were under 20, 33 percent were between 20 and 35, 34 percent between 35 and 50, with the remaining 23 percent being over 50 years old.

The gender breakdown was nearly exactly 50/50. Marital status among poor respondents was much less certain: 36 percent claimed to be legally married, but surely this figure is inexact. Brown estimates that among peasant women, for instance, "only one in a hundred has a legal marriage."[69] Only 12 percent admitted being *"plase,"* or partners in a common law marriage; seven percent were widows; while 39 percent claimed being single.

Level of education also proved difficult to gauge with any accuracy among lower-class respondents, since there is some sense of shame that accompanies illiteracy—despite it being a condition shared by the vast majority of Haitians—and few will admit to being illiterate. I suspect, therefore, that most poor respondents exaggerated their level of education. This would explain why 52 percent claimed having had some secondary school education, even though less than a quarter of under-class respondents could read the questionnaire. In any case, 42 percent attested to having been to primary school, while five percent admitted having no formal schooling. Significantly, none of the under-class respondents had ever attended university.

In terms of religious affiliation, all but six respondents professed to being Catholic. Three refused to respond to the question, while only three others admitted outright being Vodouisant, though surely many more (if not most) of this group of respondents practice Vodou. Among both poor and wealthy respondents, very few were Protestant. Their questionnaires were not included in the survey.

It deserves mention that the majority of lower-class respondents were members of some community-based, popular religious organization, either explicitly TKL (*Ti Kominote Legliz* or *Tilegliz*) or some organization with similar structure and objectives. This is significant since—despite the claim of Father Georges Charles of the Stella Maris Community in Cap-Haïtien that TKL "is not a political organization"[70]—membership in such organizations is a source of inspiration and orientation for political activism, as we saw with Guertha. A 1992 letter published by the *Komite Nasyonal TKL* (National TKL Committee) closes with a forceful and courageous declaration of its political objectives:

> Through the power of the Holy Spirit, let us continue to resist so that to Haiti:
> We make democracy return,
> We make security return,
> We make all refugees return,
> We make President Titid return,

We make justice, truth and love return.
RETURN, RETURN, RETURN, TOTALLY, AMEN![71]

Hence, given the obvious political awareness and activism of TKL members, and in light of the fact that the majority of lower-class respondents claimed membership either to TKL or to similar popular religious organizations, I expected, for this as well as other reasons, to find politicized Marian beliefs among this pool of informants. My expectation, as we'll see momentarily, proved correct.

Marian Practice Among the Haitian Poor

The most popular forms of Marian practice among the Haitian poor are the recitation of the rosary and the celebration of the Virgin's feast days. Among lower-class respondents, 88 percent attended either one or several Marian celebrations of a specific feast day, like that of *Perpétuel Secours*, June 27, which is described in chapter four. Some felt that the feast days were the Virgins' birthdays and the celebrations their birthday parties. Many consider it of dire importance to attend the feast day celebration of the Marian icon for which one holds particular devotion. Indeed, feast day attendance strikes many of these respondents as a pressing obligation, not to be neglected for fear of a consequent decline in Mary's graces. "I must be there every August 15," explained one unemployed man, "otherwise she might forget about me." Typically, my informants seemed to regard the feast day as the most opportune time to give thanks to the Virgin for blessings received or to implore her miraculous intervention to cure an ailing loved one, bring peace to Haiti, or help a business venture succeed, etc.

A slightly lower percentage (86 percent) affirmed that they pray the rosary. Often the rosary was referred to as a "weapon" ("*zam*"): "The rosary is the Christian's weapon against sin and temptation," explained a homeless woman with whom I often spoke in front of the cathedral in Port-au-Prince. Like many respondents, she felt that the rosary helped her from reverting to "old thoughts" ("*vye panse*").[72] Others noted how the rosary has a calming effect, "refreshing to the soul," that "makes you tolerant of your enemies." In sum, for the majority of poor respondents who elaborated on their employment of the rosary, this form of Marian practice is the one they most often employ for personal benefit, rather than, say, for the sake of a relative's health or the nation's progress.

The novena, which ranks next in popularity after the rosary, with 73 percent of respondents having at least once prayed it, has more public and complex objectives than the immediate and personal requests made via the rosary. It is evident that the poor employ the novena more sparingly than the rosary, some reserving the novena for the most trying of circumstances where a miracle, rather than a mere blessing, is needed. Numerous respondents indicated that they pray a novena whenever someone close to them dies, calling on the Virgin to see to the departed's soul's deliverance. Many others prayed the novena when seeking employment, and roughly two dozen attested that this had in fact worked for them. "I prayed a novena for twenty-seven days," said one young man, "and I finally got a job."

A common explanation was that the novena has the greatest potential among Marian practices for procuring the Virgin's miraculous intervention. "It is the best way to get the Virgin to perform a miracle." "The novena is the prayer which gets the most extraordinarily miraculous results."

Less common, though still evident among lower-class respondents, was the indication that the novena functions as a vehicle of fatalistic resignation. As one woman told me, "The novena is my relief from all my suffering." Another related that "the novena helps me be content with what I have." This kind of statement was strikingly typical among poor informants.

A dozen respondents offered a somewhat curious reason as to why they, although worshipful of Mary, refrained from praying the novena. "I don't pray the novena because I don't want to be brought close to the *lwas* or serve them." "If I pray the novena people will think that I am practicing Vodou, and I don't want that to happen." When pressed to elaborate, these respondents invariably gave the vaguest of explanations. "That's just the way it is." "They say that the novena is a Vodou thing." I have failed to discover the origin of this belief.

Pilgrimage was only slightly less popular than the novena, with 71 percent of lower-class respondents having at least once made pilgrimage in honor of the Virgin. Actually more than this percentage responded affirmatively to this question, though a stroll around the block or across town does not constitute pilgrimage. Without exception, obviously due to financial limitations, the poor pilgrims' destinations were limited to various Marian shrines or churches in Haiti. Wealthy Haitian Marian devotees, as we will see in the following chapter, sometimes make pilgrimage abroad to places like Lourdes or Fatima.

Under-class respondents gave a staggering variety of reasons for making pilgrimage, ranging from the possibility of finding a boyfriend—or, in the case of two prostitutes I interviewed, of the wealth of potential "johns"—among the pilgrims, to penitential asceticism and mystical enlightenment. Following is a selection of the motivations of poor Haitians who go on Marian pilgrimage:

"Pilgrimage is the best way of rendering homage to the Virgin."

"I went to Verettes to thank the Virgin for all she's done for me and to ask her to make my heart humble and pure."

"Pilgrimage is the best form of penitence"

"I felt that in going on a pilgrimage the Virgin would love me more and perhaps help me find a wife who looks like her."

"It is the most favorable way of communicating with the Virgin."

"Just as the Virgin put her life on hold to give us Jesus, I put mine on hold to give her thanks."

"Pilgrimage is an occasion for us to consecrate our lives to God."

It was somewhat surprising that less than half (45 percent) of lower-class respondents had ever made a vow of some kind to the Virgin. Of those who had, there was nothing uniquely Haitian in the kinds of vows they had made: "I promised the Virgin to name my child Marie." "I made a vow to the Virgin that I would be charitable to those who are poorer than I." "I promised to pray the rosary every Wednesday evening." These are, I suppose, standard fare wherever people make vows to Mary.

Three-fourths of poor respondents had some image of Mary on display in their homes. Roughly half of these were unable to identify which image, describing her appearance instead. *Perpétuel Secours* was, predictably, the most common Marian icon found in the homes of the Haitian poor. Fewer than 33 percent wear medals depicting the Virgin Mary. While not formally addressed in the interviews, many interjected that they wear crosses, which, in my estimation, hang around the necks of more poor Haitians than do Marian medals.

Marian Beliefs among the Haitian Poor

With a few insignificant exceptions, whoever is considered most capable of answering their prayers—be that God, Jesus Christ, or the Blessed Virgin Mary—is the figure to whom poor Haitians most often address their prayers. This is only logical. Among the 300 under-class individuals in the survey, a striking total of 65 percent prayed most often to Mary rather than to God or Jesus. Of the remainder, 19 percent prayed most often to Jesus, while only 16 percent prayed most often directly to God. This suggests precisely what I have suspected for as long as I have lived in Haiti: just as in some other poor nations of the Catholic world, like Mexico or Brazil, the Virgin Mary has eclipsed God the Father, Jesus the Christ, the Holy Spirit, and the rest of the Communion of Saints as the most important Catholic spiritual force for the popular masses. This seemingly indisputable fact raises what is perhaps the most imperative question in both sociomariology and Mariology proper: Why? How are we to explain this phenomenon which Kari Borresen refers to as "the coincidence between Mariocentricism with national economic weakness."[73] Here below, I shall weave some suggestions in response to this question out of the threads of insights shared with me by my informants from the popular Haitian masses, who most often quite simply explained that they usually prayed to Mary instead of Jesus or God because they felt that she is much closer to them. This interestingly, is the same reason that both Rosemary Radford Ruether and Marina Warner give for the rise of Marian piety in the Middle Ages in Europe:

Warner:
The intimate devotion of the last hundred years [14th Century] had made the Virgin an approachable, kindly figure who could be depended upon for pity and comfort. The cult of the *Mater Dolorosa* stressed her participation in mankind's ordinary, painful lot, and so while the repercussions of the Black Death restored a degree of majesty and terror to the personality of Christ the Judge, the Virgin herself retained the common touch.[74]

Ruether:
From the twelfth through the fifteenth centuries her star rises in medieval theology, her glory growing ever brighter in proportion to the downgrading of real women. As indicated in the preceding chapter, this development of the devotion to Mary is partly a reaction to the removal of the human from Christ, who is seen primarily as the stern judge in the Final Judgment.[75]

Reflective of a similar sense of Mary's "common touch," poor Haitians tend to address the Virgin as if they are speaking openly and informally with a relative or a close friend. This is especially true of poor women, the above description of Guertha at prayer being quite typical. While commonly the Virgin is called in prayer "*Mami Cheri*" ("Mommy Dear"), normally poor Haitians call her "*Lavyej*" ("The Virgin"). The name "*Marie*," curiously, in fact is somewhat rarely used. It seems that the respect shown to one's earthly mother in never calling her by her first name is extended to the heavenly Mother. In any case, poor Haitians often spoke of the Virgin as their mother, as the mother of all Haitians, or as everyone's mother.

Less often, lower-class respondents described their relationship with Mary in sisterly terms. After the mother/child analogy, the most popular metaphor used in describing their relationship with the Virgin was that of *domestik* (maid). Dozens of respondents employed this term. "My relationship with Mary," described the homeless woman in front of the cathedral, "is that I am her maid and I do for her whatever she asks. In return, she gives me life." It is noteworthy that while numerous lower-class respondents used this analogy, not a single wealthy Haitian did.

Thus, poor Haitians generally see the Virgin as closer to them than Jesus Christ and God, and hence her graces are more accessible through prayer. She is popularly conceived of, in a real sense, as more powerful than the men of the Trinity.[76] This, of course, is a heretical belief, one that, as illustrated in chapter three, has a long history in popular Catholicism.

Some lower-class respondents did seem to possess a more orthodox Mariology than the commonly maximalist popular position. What was striking was the ease with which many poor informants use sophisticated theological terms like "mediatrix," "intermediary graces," and "coredemptrix" when speaking of Mary, though their understanding of these terms is highly suspect. One woman, for example, after repeatedly using interchangeably the terms "intermediary" and "attorney" in reference to the Virgin, explained to me bluntly that it is Mary who "has the most pity for me and the most power to cleanse me of my sins." Once again, the Mother Goddess reigns in Catholicism on the popular level in the Virgin Mary, despite orthodoxy's efforts to delimit Mary's role in the economy of salvation. As Goethe writes in the final passage of *Faust*, "*Das ewig weibliche zieht uns heran*" ("The eternal feminine draws us ever on").

The general picture emerging here of the Haitian poor's Virgin is of a spiritual being at least equally as powerful as Jesus or God the Father, who is considered closer to humans than either Christ or God, and thus a more worthy addressee of their prayers. And for the overwhelming majority of lower-class respondents in the survey (90 percent), at some point in time, so they believe, the Virgin has answered their prayers. Interestingly, this is actually a slightly lower figure than that found in the pool of wealthy respondents (93 percent). Listed here are some typical prayers that poor Haitians believe the Virgin Mary answers:

"The Virgin gave me a boat so that I could pursue a career as a fisherman."

"She cured my son after months of serious illness. He had almost died, and the Virgin saved his life."

"I prayed for weeks to the Virgin and she finally found me a job."

"The Virgin helped my business grow and helped me sell just enough to get by during the embargo."

"She saved me from danger at sea and sent the American Coast Guard to bring us to Guantanamo [Bay, Cuba]."

"The Virgin gave me the strength and the intelligence to finish school."

"My husband used to sleep around a lot, so I prayed to the Virgin to change his ways and she has restored his fidelity."

"Once I was having serious problems at school, so I prayed to the Virgin to help me change schools. The next week this happened."

" I pray to Mary to help me understand and live according to Church doctrine."

"The Virgin has established harmony between myself, my wife, my kids, my friends, and even my enemies."

"The Virgin has made me recognize those poorer than me as needy and inspires me to acts of charity on their behalf."

"For awhile there was much shooting every night in my neighborhood. I prayed to the Virgin and she kept our home safe."

"My sister and I prayed together every night to the Virgin to stop the shooting outside, and now there is no more shooting, or much less anyway."

"I prayed daily for the Virgin to send the American soldiers to crush the motherless *macoutes*, and this has now happened, thanks to her."

It is evident that lower-class respondents prayed to Mary most often for the resolution of personal problems such as illness, unemployment, or a faulty business venture. Less often, though by no means rarely, were sick relatives or wayward spouses the subjects of their prayers. The needs of the poor are immediate, pressing, and often vital; it is the most precarious existence that inspires the least imaginative prayers. Orsi's point regarding Italian immigrants' prayers to Mary could serve with equal appropriateness in the Haitian context:

> The intensity with which the requests for help for these small problems was expressed reflects the precariousness of poor people's lives, lives in which an inflamed molar could be the beginning of a chain of consequences that could end in untold, if not unexpected suffering.[77]

Besides benefiting from the Virgin's intercessory powers to cure their ills and soothe their pains, many poor Haitians also feel that the Virgin Mary helps them understand and live in accordance with orthodox Catholic doctrine. This is something that they commonly ask of the Virgin. The frequency of such comments was initially surprising, but upon further reflection I came to realize that this is a result of the struggle over religious capital between orthodoxy and the heresiarch in the Haitian religious field, a struggle, as demonstrated in chapter two, that has a long and gripping history. When we consider orthodoxy's use of religious symbols as weapons of symbolic violence, it is understandable how Mary would function in popular Haitian Catholicism is as the custodian of orthodoxy, a vestige of the Church's unsuccessful, though influential, attempts to eliminate Vodou. In chapter four there are several examples of the Virgin employed by the Church and, in the case of Lescot, the State as champion of the anti-Vodou cause and guardian of Church doctrine in the face of a laity prone to deviation and *le mélange*. Thus, it becomes apparent why many poor Haitians feel that one of the Virgin's key functions in their lives is to help them understand Church doctrine and follow a doctrinally correct path, steering clear of heretical belief. The great irony, of course, is that their maximalist Mariology itself is generally heterodox.

Just as poor Haitians display some disregard for, if not ignorance of, orthodox Catholic Mariology, contemporary Church social teachings likewise seem to hold little significance for them, despite their prayers to the Virgin to understand them. Reflecting this, to the question as to what the Virgin has done for Haiti, one young woman responded, "She brought the pope to Haiti in 1983, and she gave us condoms so that we might protect ourselves from AIDS." I found this response altogether remarkable.

In Haitian Marianism, the most noteworthy form of heresy is that of the Virgin's assimilation with Ezili, discussed at length in chapter five. Without a doubt, the most controversial question posed to informants, both rich and poor, was one concerning whether they believed that Mary and Ezili were in some way related. A fair number of respondents, again both poor and rich alike, actually took offense—or feigned to—at my inquiry into the matter, opposed to what they perceived of as my insinuation that their Catholic faith was somehow impure or tinged with *le mélange*. "How could you dare pose that question to a Christian?"—or the like, was not an uncommon retort.

Confronted with such an attitude among a considerable number of lower-class respondents, investigation of this important matter became problematic. This was compounded by the almost traditional reticence of Haitians to reveal their Vodouisant beliefs and practices to outsiders, whence the Creole proverb: "*lè lanthropolog rive, lwa yo cache*" ("when the anthropologist shows up, the spirits go into hiding"). This is not merely the plight of foreign researchers, as Haitian sociologist of religion Laënnec Hurbon, somewhat to my relief, himself expressed frustration with this very question: "It is difficult to know whether the Vaudouisant at prayer before a statue of the Virgin in Church addresses the Virgin herself or the loa which to him the statue of the Virgin evokes or represents."[78] It must, therefore, be admitted that no single finding from my fieldwork should be approached with greater suspicion than the data regarding the identification of Mary and Ezili. The case study of Guertha, I think, offers greater insight into this question. The production of genuinely useful data on the matter through wide-scale polling, on the other hand, is an improbability.

Nonetheless, and with these misgivings in view, the survey showed that 84 percent of poor respondents answered—often in the bluntest of terms—that Mary and Ezili were entirely distinct and share nothing in common. Typical elaborations were as follows:

"The Virgin is the Mother of God and a force of light and the source of all that is good, while Ezili is the mother of Satan and a force of darkness and evil."

"The Virgin Mary is very close to God, but Ezili is rejected by God."

"The Virgin is simple, loving and generous, whereas everything you do with Ezili produces pain."

"The Virgin is God's gift to the world, unlike Ezili, who is a satanic angel. Everything about her is evil."

A highly respected Vodou priestess on the island of La Gonâve explained to me the differences between Mary and Ezili in somewhat similar terms:

> Both the Virgin and Ezili Freda are powerful women who can have a great influence over our lives. But there is an important difference. The Virgin Mary does only good things and does them unconditionally for goodness sake. There is no price; just ask her with love. She understands love. Ezili can do both good and bad things for you, but anytime she does something good, something bad must occur elsewhere. And she is expensive. You must pay if you want her to do things for you.

It is noteworthy, in any case, that in spite of the vehemence with which some poor respondents denounced Ezili as evil, distinguishing her from the Virgin Mary in terms of bad/good, darkness/light dichotomies, not a single person expressed any doubt concerning her existence. Ezili, as it were, is as real for poor Haitians as the Virgin Mary.

One of the most interesting findings of the survey was a belief expressed by roughly a quarter of those lower-class respondents who acknowledged some identity between Mary and Ezili. Thirteen individuals, all men, mentioned that President Aristide serves both the Virgin Mary and Ezili Freda, and that his example is something of a model to be followed, or it at least assures them of some form of union between the two. "I was never too sure about who Ezili was or what powers she had or if she was the Virgin," explained a dock worker, "but since Titid serves both Ezili and the Virgin, they must be the same and both of them can help us." Respondents offered no satisfactory elaborations on this intriguing matter; it appears that this belief is based on hearsay—"That is what they say." One respondent insisted to me that he knew for a fact that Aristide was a devotee of Ezili and that he even had a shrine dedicated to her in his bedroom. Whether or not there is any degree of truth to such claims, they are common fare in Haiti's exceptionally virulent rumor mill, lent credence not just by the poor: a number of rich Haitians expressed their suspicion or downright conviction that Aristide practices black magic and blood sacrifice. One young *bourgeoise* swore to me that he is "the antichrist"!

Marian Cults among the Haitian Poor

In an effort to determine which are the most important Marian cults in popular Haitian Catholicism, I listed eleven images or names of the Virgin that seemed the most common in Haiti, and asked respondents to rank them in order of personal importance: *Perpétuel Secours*, Immaculate Conception, Assumption, Mount Carmel, Lourdes, Fatima, Calvary, *Caridad del Cobre*, Czestochowa, *Altagracia*, and Guadalupe.[79] I devised a simple point system[80] by which to tabulate the rankings and discern which were the most important cults. In all, 254 lower-class respondents participated in this segment of the survey.

The following table illustrates the tabulated results from individual respondents' rankings of the various icons of Mary. They are listed in descending order of popularity. Parenthetical figures are of corresponding totals from the upper-class survey, included here for the sake of comparison. It must be kept in mind that the lower-class sample was three times larger than that of the upper-class, so to compare figures accurately from each survey group, upper-class figures should be multiplied by three.

Marian Image	1st	Total Pts.	Last
1) *Perpétuel Secours*	178 (67)	2224 (846)	0 (0)
2) Immac. Concept.	51 (12)	918 (288)	0 (0)
3) *Altagracia*	8 (8)	632 (264)	1 (2)
4) Assumption	0 (0)	428 (126)	0 (2)

5) Mount Carmel	1 (3)	317 (78)	31 (11)
6) Lourdes	3 (3)	188 (66)	2 (3)
7) Fatima	0 (0)	40 (8)	8 (0)
8) Mount Calvary	0 (1)	24 (50)	33 (15)
9) *Caridad del Cobre*	0 (1)	16 (50)	29 (13)
10) Czestochowa	0 (0)	12 (22)	18 (10)
11) Guadeloupe	0 (4)	0 (52)	45 (17)

Additionally, we asked participants which of these Virgins had the greatest concern for Haiti, and 204 answered *Perpétuel Secours*; 51, Immaculate Conception; 8, *Altagracia*; 3, Lourdes; and 1, Mount Carmel.

As expected, *Notre Dame du Perpétuel Secours* is far and away the most popular Marian icon among the Haitian poor, reflected by the 70 percent of respondents who identified her as having the greatest personal importance to them. An even higher percentage (80 percent) considered *Perpétuel Secours* as having the greatest concern for Haiti.

Perpétuel Secours, Immaculate Conception, *Altagracia*, Assumption, and Mount Carmel, in this order, are the most important Marian cults among poor Haitian Catholics. There is no significant difference in this order among wealthy Haitians. We had expected to find some disparity between cults popular among the poor and those popular among the wealthy, for a number of reasons. For instance, the oft-noted affinity of the Haitian elite for things French might have thrust Lourdes into the top five cults of elite Haitian Marianism, but our findings suggest that this is not the case. Cult popularity or the preference of one Marian image over others in general is not, as it turns out, class-specific. What agents from different socioeconomic classes do with the same image, however, is. This will be demonstrated below.

To the question as to whether my list of Marys omitted any figures that were important to them, a great number of poor respondents replied "yes"; that I had failed to mention St. Anne, St. Elizabeth, St. Rose, or St. Mary Magdalene. This suggests that in popular Haitian Catholicism all female saints are seen as manifestations of the Virgin, which is corroborated by the fact that an equally great number of poor respondents went on Marian pilgrimage or glorified Mary on the feast days and at the shrines of other female saints.

Many lower-class participants in the survey from the island of La Gonâve, where the cult of Mary Magdalene is prevalent, insisted on entering Magdalene's name on the list of Virgins. Time and again they told me that "Magdalene is the most important Virgin." The seemingly irreconcilable incompatibility between prostitution and virginity was not an issue. I came to suspect that most lower-class participants from La Gonâve simply did not know the biblical portrayal of Magdalene and took her to be the Virgin, much as elsewhere Sts. Rose, Anne, and Elizabeth are also commonly perceived by poor Haitians to be just more manifestations of the Virgin Mary. Causally, this *intra*religious conflation of female Catholic saints is akin to the *inter*religious assimilation of Catholic saints with Vodou spirits; it is entirely based upon visual identification, with little or no consideration—or perhaps even awareness of—theological or physical contradictions.

The Political Content of Popular Haitian Marianism

The single aspect of lower-class Haitian Marianism that most distinguishes it from the Marianism of wealthy Haitians is its political or ideological content. Poor and rich Haitians differ enormously in how they conceive of the Virgin Mary's role in national Haitian affairs. This is forcefully demonstrated by a juxtaposition of the percentages of respondents from each group who believe that the Virgin Mary had ousted the military junta from power, restored democracy, and returned President Aristide to Haiti. A striking 63 percent of poor respondents mentioned either the fall of the Cédras regime, the restoration of democracy, or the return of Aristide among the things that they believed that the Virgin Mary had done for Haiti. This percentage would likely have been still considerably higher had the interview included a specific question designed to elicit respondents' belief regarding their country's recent political changes. Contrarily, a mere 11 percent of wealthy participants saw Mary's hand in the unfolding of the remarkable events of September and October 1994.

This finding stands to reason. It needs to be recalled here that Aristide's support is almost entirely culled from among Haiti's poor masses, for whom the priest-turned-president is something of a prophet. His return could only seem a religious event, the people's compensation for three years of terrible suffering and earnest prayers. Mary's divine authorship of the inspirational triumph of good over evil must have struck many poor Haitians like Guertha as altogether patent. Among the wealthy, on the other hand, Aristide is generally hated and viewed as a threat to their privilege and power. To such people, some of whom financially backed the coup and the junta, Aristide's return could hardly be seen as ordained by the same spiritual forces that throughout Haitian history have sanctioned their power and privilege.

A handful of poor respondents, significantly, actually quoted the Magnificat when explaining to me the Virgin's role in the overthrow of the junta and the restoration of the once poor parish priest to the presidential palace: "He has deposed the mighty from their thrones and raised the lowly to high places." Clearly, the image of Mary in the Magnificat, here eloquently described by Boff, is appreciable in popular Haitian Marianism:

> an image of Mary as the strong, determined woman committed to the messianic liberation of the poor from the historical social injustices under which they suffer. And today we see this image taking shape, deep in the heart of an oppressed people, who long for a voice in society and liberation from its evils.[81]

To further illustrate this liberative, political dimension of popular Marianism in Haiti, it is perhaps best to let the Haitian poor speak for themselves. Following is an exemplary selection of comments made by lower-class respondents regarding what the Virgin has done for the Haitian people:

"The last miracle that the Virgin performed for the Haitian people was the Aristidian miracle."

"In 1983, the Virgin made Pope John Paul II come to Haiti, and that was the birth of our democratic movement."

"She made democracy and Titid return to Haiti."

"The Virgin Mary has shattered the teeth of the *putchists*, the thieves of our rights and dignity, the forces of darkness."

"The Virgin has caused the winds of democracy to blow once again across our land."

"In Haitian history, it is the Virgin who has chased all cruel dictators from power."

"The Virgin is the root of all liberation and the origin of the entire popular movement."

"She is a fanatic of democracy."

"She made the egg reenter the chicken's ass" ("*li fe zè la tounen na deryè poul la*").[82]

The liberative political content of poor Haitians' Mariology was equally manifest in participants' responses to the questions, "What might the Virgin Mary do for Haiti in the future?" "What is the Virgin Mary's message to the Haitian people?" Haitian culture is extraordinarily rich in proverbs, and President Aristide has been known to spin a few of his own. It was thus not surprising that many poor respondents had the Virgin quoting Aristide in articulating her message to the Haitian people: "The fork of division cannot drink of the soup of democracy" ("*Fochèt divisyon pa kabap manje soup demokrasi a*"). "No to violence, no to vengeance, yes to reconciliation." Rectifying Haiti's tense class strife toward the promotion of justice and a decent existence for all Haitians, in fact, are evidently common themes of hope at the heart of the poor's Marian devotion.

Reflective of a related theme, a few lower-class participants put the words of John F. Kennedy in the mouth of the Virgin in her message to the Haitian people: "Ask not what your country can do for you; ask what you can do for your country." Central to the recent political empowerment of the Haitian masses is their collective realization that their plight is in the main the result of the elite classes doing precisely nothing for the country, but historically arranging things so that the country does a great deal for them. In this light, the Virgin quoting JFK is implicitly subversive. From these observations we may conclude that poor Haitians, as well as many outside observers, view Haiti's class division as the root of much of what ails the nation. It would seem that Sidney Mintz's opinion is shared by the Haitian masses:

> The present situation is the outcome of 200 years of a war of attrition against the people by a ruling class.... Under the best of circumstances, Haiti cannot be changed structurally without some yielding of power by the haves.[83]

Many of the Haitian poor are counting on the Virgin Mary to perform just such a miracle.

Conclusion

To conclude this chapter, concise and direct answers to the questions enumerated above will be articulated (with the exception of question six, which has already been addressed twice):

1. *To what extent does the Virgin Mary serve poor Haitians as an "opiate," providing them with consolation in order to endure their suffering? Does this amount to fatalistic resignation?*

Undeniably, poor Haitians' Marian devotion is a great source of consolation and comfort in the face of economic deprivation and its accompanying ailments and struggles. In Guertha's case, we witnessed this clearly. Insofar as such consolation is therapeutic or anesthetic, poor Haitians' Marianism does have a narcotic effect, but no more than any other form of popular religious expression, and it does not, for most, induce a stupor of submission and fatalistic acceptance of things the way they are. Quite the contrary, for only a small percentage of lower-class respondents did Marian piety amount to either fatalistic escapism or any preclusion of political activism or belief in the attainability of positive social change.

2. *What role does the symbol of the Virgin Mary play in explaining to poor Haitians the meaning of their world and their place in it?*

This question might be best approached through a comparative analysis of several individual case studies, rather than through an attempt to draw significant conclusion from a large-scale survey. Therefore, I hesitate to venture here much further than reference to Guertha's case. Taking cue from her case—in my judgment, not an atypical one—it may be argued that an understanding of one's suffering as caused by historical circumstances rather than by divine fate is a discernible element of popular Haitian Marianism, and as such plays some role in shaping poor Haitians' understanding of their world. Furthermore, since for many under-class Haitians the Virgin is viewed as the operational force behind the nation's recent political changes and the popular democratic movement, and since they think of themselves as the Virgin's *domestik*, Marianism does indeed function for the Haitian poor as an avenue of self-recognition as agents capable of effecting political and social change.

3. *To what extent can we understand Mary to be a "factor of popular identity," or an instrument in the crystallization of class consciousness?*

As argued above in the context of Guertha's case, class consciousness and popular identity are exceptionally developed in Haiti, especially since the early eighties. Since the Haitian Church's shift toward the preferential option for the poor has played a key role in the crystallization of the revolutionary class consciousness that effected the ouster of Jean-Claude Duvalier in 1986, it is arguable that the symbol of Mary, especially as inspirational force to the TKL movement, has contributed to this process, as demonstrated in chapter four.

While this dimension of popular Haitian Marianism was certainly muted during the three years of junta rule, it remains to be seen whether it has been extinguished. Many of our under-class informants were praying to Mary to bring down the *putchists*, and some, like Guertha, drew inspiration from the Virgin to mount resistance in the face of grave danger. In general, however (as noted in chapter two), religious protest against the Cédras regime paled in comparison to the spiritually charged popular movement that sent Duvalier packing. If indeed the Virgin did return Aristide to power, she did so through U.S. military might, rather than through any popular Haitian uprising.

4. *Does popular Haitian Mariology contain expressions of protest against domination and suffering, or any appropriation of the symbol of the Virgin Mary that may be termed "ideological negation"?*

In taking up a symbol that has "served for centuries to uphold the status quo to the advantage of the highest echelons of power,"[84] and in transforming that symbol into the "promoter of the justice that liberates the oppressed,"[85] as Mary was described at Vatican II, the poor have effectively used their Marianism as an expression of protest against domination, suffering, and injustice wherever and whenever they have taken the Virgin to be on their side and supportive of their cause. The Haitian case is no exception to this. In both the religious creativity of Romaine-la-Prophétesse and the personal belief of Guertha are perceptible the oppressed's production of an element of what Gramsci referred to as a worldview "in active opposition" to the dominant, hegemonic worldview which, using the very same symbols, promotes the status quo and supports the powerful.

It is, therefore, certain that the Haitian poor have effectively negated the ideology which the military regime meant to promote by draping a banner of *Notre Dame du Perpétuel Secours* over their headquarters' balcony and by making a pompous appearance at her feast celebration in 1994, just as Romaine-la-Prophétesse succeeded two hundred years early in stripping the symbol of its legitimizing force for the European slave regime and appropriating it to inspire some of the slave insurrections that made a racist white world tremble with fear.

5) *Are there discernible religious interests or needs among the Haitian poor to which the symbol of the Virgin responds? How do these needs and interests influence the forms and types of Marian devotion preferred or created by poor Haitians?*

If Bourdieu is correct, as I believe he is, in asserting that agents' religious habiti are determined in the main by the "material conditions of their existence," then it is upon the existential needs, pains, and uncertainties that accompany poverty that our attention must focus in order to identify the poor's religious needs. Bourdieu is indebted to Weber for this insight. Weber identifies three kinds of religious needs in "disprivileged groups": (1) "[the] need for release from suffering;" (2)"[the] need for just compensation;"[86] and, concomitantly, (3) "a hunger for a worthiness which has not fallen to their lot, they and the world being what it is."[87] These needs are readily discernible in the religious habitus of the Haitian poor and are met through popular forms of Marian piety and their Mariological substructure. The interviews we conducted with several hundred impoverished Haitian men and women, most of whom mentioned finding in the Virgin personal consolation for their ills and hope for the restoration of democracy, have demonstrated this. As compensation for their suffering and struggle, and in order to sate their hunger for worthiness, poor Haitians have pinned their hopes and aspirations on democratization, which, as the fieldwork reveals, is a process most believe is being realized through the Virgin Mary's divine intervention.

A fourth religious need of the poor that Weber identifies is the need for "saints, heroes or functional gods…the veneration of which constitute(s) the real religion of the masses in everyday life."[88] Over and above "the concept of an absolutely transcendent god,"[89] the religious habitus of the oppressed disposes them to preference spiritual beings with whom they, in their existential plight, may identify and to whom they feel close enough to speak with. This goes far in explaining not only why 65 percent of under-class respondents pray most often to the Virgin Mary—since they consider her to be closer to them than God or Jesus, and hence abler to answer their prayers—but also why the cult of saints in Haiti is so vigorous, and why Vodou, with its pantheon of anthropomorphic spirits, maintains such an extraordinary appeal for the Haitian masses.

NOTES

1. Interviews were conducted and questionnaires distributed between September of 1993 and December of 1996, roughly one-fourth by a research assistant, the remainder by myself. Besides Port-au-Prince, where most of our fieldwork was conducted, we interviewed people in Jacmel, Les Cayes, Bombardopolis, Gonaïves, and on the island

of La Gonâve, as well as Haitian refugees in Guantanamo Bay, Cuba. About thirty-five interviews took place at sea aboard a U.S. Coast Guard cutter transporting Haitian refugees to Cuba during the summer of 1994. Anonymity was guaranteed in regard to date as well as identity, since many of my informants were in hiding, hence no dates of interviews are recorded in this book.

2. Edouard Françisque, following Jean Price-Mars and others, notes that the basic radical division of Haitian society into the somewhat hermetic classes of elite and mass "is one of the gravest consequences of the colonial fall-out." Quoting Price-Mars' classic *Ainsi parla l'oncle*, Françisque concludes that the Haitian Revolution in reality changed very little: "The change was more apparent than real, transpiring more on the surface than within…there only occurred but a change in masters…in fact, the social strata remained unchanged." *La structure économique et sociale d'Haïti* (Port-au-Prince: Deschamps, 1986), pp. 203-4. For additional useful statistics on poverty in Haiti, see CRESDIP, NCHR, HSI, *Haïti, pays escorché* (Port-au-Prince: CRESDIP, 1990); and Simon M. Fass, *Political Economy in Haiti: The Drama of Survival* (New Brunswick: Transaction Publishers, 1990).

3. "The Haitian middle-class represents a very slender, quite unsettled fringe with uncertain and hazy boundaries somewhere between the new bourgeoisie and what we call 'the people.'" Françisque, *La structure économique et sociale d'Haïti*, p. 225.

4. Sidney W. Mintz, "Can Haiti Change?" *Foreign Affairs*, Jan/Feb 1995, pp. 73-86, pp. 82-83.

5. Richard Leyburn, *The Haitian People* (New Haven: Yale University Press, 1941), pp. 3-4.

6. Mintz, "Can Haiti Change?" p. 83.

7. Michel-Rolph Trouillot, *Haiti: State Against Nation: Origins and Legacy of Duvalierism* (New York: Monthly Review Press, 1990), p. 81.

8. Ibid., pp. 114-115.

9. Ibid., p. 115.

10. Ibid.

11. Christian Parker, "Popular Religion and Protest against Oppression: The Chilean Example," in N. Greinacher, and N. Mette, (eds.), *Popular Religion, Concilium*, 186, 1986, 28-35, p. 29.

12. Karl Marx, *Early Writings* (New York: Vintage, 1975), p. 244.

13. Ibid.

14. Marx, *The Communist Manifesto* (New York: Norton, 1988) , p. 73.

15. Marx, *Early Writings*, p. 243.

16. For a useful discussion of Marxist perspectives on religion, see Bryan S. Turner, *Religion and Social Theory: Materialist Perspectives* (London: Heinemann, 1983).

17. Marx, *Early Writings*, p. 243.

18. Ibid.

19. Hans Küng, *Does God Exist?* (New York: Doubleday, 1978), p. 229.

20. Marx, *The Communist Manifesto*, p. 55.

21. Dwight B. Billings, "Religion as Opposition: A Gramscian Analysis." *American Journal of Sociology*, 66: 1990, pp. 1-31, p. 4.

22. Lucia Chiavola Birnbaum, *Black Madonnas: Feminism, Religion, and Politics in Italy* (Boston: Northeastern University Press, 1993), p. 19.

23. Antonio Gramsci, *Lettere dal Carcere*, p. 455, as quoted in John Fulton, "Religion and Politics in Gramsci, An Introduction," *Sociological Analysis*, 48: 1987, pp. 197-216, p. 201.

24. Antonio Gramsci, *Scritti Giovanilli*, pp. 1-2, as quoted in John Fulton, "Religion and Politics in Gramsci: An Introduction." *Sociological Analysis*, vol. 48, no. 3, 1987, 197-216, p. 201.

25. Antonio Gramsci, *Sotto la Mole*, p. 71, as quoted in Fulton, ibid., p. 202.

26. Antonio Gramsci, *Selections from the Prison Notebooks*, (New York: Lawrence and Wishart, 1971) p. 420.

27. See Fulton, "Religion and Politics in Gramsci," p. 203.

28. Ibid., p. 204.

29. Ibid., 214.

30. In particular, Gramsci points to certain medieval heretical movements in Europe, the Reformation itself, Protestantism's entrepreneurial bent, and the popular religious contributions to the workers' movement in prefascist Italy.

31. Parker, "Popular Religion and Protest against Oppression," p. 33.

32. Marcus speaks of "letting ethnography demonstrate that the most powerful criticisms of capitalist society lie embedded in the everyday conditions and talk of ethnographic subjects.... The ethnographer is the midwife, as it were, who delivers and articulates what is vernacularly expressed...." Georges E. Marcus "Ethnography in the Modern World System," in James Clifford, and George E. Marcus, *Writing Culture: The Poetics and Politics of Ethnography* (Berkeley and Los Angeles: University of California Press, 1986), 165-193, p. 180.

33. See especially Gellner's "Concepts and Society," in B. R. Wilson, (ed.), *Rationality* (Oxford: Blackwell, 1970), pp. 18-49.

34. Clifford Geertz, *The Interpretation of Cultures* (New York: Basic Books, 1973), p. 15.

35. Ibid., p. 125.

36. Paul Willis, *Learning to Labour: How Working Class Kids Get Working Class Jobs* (New York: Columbia University Press, 1981), pp. 202-203.

37. James Scott, *Domination and the Arts of Resistance: Hidden Transcripts* (New Haven: Yale University Press, 1990), p. 14.

38. See Albert Raboteau, *Slave Religion: The "Invisible Institution" in the Antebellum South* (Oxford: Oxford University Press, 1978), chapter four.

39. I.M. Lewis, *Ecstatic Religion: An Anthropological Study of Spirit Possession and Shamanism* (Harmondsworth: Penguin Books, 1971), p. 203.

40. Ibid.

41. Lewis demonstrates that women are more often the victims of oppression than men and are thus more prone to spirit possession. It strikes me, as it does Orsi and others, that the cult of the Virgin Mary is "largely a women's devotion," thus suggesting that the oppressed have a greater proclivity to Marian devotion than others. To determine whether this has been the case throughout the cult's history would demand extensive and painstaking research, though the fact that the periods of exaggerated rise in Marianism's popularity are also periods of heightened oppression against women would suggest that women have historically made up the majority of Marian devotees. I, thus, find questionable Michael P. Carroll's assertion that "the Mary cult over the centuries has probably appealed more to males than to females"(p. 111). It seems Carroll finds himself obliged to stretch this point in order to support his somewhat curious and unconvincing Freudian argument "that a son's repressed desire for the mother (however strong) is everywhere the mainstay of the Mary cult" (p. 68, *The Cult of the Virgin Mary*).

42. Scott, *Domination and the Arts of Resistance,* p. 140.

43. Métraux, *Voodoo in Haiti,* p. 326. "Whereas the *loa* reveal themselves in possessions no one to my knowledge was ever possessed by a saint." One possible exception is that of Haitian revolutionary hero Jean-Jacques Dessalines, who, according to one obscure legend, was possessed by the Virgin Mary when he ripped the white out of the French *tri-couleurs* to form the red and blue of the Haitian flag. Joan Dayan pulls from Timoleon Brutus' 1946 novel *L'Homme d'airain* the following interesting rendition of the tale: "It was not a spirit of African origins that possessed Dessalines, but 'the Holy

Virgin, protectress of the Blacks.' Then Dessalines cursed in 'Congo *language*' (the sacred language for direct communication with the spirits) and 'then in French against the Whites who dared believe that "the Independents wanted to remain French." Brutus concludes, 'He was in a mystic trance, possessed by the spirit when he said: *'Monsieur, tear out the white from the flag.'*" *Haiti, History, and the Gods*, (Berkeley: University of California Press, 1995), p. 52.

44. Scott, *Domination and the Arts of Resistance*, p. 118.
45. "Class consciousness involves, first of all, the recognition, however vaguely defined, of another class or of other classes: perception of class identity implies cognizance of characteristics which separate the class of which one is a member from another or others.... [R]evolutionary class consciousness...involves a recognition of the possibility of an overall reorganization in the institutional mediation of power and a belief that such a reorganization can be brought about through class action." Anthony Giddens, "Class Structuration and Class Consciousness," in Giddens and Held, eds., *Classes, Power, and Conflict*, pp. 157-174.
46. Johan Galtung, *The True Worlds: A Transitional Perspective* (New York: The Free Press, 1980), p. 1.
47. Ibid.
48. The coup d'état that overthrew the Aristide government and forced him into exile in Washington occurred on September 30, 1991. With the blessings of the UN Security Council, and on the heels of an eleventh hour accord signed between Jimmy Carter and the *putchist* high command, the U.S. military occupational force arrived in Haiti on September 14, 1994. One month later, on October 15, 1994, President Aristide himself returned to Haiti. The field research for this book was conducted from July of 1992 to January of 1996.
49. Galtung, *The True Worlds*, p. 1.
50. During the systematic wave of oppression unleashed by the Cédras regime against pro-Aristide activists, thousands of Haitians were forced into hiding. One human rights expert estimates that the city of Port-au-Prince absorbed as many as a quarter-million such *mawon* (exiles), or refugees fleeing persecution in the provinces.
51. In the summer of 1994, I took on employment as director of a relief program for victims of political persecution, of which Guertha became a beneficiary. The majority of the several hundred families in this program were recently arrived migrants in Port-au-Prince, on the run from hostile forces in their native provincial villages. Of the adult female beneficiaries, between one-quarter and one-third had been raped by their persecutors.

52. "The core of my approach to Mary is a paradigm, a four-celled "model" that represents four aspects of the Mary myth—the Madonna, Sponsa, Virgo, and Pieta—which correspond to four elements of the human "limit experience" of sexual differentiation." Greeley, *The Mary Myth*, p. 21.

53. Hurbon, *Dieu dans le vaudou haïtien*, p. 87.

54. Ira Paul Lowenthal, "Marriage is 20, Children are 21: The Cultural Construction of Conjugality and the Family in Rural Haiti," Ph.D. diss., Johns Hopkins University, 1987, pp. 92-104. Lowenthal defines the 'conjugal contract' as "an effective contractual arrangement between a man and a woman that pertains directly, and quite explicitly, to the substance of their interaction, both sexually and with respect to the organization of effort. Once entered into, this conjugal contract simultaneously transforms the tenor of their sexual relations, and indicates the full range of their labor relations.... The man, for his part, assumes his *devwa* (duties) vis-à-vis the woman. What might once have been an 'appreciation' (*apresyasyon*), a gift (*kado*), or some 'help' (*konkou*) now becomes a generalized, diffuse and enduring responsibility for the male partner."

55. In *Mama Lola*, Brown demonstrates the effectiveness of devotee/ *lwa* relations in dealing with certain problems of Haitian immigrants in New York City. These difficulties would have been unknown to them in Haiti, and thus the adaptability of the Vodou *lwas* to changing needs encountered in the immigrant experience is apparent. The oppression suffered by Guertha, however, amounted to difficulties far graver than any encountered by Brown's subjects, and Ezili's adaptability, it would seem, had reached its limit, leaving Guertha's amplified religious needs unmet through traditional Vodou channels.

56. Brown, *Mama Lola*, p. 37.

57. Robert Anthony Orsi, *The Madonna of 115th Street: Faith and Community in Italian Harlem, 1880-1950* (New Haven: Yale University Press, 1985), p. 206.

58. Ibid., p. 204.

59. Ibid., p. 207.

60. According to Sister Maria Lucia's unpublished manuscript "Notre Dame du Perpétuel Secours," in 1950 the miraculous Bel-Air painting was restored, and in 1954 it was newly framed. In 1961 the original painting, now deteriorating, was replaced with a copy.

61. Guertha's recitation of official Catholic prayers to invoke the Virgin's presence is perhaps influenced by the typical approach to prayer exhibited in Vodou ceremonies, which usually begin with invoca-

tions in the form of routine and orthodox Catholic prayers, like the "Hail Mary" and the "Our Father." In *Voodoo in Haiti* (pp. 327-8), Métraux writes, "it is customary for most services to be proceeded by the Thanksgiving...[wherein] priest or priestess recites Paters, Confiteors and Ave Marias followed by hymns to the Virgin and to the saints...to stir the *loa* up...in other words to attract their benevolent attention." As with Guertha's Marian devotions, in Vodou ceremonies official Catholic prayers are normally thereafter dispensed with after these initial invocations.

62. Greeley, *The Mary Myth: On the Femininity of God* (New York: Seabury, 1977), pp. 25-26.

63. Ibid., p. 27.

64. Ibid., p. 221.

65. Scott, *Domination and the Arts of Resistance*, p. 118.

66. Weber, *The Sociology of Religion*, p. 108.

67. Ibid.

68. It is noteworthy that in Guertha's "theodicy of compensation," it is the Virgin, rather than Jesus, who brings the unrighteous to judgment. In this case, which is hardly atypical on the popular level, Mary supplants Jesus not only as "divine friend" but also as stern judge.

69. Brown, *Mama Lola*, p. 83.

70. Gilbert Charles, "Les Communautés Ecclesiales de Base dans l'archdiocèse du Cap-Haïtien," in Gabriel Charles, Gilles Danroc, Carlos Mesters, Pierre Salvetti, and Yves Voltaire, (eds.), *Evangelisation d'Haiti, 1492-1992, Tome 3: Les TKL et la nouvelle évangelisation* (Port-au-Prince: Le Natal, 1992), pp. 139-148, p. 147.

71. Komite Kontak Nasyonal TKL yo, "Mesaj Ti Kominote Legliz yo, Nan okasyon Fèt Pannkòt 1992 lan. Dimanch 7 jen 1992." Cited in ibid., pp. 177-8.

72. *Vye panse,* in the religious context, might best be translated as "sinful ways." Implicit in this expression, it would seem—especially given the Haitian Church's elevation of Vodou practice to the summit of all sins—is Vodou belief and practice. In fact, the Church has succeeded in molding the Virgin into the guardian of Catholic doctrinal and symbolic purity against syncretism with Vodou belief and ritual. Many of my informants, both rich and poor alike, indeed conceive of Mary as such.

73. Borresen, "Mary in Catholic Theology," Hans Küng, and Jürgen Moltmann, (eds.) *Mary in the Churches, Concilium 168*, pp. 48-56, p. 55.

74. Warner, *Alone of All Her Sex*, p. 216.

75. Ruether, *Mary: The Feminine Face of the Church*, p. 54.

76. For an interesting discussion of biblical and Catholic traditions where the Holy Spirit is considered to be female, see Leonard Swidler, *Biblical Affirmations of Women* (Philadelphia: Westminster Press, 1979).

77. Orsi, *The Madonna of 115th Street*, p. 176.

78. Hurbon, *Dieu dans le vaudou haïtien*, p. 104.

79. During the course of my fieldwork it became apparent that three other Marian icons should have been included in this list, as they are of at least minor importance in the Haitian religious field: Our Lady of Victories, Our Lady of the Nativity, and Our Lady of Wisdom. Guadeloupe, on the other hand, was known by very few informants, despite her painting in the national cathedral.

80. Points were awarded as follows: ten points for first place votes; seven points for either second or third place votes; five points for either fourth or fifth place votes; three points for sixth through eighth place votes; and two points for either ninth or tenth place votes.

81. Boff, *The Maternal Face of God*, p. 189.

82. This expression is an sarcastic adaptation of a comment made by a *putchist* military officer when asked by a journalist if Aristide could ever return to Haiti. His response: "Can the egg reenter chicken's ass?"

83. Mintz, "Can Haiti Change?" p. 86.

84. Warner, *Alone of All Her Sex*, p.104.

85. *Lumen gentium*, no. 37.

86. Weber, *The Sociology of Religion*, p. 108.

87. Ibid., p. 106.

88. Ibid., p. 104.

89. Ibid., p. 103.

CHAPTER SEVEN

THE MARIAN DEVOTION
OF THE HAITIAN ELITE

For the élite (who insist on French sermons), well groomed,
sitting with his missal in a seat bearing his name plate,
the psychic elation to be derived from hearing a sermon
preached in a language which the rabble seated around
him does not know must be very great—and very Christian.

— Richard Leyburn, *The Haitian People*

Weber's Theory of the Religion of Elite Classes

Thus far we have cited elements of Weber's sociology of religion in
three contexts: (1) its influence on Bourdieu's theory of religious
habitus and field; (2) the degree to which his notion of charisma is
applicable to an understanding of Romaine-la-Prophétesse; and (3)
the understanding of the religious needs of the oppressed. While all
of these areas are vital to the present study and reflect the great
richness of Weber's contribution to the sociological study of religion, the most important aspect of his theses for our purposes remains to be analyzed, applied, and tested against the empirical data
generated through our fieldwork. Throughout the fifth and sixth
chapters of his seminal study *The Sociology of Religion*, Weber's
articulates his thesis on the religion of elite classes, which shall
provide the theoretical framework for the present analysis of the
Marianism of upper-class Haitians.

As Brian Morris writes, a paramount objective of Weber's sociology of religion is "to explore the interrelationship between religious culture and the economic interests of specific social groups."[1] For instance, to summarize cursorily his famous argument in *The Protestant Ethic and the Spirit of Capitalism*, the development of capitalism produced a social group of large-scale property owners whose inordinate accumulation of capital was served by the justification and contingency provided by the concomitant development of the Calvinist-based Protestant work ethic, which turned work into a virtue and wealth into a mark of the elect. The Protestant work ethic thus functioned as an instrument of *legitimierende Macht* nonpareil for capitalists' augmentation of profit and accumulation of wealth. For Weber, "the development of that type of economic system which he called rational capitalism which has come to dominate by far the greater part of the globe and which has stimulated such a remarkable growth in technology and production is rooted in part in religious developments at the time of the Reformation,"[2] particularly in ascetic Calvinism and the Calvinist version of the doctrine of the elect.[3]

Whereas on the surface it might appear that in his sociology of religion, "Weber's "emphasis tends to be on interest groups,"[4] and on economic and social forces, there is a stronger psychological undercurrent to his discussions of religious needs and interests, wherein "the fundamental unit of analysis...is the individual."[5] Individuals are, of course, likely to share many interests and needs, religious or other, with other agents of their social group; these needs and interests, nevertheless, are in the last analysis subjective and, as Weber puts it, "rooted in certain basic psychological patterns."[6] Moreover—and this is a crucial point for the present analysis, one taken up in Bourdieu's notion of religious *habitus*—these religious needs and interests are determined principally by one's socioeconomic circumstances; i.e., by the material conditions of his or her existence. Thus in spite of the "long epic campaign"[7] against Marxist thought that Weber waged, "the way in which he related religious beliefs to the class or status position of believers has understandably led some writers to describe Weber as a crude materialist."[8]

In one sense, this description is correct, for Weber clearly developed arguments that the material conditions of any agent's existence determine to a large extent the style or form of religious belief and practice which that agent adopts or prefers. And just as agents of a distinct class have similar life experiences, customs, and tastes, they also demonstrate similar religious needs. Incidentally, Bourdieu refines this argument, in his discussion of the class-determination of the religious habitus, which is the depository of agents' predispositions in the religious field. The suggestion that religious dispositions are conditioned by agents' socioeconomic background raises an important question: What specifically are the religious needs of the dominant, and what characterizes their religious belief and practice? Unlike agents of "disprivileged groups," whose "particular need is for release from suffering" and for some assurance of compensation,[9] as we turn "to the 'sated' and privileged strata," Weber argues, "the need for salvation is remote and alien...."[10] Thus, for Weber, the wealthier the individual, the less likely s/he will demonstrate a need for the promise of a future, otherworldly salvation. The causal explanation for this is ultimately psychological and hinges upon the degree to which one's "hunger for a worthiness," for a "sense of honour," or for a "sense of self-esteem" is or is not met by his/her economic circumstances and social status. In an essential passage Weber discusses this most impressively. It is worth quoting here at length:

> The specific importance of salvation religion for politically and economically disprivileged social groups, in contrast to privileged groups, may be viewed from an even more comprehensive perspective.... Their sense of self-esteem rests on their awareness that the perfection of their life pattern is an expression of their underived, ultimate, and qualitatively distinctive *being*; indeed, it is in the very nature of the case that this should be the basis of the elite's feeling of worth. On the other hand, the sense of honor of disprivileged classes rests on some concealed promise for the future which implies the assignment of some vocation to them. What they cannot *be*, they replace by the worth of that which they will one day *become*, to which they will be called in some future life here or hereafter; or replace...by their sense of what they signify and achieve in the world as seen from the point of view of providence. Their hunger for a worthiness that has not fallen to their lot, they and the world being what it is, produces this conception

> from which is derived the rationalistic idea of providence,
> a significance in the eyes of some divine authority pos-
> sessing a scale of values different from the one operating
> in the world of man.[11]

Thus, this primary function of religion for the under-class—this provision of a sense of honor, worth, and self-esteem—consists in the promise of something greater "which they will one day *become* in some future life here or hereafter." Insofar as the dominant find their own sense of honor, worth, and self-esteem in "their underived, ultimate, and qualitatively distinctive *being*," they have no such use of religion. Why, then, do they need religion at all? What, for Weber, is religion's primary function for the elite?

> Other things being equal, classes with high social and eco-
> nomic privilege will scarcely be prone to evolve the idea
> of salvation. Rather they assign to religion the primary
> function of legitimizing their own life pattern and situa-
> tion in the world. This universal phenomenon is rooted in
> certain basic psychological patterns. When a man who is
> happy compares his position with that of one who is un-
> happy, he is not content with the fact of his happiness, but
> desires something more, namely the right to his happi-
> ness, the consciousness that he has earned his good for-
> tune, in contrast to the unfortunate one who must equally
> have earned his misfortune.... What the privileged classes
> require of religion, if anything at all, is this psychological
> reassurance of legitimacy.[12]

Following Weber's argument, upon careful analysis it should emerge as clear that the rich and the poor of any society have radically different religious needs and, thus, use religion for divergent ends. For the poor, religion functions primarily as consolation, release, and a bolstering of one's sense of worth through the belief in some future compensation or higher quality existence, whereas for the rich, religion meets a psychological need for the legitimization of their economic power and social prestige. Logically, different religious needs breed different religious beliefs and practices. Hence, while popular religion—and this is especially true in Haiti—tends to be ecstatic and somewhat licentious, for the elite, as Francis

Schüssler Fiorenza explains, "religious experience tends to be less ecstatic or dreamlike in nature...."[13] The privileged, as it were, consider themselves "above" popular forms of religious expression, like Vodou, whose ecstatic forms have historically been a source of painful embarrassment for the Haitian elite. Haiti's upper-class—as, for Weber, the privileged groups of any society—therefore, are usually possessed of "a profound disesteem of all irrational religion combined, however, with a recognition of the usefulness of this type of religion as a device for controlling the people."[14] Indeed, this last passage reads almost as if Weber had Haiti in mind.

To summarize, in Weber's sociology of religion there are basically four characteristics or tendencies found in the religious beliefs and practice of the economically privileged: (1) A primary need for "the psychological reassurance of legitimacy"; (2) an absence of ecstatic expression or ritual performance; (3) an absence of the need for salvation; and (4) a "profound disesteem for," and hence a cultivated disassociation from, popular forms of religious expression. Central to the overall aims of this chapter is the application and testing of these four elements of Weber's theory of the religion of the elite against the empirical data from our fieldwork to develop an understanding of upper-class Haitian Marianism. To proceed with this endeavor, they may be translated into question form and employed as guidelines for this discussion:

1) *Does their Marian devotion provide the Haitian elite with "the psychological reassurance of legitimacy"?*

2) *Is the Marian devotion of the Haitian upper-class devoid of ecstatic expression?*

3) *Is Mary's influence on the economy of salvation of little or no importance to wealthy Haitians?*

4) *Do upper-class Haitians exhibit a "profound disesteem" for certain ways in which the symbol of Mary is employed on the popular level?*

Before referring to the data produced through my fieldwork among the Haitian upper-class in an effort to answer these and other related questions of import, it is expedient to first inform our investigation with a brief survey of the various representations of the religious life of the Haitian wealthy as found in scholarly literature.

Portrayals of the Religious Life of the Haitian Elite in Scholarly Literature

The general assessment of the religious life of the Haitian elite in the accounts of leading scholars of Haitian religion is, on the whole, inadequate, with little or no rooting in any substantial field research among the population in question. In the way of support for their generalizations and passing comments on the religion of Haiti's wealthy, Maya Deren, Alfred Métraux, Karen McCarthy Brown, and others make usually second-hand references to few and scattered informants without ever, apparently, having taken the pains to engage in any formal participant/observation to test their assumptions. Otherwise careful scholars tells us this or that about the religious belief and practice of the Haitian elite while rarely divulging their sources of information or methodology. This gives the careful reader the impression that many of their claims are mere speculation rooted in hearsay. In effect, the overall image of the Haitian elite that emerges out of scholarly texts, not only regarding their religious belief and practice, is anything but flattering, sometimes pejorative and almost sanctimonious, to a degree unfair, and, by the standards of social science, poorly developed and thus inadequate.

Generally speaking, two positions concerning the nature of upper-class Haitian religious life predominate in the literature, each reflective of the epic tension in Haitian society between Catholicism and Vodou, which was detailed in chapter two. The first claim is that the Haitian elite are altogether embarrassed by Vodou, which they deem an amalgam of superstitious vestiges of their African roots that they would rather see wholly eclipsed by their French cultural ties. Historically, many of the elite have been concerned with how Vodou taints Haiti's image abroad, an attitude typified by President Lescot, as we saw in chapter four. This position holds that the Haitian elite are in reality quite ignorant, afraid, and scornful of Vodou, and that they have been the driving force behind every systematic effort to eradicate the popular African-derived religion from Haitian society. For obvious social and cultural reasons, the

Haitian elite are Catholic and take pains to appear so as orthodox as possible, having steadfastly "upheld their religion's strict traditions and official order."[15]

The second position, basically stated, is that the Haitian elite ostensibly reject Vodou so as not to tarnish the orthodoxy of their Catholicism and French-ness, and scorn it as something primitive and woefully inferior to their own more "civilized" European cultural traditions. However, under the surface, this argument continues, the elite are often secretly devoted to the *lwas* and consult *oungans* and *mambo*s underground. This view is reflected in a quasi proverb—one that is quoted, usually uncritically, by many who have written about Haiti—that states that "Haiti is 90 percent Catholic, 10 percent Protestant, and 100 percent Vodouisant."

Maya Deren's eloquent *The Divine Horsemen* ranks among the most popular books on Haitian Vodou. Deren, who first went to Haiti in 1947 to film a documentary on dance, was so struck by the nation's stark class divisions and the radical differences between life for the masses and life for the elite that she saw fit to preface her entire book with an introductory note explaining to her reader that "influenced by the conventional criteria of civilized culture and buckling under the pressures of the Catholic Church, the Haitian elite have altogether abandoned Vodou."[16] One problem with this statement is Deren's word choice, for to say that the elite "have altogether abandoned Vodou" is to imply that as a group they once embraced it as their religion, a view that is not necessarily supported by historical evidence. Deren proceeds to tell us that "they are largely ignorant of Vodou,"[17] without explaining just how it is she knows. But the most arresting element of Deren's "Introductory Note" is her decision that when she employs the term "Haitian" throughout her text, the term is not referentially inclusive of the upper-class! It would seem that being Haitian, for Deren, requires being poor and Vodouisant, a requirement that eliminates a small, but very powerful sector of the nation's population who are in fact *Haitian*! Clearly, therefore, Deren exemplifies the first position enumerated above.

Another writer who, despite making no claims to include the Haitian elite in her research, has difficulty, nonetheless, concealing her contempt for Haiti's upper-class is Karen McCarthy-Brown, in whose *Mama Lola* the reader is offered a rather condescending portrayal of wealthy Haitian mulatto women:

> These women are light-skinned—some are actually blond and blue-eyed—and they marry in white dresses in big Catholic churches and return to homes that have bedroom sets and dining room furniture and servants. These women never have to work. They spend their days resting and visiting with friends; at night, they emerge on the arms of their men, dressed like elegant peacocks and affecting an air of haughty boredom.[18]

While neither Deren nor Brown formally addresses the question of the religion of the Haitian elite, they both hold to what I refer to as the "seepage theory." This theory states that even if a wealthy Haitian family is itself not involved with Vodou on the formal level, and even if the family elders take pains to cultivate their children's Catholicism and French cultural traits, the fact that their children's upbringing is largely left to under-class Vodouisant nannies, with whom the children wind up spending most of the time in their formative years, allows for the mythological world of Vodou spirits and all its accompanying fears and aspirations—elements of the Vodouisant *habitus*, as it were—to seep into the psyche of the wealthy's children. Deren cites as evidence of this phenomenon expressions that are regularly pronounced by the elite in both French and Creole that are plainly reflective of the Vodouisant worldview: "*on se maintien*" (literally: "one maintains oneself"); "*pas plus mal*" (literally: no worse)—two common responses to the salutation, "How are you doing?" Brown, meanwhile, makes reference to a wealthy white Haitian woman who, during a period of heightened political crisis in 1988, commented that "Haiti is losing its life force," a comment which might likewise reflect a fundamentally Vodouisant understanding of existence.[19]

Alfred Métraux, whose *Voodoo in Haiti* is perhaps the most widely read text on religion in Haiti, also holds to the seepage theory. He distinctly articulates the argument that the upbringing of elite children by nannies of lower-class backgrounds, who are themselves deeply Vodouisant, ineluctably paints the *habitus* of the wealthy Haitian with the colors of the nation's popular religion.[20]

In Métraux's view, interestingly, the starkness of Haiti's class divisions "have been greatly exaggerated,"[21] and he has noted that it is not altogether uncommon for wealthy Haitians to be found serving the *lwas* side-by-side with the poor in Vodou ceremonies. As evidence of this, Métraux cites an example of three Catholic clergymen who expressed despair at the sight of the wealthy of their flock running off to the Vodou priest for counsel. It is telling to note that Métraux's polling of three priests represents the most extensive field work yet conducted toward an understanding of the religion of the Haitian elite![22]

A disputably more sober approach to the question at hand is offered by the godfather of Haitian intellectuals, Jean Price-Mars, whose classic *Ainsi parla l'oncle* is considered by many Haitians to be the best single-volume insight into their culture. While Price-Mars offers some reflection on the worldview and religious dispositions of the Haitian elite in his famous book, it is to his much less-often cited *La vocation de l'élite* to which we must turn for a fuller expression of his thought on this question. As a champion of the *Negritude* movement and promoter of Pan-Africanism, Price-Mars felt that Vodou, long disdained by the Haitian upper-class and intellectuals, should be reclaimed by all Haitians as a great source of pride and cultural richness. Vodou is especially propitious to the Pan-African ideal, he rightly felt, since it is a repository of originally African traditions and hence ties Haitians intimately to their brothers and sisters of other lands of the African Diaspora and the mother continent itself. Moreover, in order for Haiti to develop on all levels, the disdain which the upper-classes, and hence the best educated and the professional class, hold toward Vodou—which is itself a root source of social rupture and class strife—must be overcome. If not, the concerned involvement of the wealthy and professional classes in the improvement of the living conditions of the nation's poor could never be effectively solicited, and true national unity and development would forever remain an impossibility.

Price-Mars asserted that the Haitian elite suffer from a collective psycho-social malady that he refers to as "*Bovarisme collectif*" ("collective Bovarism").[23] Coined by a French sociologist in reference to the idiosyncrasies of the lead character in Gustave Flaubert's classic novel *Madame Bovary*, by *Bovarisme collectif* Price-Mars meant the condition of a social group that denies aspects of its true identity so as to take on a more desirable identity. Such an abnormality is reflected as much in the Haitian elite's preference for French over Creole as in their condescending attitude toward Vodou. Price-Mars saw such predilections and attitudes as rooted in the elite's *mentalité de l'eclairissement* (literally: "lightening mentality," an allusion to the calculating efforts of certain families of Haiti's mulatto elite to assure the lightening of their descendants' skin tone through carefully planning marriages exclusively with partners of lighter skin tone than that which they have already achieved through this inherently racist trans-generational endeavor!)[24]

For their efforts to punish Vodou, Price-Mars accused the Haitian elite of having a "presumptuous soul,"[25] and he viewed their devotion to the Catholic Church as nothing short of hypocrisy that masked a deep-seated inferiority complex; hypocrisy since in reality (in Price-Mars's judgment) many wealthy Haitians do in fact practice Vodou, largely, though not exclusively, for medical purposes. As a physician himself, Price-Mars referred to several of his medical colleagues who agree that the Haitian wealthy generally see Vodou's herbalism as a bona fide alternative to western medicine. But ultimately, his argument concludes, it is more than just the prospect of physical healing that ever draws the elite to Vodou: "even among the elite who pride themselves on being pious Catholics there exists a cooperation and a juxtaposition between two beliefs as a mutual counter insurance against the mysterious beyond."[26]

In *Haïti: couleurs, croyances, créole*, Leon-François Hoffmann also makes note of the Haitian elite's deep-seated interest in the healing arts and sciences that are so fundamental to Haitian Vodou. Hoffmann cites a Haitian physician who caters mostly to a wealthy clientele, and comments that "in the face of extreme cases of illness, even my richest patients are prone to running off to the Vodou priest rather than putting their trust in modern medical science."[27] Yet, Hoffmann adds, even if their consultation with the Vodou priest is strictly for medical purposes, the Haitian elite must take care to avoid detection, for fear of the shame that such an action would bring upon them in the eyes of "their kind:"

> For a bourgeois to serve the lwas is considered a sort of scandalous perversion, and the guilty are considered traitors not only against their social class but against the coun-

try itself, since, as common opinion has it, the existence
of Vodou has brought Haiti into disrepute in the eyes of
foreigners. Thus, bourgeois practitioners are subject to
derision and misunderstanding…those of the masses
arouse pity.[28]

From our summary it, thus, seems that in the scholarly literature
there is a scarcity of concrete examples on which to base any sociological theory of the religion of the Haitian elite.[29] In light of this,
and given the fact that certain writers have nevertheless paraded
assumptions as sound conclusions, it is almost refreshing to come
across Desmangles's complaint about the difficulty in conducting
fieldwork among the Haitian elite (apparently here is one researcher
who finally has seen fit to try!). Avoiding the sweeping generalizations of which some of his peers and predecessors are guilty,
Desmangles carefully begins his discussion of upper-class religion
in Haiti by informing us that "Catholics make up the bulk of the
Haitian elite, who themselves consist of 15 percent of the population," and that some of these people "are not religious at all," while
others "are only marginally Catholic, attending Mass only on occasion." However, it strikes Desmangles as warranted to question
whether the wealthy attend Mass "for the right reasons," or instead
participate as if it were a social gathering of more secular than
religious import, "a place for the practicing of cultural refinement
where the rules of etiquette are observed with religious devotion."[30]

Regarding the elite's attitude toward Vodou, Desmangles is again
careful to avoid making baseless claims. Some, he explains, are
embarrassed by it, others "know little about it," while others still
"are intensely drawn to Vodou, adhering to its teachings and secretly consulting oungans on occasion."[31] Based upon his observations, Desmangles estimates, in any event, that the number of elite
who practice Vodou is actually on the rise.

It may be concluded that the religious beliefs and practices of
the wealthy remain an area largely untouched by scholars of Haitian religion, who for the most part have preferred analyzing Vodou
as it is practiced by the Haitian peasantry and urban poor, as well
as the relationship between Vodou and Catholicism and the role of
Vodou and the Catholic Church in Haitian politics. Some, like Deren,
avoid the subject altogether, while others treat the religion of the

elite as tangential to Haitian religious life. This is a misleading position, for the understanding of the relationship between religion and power in Haiti is thereby limited to focus on the struggle between the Church and Vodou on mainly the politicoideological and doctrinal levels, to the neglect of the divergence between upper and lower-class lay uses of religion, which usually emerges as an important structural determinate in any religious field. In other words, it may very well be vital, depending on the sociohistorical realities of the case in question, for the sociological understanding of religion to analyze the ideologicoreligious "guerrilla warfare," to adapt Michel-Rolph Trouillot's apt term ("cultural guerilla warfare"), that rages not just between the people and the Church, but also between the masses and the elite.

The Case of Marie-Carmel

Marie-Carmel, a stylish 34-year-old Port-au-Prince business woman, was raised as the daughter of a successful Port-au-Prince merchant with strong ties to the leading families of the Haitian elite. Like most of the people in this "status group,"[32] Marie-Carmel's family are light-skinned mulattos who make every effort to cultivate their European cultural ties, which means, among other things, proscribing the use of Creole in the home and practicing exclusively Catholicism *sans mélange*. This family would thus represent a good case study in *Bovarisme collectif*. As Marie-Carmel insisted, they find not the least attraction in Vodou: "We have always been Catholic and have never been involved with any superstitious paganism or black magic." For Marie-Carmel, her mother, and her siblings, being religious meant being Catholic, which, as we shall see, consisted mainly in Marian devotion.

Marie-Carmel's father, whose amassed his fortune through various import/export and manufacturing enterprises, was by her accounts somewhat indifferent to things religious, although he did make an occasional appearance at church on certain holy days, or for weddings, baptisms, and funerals. Marie-Carmel's mother (we'll call her Florence), on the other hand, was very pious and possessed of an especially deep devotion to Our Lady of Mount Carmel. Marie-Carmel recounted that for as long as she could remember her mother "prayed the rosary every day, usually three times, morning, noon, and night. And each time someone close to her died or when some grave problem arose, she would also pray the novena, and at times she would only dress in blue and white for long periods of time. In fact, she did this to me for several entire years—dressed me exclusively in blue and white."

The last of the above devotions, that of dressing herself and Marie-Carmel only in blue and white, a practice not uncommon in Haiti, seems to have been part of a promise that Florence had made to Our Lady of Mount Carmel around the time of Marie-Carmel's birth. From the details Marie-Carmel could recall, one dry summer day in 1961, a fire broke out in a building adjacent to the family's Port-au-Prince home. Florence, then eight months pregnant with Marie-Carmel and suffering from severe leg cramps that often confined her to bed, was home alone at the time, save for two or three members of the household staff. Alarmed by the smoke and commotion outside, Florence made every effort to get out of bed, but was rendered impotent by a combination of the cramps and her excessive weight. Afraid that her cries for help were unheeded, and quite sure that she was about to burn to death, Florence reached for her rosary and prayed to the Virgin for succor.

Moments later, with the flames now igniting in her own house, Florence was relieved at the sight of her maid running into her room screaming "Fire, fire!!" This relief, however, vanished at once with the realization of the physical impossibility that the frail, toothless old maid in bifocals could ever manage even to lift the heavyset pregnant woman from her bed, let alone carry her down two flights of stairs to safety. Yet somehow—Marie-Carmel believes by virtue of the Virgin's intervention—this is precisely happened.

By the following morning, the fire was extinguished, and the clearing smoke revealed substantial structural damage to the house, but "everything that was really important to my mother was untouched." Florence believed, interestingly, that not only her life but her dearest material possessions were spared from the flames by the miraculous intervention of the Virgin Mary. Among these possessions, which now belong to Marie-Carmel, are a collection of valuable antique jewelry, a complete set of fine china, French silverware and crystal glasses for a seven-course meal to serve a dozen people, and a volume of prayers to the Virgin that was given to Florence by her godmother at her first communion.

The very next Sunday after the fire was the feast of Our Lady of Mount Carmel, July 16, 1961,[33] and Florence went to one of the capital's several churches named for this manifestation of the Virgin. Unshakably convinced that the Virgin Mary had intervened to save both her and her unborn child, Florence became driven by a desire to thank the Virgin for the miraculous events of days prior, a desire that would color her Marian devotion for the rest of her life. Thus, a trip to a church consecrated to Our Lady of Mount Carmel, particularly on her feast day, was doubtless in order. As Marie-Carmel explained, "It was there that she had a mystical vision of Our Lady of Mount Carmel, who explained to my mother that her thanks was accepted and that her child would be a healthy girl, whom she was to consecrate to her. That is why my name is Marie-Carmel." Marie-Carmel knew no further details than these concerning her mother's "mystical vision," though she felt that the Virgin Mary may then also have asked Florence to always dress her daughter in blue and white. "Also, my mother was always very concerned that a blue and a white dress were always hanging in each of our closets."

Thus having been dedicated to Our Lady of Mount Carmel at birth, Marie-Carmel's mother regularly reminded her of the fact throughout her childhood, and even on occasion during her adult life. As Florence lay dying in a Miami hospice a few years ago, in fact, she asked Marie-Carmel to vow to the Virgin in prayer before her that she too would dedicate her first daughter to the Virgin, a request that Marie-Carmel would ultimately meet.

Marie-Carmel thus inherited the Marian devotion that her mother had practically imposed upon her. Neither her younger brother nor sister was spared this, as each was dedicated at birth to some other image of the Virgin Mary that Florence believed to have performed some miracle, however small, for each of them. Marie-Carmel is doubtful, however, that her siblings' cases involved either the visions or strict observances that characterized her own.

While Marie-Carmel herself clearly makes the Virgin the center of her religious life, she has never adopted her mother's style, regularity, or intensity of worship. "I hate to say it," she explained, "but my mother was a bit fanatical." Marie-Carmel, in fact, would only gradually feel free to approach the Virgin Mary in ways different from the devotions that her mother had taught her. Two-and-a-half years of pre-med studies at a Mexican university brought Marie-Carmel into contact with Our Lady of Guadalupe,[34] of whom she would become particularly enamored. This new devotion, however, she feared might anger her mother:

> At first, I felt somewhat guilty that I was praying to Guadalupe and not to Mount Carmel, especially when I bought her icon and placed it in my home. I actually felt that I was doing something wrong! Then one day I spoke with a priest about my feelings. He assured me that there was ultimately no difference between Guadalupe and Mount Carmel and that the icons were tools that help us to love the Virgin and bring her into our lives. So, I was relieved, though still reluctant to reveal my love for Guadalupe to my mother. I just found Guadalupe so peaceful and so beautiful, and somehow I could identify with her more than I ever could with Mount Carmel. Maybe it's because she looks more like me, I don't know. Maybe because I felt so lonely in Mexico. All I do know for sure is that she was always there for me, and I saw her perform so many miracles for the Mexican people.

A young woman in a foreign land, negotiating a strange language and unfamiliar customs, Marie-Carmel's uncertainties in Mexico were many and weighty. She turned to Guadalupe for guidance, and though she never had a vision or heard the Virgin's voice, she is unwavering in her conviction that Guadalupe wanted her to return to Haiti and raise a family. "I also felt that Guadalupe was telling me that the medical profession was not my path—and, you know, I finally realized that it was my mother all along who was pushing me to become a doctor anyway. Guadalupe really helped me find myself."

It seemed to Marie-Carmel more apparent each day that she would not meet her future husband in Mexico and that she should abandon her medical studies. With little planning, she left for Paris, where eventually she took up university studies in business administration. She was able to do this thanks to her father's very generous financial backing, perhaps because he deemed such a change in curriculum beneficial to the family business. Her mother's graces were more obdurent, though eventually Marie-Carmel managed to convince Florence that it was the Virgin who had guided her to change in plans—she was careful not to mention which Virgin—and with that, her mother came to approve of Marie-Carmel's move to Paris and her change in majors.

Both more interested in the subject matter and more at ease in her native French, Marie-Carmel excelled in her studies while in Paris, eventually graduating with distinction. The move to Paris would also prove fortuitous to her plan to soon start a family, for while there she fell in love with a Canadian doctoral student, whom she would ultimately marry. The happy fruits of her decision to leave Mexico for France would also serve to deepen her Marian devotion, since it was a decision she believed that by Our Lady of Guadalupe had guided. "When I think of all of the happiness that I have had because of Guadalupe's help in going to France, I am filled with such love for her, and I renew my promise to live for her honor."

After finishing her studies, Marie-Carmel and her new husband moved for a time to Miami, where they resided in a townhouse that her family owned. While there, she tended to some of her mother's needs; Florence was now in the terminal stages of lung cancer, bed ridden in a hospice. She also took up the management of the states-side end of her father's business ventures. Her husband, newly armed with a doctorate in third world development, and with four years of development experience in Niger, began to market his candidature for employment overseas. Coincidentally—or as Marie-Carmel believed, by virtue of the Virgin's intervention in his job search—he received an offer for a lucrative position with a humanitarian project in Haiti. This gave Marie-Carmel and her husband the ideal opportunity to move to Haiti in the summer of 1987, just after Florence's death.

The young coupled quickly settled into one of Marie-Carmel's family's several comfortable hillside homes a few miles from downtown Port-au-Prince. Financially stable, and thus able to withstand the quotidian effects of a series of national political and economic crises, including the 1991 coup d'état and ensuing economic embargoes imposed upon Haiti by the OAS and the UN, Marie-Carmel and her husband made the transition to upper-class Haitian life with relative ease. They now have two children; a five year-old son and a year-old daughter named Natasha Guadalupe.

Judging from her own accounts, the central aspect of Marie-Carmel's Marianism is her belief that it is the Virgin Mary who has secured for her so many blessings and comforts in life and her sense of indebtedness for them: from saving her from the flames while still in her mother's womb, to her wealthy upbringing in a stable home; from her lucrative move to Paris, to the health of her own children and the comfortable life that she and her family now lead. This need to express her gratitude is the driving force that brings Marie-Carmel to most of the major Marian celebrations around Port-au-Prince, and which twice has led her back to Guadalupe's pilgrimage center in Mexico City during the last five years.

Existential suffering has been almost entirely unknown to Marie-Carmel on a personal level, although witnessing her mother's slow and painful death was a terrible experience and a source of some measure of spiritual angst:

> I cried every night, not understanding how the Virgin could allow her to suffer after all the devotion she had received from my mother. She did everything that the Virgin ever asked of her. But mother reassured me that she looked forward to seeing Mary again, just as she did after the fire, only now it would be not a fleeting glimpse, but forever.

Yet personally, Marie-Carmel had never really known suffering. Hers was a life of privilege and luxury, during which she had never once lacked, or been anxious over, the basic necessities for a comfortable existence. She was even accompanied by a maid during her years of study in Mexico and Paris. Marie-Carmel very rarely called upon the Virgin's warm consolation, so central to the Marianism of the Haitian poor. Sometimes she would pray to the Virgin "to bring comfort and hope to the bereaved," but the invocation of the Virgin's consolatory grace was at best tangential to Marie-Carmel's Marian devotion. Moreover, when she did pray to the Virgin to provide such solace, it was almost never for herself.

On occasion, the others for whom Marie-Carmel prayed to the Virgin included 85 percent of the Haitian population. "Only Mary can help my people. They suffer so much that they need spiritual help to carry on. This is why they love Mary so much—she alone provides them with the solace and strength to carry on." Struck by her use of the word strength, I asked Marie-Carmel whether the Virgin might strengthen the poor so that they could one day fight for their rights and for social and political change. Her reply was blunt and reflected some offense. "No! The Virgin has nothing to do with politics."

Indeed, Marie-Carmel's own Mariology is devoid of political content. When I explained to her that many of my poor informants believe Mary to be behind the popular democratic movement and the force that effected President Aristide's return, she seemed to judge this finding a mere reflection of the people's ignorance and thus as unworthy of serious consideration:

> People will believe what they want to believe, but Aristide has done tremendous harm to my country, and the poor are ignorant; that's why they foolishly look at him as their savior. The Virgin would never bring such a violent hypocrite to power. As for democracy, I think in Haiti it is very dangerous, since most Haitians can't read and they take democracy to mean license—that they can do what they please and that they don't have to respect people whom they should respect. Perhaps the Virgin will save Haiti from such people.

The diametric opposition between Marie-Carmel's understanding of the relationship between the Virgin and Haitian politics and Guertha's is altogether impressive and forcefully illustrates what is arguably the main difference between popular and elite Haitian Marianism: its ideological function. While for the poor, the Virgin is on their side and serves as a force of both empowerment and for the realization of their political agenda, for the rich, Mary might actually intervene to save Haiti (i.e., *them*) from the threatening (to *them*) implications of such political change. Thus, just as Mary, as we saw in chapter four, has made appearances for opposing forces on Catholic history's battlefields, for opposing forces in Haiti's class struggle she is a contested symbol, being for each the spiritual guarantor of victory.

As is the case for most Haitian Marian devotees of either class, Marie-Carmel's Mariology exhibits a strong nationalist element.

Of course, given her upper-class status, in Marie-Carmel's case this is a distinctly elite brand of nationalism, one which accepts that Mary provides the subjugated with bread and consolation but nothing in the way of political empowerment. "The Virgin loves Haiti. Just look at the miracle she performed to save the people from small pox and other diseases." To the question as to what the Virgin might do for Haiti in the future, Marie-Carmel replied:

> She will help us find peace and calm the people. They are disillusioned with Aristide and all the nonsense he has put into their heads. They are foolish to believe he can save them. They have forgotten how much better off they were under François Duvalier. The Virgin will teach them to stop hating so much the bourgeois. After all, if it weren't for people like my father and the Mews (one of Haiti's wealthiest families), they would have no work at all.

In part it is to pray for national peace, which in Marie-Carmel's judgment will only be achieved through the tranquilization of the newly politicized masses, that Marie-Carmel attends *Perpétuel Secours'* feast celebration in Bel-Air each June 27. This is, of course, the church of the nation's patroness, and June 27th is thus the ideal occasion on which to appeal to the Virgin to let peace reign in Haiti. On another level, there is a second function performed for Marie-Carmel through attending such a popular religious gathering: Marie-Carmel experiences a superficial feeling of unity with the Haitian poor, who are, after all, singing the same songs of praise to *Perpétuel Secours* for the benefit of the entire nation. This sentiment serves to render her social privilege more palatable to—if not cathartic for—her conscience, psychologically reassuring her, to use Weber's provocative term, that her wealth and advantages are legitimate. "One of the most beautiful things about *Perpétuel Secours'* feast is that it brings all Haitians together as one, rich and poor alike, praying and singing together, sharing their love for the Virgin. *Perpétuel Secours* makes us remember that we are all Haitians and that she and God love us all equally." Thus for Marie-Carmel, as I would suspect for elites in general, participation in national religious celebrations, where the majority of participants are poor, has a double function: First, through the feelings of unity with the poor that they otherwise would rarely be afforded, it has a soothing effect that makes it easier for the wealthy "to live with themselves" in such a terribly impoverished land. Second, it also functions to lead the subjugated to misrecognize this temporary and superficial ceremonial unity evoked by elite participation as authentic and reflective of a greater social unity that transcends the religious ceremony. The second of these functions, as witnessed in the case of Guertha, is not always effective. Whether this is the conscious intent of the elite is difficult to say.

In late 1993, the belief content of Marie-Carmel's Marianism underwent an interesting transformation of sorts as she became aware of, and responsive to, a series of visions and messages of the Virgin that a Haitian nun named Sister Altagrâce was receiving with some regularity. Some believe these messages and apparitions, or "*manifestations*," to have numbered around sixty over a two-year period. The messages, usually accompanied by a brief description of the Virgin's appearance, were typed up, photocopied, and circulated among a group of mostly middle- and upper-class Haitian women. Appropriately, the Virgin spoke in French. While for various reasons I never conducted any extensive research of this group, it did strike me that they lent great credence to the messages as authentic, hence opening the door for the messages to become, at least temporarily, a central element of their Mariology. Although Marie-Carmel never herself actually saw or heard Sister Altagrâce, who remains by one account quite inaccessible, Marie-Carmel, too, would come to believe in the veracity of the *manifestations*, which led to an overall intensification, and slight politicization, of her Marian devotion. In concert with the others in this group, for instance, Marie-Carmel began to pray the novena with much greater frequency than ever before, had her miraculous Marian medal blessed anew, and kept her rosary with her at all times for frequent use.

To suggest that Marie-Carmel's belief in the authenticity of these apparitions politicized her Mariology, however, is to risk an overstatement, for in her eyes the Virgin was interested mainly in the salvation of souls and the guardianship of Catholic orthodoxy. Nevertheless, Marie-Carmel's characteristically upper-class opposition to any American intervention in Haiti to return Aristide to power found religious reinforcement in certain elements of some of the Virgin's messages to Sister Altagrâce. In one message, for example, the nun reports that Mary spoke out strongly against "the American power," who in spite of the "warnings of anger they have had from my dearly beloved son," continued to take measures to drive the *putchist* regime from power in Haiti, to which the Virgin refers as "my hot land...the center of the universal conversion."[35]

In opposition to the "American power," the Virgin, through Sister Altagrâce, exhorted her devotees "to continue to pray, to fast, also making sacrifices and mortifications."[36] Given her implicit support for the de facto military regime, it would seem that the Virgin who spoke to Sister Altagrâce was hardly the Virgin who spoke the Magnificat. Indeed, the very concordance between the Virgin's message regarding the Haitian crisis as it unfolded dramatically in 1993/94 and the anti-Aristide/pro*putchist* position of most of the elite, Marie-Carmel included, certainly enhanced the messages' appeal to the elite. Such would reflect Bourdieu's logic of the dialectics between prophet, message, and believer, which is discussed in chapter four. The message appeals, in effect, to those whose interests it reflects.

The Contested Virgins of Marie-Carmel and Guertha

To conclude this analysis of the case of Marie-Carmel, we may draw out differences between her Mariology and Marian devotion and that of Guertha. This synopsis will contribute to the disclosure of key differences between elite and popular Marianism in Haiti in general, which is, of course, the central objective of this book. Specifically, this comparison, in order to make such a contribution, must focus attention on the respective religious needs and interests of each Marie-Carmel and Guertha to which this form of devotion responds, on the respective ideological substructures of the Marianism of each, and on the forms of practice that each prefers.

Taking cue from Weber, in Guertha's case we identified three primary religious needs that were filled by her Marian devotion: (1) The need for consolation from suffering; (2) the need for the assurance of compensation; and (3) the need for "functional gods" over and above a single transcendent God. We noted that the need for other-worldly salvation or personal sanctification is an almost totally imperceptible feature of Guertha's religious habitus. Marie-Carmel, on the other hand, and contrary to Weber's thesis, often mentioned Jesus' mercy as that which she hoped to secure through her devotion to the Virgin:

> We are all sinners, yet Jesus died for our sins. His grace of divine forgiveness is offered to us, and when his Mother asks him to bestow it upon her loved ones, he cannot refuse. She is our mediatrix.

Marie-Carmel's Marianism thus consisted of a predominant and personal soteriological solicitude, virtually absent from Guertha's. As already noted, physical suffering and deprivation are entirely unknown to Marie-Carmel, hence she demands little or nothing in the way of consolation from Guadalupe, her preferred Marian icon. Her principal need is, instead, for the assurance of her personal sanctification. This finding, significantly, is precisely the opposite of what Weber's thesis on class and the tendency toward salvation religion would have us expect, for such a need, in his argument, "is remote and alien" to the privileged.

Marie-Carmel's devotion to the Virgin Mary also met her "psychological need for the reassurance as to the legitimacy or deservedness" of her considerable wealth and social privilege. It did so in two ways. First, through the creation of a sense of unity with the Haitian poor, especially pronounced during Marian feast celebrations, the glaring social differences and class strife so endemic to Haitian society were obscured, and Marie-Carmel felt at one in love, song, and prayer with the under-class. In a sense, her pangs of conscience were thereby effectively muffled, since the Virgin accepts rich and poor alike—as evidenced by their physical unification during the ceremony—and hence being personally wealthy in an impoverished land is okay after all. Second, compounding the entrepreneurial ethic of material self-enrichment being the reward for diligent work with the conviction that Mary had arranged for rewards of comfort and wealth for Marie-Carmel and her mother because of their devotion, Marie-Carmel's belief in the "legitimacy or deservedness" of their elite status was indeed reassured. The poor, meanwhile—and this is the other side of Weber's equation—were poor, in Marie-Carmel's mind, not for want of devotion to Mary but for impurities in their devotion and for their incorrigible laziness. "The poor are poor very simply because they are lazy.

My great-grandfather came from Europe virtually penniless, and through hard work he nonetheless managed to provide a good life for his wife and children." The poor's fate, that is to say, is deserved, just as is Marie-Carmel's own socioeconomic privilege. When I asked her how the Virgin could, as Marie-Carmel believed, help her quit smoking and at the same time allow thousands of her poor devotees to struggle helplessly in misery, Marie-Carmel replied that "they need to understand that the Virgin does not want them to sacrifice chickens for her, but just to love her, her son, and follow Church doctrine." Orthodoxy is thus here seen as requisite to social well-being and economic ease, as well as the Virgin's favor.

To say that Marie-Carmel's Mariology is more orthodox than Guertha's would be an understatement. More important is how their respective orthodox and heterodox Mariologies are propitious to the satisfaction of certain religious needs specific to each. In Guertha's case, for example, the heretical belief that Mary, rather than God or Jesus, is the vengeful lord of the universe who orchestrated the ouster and punishment of the Cédras regime, and who rewarded Guertha and thousands like her for their devotion with the restoration of President Aristide and democracy, facilitated the satisfaction of Guertha's need for the assurance of compensation not only in the form of her reward but also in the form of "punishment for the unrighteousness of others."[37] For Marie-Carmel, meanwhile, the recognition of her own Mariological beliefs as being orthodox (to recall, Marie-Carmel understood the Virgin to be her unfailing attorney before Jesus, and all graces were ultimately from Christ through Mary's supplication on her behalf), and hence distinguished from those of the popular masses, served to reassure her of the "deservedness" of both her own worldly advantages and the miserable lot of the poor. The decisive point that these observations indicate is that both Guertha and Marie-Carmel perceive of the Virgin Mary in ways salutary to their own interests and needs, making the Virgin Mary a contested symbol in Haiti's class struggle. Some of these needs, as we have seen, are extrareligious, psychological, or political. They are all, meanwhile, largely class-determined and distinctly characteristic of agents of their respective socioeconomic classes.

This divergence in religious interests and the resultant divergence in the perception and uses of a religious symbol may be, in my judgment, best understood in Bourdieuean terms. In brief, Guertha and Marie-Carmel, being of radically different socioeconomic backgrounds, are each possessed of a religious habitus that reflects "the material conditions of existence" in which each was raised, educated, and socialized. There is a pervasive insistence in Bourdieu's work that "cultural needs are the product of upbringing and education," a point which is demonstrated by "scientific observation:"..."surveys establish that all cultural practices . . . and preferences . . . are closely linked to education level . . . and secondly to social origin."[38] Consequently, the religious habitus of both Guertha and Marie-Carmel, being the "depository" of their religious needs and dispositions, "predisposed" each to perceive of and use the symbol of the Virgin Mary in ways satisfactory to their own interests.

One of the reasons that I chose each Marie-Carmel and Guertha from among hundreds of informants as exemplary case studies representing the wealthy and the poor, respectively, is that on two occasions I had the opportunity to observe them both during the very same Marian feast celebrations.[39] Their styles of participation both during and after these ceremonies differ considerably, reflective of a divergence both in their conceptions of their relationships with the Virgin and of differently cultivated religious tastes. Unlike Guertha, for instance, Marie-Carmel never prays aloud to the Virgin and usually remains seated throughout the course of her prayers, which are always accompanied by a careful passing of her rosary through her fingers. "I prefer reciting the Hail Mary on the rosary," explained Marie-Carmel. "It is such a beautiful prayer and Mary is best praised through it." On the other hand, Guertha's expressed her devotion more often in church than at home, unlike Marie-Carmel, who often recited the rosary and petitioned the Virgin before a small altar in her bedroom. It is plausible that this difference itself has more to do with living space than anything else. Other differences in practice, such as frequency and destination of pilgrimage, also seem more determined by economic resources than underlying beliefs; Guertha had once been to Saut-d'Eau, a trip that caused her most untimely financial stress, while Marie-Carmel has twice returned to Mexico City and had been both to Fatima and Lourdes as a child with her mother. Marie-Carmel had also several times visited Saut-d'Eau in mid-July, though her disdain for Vodou made her too uncomfortable to pass much time by the waterfalls. Guertha, meanwhile, explained to me that she reserved her prayers to Mary for the village church, while at the falls she participated in a number of Vodou ceremonies, where she was even herself possessed.

While Marie-Carmel would at times speak of the Virgin as her "spiritual mother," it was evident that she conceived of her relationship with the Virgin in less intimate and much more orthodox terms than Guertha. Marie-Carmel reflected this conception when she spoke of what she prayed for and of the powers she believed the Virgin to possess:

> The Virgin is a spiritual mother, who made great sacrifices for us. As God's mother, she has great influences over whose sins Jesus forgives. Jesus has a real soft spot for his mother, and for those of us who really love her, he will deliver us.

Compared with Guertha's answers to the same questions, Marie-Carmel's have led me to conclude that while Guertha aimed ultimately to serve Mary, Marie-Carmel principally sought to glorify the Virgin for the benefit it would garner toward her own personal sanctification. It is plausible that the primacy of serving Mary, for Guertha, reflects her Vodouisant background, for service of the *lwas* in return for their involvement in believers' lives is a central element of Vodou.[40]

It may be argued that the dissimilarity in their attitudes toward Vodou are at the root of the different ways in which the two women pray to the Virgin while in church and of the different ways each conceives of the Virgin in general. As already described, Guertha would stand and sway, praying aloud with much emotion, often in tears, with a lighted candle in one hand and a photo of her dead husband in the other. Her display, arguably, reflected some of the ecstatic fervor characteristic of Vodou, a religion that Guertha herself practiced. In such a trance-like state, Guertha at prayer front and center before the altar is markedly more conspicuous than Marie-Carmel, who preferred sitting several pews deep, silently praying just as she had learned as a school girl under the French nuns. Yet, while their practice did differ in style and preference, a difference of much greater importance in their Marianism lies, as we have seen, on the level of belief, particularly its ideological function. In a word, for Marie-Carmel, the Virgin's graces, which are ultimately from Jesus, operate according to a logic of merit: one is blessed materially because of the orthodoxy of one's religious belief and practice and hard and honest work. By the same operative logic, tarnishing Catholicism with Vodouisant "superstition" and simple laziness are the causes of poverty. Marie-Carmel's Virgin, nevertheless, does provide the poor with enough bread to survive and with the solace to endure their painful lot. Guertha's Virgin, on the other hand, is in the process of turning Haiti's social and political tables and, in the end, will wreak havoc on those responsible for the plight of Haiti's oppressed masses.

Upper-class Survey: Demographic Profile

Unlike the process of the categorization of under-class respondents, combining variables to determine upper-class status was quite unnecessary, as these respondents were usually unambiguous about their membership in the "elite" or "favored class." Many circled both. Moreover, I personally know, am acquainted with, or know something of the background of nearly half of the wealthy survey participants, which further facilitated direct and accurate categorization of this study group.

Of the 100 informants grouped as representative of the Haitian wealthy, roughly 75 percent were residents of Port-au-Prince or its suburbs, 20 percent from other Haitian cities, and the remaining 5 percent from small provincial towns. Nearly 70 percent of wealthy informants were female, 20 percent more than among the under-class pool. Of upper-class respondents 45 percent were married; 10 percent, single; with a nearly equal 15 percent being each divorced, widowed, or partners in a common law marriage.

As expected, the greatest variances between the demographic profiles of the poor and the wealthy groups, besides, of course, income, were found on the level of education and employment. Of wealthy respondents, 60 percent had at least some university training, and all had finished secondary school, usually at a private Catholic institution or at the *Lycée Français* or Union School, respectively the leading French and American schools in Port-au-Prince. No poor respondents, as noted in the previous chapter, had ever attended university. Roughly two-thirds of the upper-class group were employed, mainly in family-owned business enterprises. A number of doctors and lawyers were also counted among employed upper-class participants. The remaining third were either home-makers, students, or retired.

With one-third of wealthy respondents aged over 50, the upper-class group was slightly older than the poor. Thirty-eight percent aged between 35 and 50, 21 percent between 20 and 35, while the remaining approximately 10 percent were teenagers.

Marian Practice Among the Haitian Elite

On the level of practice, dissimilarities in preferred forms of Marian devotion between rich and poor Haitians are ultimately negligible. Approaches to the same devotion, however, do vary significantly, as demonstrated above in the brief comparison of Guertha and Marie-Carmel at prayer in church.

As was the case with the lower-class group, attendance at the Virgin's feast day celebrations is the most popular form of Marian devotion among the Haitian wealthy. Of the upper-class survey participants, 90 percent had at least once attended such a Mass or do so with some regularity. Their reasons for attending hardly differed from of the poor, with the exception that no wealthy respondents took the occasion to mark the Virgin's birthday. Wealthy and poor respondents alike tended to view the feast day celebrations as something of an obligation, especially celebrations dedicated to whichever manifestation of the Virgin to whom one feels most indebted, and as the prime occasion for rendering thanks to Mary or for securing her blessings.

The rosary ranked second in popularity among forms of Marian devotion for upper-class respondents. While it ranked second in popularity among the lower-class study group as well, the percentage of wealthy informants (70 percent) who pray the rosary was considerably lower than that of the poor (86 percent). There was a slightly greater disparity regarding the novena, with only 55 percent of upper-class participants having at least once prayed it, compared to a figure of 73 percent for the under-class. It is feasible that since the rosary and especially the novena are commonly regarded as means to secure the Virgin's intervention in believers' lives in times of need, the wealthy therefore engage in these forms of devotion less than the poor, because their experience of need is far less pronounced. As the wife of one of Haiti's wealthiest men explained, "I don't ever need to pray the novena, because things have always gone very well for me."

Nevertheless, in spite of the absence in the lives of the rich of that painful want that brings Catholics the world over to pray the rosary and the novena, these forms of devotion remain popular among the wealthy in Haiti. From this observation one may deduce that the rosary and the novena play other roles for the wealthy than they do for the poor. My suspicion is that this function lies, for the wealthy, in the need for the assurance of the maintenance of their well-being, and the need to express their gratitude for their positions of power and privilege. The case of Marie-Carmel, in any event, would corroborate my suspicion here, as, again, thanksgiving to the Virgin and petition of the Virgin to keep her family well are the main themes in her Marian devotion, which most often took the form of the recitation of the rosary.

Among rich and poor Haitians alike, there is a strong association between the novena and work. Whereas employing the novena to find work was typically a strategy of the poor, belief in the novena's power to bring clients and enhance profits was evident across the boundaries of socioeconomic class. Whether for selling cigarettes and candles one by one in the streets or for importing new Land Rovers for retail, the novena, for Haitian Marian devotees, is endowed with positive capitalistic efficacy. Another motivation for praying the novena, as suggested by several bourgeois respondents, is that in times of heightened social unrest, which are frequent in Haiti, the novena offered a sense of security. Two downtown shop owners, in fact, resorted to novenas during a week-long period of looting in October of 1994, just after the landing the US military landing. Unable to go downtown, one explained, "I prayed the novena so that my store would be spared from the *dechoukaj* (destructive looting)." It would be no exaggeration to suggest that the novena, for the wealthy, thus offers protection from the decreasingly passive Haitian masses.

Upper-class respondents (67 percent) were more likely to make pilgrimage in Mary's honor than to pray the rosary. The reverse was true for the poor. This variance is probably explicable in terms of financial means, as pilgrimage is by far the most economically demanding of Marian devotions. Yet in spite of their economic disadvantage, a higher percentage of poor (71 percent) than wealthy informants had at least once been on Marian pilgrimage.

While reasons for making pilgrimage were similar among wealthy and poor informants, there was apparently a much greater variety in destination for the upper-class group. Whereas lower-class pilgrims had without exception never left Haiti in the name of Mary, roughly 20 percent from the upper-class group, almost all women, had made pilgrimage abroad. Their foreign destinations included Higuey in the Dominican Republic, the Shrine of Our Lady of Caridad in Miami, Lourdes, Fatima, Medjugorje, Mexico City, Caracas, Rome, and Jerusalem. One women of unspeakable wealth told me that she had vowed to Mary to visit all of her main shrines. "I have already been to Guadalupe, Lourdes, and Fatima," she explained with pride. "But I am planning to go to Medjugorje [Yugoslavia] as soon as it is safe."

Having made some kind of vow to the Virgin, this woman ranks in the minority among her study group; a mere 30 percent of whom had done the like. As with the under-class, those wealthy respondents who had made vows to the Virgin often did so in an effort to become more charitable and compassionate individuals. To quote a wealthy factory owner, "I vowed to Mary that I would give my employees a larger Christmas bonus each year." Vows among both classes also take the form of exchange of devotions for graces. In the case of Marie-Carmel's mother, always keeping a blue and white dress in her closet was a form of repayment to the Virgin for having steered her through a difficult period. Guertha, likewise, had promised to visit Saut-d'Eau if the Virgin would help her find lodging in Port-au-Prince, which she did, albeit temporarily. Haitians, generally, do not take vows with the saints lightly, and grave consequences are feared in the event of broken ones, which is plausibly to some extent evidence of Vodouisant coloring of Haitians' understanding of their relationship with the saints, since fear of ancestors' or *lwas*' retribution against the wayward and ungrateful is one of the strongest characteristics of not only Haitian Vodou but of African-based and African religions in general. It was not only poor respondents, as it were, who made reference to the Virgin's capacity for anger and punishment administration.

An almost equal percentage of poor and wealthy respondents (75 percent) had one or another Marian icon on display in their home, which the rich could more readily identify by name than could the poor. As for Marian medals, on the other hand, the percentage of upper-class respondents who owned or wore one (60 percent) was, somewhat surprisingly, almost double that of the under-class (33 percent). Michael P. Carroll calls the miraculous medal "— after the rosary and the Brown Scapular—the most popular of all Marian cult objects. Hundreds of millions of these medals have been distributed, and the wearing of these medals has been credited with thousands of miraculous cures."[41] For the wealthy participants in my survey, however, the medal seemed more an instrument of protection than a purveyor of miracles. "The miraculous medal keeps me safe from all dangers. I never worry about my own safety, as I always have it on," wrote one woman, the owner of a Port-au-Prince bakery. I myself was twice given a miraculous medal, along with a guide to its corresponding "Perpetual Novena," by upper-class couples when I first moved to Haiti. "Haiti is full of dangers and dark forces," one of the wives warned me. "Always keep this on, and the Virgin will protect you from them." When asked what she meant by dark forces, I was offered a most telling response: "Black magic and democracy!" The Haitian elite, as it were, are threatened by democratic progress, and thus it is only logical that they would turn to the Virgin to protect them from such a menace.

The miraculous medal also comes in the form of an ovular blue and white decal designed for adhesion to automobile windshields. The image is of Our Lady of the Assumption, surrounded by the plea *"Notre Dame, Soyez Notre Refuge"* (Our Lady, Be Our Refuge). It common to take it to a Catholic priest for a blessing prior to pasting it on the windshield. These stickers are remarkably diffuse on Haitian roadways. I once counted three dozen vehicles adorned with a miraculous Marian decal pass by during a thirty-minute period on a busy-but-flowing Port-au-Prince street one Wednesday afternoon! The decal is appreciably more popular among the wealthy than the poor, most of whom, of course, either do not own cars or cannot spare an extra seventeen gourdes (about US$1) for the holy trimming. The decal, as understood by wealthy drivers, protects against not only vehicular dangers, but also against the increasingly-feared masses: "Those people were beating on my car, and I thought they were going to drag me into the streets, rape and murder me," one affluent housewife recounted. "I prayed to Mary, who is always watching over me when I drive [a late-model Range Rover with one of the miraculous blue stickers on each of the upper corners of her smoked windshield], and she delivered me." It is indeed somewhat more common to see these decals stuck on newer, expensive vehicles than on the teeming multitude of decrepit jalopies that pack and smoke up the city streets. This is not to imply that the images of Mary are not used to protect Haiti's poor voyager. On the contrary, no other figure, not even Rambo or Jesus, is more commonly painted on the maddeningly colorful public buses and trucks into and onto which the impecunious masses cram themselves to journey across town or about the provinces.

At the outset of my fieldwork, I had expected to find a greater divergence between forms of Marian devotion that the wealthy and the poor in Haiti prefer. The survey, however, revealed the differences to be negligible. To be sure, just as they appear unalike in virtually everything they do, the ways in which agents from opposing classes carry themselves during Mass at a Marian feast day celebration, for example, are dissimilar. Yet of far greater moment than the apparent dissimilarities between upper and lower-class embellishments and styles of the same Marian devotions are their sometimes radically disparate perceptions and uses of the symbol of the Virgin Mary. It is clearly on the level of belief, or Mariological substructure, that elite and popular Haitian Marianism are most thorough-goingly divergent, as will be made apparent in the following section, which summarizes of upper-class Haitian Marian belief.

Marian Beliefs of the Haitian Elite

The Virgin Mary is the most common addressee of upper-class respondents' prayers, with 60 percent usually praying to her rather than God (30 percent) or Jesus (10 percent). Almost without exception, they do so because they perceive of the Virgin Mary as the closest to them among Catholicism's pantheon of spiritual beings and, as such, the most capable of ensuring effective response to their prayers. While a similar percentage of under-class informants likewise pray most often to the Virgin, they mostly do so believing that she personally is endowed with the power of answering their prayers and performing miracles, which is, of course, a heterodox belief. Wealthy Haitian Catholics, meanwhile, are much more carefully orthodox in their explanations. As one woman from an elite family explained, "I don't pray to the Virgin, I pray with her, and she sees that God responds to my prayers. But it is definitely God who ultimately answers my prayers, not the Virgin." A number of rich informants made similar disclaimers, and yet ostensibly their Catholicism consists in Marianism and little else, save Communion, which, after all, it would be difficult even for the most mariologically maximally inclined to misconstrue as somehow a Marian ritual. Be that as it may, both upper-class and lower-class Haitians cultivate a prayer life that clearly places Mary at the center, only the wealthy tend to be carefully orthodox in their explanation of the function of such prayer.

Besides the underlying difference in the degree of orthodoxy of each upper and lower-class Haitians' understanding of the dynamics of Marian prayer, the content of the prayers of each group also differed in degree of demand. Poor Haitians exhibit a greater tendency to ask the world of Mary, often praying for life and social change—things of the gravest moment imaginable. The wealthy—who do, of course, sometimes pray to Mary for matters of great import—far more frequently than the poor reported addressing to the Virgin generally much less significant, more mundane requests. Like three other rich informants, one woman, for instance, explained, "I prayed to the Virgin Mary to help me quit smoking, and I haven't had a cigarette in five years." Another recounted that, "For months the passenger door of my car was stuck, but just this morning it dawned upon me to say a little prayer to the Virgin, and when I got into my car, the door opened."

Commonly, wealthy respondents seemed to pride themselves on the orthodoxy of their Mariology. For some, this seemingly operated to reinforce their sense of distinction from the masses, suggesting thus that orthodox or "correct" beliefs are themselves a central religious feature of what Scott refers to as "the necessary posing of the dominant:"[42] "As an integral part of their claim to superiority, ruling castes are at pains to elaborate styles of speech, dress, consumption, gesture, carriage, and etiquette that distinguish them as sharply as possible from the lower orders." Later he further elaborates this thesis. "The culture of the aristocrat, lord, slave masters, and higher castes is, after all, designed to distinguish these ruling groups from the mass of peasants, serfs, slaves, and untouchables beneath them."[43] Such a design, for the Haitian upper-class, results in that "psychic elation" to which Leyburn referred some fifty years ago while commenting on elite Haitian culture in the quotation that opens this chapter.

Scott's argument, which owes much to Bourdieu and perhaps something to a reading of his Yale forefather Leyburn, gives insight into why so often wealthy respondents in my survey expressed horror at those questions that they found suggestive that they, for instance, believed in many Marys or that they confused the Virgin with Ezili. One woman wrote, "This questionnaire upset me very much...it makes us seem like blind 'picture' worshippers." Her Mariology is, of course, free of such idolatry and polytheistic superstition, and, following Scott's argument, contributes to her distinction from the common people, thereby reassuring her of her superiority over them. This woman's attitude was rather typical among the upper-class group. Consequently, the question that most offended them was, as expected, that regarding their understanding of the relationship between the Virgin Mary and Ezili. Some expressed outright indignation. "How dare you insinuate that I might even dream of identifying God's Mother with Satan's daughter," shrieked one woman. She thereafter refused to continue with the interview, mumbling something as she stormed off about how white people are so judgmental and could never understand Haitian culture in all its "*grandeur*." Fortunately, I had foreseen the possibility of such a scenario and therefore always saved this question for the end. Another man, a veritable modern aristocrat sporting a silk scarf, with a snicker protested, "Now really, you don't think that you can make me believe that there's any substance to such nonsense?" This is something of a unique response in the sense that it actually brings into question Ezili's existence. Most of the wealthy did not and typically looked at the phenomenon of syncretism as some criminal form of sacrilege. As the woman who was offended by the questionnaire's insinuation that her belief might be idolatrous put it,

"It is such a pity that they [Vodouisants] use such a pure heart for Voodoo purposes."

It thus appears that the attitude of the Haitian elite toward Vodou has changed little in the last half-century. Métraux, writing of how upper-class Catholics reacted to the Church's insistence that they take an anti-superstitious oath in 1939, notes that "Members of the 'elite' and even of the middle classes, were outraged that they should be required to take an oath which suggested they were suspect of sharing peasant beliefs and practices. Their indignation knew no limits."[44] Such a persistent insolence toward Vodou among the Haitian wealthy corroborates Weber's argument that the dominant "class is usually characterized by a profound disesteem of all irrational religion."[45]

The Cults of Mary Among the Haitian Elite

The survey revealed differences between upper- and lower-class respondents' preferential rankings of the various cults of Mary to be inconsiderable. The same five leading Marian cults for the poor, in the same exact descending order of popularity, turned out to be consistent with those of the wealthy: (1) *Perpétuel Secours*; (2) Immaculate Conception; (3) Altagracia; (4) Assumption; and (5) Mount Carmel. There were notable differences in cult predilection only in the slightly greater variety of Virgins holding primary importance in the religious lives of individual upper-class respondents. Specifically, eight different Marian icons were at least once deemed most important by wealthy informants, against five for the poor. This variation is revealed to be even more significant when one recalls that the poor group outnumbered the upper-class group by three to one.

Our Lady of Guadalupe, whom the under-class group ranked lowest overall among the eleven Virgins listed in the survey, was ranked seventh by the wealthy, thanks mainly to her four first-place votes. These votes were all from respondents who had spent extended periods of study at Mexican universities, Marie-Carmel included. Of wealthy respondents, 67 percent held *Notre Dame du Perpétuel Secours* to be the most meaningful image of Mary in their lives, a figure roughly equal to that of the lower-class pool (70 percent). Likewise, the percentage of wealthy and poor respondents who considered *Perpétuel Secours* the Marian image who has the greatest concern for Haiti (80 percent) was consistent. As noted in the previous chapter, class distinctions in cult preferences are minimal in Haitian Marianism, with noted divergences being explicable in terms of wealthy respondents having been exposed through travel and residence abroad to a greater variety of Marian cults, as evidenced in the unique popularity of Guadalupe among four upper-class respondents who had lived for a time in Mexico.

Listed below is the tabulated breakdown of Marian cult preferences among upper-class respondents in the survey. Figures in parentheses are corresponding totals from the lower-class group, whose sampling was three times larger:

Marian Image	**1st**	**Total Points**	**Last**
1) *Perpétuel Secours*	67 (178)	846 (2224)	0 (0)
2) Immac. Concept.	12 (51)	288 (918)	0 (0)
3) *Altagracia*	8 (8)	264 (632)	2 (1)
4) Assumption	0 (0)	126 (428)	2 (0)
5) Mount Carmel	3 (1)	78 (317)	11(31)
6) Lourdes	3 (3)	66 (188)	3 (2)
7) Guadalupe	4 (0)	52 (0)	17 (45)
8) Mount Calvary	1 (0)	50 (24)	15 (33)
9) *Caridad del Cobre*	1 (0)	50 (16)	13 (29)
10) Czestochowa	0 (0)	22 (12)	10 (18)
11) Fatima	0 (0)	8 (40)	0 (8)

Upper-class Perceptions of the Virgin Mary in Haitian Politics

In light of the data produced through our fieldwork, it may be convincingly argued that the most glaring and significant difference between the ways that wealthy and poor Haitians understand the Virgin Mary is manifest on the level of the politicoideological content of their respective Mariologies. Whereas 63 percent of underclass respondents believed the Virgin Mary to be the driving force behind the restoration of democracy and the concomitant return of President Aristide from exile, a mere 11 percent of wealthy respondents shared this or similar beliefs. Although Marie-Carmel's judgment that, if anything, the Virgin might spare the Haitian people form the "Aristidean delusion" is perhaps extreme and atypical, it did emerge as evident that many wealthy Marian devotees do look to the Virgin for protection against the masses, who certainly have been emboldened by Aristide, and it would strike many wealthy Haitian Catholics as abhorrent to suggest that the nation's patroness could choose for Haiti such a fate as the return of the nation's first truly democratically-elected president. Some, like the members in the prayer groups that emerged around Sister Altagrâce's visions, to be sure, believed the Virgin to be opposed to the U.S. intervention in Haiti, though, to portray such a belief as typical of upper-class Haitian Catholics would be irresponsible, as my research of this group was limited to discussions with only two members and an analysis of the published messages received by the nun. Furthermore, in an effort not to allow the content of my questions to introduce new ideas to respondents who might in turn be mistaken for, or misrepresented as, their own long-standing beliefs, I was careful not to formulate direct questions regarding contemporary Haitian political affairs, allowing respondents instead to volunteer their own slant on the relationship between Mary and politics in the context of more general questions such as, "What has the Virgin Mary done for Haiti?" In other words, had the question been posed to upper-class respondents specifically whether they believed the Virgin to be opposed to the Aristide presidency, it is reasonable to assume that a fairly considerable percentage would have answered yes, and this percentage could in turn be used to reinforce my main conclusion. However, such a move would be misleading, as the question itself might have been the cause of their initial reflection on the matter, and hence care was taken to avoid such a methodological misstep.

In any case, a small minority of upper-class respondents actually believed that the Virgin Mary had willed the restoration of democracy in Haiti and restored Aristide to the presidential palace. Another equally small minority expressly stated that the Virgin is opposed to this transition of power, while the Mariology of the majority of rich participants displayed no substantial political content. This is not to suggest that they see the Virgin as ambivalent to Haitian affairs. Quite the contrary, upper-class Haitians believe as strongly as the poor especially in *Perpétuel Secours'* maternal concern for the nation; as far as the wealthy are concerned, however, this concern is manifest among the poor in the form of the providence of bread and consolation, rather than wealth distribution and subversive populist ideology. A few elite respondents, in fact, actually claimed that the Virgin Mary abets the poor in resigning themselves to their fate and hence soothes the pain of their suffering. Following is an exemplary selection of statements from wealthy Haitians regarding the expected manifestations of the Virgin Mary's concern for Haiti:

"The Virgin will continue to make the people's suffering less hard, almost bearable."

"She will rid Haiti of the devil!!"

"The Virgin will demonstrate to the Haitian people that what they really need is the Gospel of resignation rather than the Gospel of liberation"

"She will bring all Haitians to learn how to read and write and ensure that they all have access to decent health care."

"It is thanks to the Virgin that the poor of this country have anything to eat at all."

"*Notre Dame* loves Haiti, but is saddened by the state of the country. The country is sick. She has cured it before, and I trust that she will cure it again."

"The Virgin will help the Haitian people understand that democracy does not give them the right to loot and steal."

"Haiti suffers because the people are superstitious and involved in Vodou and black magic. *Notre Dame* will show the people the right path."

"Haiti is a poor country, which is why Haitians love the Virgin so much—she helps them get by."

Thus, it is clear that wealthy Haitians, contrary to the poor, await no grandiose political or social transformation to be brought about by the Virgin Mary, who may even resist such change or at least protect the elite from harm once it occurs. True social change in Haiti would, of course, be counter to their short-sighted, myopic interests. The most potentially subversive deed that Mary might do for the poor, it would seem, is to teach them to read and write. In the elite's perspective, Mary's involvement in Haitian history—through inspiring resignation in the poor and providing them with bread, consolation, and little else—would serve, then, to perpetuate the status quo and their positions of power and privilege. Insofar as popular Haitian Marianism takes the form of resignation and instills quiescence in the masses, as argued in the previous chapter, it indeed is effective in performing precisely this function. However, as we have seen, in Haiti as elsewhere, such has not always been the case. Radical forms of Haitian Marianism are but specific examples of a politically potent trend in "folk Catholicism" throughout the world and over the ages. Scott makes this point forcefully:

> Any argument claiming that the ideological efforts of ruling elites are directed at *convincing* subordinates that their subordination is just must confront a good deal of evidence suggesting that it often fails to achieve its purpose. Catholicism, for example, is the logical candidate for the hegemonic ideology of feudalism. But it is abundantly clear that the folk Catholicism of the European peasants, far from serving ruling interests, was practiced and interpreted often in ways that defended peasant property rights, contested large differences in wealth, and even provided something of a millennial ideology with revolutionary import. Rather than being a "general anesthesia," folk Catholicism was a provocation—one that, together with its adherents in the lower clergy, provided the ideological underpinning for countless rebellions against seigneurial authority.[46]

In the Haitian religious field, it would seem that the "ideological efforts of the ruling elites" have met with greater success than in most cases, and yet Haitian "folk Catholicism" has since 1983 made great strides toward balancing the scale. What is clearer now than ever, in any case, is that "the ideological underpinning" of popular Haitian Marianism stands "in active opposition" to the "hegemonic ideology" embodied by the Virgin who offers the poor but morsels of bread and the promise of other-worldly salvation in return for their devotion and subservience.

Besides this divergence in politicoideological content, elite and popular Haitian Marianism also differs regarding the importance each places on the Virgin's soteriological clout. Convinced of Mary's influence over the economy of salvation, the Mariology of many wealthy Haitians demonstrated a decidedly soteriological emphasis (which is not at all prevalent among the poor). This was evinced by over a dozen wealthy informants who expressed a keen desire for the Virgin to aid them "at the hour of our death." Significantly, no lower-class respondent expressed such a desire. Interestingly, the elite's concern for their own sanctification is a guiding force not only of their Marianism but of other elements of their religious lives. Suze Marie Mathieu, whose dissertation explores the socioeconomic class structure of religious group membership in Haiti and the influence of socioeconomic class on Haitian Catholics' personal ecclesiology, concludes that for upper-class Haitians active in prayer groups or religiously-based charitable organizations, "their primary goal is their own sanctification."[47] Doing good for the less fortunate, much like praying the rosary or making pilgrimage to Lourdes, it would seem, operates for the wealthy as a vehicle of assurance not only of the legitimacy of their this-worldly riches, as we have argued, but of blessed eternity in the hereafter.

It should be borne in mind that while Weber's argument that the need for the "psychological reassurance of legitimacy" is *the* reason affluent and powerful individuals are religious is provocative, it is clearly limited. Religion is far too complex and multilayered to permit such a reductionist explanation as final. While many of the upper-class Haitians studied in this project did exhibit this form of religious need, few, if any, exhibited *only* this form of need, as illustrated, for example, by the soteriological angst that lies close to the heart of their Marian devotion. Furthermore, agents from either class often spoke of Mary's beauty as something utterly appealing and soothing, which suggests that there is also an aesthetic dimension to all people's devotion to the Virgin Mary, regardless of socioeconomic background or psychological need.

Nevertheless, the portrayal of upper-class Haitian Marianism that emerges out of our fieldwork and the case study of Marie-Carmel confirm, on three of four counts, Weber's thesis on the religion of elite classes. In this chapter it has been demonstrated that in Haiti: (1) Marian devotion does provide the elite with "the psychological reassurance of legitimacy; (2) forms of Marian devotion practiced by the elite tend to be reserved and are rarely, if ever, expressed in ways that could be defined as ecstatic; and (3) in general, wealthy Haitians exhibit "a profound disesteem for" any popular forms of Marian devotion that they suspect of being tinged with Vodouisant belief, symbolism, or ritual. In addition, a point that Weber implies in *The Sociology of Religion* is that the lower a group's socioeconomic standing, the more likely they are to stray from orthodoxy.488 Such a tendency is, too, evident in Haitian Marianism, as the Mariology of the upper-class is plainly more orthodox than that of the under-class.

The fourth count, the only count on which our field research reveals a characteristic of upper-class Haitian Marianism that contradicts Weber's thesis, concerns the diverse predilections of different social groups for "salvation religion." Whereas according to Weber's argument, among the religious needs of elite classes "the need for salvation is remote and alien,"[49] our survey of one hundred upper-class Haitians and Marie-Carmel's case revealed that the concern for personal salvation is not an uncommon feature in the Marian devotion of wealthy Haitians, and is in effect anything but "remote and alien." As for the under-class, Weber writes, "The lower the social class, the more radical are the forms assumed by the need for a savior," and the greater variety of forms (sometimes nonreligious forms) their quest for salvation takes.[50] For poor Haitians, this need took a religious form in the context of their Marianism in an indirect and collective way. While poor informants' Mariology seldom exhibits personal soteriological concerns like those of the wealthy, their Mariology did nonetheless meet their real need for salvation in the sense that the Virgin represented their source of hope for the return of President Aristide. It is no exaggeration to add that this was indeed equivalent to salvation for the Haitian under-class, albeit not in a purely religious but a very this-worldly form.

For the "disprivileged" of Haitian society, then, the need for salvation took on a politicomariological form. That it was not a purely religious form is actually consonant with Weber's thesis: "They (the disprivileged) do not always experience this need for salvation in a religious form, as shown by the example of the modern proletariat."[51] Furthermore, this need for salvation among the under-class "may be conjoined with a need for just compensation,"[52] which clearly is also a feature of contemporary popular Haitian Mariology, as illustrated in chapter six. In any case, the Marianism of the Haitian upper-class exhibits a greater concern with personal salvation than does the Marianism of the poor, and this is a finding that is contrary to Weber's argument concerning the relationship between social class and personal soteriological interest.

One additional conclusion—as illuminating as it is ironic—may be drawn from the detailed observations made over the course of these last two chapters: Since Marian devotion in Haiti, as we have seen, serves to politically embolden the poor—giving them strength to carry on resistance activities in the face of persecution—while tending to numb the conscience of the wealthy so as to render their power and privilege acceptable *to themselves* as well as to the poor, Marianism, in the end, is more an opiate for the ruling elite than for the masses.

NOTES

1. Brian Morris, *Anthropological Studies of Religion: An Introductory Text* (Cambridge: Cambridge University Press, 1987), p. 79.
2. Malcolm B. Hamilton, *The Sociology of Religion: Theoretical and Comparative Perspectives* (London: Routledge, 1995), p. 147.
3. Martin Luther originally developed the doctrines of calling and of the elect, although it was Calvinist theology, which "thought that the devout could seek some sign of being among the elect" (Morris, p. 151), that represented for Weber the ultimate connection between the Protestant ethic and the spirit of capitalism.
4. Morris, *Anthropological Studies of Religion*, p. 59.
5. Ibid.
6. Max Weber, *The Sociology of Religion* (Boston: Beacon, 1953), p. 107.

7. J. Lewis, *Max Weber and Value-Free Sociology*, p. 13, as cited in Morris, *Anthropological Studies of Religion*, p. 59.

8. Morris, *Anthropological Studies of Religion*, p. 59.

9. Weber, *The Sociology of Religion*, p. 108.

10. Ibid., p. 110

11. Ibid., p. 106.

12. Ibid., p. 107.

13. Francis Schüssler Fiorenza, "Religion and Society: Legitimation, Rationalisation or Cultural Heritage," in Johannes Baptist Metz, (ed.), *Christianity and the Bourgeoisie*; *Concilium 125*, June, 1977, pp. 24-32, p. 28.

14. Weber, *The Sociology of Religion*, p. 89.

15. Leslie G. Desmangles, *The Faces of the Gods: Vodou and Roman Catholicism in Haiti* (Chapel Hill: The University of North Carolina Press, 1992), p. 3.

16. Maya Deren, *The Divine Horsemen: The Living Gods of Haiti* (London and New York: Thames and Hudson, 1953), p. 15.

17. Ibid.

18. Karen McCarthy Brown, *Mama Lola: A Vodou Priestess in Brooklyn* (Berkeley and Los Angeles: University of California Press, 1992), p. 249.

19. Ibid., p. 309.

20. Alfred Métraux, *Voodoo in Haiti* (New York: Schocken Books, 1972), p. 58.

21. Ibid. pp. 58-59.

22. During the research for her 1991 Ph.D. dissertation, Suze Marie Mathieu interviewed twenty-seven individuals from the "upper-class," though some of the criteria employed in her classification of these individuals is suspect. For instance, some of Mathieu's "upper-class" respondents reported monthly incomes of $100, which is hardly suggestive of true upper-class status in Haiti. Suze Marie Mathieu, "The Transformation of the Catholic Church in Haiti," Ph.D. diss., Indiana University, 1991.

23. Jean Price Mars, *Ainsi parla l'oncle*, as cited in Lyonel Paquin, *The Haitians: Class and Color Politics*, p. 252.

24. Ibid.

25. Ibid.

26. Jean Price Mars, *La vocation de l'élite* (Port-au-Prince: Imprimerie La Presse, 1919), p. 81.

27. Léon Audain, *Mouers haïtiennes*, as cited in Leon-François Hoffmann, *Haïti: couleurs, croyances, créole* (Montréal: CIDHICA, 1990), p. 152.

28. Ibid., p. 153.
29. While my knowledge of Haitian fictional literature is limited, it is possible, as Hurbon suggests, that certain novels offer useful portrayals of elite Haitians' attitudes toward Vodou. See Hurbon, *Dieu dans le vaudou haïtien*, pp. 38-45.
30. Desmangles, *The Faces of the Gods*, p. 58
31. Ibid. p. 6.
32. "Status group" is the English translation often used for Weber's *Stand*, which, as Anthony Giddens and David Held explain, is distinguished from "the purely economically determined" notion of class insofar as status group membership has as much to do with "style of life" and "social estimation of *honor*" as anything else. In this respect, it is appropriate to conceive of the Haitian elite as a *Stand*, not, mind you, over and above, but complimentary to conceiving of them as a "class." Anthony Giddens and David Held, eds., *Classes, Power, and Conflict*, p. 65.
33. To recall, July 16th is one of the two most important dates in Haitian Marianism (the other June 27th) because of the Saut-d'Eau pilgrimage that culminates on this day, as well as the extensive pilgrimage traditions of Haitians in the diaspora to Mount Carmel's churches, like the one on 115th Street in Harlem that is the subject of Robert Anthony Orsi's study.
34. Our Lady of Guadalupe is the patron saint of Mexico and of all the Americas. Her cult in Haiti, however, is virtually nonexistent and devotion to her seems limited to a few wealthy individuals who had spent extended periods of time in Mexico. There is a large painting of Guadalupe in the national cathedral in Port-au-Prince, though it is hung in a side corridor and rarely attracts many faithful.
35. "*59ème Manifestation: de Marie, Mère de Dieu, Mère des Hommes, Corédemptrice de Genre humain, à Soeur Altagrâce Doresca, o.v.c., le 25 Mars 1993 (l'ANNONCIATION) de 5:00 à 6:30 A.M., à la "Chambre de Jésus."* I have quoted passages as they appear in an unpublished flyer that circulates informally in certain Catholic circles in Port-au-Prince.
36. Ibid.
37. Weber, *The Sociology of Religion*, p. 108.
38. Pierre Bourdieu, *Distinction: A Social Critique of the Judgement of Taste* (Cambridge: Harvard University Press, 1984), p. 1. Although in this discussion Bourdieu is primarily concerned with art, I think that he would agree that the same holds true for religious preferences.

39. On June 27, 1994, I met Guertha at Bel-Air for the feast of *Notre Dame du Perpétuel Secours*. It was by coincidence that Marie-Carmel also happened to be there. Although I was already acquainted with Marie-Carmel, it was not until I saw her on this morning that I decided to ask her if she would agree to become a case study for this dissertation. The following summer the same coincidence occurred on August 15, 1995, this time at the Cathedral during the feast of *Notre Dame de l'Assomption*. Guertha and Marie-Carmel have never met. The *Assomption* feast, incidentally, is as popular as that of *Perpétuel Secours*, with thousands of people taking part in the procession that follows the Masses, reciting the rosary in unison as they wind about the neighborhood in the path of the statue of the Virgin, which sits in the bed of a Toyota pickup surrounded by burly body guards sporting black berets and submachine guns.

40. Deren explains that service is very much the essence of Vodou practice, thus inspiring the suggestion that lower-class Haitians, since more likely to be possessed of a Vodouisant religious habitus, are thus more likely to conceive of their relationship with the Virgin Mary in similar terms. "The Haitian thinks of his religion in working terms. To ask whether he "believes" in Voudoun is to pose a meaningless question. He answers, "I serve the loa", and more than likely, he will say, "I serve so-and-so...." *The Divine Horsemen*, pp. 73-74.

41. Carroll, *The Cult of the Virgin Mary*, p. 148.

42. Scott, *Domination and the Arts of Resistance*, p. 11.

43. Ibid. p. 158.

44. Métraux, *Voodoo in Haiti*, p. 341.

45. Weber, *The Sociology of Religion*, p. 89.

46. Scott, *Domination and the Arts of Resistance*, p. 11.

47. Suze Marie Mathieu, "The Transformation of the Catholic Church in Haiti," Ph.D. diss, Indiana University, 1991, p. 97.

48. See Weber, *The Sociology of Religion*, esp. pp. 95-104.

49. Ibid., p. 101

50. Ibid., p. 102.

51. Ibid., p. 108.

52. Ibid.

CHAPTER EIGHT

STONES, WATER, SUN, AND FIREFLIES:
A BRIEF CONCLUSION

> Conquerors and conquered, owners and workers, religious
> and lay people have experienced their relationship with
> Mary over the centuries-long history of Christian faith in
> Latin America. Impelled by its own interests, each group
> has claimed Mary for its own, and so she has taken part in
> the conflicts of life and death, victory and defeat of differ-
> ent groups within the complex Latin American social fab-
> ric.[1]

The above passage is as true regarding Haiti as anywhere else. In
this study, we have seen efforts by the politically, the religiously, the
sexually, the economically, and the socially dominant to manipulate
the symbol of Mary and popular Marian devotion to legitimize their
power and privilege. The Spanish conquest of the New World, with
its virtual extermination of indigenous peoples and development of
the transatlantic slave trade, was considered from the outset—at
least by Queen Isabella, Columbus, and the ensuing waves of missionaries and conquistadors—the Virgin Mary's triumph. Thus
began a recurrent theme in the history of Haitian Marianism, one
most recently manifest in the brutally oppressive Cédras junta's attempt to give their illegitimate de facto regime the veneer of *Notre
Dame du Perpétuel Secours'* sanction. Yet at times in Haitian history, the Marianism of the subjugated has displayed that revolutionary capacity that Gramsci felt to be characteristic of popular

religion. From Romaine-la-Prophétesse's radical appropriation of the Virgin to inspire violent slave insurrections in 1791 to the hundreds of thousands of oppressed Haitians praying to *Perpétuel Secours* to topple the Cédras regime two hundred years later, popular Haitian Marianism has on occasion exhibited this capacity to serve as a motivational force for resistance against abusive and dominant powers. Thus, in Haiti as elsewhere, while the forces "who wield power have always tried to take over the devotion to Mary and subject the poor to their organizations and demands,"[2] popular Marianism, far from being a merely passive and diluted adoption of forms of devotion sanctioned by the Church, has sustained a subversive originality that, given fortuitous circumstances, may be actualized in the form of social and political activism, or outright insurgence and revolt.

This study has demonstrated that struggle is central to the history and structure of both the Haitian religious field in general and to Haitian Marianism in particular. Basically, this struggle over Mary between the dominant and the subjugated tends to take three dualistic forms: (1) Struggle by the dominant for the legitimization of political, social, and economic power, or by the subjugated for the inspiration of resistance or action toward social or political change; (2) struggle by orthodoxy to maintain a purely Catholic Mary operative in the Church's epic campaign against the Vodou heresiarchy, which has itself seized the symbol of Mary and elements of Marian devotion, freely adapting them in its own liturgy, symbolism, and ritual; and (3) a mainly lay-level struggle by each of the two main opposing classes in Haitian society to appropriate Mary to meet their own class-specific religious needs; i.e., needs, following Weber, that we discovered to be largely psychological. Hence, our analysis of this episodic yet constant struggle over Mary on the political, religious, and psycho-ideological levels reveals that throughout the entire course of Haitian history "devotion to Mary retains an anthropological and ideological substrate common to all adherents, which is expressed in the pursuit of their needs and in defense of their interests."[3] A comparison of the results of this study's upper-class and lower-class surveys, especially when personalized through a referential comparison of the case studies of Guertha and Marie-Carmel, illustrates this conclusion amply.

Stated generally, chapters six and seven showed that regarding devotional practice (i.e., rosary, feasts, pilgrimage, etc.), there is not a marked divergence between elite and popular Haitian Marianism. Percentages of poor and rich respondents who prefer celebrating Mary's feast days, making pilgrimage, or praying the rosary were roughly proportionate. The same holds true for cult preferences, with *Perpétuel Secours*, Immaculate Conception, *Altagracia*, Assumption, and Mount Carmel being the Marian icons of choice for each class. It was also demonstrated that belief in *Notre Dame du Perpétuel Secours* as the Mary most concerned with Haiti is uniform across socioeconomic class divisions. In light of her status as national patroness, this much was to be expected. What each class believes *Perpétuel Secours* has done and will do for Haiti, however, is quite different. Perhaps nothing more forcefully illustrates the respective ideological functions that Marianism performs for each class than the diametrically opposed stances that each group, the elite and the masses, believed Mary to have taken in the Aristide saga.

Therefore, the most significant disclosure of our fieldwork—that the greatest difference between elite and popular Haitian Marianism lies on the level on the ideological content of their respective mariological substructures—is, as the historical analyses in chapters two and four demonstrated, but the latest manifestation of the conflict that has been inherent to Haitian Marianism for half a millennium. Current sociocultural incarnations of this struggle differ from those of other ages only insofar as the sociocultural realities for each dominant and the subjugated have also changed. The underlying constant is a radical split between the elite and the masses, the dominant and the subjugated, the conquering and the conquered. This, I would argue, is the major determinant of the various forms that Haitian Marianism has taken over the course of five hundred years. In effect, one can read the story of Haiti's epic class struggle in the history of its cult of the Virgin Mary.

To be sure, other factors besides socioeconomic class struggle have influenced both the development of the different forms that Marian devotion takes in the Haitian religious field, and the ways in which Haitians perceive of and appropriate the symbol and myth of the Virgin. Undoubtedly, the Vodouisant worldview that permeates many aspects of Haitian culture has influenced, to varying degrees, both popular and elite perceptions of Mary. The Virgin is a subject of choice among many Haitian painters, for example, who often enrich her image with characteristics of Ezili, as in the painting that graces the cover of this book. Similarly, the Virgin Mary is embellished in the Haitian religious habitus. For example, the notion that the different manifestations of the Virgin Mary sometimes struggle with one another over the devotion of the faithful, and that some Virgins are prone to fits of jealous rage when their devotees unfaithfully seek the succor of another Virgin, is arguably rooted in the Vodouisant conception of spiritual beings. Significantly, moreover, this is not merely a belief of the popular classes; while Vodouisant influences on perceptions of the Virgin Mary's potencies and characteristics are considerably more prevalent among the poor, belief in Mary's capacity for jealousy and vengeance is one noteworthy exception, as more than a few rich Haitians share this conception.

Where the Vodouisant influence on Marianism is more appreciable among the poor than the wealthy, however, is in the poor's conception of their relationship with Mary in terms of service. Commonly underclass informants spoke of themselves as being the Virgin's *domestik*, or as the instrument of her will. The wealthy seemed more selfishly calculating in their approach to Marian devotion, usually fixing their sights on the personally lucrative potential of their piety. It is plausible that since Vodou practice is more common among the poor than the rich, since service of the *lwas* is central to Vodou, and since the Vodouisant perception of one's relationship with the spirits translates itself into Catholic devotion, the underclass, thus, conceive of their commerce with Mary in such terms of service. Maya Deren offers insight into this feature of the Vodouisant's relationship with the spirits:

> The Haitian thinks of his religion in working terms. To ask him whether he believes in Voudoun is to pose a meaningless, irrelevant question. He answers, "I serve the loas", and, more than likely, he will say, "I serve so-and-so", giving even to general divine power a specialized focus.[4]

For the impoverished Haitian Marian devotee, more so than the ornately bejeweled woman who drives to the church at Bel-Air in her late-model BMW, this specialized focus is fixed interchangeably on the Virgin Mary and Ezili. Degrees of syncretism conflating the two, of course, vary from individual to individual, but it is certainly more likely to be a feature of popular rather than elite Haitian Marianism, which, as demonstrated in chapter seven, is far more concerned with orthodoxy. In summary, certain features of Haiti's Mary cult, such as syncretism with Ezili, the conception of the devotee as Mary's servant, and the belief that different incarnations of the Virgin may become jealous of one another over their devotees, are each demonstrably rooted in Vodou. Each of these features, moreover, is more likely to be discernible in popular rather than elite Haitian Marianism. Class struggle and Vodou, thus, go far in explaining the nature of Haitian Marianism.

Yet beyond these influences that have been very much the focus of our analysis, Marian piety in Haiti, as with most any form of religious devotion in any society, is driven mainly by a people's response to something or someone they experience as a real spiritual force. Historical analysis, for its insistence on concrete facts, and the sociology of religion, for its "methodological atheism,"[5] are somewhat predisposed to overlook the noumenal and aesthetic dimensions of religious devotion. It would be a great injustice to the Haitian people to end this study without affirming that the Virgin Mary is to them very real. The theories advanced throughout this study, I fear, tend to belie this very essential fact. Class differences, legitimation, syncretism, "the psychological reassurance of legitimacy," the "opium of the people," and existential suffering aside, Haitians are, in general, unshakably convinced that the Virgin Mary intervenes in the world to help them through whatever trials they encounter on life's way. I am perfectly aware of the possibility that Guertha, Marie-Carmel, and other of my informants might find my explanations of their devotion curious, if not offensive; to me this is acceptable. I will only add that the sincerity of their devotion is unquestionable, and certain Haitian expressions of devotion to Mary are as beautiful and moving as religion gets.

As a trained sociologist of religion, I suppose I was predisposed, however, to find the influence of class on Haitian Marian devotion as striking as this devotion is beautiful. To return, then, to our "explanatory reduction,"[6] the theoretical premises of this study, influenced mainly by Gramsci, Weber, and Bourdieu, prefigured especially the discoveries of those differences between elite and popular Haitian Marianism that are shaped by class struggle. Gramsci's suggestive reclamation from Marx of the political potency of popular religion—which represents a worldview in opposition to that which has for centuries served to legitimize the domination to which the oppressed are subjected—inspired the question as to whether such a revolutionary capacity might exist in popular Haitian Marianism. The research undertaken here indicates that indeed it does. Weber's enumeration of class-distinct religious needs and interests suggested investigating and comparing those needs of each poor and wealthy Haitians to which their Marian devotion responds. With one exception in regards to the soteriological concerns of elite Haitian Marianism, the findings in this study emerge as consistent with Weber's thesis on class and religious needs. Finally, Bourdieu's refinement of several components of Weber's sociology of religion were likewise germane to the objectives of this study. For one, we fruitfully followed Bourdieu's suggestion that the analysis of the structures of the religious field and of their relationship to agents' religious habiti should be the primary methodological step for any sociological study of religion. Bourdieu's emphasis on the unsurpassed determining force of struggle on these structures also has had a vital impact on this study. Thus taking Marianism to be a major subfield of the Haitian religious field positioned our analysis well to reveal struggle on various levels between the dominant and the subjugated to be the main structural determinant of Haitian Marianism. As Bourdieu suggests, once the structures of the religious field or of any of its subfields are in view, "we can arrive at the principle which explains the direct interactions between social agents and the strategies they may employ against each other."[7] The symbol of Mary and Haitians' Marian devotion, as we have stressed, have been irreplaceable components of such "strategies" that the powerful and the weak in Haiti have always employed and continue to "employ against each other."

What this amounts to in reality is a schism in Haitian Marianism so severe that we may correctly speak of what are *essentially* two different cults of Mary in the Haitian religious field: one of the actually powerful and one of the potentially powerful, or one of the dominant and one of the subjugated. These are especially divergent in terms of the ideological substructure of their belief content. This, in my view, represents this study's most important conclusion. Two implications of this conclusion deserve note: (1) In other "Catholic countries" with similar class structures to Haiti's—especially in Latin America and the Caribbean—it is likely that at the core and historically there exists such an ideologically-based schism between elite and popular Marianism; and (2) in Haiti, as elsewhere, this socioideologically schismatic dimension of Catholicism's most important cult will probably characterize Marianism for as long as the radical division between rich and poor that marks Haitian society perpetuate the conditions that promote it.

It remains now but to end where we started, only conclusively stringing together the three quotations with which we began in a way that sums up what we have learned. To those who might find suspect the very idea of mixing Goethe with Haitian proverbs, I only suggest that true wisdom transcends cultural differences.

> *Das ewig weibliche zieht uns heran.*
> [However], *roch na dlo pa kon doulè roch na sole*y,
> [and thus], *jipon Lavyej plen koukouy.*

The eternal feminine draws us on. However, the stone in the water knows not the pain of the stone in the sun, and thus, the Virgin's slip is full of fireflies.

NOTES

1. Ivone Gebara, and Maria Clara Bingemer, *Mary: Mother of God, Mother of the Poor* (Maryknoll: Orbis, 1989), p. 128.
2. Ibid., p. 157.
3. Ibid., p. 135.
4. Deren, *The Divine Horsemen: the Living Gods of Haiti* (New York and London: Thames and Hudson, 1953), pp. 73-74.
5. The term "methodological atheism" was adopted by Peter Berger in his classic *The Sacred Canopy* (New York: Doubleday, 1967). Berger explains this theoretical standpoint thus: "sociological theory must, by its own logic, view religion as a human projection, and by the same logic can have nothing to say about the possibility that this projection may refer to something other than the being of its projector (p. 180)."

6.   In the sociology of religion the term "explanatory reduction" is distinguished from "descriptive reduction." The latter is a description based on observation of the religious practice of the subjects of sociological analysis. Generally sociologists agree that it is crucial that such descriptions be understandable to the subjects themselves, i.e., that, should the subject read or be read the description, they would agree that it accurately depicts their practice. An "explanatory reduction," on the contrary, is not contingent upon the subject's hypothetical accordance and may explain the underlying meaning of religious belief and practice in ways that the subjects themselves might find inaccurate. For a useful discussion of these terms see Malcolm B. Hamilton, *The Sociology of Religion: Theoretical and Comparative Perspectives* (London and New York: Routledge, 1995), Chapter One.

7.   Pierre Bourdieu, "Legitimation and Structured Interest in Weber's Sociology of Religion," in S. Whimster and S. Lash, eds., *Max Weber, Rationality, and Modernity* (London: Urwin and Allen, 1971), pp. 119-136, p. 121.

BIBLIOGRAPHY

PRIMARY SOURCES

News Articles

Agence Haïtienne de Presse. *1993 au quotidien*. Port-au-Prince: AHP, 1994.

_____. *1993 au quotidien*. Port-au-Prince: AHP, 1995.

Bataille, Frantz. "Marie-Flor Thélus nous raconte." *Le Nouvelliste*, 30 mai 1976.

French, Howard. "Haiti's Curse: Power Means Brutality: Practice Makes Perfect." *The New York Times*, 17 October 1993.

Innocent, Henry-Claude, "Une vierge noire pour Haïti aussi." *Le Nouvelliste*, 18-19 November, 1995.

Kyss, Jean-Mary, "La nouvelle cathédrale de l'Immaculée Conception de Hinche," *Le Nouvelliste*, 14 November 1995.

Maisonneuve, Gérard. "Notre Dame du Perpétuel Secours." *Le Nouvelliste*, 6 December 1992.

_____. "Informations religieuses." *Le Nouvelliste*, 7 May 1995.

_____. "Informations religieuses." *Le Nouvelliste*, 14-15 June 1995.

_____. "Informations religieuses." *Le Nouvelliste*, 14-16 July 1995.

_____. "Informations religieuses." *Le Nouvelliste*, 6 September 1995.

_____. "Informations religieuses." *Le Nouvelliste*, 12 December 1995.

Saint-Gérard, Y. "Histoire et religion: les fondements du pouvoir théologique haïtien et ses contradictions." *Haiti-Observateur*, 1-8 February 1995.

Tomson, Ian. "A devil-may-care voodoo society." *Financial Times*, 22 February 1993.

BOOKS

Abbot, Walter J., ed. *The Documents of Vatican II*. London: Geoffrey Chapman, 1966.

Anonymous. *Supplique et neuvaine à Notre Dame du Perpéteul Secours.* Québec: Librarie de la Bonne Sainte Anne, 1963.

Bonnardot, Michel-Luc, and Gilles Danroc, eds. *La chute de la maison Duvalier: textes pour l'histoire.* Paris: KARTHALA, 1989.

Breathett, George, ed. *The Catholic Church in Haiti (1704-1785): Selected Letters, Memoires and Documents.* Salisbury: Documentation Publications, 1982.

Gremillon, Joseph, ed. *The Gospel of Peace and Justice: Catholic Social Teaching since Pope John.* Maryknoll: Orbis, 1976.

Lig Nòtre Dam Pepètyèl Sekou. *An'n chante Manman Pètyèl: Koze, lapriyè ak chan pou Mari Patwòn e Rèn Dayiti.* Port-au-Prince: Le Natal, 1992.

SECONDARY SOURCES

Unpublished Manuscripts

Lowenthal, Ira P. "Haiti: A House Divided." 1995.

Soeur Maria Lucia. "Notre Dame du Perpétuel Secours." Archives des Filles de Marie de Bel-Air. 1982.

Vadeboncouer, Paul-Emile. "Notre Dame du Perpétuel Secours." Archives des Filles de Marie de Bel-Air. Undated.

Woodson, Drexel G. "Which Beginning Should be Hindmost?: Surrealism in Appropriations About Haitian 'Contact Culture.'" 1993.

BOOKS

Ardouin, Beaubrun. *Etudes sur l'histoire d'Haïti.* Port-au-Prince: Dalencour, 1958.

America's Watch and National Coalition for Haitian Refugees. *Silencing a People: The Destruction of Civil Society in Haiti.* New York: Human Rights Watch, 1993.

Aristide, Jean-Bertrand. *In the Parish of the Poor: Writings from Haiti.* Maryknoll: Orbis, 1991.

Baring, Anne and Jules Cashford. *The Myth of the Goddess: Evolution of an Image.* London: Penguin Books, 1993.

Bastide, Roger. *African Civilisations in the New World.* New York: Harper Torchbooks, 1971.

_____. *Les amériques noires, les civilisations africaines dans le Nouveau Monde.* Paris: Payot, 1967.

_____. *The African Religions of Brazil: Toward a Sociology of the Interpenetration of Cultures.* Baltimore: Johns Hopkins University Press, 1960.

Beauvoir-Dominique, Rachel. *L'Ancienne cathédrale de Port-au-Prince: Perspectives d'un vestige de carrefours.* Port-au-Prince: Editions Henri Deschamps, 1991.

Bébel-Gisler, and Laënnec Hurbon. *Cultures et pouvoir dans la Caraïbe: langue créole, vaudou, sectes religieuses en Guadeloupe et en Haïti.* Paris: L'Harmattan, 1987.

Benko, Stephen. *The Virgin Goddess: Studies in the Pagan and Christian Roots of Mariology.* Leiden and New York: E.J. Brill, 1993.

Berger, Pamela. *The Goddess Obscured: The Transformation of the Grain Protectress From Goddess to Saint.* Boston: Beacon Press, 1985.

Berger, Peter. *The Social Reality of Religion.* Harmondsworth: Penguin Books, 1973.

Bien-Aimé, Gabriel. *Eglise pour changer.* Port-au-Prince: St. Gérard, 1987.

Boff, Leonardo. *Church: Charisma and Power: Liberation Theology and the Institutional Church.* New York: Crossroad, 1985.

_____.*Ecclesiogenesis.* Maryknoll: Orbis, 1986.

_____.*The Maternal Face of God: The Feminine and Its Religious Expressions.* New York: Harper and Row, 1987.

Boff, Leonardo, and Virgil Elizondo, eds. *Option for the Poor: Challenge to the Rich Countries.* Edinburgh: T.& T. Clarke, 1986. Concilium 187.

Bokenkotter, Thomas. *Essential Catholicism: Dynamics of Faith and Belief.* New York: Doubleday, 1986.

Bourdieu, Pierre. *Outline of a Theory of Practice.* Cambridge: Cambridge University Press, 1977.

_____. *Language and Symbolic Power.* Cambridge: Harvard University Press, 1991.

_____.*Distinction: A Social Critique of the Judgement of Taste.* Cambridge: Harvard University Press, 1991.

Bourdieu, Pierre, and Loïc J. D. Wacquant. *An Invitation to Reflexive Sociology.* Chicago: The University of Chicago Press, 1992.

Brinbaum, Lucia Chiavola. *Black Madonnas: Feminism, Religion, and Politics in Italy.* Boston: Northeastern University Press, 1993.

Brown, Karen McCarthy. *Mama Lola: A Vodou Priestess in Brooklyn.* Berkeley and Los Angeles: University of California Press, 1992.

Bulletin de la Societé Française d'Etudes Mariales. *La Vierge Marie dans la piété du peuple chrétien depuis Vatican II.* Paris: Mediaspaul, 1992.

Cabon, Adolphe. *Notes sur l'histoire religieuse d'Haïti, de la révolution au concordat (1789-1860)*. Port-au-Prince: Petit Séminaire Collège St Martial, 1933.

Calhoun, Craig, Edward LiPuma, and Moishe Postone, eds. *Bourdieu: Critical Perspectives*. Chicago: The University of Chicago Press, 1993.

Campbell, Joseph. *The Masks of the Gods: Oriental Mythology*. Harmondsworth: Penguin Books, 1970.

Canizares, Raoul, *Walking with the Night: The Afro-Cuban World of Santería*. Rochester: Destiny Books, 1993.

Carroll, Michael P. *The Cult of the Virgin Mary: Psychological Origins*. Princeton: Princeton University Press, 1986.

Clifford, James, and George E. Marcus. *Writing Culture: The Poetics and Politics of Ethnography*. Berkeley and Los Angeles: University of California Press, 1986.

Conférence Haïtienne des Religieux. *Evangelisation d'Haïti, 1492-1992: Introduction*. Port-au-Prince: Le Natal, 1991.

_____. *Evangelisation d'Haïti, 1492-1992, tome 1: Esclavage et évangelisation*.Port-au-Prince:Le Natal, 1991.

_____. *Evangelisation d'Haïti, 1492-1992, tome 2: Révolution de 1791*. Port-au-Prince: Le Natal, 1992.

_____. *Evangelisation d'Haïti, 1492-1992, tome 3: Les TKL et la nouvelle vangelisation*. Port-au-Prince: Le Natal, 1993.

_____.*Haïti et l'Amérique Latine*. Port-au-Prince: Le Natal, 1995.

Corvington, Georges. *Port-au-Prince au cours des ans: Sous les assauts de la révolution, 1789-1804*. Port-au-Prince: Editions Henri Deschamps, 1992.

_____.*Port-au-Prince au cours des ans: La Métropole haïtienne du XIXe siècle, 1804-1888*. Port-au-Prince: Editions Henri Deschamps, 1993.

Courlander, Harold. *The Drum and the Hoe*. Berkeley: University of California Press, 1960.

_____. and Remy Bastien. *Religion and Politics in Haiti*. Washington: Institute for Cross-Cultural Research, 1966.

Crow, John A. *The Epic of Latin America*. Garden City: Doubleday, 1946.

Daly, Mary. *Beyond God the Father: Toward a Philosophy of Women's Liberation*. Boston: Beacon Press, 1973.

_____.*Pure Lust: Elemental Feminist Philosophy*. San Francisco: Harper, 1984.

Davis, Elizabeth Gould. *The First Sex*. New York: G.P. Putman's Sons, 1971.

Davis, Wade. *The Serpent and the Rainbow*. New York: Simon and Schuster, 1985.

Dayan, Joan. *Haiti, History, and the Gods*. Berkeley and Los Angeles: University of California Press, 1995.

Dejean, Paul. *Willy Romélus: L'Evêque-Courage*. Québec: Editions Hurtubise, 1995.

Denis, Lorimer, and François Duvalier. *Le Problème des classes à travers l'histoire d'Haïti*. Port-au-Prince: Au service de la jeunnesse, 1948.

Deren, Maya. *Divine Horsemen: The Living Gods of Haiti*. London and New York: Thames and Hudson, 1953.

Desmangles, Leslie G. *The Faces of the Gods: Vodou and Roman Catholicism in Haiti*. Chapel Hill: The University of North Carolina Press, 1992.

Desquiron, Lilas. *Racines du vodou*. Port-au-Prince: Editions Henri Deschamps, 1990.

Diedrich, Bernard, and Al Burt. *Papa Doc and the Tonton Macoutes*. Port-au-Prince: Editions Henri Deschamps, 1986.

Duvalier, François. *Mémoires d'un leader du tiers monde*. Paris: Hachette, 1969.

Eckstein, Susan, ed. *Power and Popular Protest: Latin American Social Movements*. Berkeley and Los Angeles: University of California Press, 1989.

Eliade, Mircea. *The Sacred and the Profane: The Nature of Religion*. New York: Harvest/HBJ, 1959.

Farmer, Paul. *The Uses of Haiti*. Monroe: Common Courage Press, 1994.

Fass, Simon M. *Political Economy in Haiti: The Drama of Survival*. New Brunswick: Transaction Publishers, 1988.

Fick, Carolyn E. *The Making of Haiti: The Saint-Domingue Revolution from Below*. Knoxville: The University of Tennessee Press, 1990.

Fouchard, Jean. *Les Marrons de la liberté*. Port-au-Prince: Editions Henri Deschamps, 1988.

————. *Les Marrons du syllabaire*. Port-au-Prince: Editions Henri Deschamps, 1988.

Françisque, Edouard. *La structure économique et social d'Haïti*. Port-au-Prince: Editions Henri Deschamps, 1986.

Galtung, Johan. *The True Worlds: A Transitional Perspective*. New York: The Free Press, 1980.

Gebara, Ivone, and Maria Clara L. Bingemer. *Mary: Mother of God, Mother of the Poor*. Maryknoll: Orbis, 1989.

Geertz, Clifford. *The Interpretation of Cultures*. New York: Basic Books, 1973.

Genovese, Eugene. *Roll, Jordan, Roll: The World the Slave Made*. New York: Random House, 1976.

Giddens, Anthony, and David Held, eds. *Classes, Power, and Conflict: Classical and Contemporary Debates*. Berkeley and Los Angeles: University of California Press, 1982.

Gramsci, Antonio. *Selections from the Prison Notebooks*. New York: Lawrence and Wishart, 1971.

————.*Pre-Prison Writings*. Cambridge and New York: Cambridge University Press, 1994.

Greeley, Andrew. *The Mary Myth: On the Femininity of God*. New York: Seabury, 1977.

Greene, Anne. *The Catholic Church in Haiti: Political and Social Change*. East Lansing: Michigan State University Press, 1993.

Greene, Graham. *The Comedians*. New York: Viking Press, 1966.

Greinacher, Norbert, and Norbert Metz, eds. *Popular Religion*. Concilium 186. Edinburgh: T.& T. Clarke, 1986.

Gutiérrez, Gustavo. *The Power of the Poor in History*. Maryknoll: Orbis, 1983.

Hamilton, Malcolm B. *The Sociology of Religion: Theoretical and Comparative Perspectives*. London and New York: Routledge, 1995.

Hamington, Maurice. *Hail Mary? The Struggle for Ultimate Womanhood in Catholicism*. London and New York: Routledge, 1995.

Herskovits, Melville J. *Life in a Haitian Valley*. Garden City: Anchor, Doubleday, 1971.

Hoffmann, Leon-François. *Haïti: couleurs, croyances, créole*. Montréal: CIDIHCA, 1990.

————.*Haïti : lettres et l'être*. Toronto: GREF, 1992.

Hurbon, Laënnec. *Dieu dans le vaudou haïtien*. Paris: Payot, 1972.

————. *Culture et dictature en Haïti: l'imaginaire sous controle*. Paris: L'Harmattan, 1979.

————. *Comprendre Haïti: Essai sur l'Etat, la nation, la culture*. Port-au-Prince: Editions Henri Deschamps, 1987.

————. *Les mystères du vaudou*. Paris: Gaillimard, 1993.

Hurbon, Laënnec, ed., *Le Phénomène religieux dans la Caraïbe*. Montréal: CIDHICA, 1989.

Jahn, Janheinz. *Muntu: Afrcian Culture and the Western World*. New York: Grove Press, 1961.

James, C.L.R. *The Black Jacobins: Toussaint L'Ouverture and the Saint-Domingue Revolution*. 2d ed. New York: Random House, 1963.

Jan, Jean-Marie. *Documents pour l'histoire religieuse d'Haïti*. Port-au-Prince: Editions Henri Deschamps, 1956.

_____. *Collecta pour l'histoire religieuse du diocèse du Cap-Haïtien*, *Tome 1*. Port-au-Prince: Editions Henri Deschamps, 1958.

_____. *Collecta pour l'histoire religieuse du diocèse du Cap-Haïtien*, *Tome 2*. Port-au-Prince: Editions Henri Deschamps, 1960.

Collecta pour l'histoire religieuse du diocèse du Cap-Haïtien, *Tome 3*. Port-au-Prince: Editions Henri Deschamps, 1958.

_____.*Les congregations religieuses au Cap-Français, Saint-Domingue: 1681-1793*. Port-au-Prince: Editions Henri Deschamps, 1951.

Jenkins, Richard. *Pierre Bourdieu*. London: Routledge, 1992.

Joseph, Dieuveuil. *La Vierge Marie et l'independance d'Haïti*. Port-au-Prince: Editions Henri Deschamps, 1990.

Küng, Hans. *On Being a Christian*. New York: Doubleday, 1984.

_____.*Global Responsibility: In Search of a New World Ethic*. New York: Crossroad, 1991.

_____. *Reforming the Church Today: Keeping Hope Alive*. New York: Crossroad, 1992.

Küng, Hans, and Jürgen Moltmann, eds. *Mary in the Churches*. New York: Seabury, 1983. Concilium 168.

_____. and Leonard Swidler, eds. *The Church in Anguish: Has the Vatican Betrayed Vatican II?* San Francisco: Harper and Row, 1987.

Lafaye, Jacques. *Quetzacóatl and Guadalupe: The Formation of Mexican National Consciousness, 1531-1813*. Chicago: The University of Chicago Press, 1976.

Laguerre, Michel. *Voodoo and Politics in Haiti*. New York: St. Martins, 1981.

Lanternari, Vittorio. *The Religions of the Oppressed*. London: McGibbon & Key, 1968.

Lescot, Elie. *Avant l'oubli: Christianisme et paganisme en Haïti et autres lieux*. Port-au-Prince: Editions Henri Deschamps, 1974.

Levine, Daniel H. *Popular Voices in Latin American Catholicism*. Princeton: Princeton University Press, 1992.

Lewis, I. M. *Ecstatic Religion: An Anthropological Study of Spirit Possession and Shamanism*. Harmondsworth: Penguin Books, 1971.

Leyburn, James. *The Haitian People*. New Haven: Yale University Press, 1966.

Limberis, Vasiliki. *The Divine Heiress: The Virgin Mary and the Creation of Christian Constantinople*. London and New York: Routledge, 1994.

MacGaffey, Wyatt. *Religion and Society in Central Africa*. Chicago: The University of Chicago Press, 1986.

Macquarie, John. *Mary for All Christians*. Grand Rapids: Wm. B. Eerdmans Publishing, 1990.

Madiou, Thomas. *Histoire d'Haïti: Tome 1: 1492-1799*. Port-au-Prince: Editions Henri Deschamps, 1989.

_____.*Histoire d'Haïti, Tome 5: 1811-1818*. Port-au-Prince: Editions Henri Deschamps, 1989.

Marcus, George E., and Michael M.J. Fischer. *Anthropology as Cultural Critique: An Experimental Moment in the Human Sciences*. Chicago: University of Chicago Press, 1986.

Marx, Karl. *Early Writings*. New York: Vintage, 1975.

_____.*The Communist Manifesto*. New York: W.W. Norton & Co., 1988.

Maxmilien, Louis. *Le vodou haïtien: rite radas-canzo*. Port-au-Prince: Editions Henri Deschamps, 1945.

Mbiti, John S. *African Religions and Philosophy*. Oxford: Heinemann, 1969.

McBrien, Richard P. *Catholicism*. San Francisco: Harper, 1994.

Métraux, Alfred. *Voodoo in Haiti*. New York: Schocken Books, 1972.

Mintz, Sidney W. *Caribbean Transformations*. Baltimore: Johns Hopkins University Press, 1974.

_____. and and Sally Price, eds. *Caribbean Contours*. Baltimore: The Johns Hopkins University Press, 1985.

Miravalle, Marc. *Marie: coredemptrice, mediatrice, avocate*. Santa Barbara: Queenship Publishing, 1993.

Nérestant, Micial M. *Religions et politique en Haïti*. Paris: KARTHALA, 1994.

Orsi, Robert Anthony. *The Madonna of 115th Street: Faith and Community in Italian Harlem, 1880-1950*. New Haven: Yale University Press, 1985.

Pamphile, Leon Denius. *La Croix et la glaive: L'Église Catholique et l'occupation américaine d'Haïti 1915-1934*. Port-au-Prince: Editions des Antilles, S.A., 1991.

Paquin, Lyonel. *The Haitians: Class and Color Politics*. Brooklyn: Multi-Type, 1983.

Peters, Carl E. *La coix contre l'asson*. Port-au-Prince: Telhomme, 1960.

Perry, Nicholas and Loreto Echeverría. *Under the Heel of Mary*. London and New York: Routledge, 1988.

Price-Mars, Jean. *Ainsi parla l'oncle*. Ottawa: Lemeac, Collection Caraïbes, 1973.

_____. *La vocation de l'élite*, Port-au-Prince: Imprimerie La Presse, 1919.

Raboteau, Albert J. *Slave Religion: The "Invisible Institution" in the Antebellum South.* New York and Oxford: Oxford University Press, 1978.

Rigaud, Milo. *La tradition vaudou et vaudou haïtien: son temple, ses mystères, sa magie.* Paris: Editions Niclaus, 1953.

Rodriguez, Jeanette. *Our Lady of Guadalupe: Faith and Empowerment among Mexican-American Women.* Austin: University of Texas Press, 1994.

Romain, Charles Poisset. *Le protestantisme dans la societé haïtienne: Contribution à une Étude sociologique d'une religion.* Port-au-Prince: Editions Henri Deschamps, 1986.

Ruether, Mary Radford. *Mary: The Feminine Face of the Church.* Philadelphia: Westminster Press, 1977.

_____. *Sexism and God-Talk: Toward a Feminist Theology.* Boston: Beacon Press, 1983.

Schillibeeckx, Edward. *Mary: Mother of Redemption.* New York: Sheed and Ward, 1964.

_____. and Catharina Halkes. *Mary: Yesterday, Today, Tomorrow.* New York: Crossroad, 1993.

Scott, James C. *Domination and the Arts of Resistance: Hidden Transcripts.* New Haven: Yale University Press, 1990.

Simpson, George E. *Religious Cults of the Caribbean: Trinidad, Jamaica and Haiti.* San Juan: Institute of Caribbean Studies, University of Puerto Rico, 1980.

Sloyan, Gerard. *Jesus in Focus: A Life in its Setting.* Mystic: Twenty-Third Publications, 1983.

Swidler, Leonard. *Biblical Affirmations of Woman.* Philadelphia: Westminster Press, 1979.

_____. *The Meaning of Life at the Edge of the Third Millennium.* Mawah: Paulist Press, 1972.

Thompson, Vincent Bakpetu. *The Making of the African Diaspora in the Americas: 1441-1900.* New York: Longman, 1987.

Trouillot, Henock. *Introduction à une histoire du Vaudou.* Port-au-Prince: Editions Fardin, 1983.

Trouillot, Michel-Rolph. *Haiti, State Against Nation: Origins and Legacy of Duvalierism.* New York: Monthly Review Press, 1990.

Turner, Bryan S. *Religion and Social Theory: Materialist Perspectives.* London: Heinemann, 1983.

Valdman, Albert, et. al. *Haitian Creole—English—French Dictionary.* Bloomington: Creole Institute, University of Indiana, 1981.

Warner, Marina. *Alone of All Her Sex: The Myth and Cult of the Virgin Mary.* New York: Knopf, 1976.

Weber, Max. *The Protestant Ethic and The Spirit of Capitalism.* London: Allen & Unwin, 1933.

_____. *The Sociology of Religion.* Boston: Beacon Press, 1963.

Zidmas-Swartz, Sandra L. *Encountering Mary.* New York: Avon Books, 1992.

Articles

Adrien, Antoine. "Notes sur le clergé du Nord et la révolte des esclaves en 1791." In Conférence Haïtienne des Religieuses. *Evangélisation d'Haïti 1492-1992, tome 2: Revolution de 1791.* 47-56. Port-au-Prince: Le Natal, 1992.

Badone, Ellen. "Introduction." In Ellen Badone, ed. *Religious Orthodoxy and Popular Faith in European Society.* Princeton: Princeton University Press, 1990, 3-23.

Billings, Dwight B. "Religion as Opposition: A Gramscian Analysis." *American Journal of Sociology* 66, 1990, 1-31.

Boff, Leonardo, and Virgil Elizondo. "Editorial: Theology From the Viewpoint of the Poor." In Leonardo Boff and Virgil Elizondo, eds. *Option for the Poor: Challenge to the Rich Countries,* ix-xii. Concilium 187. Edinburgh: T.& T. Clarke, 1986.

Borresen, Kari. "Mary in Catholic Theology." In Hans Küng and Jürgen Moltmann, eds. *Mary in the Churches.* Concilium 168. New York: Seabury, 1983, 48-56.

Bourdieu, Pierre. "Genèse et structure du champ religieux." *Revue française de sociologie,* 12, no. 3. julliet-septembre, 1971, 294-334.

_____. "Legitimation and Structured Interests in Weber's Sociology of Religion." In Sam Whimster and Scott Lash, eds. *Max Weber, Rationality, and Modernity.* London: Allen and Unwin, 1987, 119-136.

Brown, Karen McCarthy. "Olina and Ezili: A Woman and a Goddess in Haitian Vodou." *Anima* 5 (Spring 1979), 110-116.

_____. "Mama Lola and the Ezilis: Themes of Motherhood and Loving in Haitian Vodou." In Nancy A Falk, and Rita M. Gross, eds. *UnspokenWorlds: Women's Religious Lives.* Belmont, CA: Wadsworth Publishing Co., 1989, 235-245.

_____."Afro-Caribbean Spirituality: A Haitian Case Study." In Lawrence Sullivan, ed. *Healing and Restoring: Medecine and Health in the World's Religious Traditions.* New York: MacMillan, 1989, 255-285.

Calhoun, Craig. "Habitus, Field, and Capital: The Question of Historical Specificity." In Craig Calhoun, Edward LiPuma, and Moishe Postone, eds. *Bourdieu: Critical Perspectives*. Chicago: The University of Chicago Press, 1993, 61-88.

Castillo, Fernando. "Christianity: Bourgeois (*Burgesa*) Religion or Religion of the People?" In Johannes Baptist Metz, ed. *Christianity and the Bourgeoisie*, 51-60. Concilium 125. Edinburgh: T.& T. Clarke, 1977.

Charles, Gabriel. "Les communautés ecclesiales de base dans l'archdiocèse du Cap-Haïtien." In Conférence Haïtienne des Religieuses. *Evangélisation d'Haïti, tome 3: Les TKL et la nouvelle évangélisation*, 139-148. Port-au-Prince: Le Natal, 1993.

Chauleau, Liliane. "Le baptême à la Marrtinique au XVIIe siècle." In Laënnec Hurbon, ed. *Le Phénomène religieux dans la caraïbe*. Montréal: CIDHICA, 1989. 57-71.

Danroc, Gilles. "Les relations Catholicisme et Vodou à la lumière de Vatican II." In Conférence Haïtienne des Religieuses. *Evangélisation d'Haïti 1492-1992, tome 2: Revolution de 1791*. 47-56. Port-au-Prince: Le Natal, 1992.

Davis, Natalie Zemon. "Some Tasks and Themes in the Study of Popular Religion." In Charles Trinkaus and H.A. Oberman, eds. *The Pursuit of Holiness in Late Medieval and Renaissance Religion*. Leiden: E.J. Brill, 1974, 307-336.

Droogers, André. "Syncretism: The Problem of Definition, the Definition of the Problem." In J. Goort, H. Vroom, R. Feinhort, and A. Wessels, eds., *Dialogue and Syncretism: An Interdisciplinary Approach*. Grand Rapids: Wm. B. Eerdmans Publishing, 1989.

Dussel, Enrique. "Popular Religion as Oppression and Liberation: Hypotheses on its Past and Present in Latin America." In Norbert Greinacher and Norbert Metz, eds. *Popular Religion*, 82-94. Concilium 186. Edinburgh: T. & T. Clarke, 1986.

Eckstein, Susan. "Power and Popular Protest in Latin America." In Susan Eckstein, ed. *Power and Popular Protest: Latin American Social Movements*. Berkeley and Los Angeles: University of California Press, 1989, 1-60.

Elizondo, Virgil. "Mary and the Poor: A Model for Evangelising Ecumenism." In Hans Küng and Jürgen Moltmann, eds. *Mary in the Churches*. Concilium 168. New York: Seabury, 1983, 48-56.

_____. "Popular Religion as Support of Identity; A Pastoral-Psychological Case-Study Based on the Mexican American Experience in the USA." In Norbert Greinacher, and Norbert Metz, eds. *Popular Religion*, 36-43. Concilium 186. Edinburgh: T. & T. Clarke, 1986.

Fiorenza, Francis Schüssler. "Religion and Society: Legitimation, Rationalisation, or Cultural Heritage. In Johannes Baptist Metz, ed. *Christianity and the Bourgeoisie*, 24-32. Concilium 125. Edinburgh: T.& T. Clarke, 1977.

Fulton, John. "Religion and Politics in Gramsci: An Introduction." *Sociological Analysis, vol.* 48, no. 3, 1987, 197-216.

Gellner, Ernst. "Concepts and Society," in B.R. Wilson, ed., *Rationality*. London: Blackwell, 1970, pp. 18-49.

Giddens, Anthony. "Class Structuration and Class Consciousness." In Anthony Giddens, and David Held, eds. *Classes, Power, and Conflict: Classical and Contemporary Debates*. Berkeley and Los Angeles: University of California Press, 1982, 157-174.

Gisler, Antoine. "L'Église et l'esclavage aux Antilles françaises." In Conférence Haïtienne des Religieuses. *Evangélisation d'Haïti, Introduction*, 40-58. Port-au-Prince: Le Natal, 1992.

Gutiérrez, Gustavo. "Vers le cinquième centenaire." In Conférence Haïtienne des Religieuses. *Evangélisation d'Haïti, Introduction*, 40-58. Port-au-Prince: Le Natal, 1992.

Halkes, Catharina. "Mary and Women." In Hans Küng and Jurgen Moltmann, eds. *Mary in the Churches*, 66-73. Concilium 168. New York: Seabury, 1983.

Herskovits, Melville J. "African Gods and Catholic Saints in New World Religious Belief."*American Anthropologist*, 39, 1937, 635-643.

_____. "What is Voodoo?" *Tomorrow* 3, 1954, 11-20.

Hurbon, Laënnec. "Enjeu politique de la crise actuelle de l'église." *Chemins Critiques* 1, no.1, 1989,13-22.

_____. "Présentation: Le continent "religion" dans les iles de la Caraïbe." In Laënnec Hurbon, ed. *Le Phénomène religieux dans la caraïbe*. Montréal: CIDHICA, 1989, 11-17.

_____."Les nouveux movements religieux dans la Caraïbe." In Laënnec Hurbon, ed. *Le Phénomène religieux dans la caraïbe*. Montréal: CIDHICA, 1989, 307-354.

_____. "Evangelisation et Esclavage: Point de départ pour une méthodologie de l'histoire de L'Église d'Haïti." In CHR. *Evangelisation d'Haïti, 1492-1992, tome 1: Esclavage et évangelisation*, 43-71. Port-au-Prince: Le Natal, 1991.

Johnson, Elizabeth A. "The Symbolic Character of Theological Statements about Mary." *Journal of Ecumenical Studies*, vol.22, no.2 (Spring 1985), 312-335.

Laguerre, Michel S. "Voodoo as Religion and Political Ideology." *Freeing the Spirit* 3, 1974, 23-28.

_____."The Place of Voodoo in The Social Structure of Haiti." *Caribbean Quarterly*, vol. 19, no. 3, 1973, 10-24.

Lafleur, Gérard. "L'Église dans la societé du XVIIe siècle au Antilles françaises du Vent. In Laënnec Hurbon, ed. *Le Phénomène religieux dans la Caraïbe*. Montréal: CIDHICA, 1989. 21-40.

Larose, Serge. "The Meaning of Africa in Haitian Vodu." In I.M. Lewis, ed. *Symbols and Sentiments: Cross-Cultural Studies in Symbolism*. New York: Academic Press, 1977, 85-116.

Lanternari, Vittorio. "La religion populaire: perspective historique et anthropologique." *Archives de sciences sociales des religions*, 127, 1982, 121-143.

Lash, Scott. "Pierre Bourdieu: Cultural Economy and Social Change." In Craig Calhoun, Edward LiPuma, and Moishe Postone, eds. *Bourdieu: Critical Perspectives*. Chicago: The University of Chicago Press, 1993, 193-211.

Lee, Rebecca. "The Jerusalem Syndrome." *The Atlantic Monthly*, May 1995, 24-38.

Levine, Daniel H., and Scott Mainwaring. "Religion and Popular Pretest in Latin America: Contrasting Experiences." In Susan Eckstein, ed. *Power and Popular Protest*. Berkeley and Los Angeles: University of California Press, 1989, 203-240.

LiPuma, Edward. "Culture and the Concept of Culture in a Theory of Practice." In Craig Calhoun, Edward LiPuma and Moishe Postone, eds. *Bourdieu: Critical Perspectives*. Chicago: The University of Chicago Press, 1993, 14-34.

Lowenthal, Ira P. "Ritual Performance and Religious Experience: A Service for the Gods in Southern Haiti." *Journal of Anthropological Research* 34, no. 5 (Fall 1978), 392-414.

Krais, Beate. "Gender and Symbolic Violence: Female Oppression in the Light of Pierre Bourdieu's Theory of Social Practice." In Craig Calhoun, Edward LiPuma, and Moishe Postone, eds. *Bourdieu: Critical Perspectives*. Chicago: The University of Chicago Press, 1993, 156-177.

Küng, Hans. "Editorial: Mary in the Churches." In Hans Küng and Jürgen Moltmann, eds. *Mary in the Churches*. Seabury, Concilium 168, 1983, viii-xi.

Maldonado, Luis. "Popular Religion: Its Dimensions, Levels and Types." In Norbert Greinacher and Norbert Metz, eds. *Popular Religion*, Concilium 186. Edinburgh: T. & T. Clarke, 1986. 3-11.

Mennesson-Rigaud, Odette. "Le rôle du Vaudou dans l'indépendance d'Haïti." *Présence Africaine*, 17/18 (fév-mai 1958), 43-67.

Midy, Franklin. "L'Affaire Aristide en perspective: Histoire de la formation et du rejet d'une vocation prophétique." *Chemins Critiques* 1,
no.1, 1989, 45-57.

_____. "Haiti, la religion sur les chemins de la démocratie." *Chemins
Critiques* 1, no.1, 1989, 23-43.

Mintz, Sidney W. "Can Haiti Change?" *Foreign Affairs*, vol. 74, no. 1
(Jan/Feb. 1995), 73-86.

Moltmann, Jürgen. "Editorial: Can there be an Ecumenical Mariology?"
In Hans Küng, and Jürgen Moltmann, eds. *Mary in the Churches*,
xii-xv. Concilium 168. New York: Seabury Press, 1983.

Nesti, Arnaldo. "Gramsci et la religion populaire." *Social Compass* 22,
no. 3-4, 1986, 342-354.

Oliveira. Pedro A. Ribeiro de. "Catholicisme populaire et hégémonie
bourgeois au Brésil."*Archives de sciences sociales des religions* 24,
1979, 53-79.

Orsi, Robert. "The Religious Boundaries of an Inbetween People: Street
Feste and the Problem of the Dark-Skinned Other in Italian Harlem,
1920-1990." *American Quarterly*, vol. 44., no.3 (September 1992),
313-347.

Parker, Christian. "Popular Religion and Protest against Oppression:
The Chilean Example." In Norbert Greinacher and Norbert Metz,
eds. *Popular Religion*, 28-35. Concilium 186, 1986.

Postone, Moishe, Edward LiPuma, and Craig Calhoun. "Introduction:
Bourdieu and Social Theory." In Craig Calhoun, Edward LiPuma,
and Moishe Postone, eds. *Bourdieu: Critical Perspectives*. Chicago:
The University of Chicago Press, 1993, 1-13.

Poulantzas, Nicos. "On Social Classes." In Anthony Giddens and David
Held, eds. *Classes, Power, and Conflict: Classical and Contempo-
rary Debates*. Berkeley and Los Angeles: University of California
Press, 1982, 101-111.

Smith, Raymond T. "Race and Class in the Post-Emancipation Caribbean." In Robert Ross, ed. *Essays on Ideology and Social Structure*.
The Hague and Boston: Martinus Nijhoff Publishers, 1982, 93-119.

Smucker, Glenn R. "The Social Character of Religion in Rural Haiti."
In Charles R. Foster and Albert Valdman, eds. *Haiti—Today and
Tomorrow: An Interdisciplinary Study*. New York and London, Uni-
versity Press of America, 1984, 35-56.

Spivak, Gayarti. "Can the Subaltern Speak?" In C. Nelson and L.
Grossberg, eds. *Marxism and the Interpretation of Culture*. Urbana:
University of Illinois Press, 1988, 134-155.

Suess, Paulo. "The Creative and Normative Role of Popular Religion in
the Church." In Norbert Greinacher and Norbert Metz, eds. *Popu-*

lar Religion, 122-131. Concilium 186. Edinburgh: T. & T. Clarke, 1986.

Barthélémy, Gérard, Jean-Yves Blot, Georges Castera, Gilles Danroc, Laënnec Hurbon, Jean-Claude Jean, Yanick Lahens, Vernet Larose, Franklin Midy, Marc Maesschalk, Bérard Sénatus, and William Smarth. Table Ronde: "Religion et politique en Haïti."*Chemins Critiques* 1, no.1, 1989, 61-83.

Thompson, John B. "Editor's Introduction." In Pierre Bourdieu. *Language and Symbolic Power*. Cambridge: Harvard University Press, 1991, 1-31.

Trouillot, Michel-Rolph. "The Caribbean Region: An Open Frontier for Anthropological Theory." *Annual Review of Anthropology*, 21, 1992, 19-42.

_____."Haiti's Mightmare and the Lessons of History." *NACLA Report on the Americas*, vol. 27, no. 4 (Jan/Feb. 1994), 46-52.

Wacquant, Loïc J.D. "Toward a Social Praxeology: The Structure and Logic of Bourdieu's Sociology." In Pierre Bourdieu and Loïc J. D. Wacquant. *Invitation to Reflexive Sociology*. Chicago: The University of Chicago Press, 1992, 1-59.

_____."Toward a Reflexive Sociology: A Workshop with Pierre Bourdieu." *Sociological Theory*, 7, no. 1 (Spring 1987), 26-63.

Dissertations

Conway, Frederick J. "Pentecostalism in the Context of Haitian Religion and Health Practices." Ph.D. dissertation, American University, 1978.

Lowenthal, Ira Paul. "Marriage is 20, Children are 21: The Cultural Construction of Conjugality and the Family in Rural Haiti." Ph.D. dissertation, Johns Hopkins University, 1987.

McClure, Marian. "The Catholic Church and Rural Social Change: Priests, Peasant Organizations, and Politics in Haiti." Ph.D. dissertation, Harvard University, 1985.

Mathieu, Suze Marie. "The Transformation of the Catholic Church in Haiti." Ph.D. dissertation, Indiana University, 1991.

Murray, Gerald F. "The Evolution of Haitian Peasant Land Tenure: A Case Study in Agrarian Adaptation to Population Growth," 2 vols. Ph.D. dissertation Columbia University, 1977.

Woodson, Drexel G. "*Tout Moun sé Moun, Men tout Moun pa Menm*: Microlevel Sociocultural Aspects of Land Tenure in a Northern Haitian Locality," 3 vols. Ph.D. dissertation, The University of Chicago, 1990.

INDEX